The Gospel of MATTHEW

Also by James Montgomery Boice

Witness and Revelation in the Gospel of John
Philippians: An Expositional Commentary
The Minor Prophets: An Expositional Commentary (2 volumes)
How to Live the Christian Life (originally, *How to Really Live It Up*)
Ordinary Men Called by God (originally, *How God Can Use Nobodies*)
The Last and Future World
The Gospel of John: An Expositional Commentary (5 volumes)
The Epistles of John: An Expositional Commentary
"Galatians," in the *Expositor's Bible Commentary*
Can You Run Away from God?
Our Sovereign God, editor
Our Savior God: Studies on Man, Christ and the Atonement, editor
Does Inerrancy Matter?
The Foundation of Biblical Authority, editor
Making God's Word Plain, editor
The Sermon on the Mount
Genesis: An Expositional Commentary (3 volumes)
The Parables of Jesus
The Christ of Christmas
The Gospel of Matthew: An Expositional Commentary (2 volumes)
Standing on the Rock
The Christ of the Empty Tomb
Foundations of the Christian Faith (4 volumes in one)
Christ's Call to Discipleship
Transforming Our World: A Call to Action, editor
Ephesians: An Expositional Commentary
Daniel: An Expositional Commentary
Joshua: An Expositional Commentary
Nehemiah: An Expositional Commentary
The King Has Come
Romans: An Expositional Commentary (4 volumes)
Mind Renewal in a Mindless Age
The Glory of God's Grace (originally, *Amazing Grace*)
Psalms: An Expositional Commentary (3 volumes)
Sure I Believe, So What?
Hearing God When You Hurt
Foundations of God's City (originally, *Two Cities, Two Loves: Christian Responsibility in a Crumbling Culture*)
Here We Stand!: A Call from Confessing Evangelicals, editor with Benjamin E. Sasse
Living by the Book: The Joy of Loving and Trusting God's Word
Acts: An Expositional Commentary
The Heart of the Cross, with Philip G. Ryken
What Makes a Church Evangelical?
The Doctrines of Grace, with Philip G. Ryken

The Gospel of MATTHEW

Volume 1

The King and His Kingdom

Matthew 1–17

JAMES MONTGOMERY BOICE

BakerBooks
Grand Rapids, Michigan

Published by Baker Books
a division of Baker Publishing Group
P.O. Box 6287, Grand Rapids, MI 49516-6287
www.bakerbooks.com

Paperback edition published 2006
ISBN 978-0-8010-6643-6

Printed in the United States of America

The Library of Congress has cataloged the hardcover edition as follows:
Boice, James Montgomery, 1938–2000
The Gospel of Matthew / James Montgomery Boice.
p. cm.
Includes bibliographical references (v. 1, p.) and indexes.
Contents: v. 1. The King and his kingdom (Matthew 1–17).
ISBN 10: 0-8010-1201-5 (cloth)
ISBN 978-0-8010-1201-3 (cloth)
1. Bible. N. T. Matthew—Commentaries. I. Title.
BS2575.53.B65–2001
226.2′077—dc21 00-064147

In keeping with biblical principles of creation stewardship, Baker Publishing Group advocates the responsible use of our natural resources. As a member of the Green Press Initiative, our company uses recycled paper when possible. The text paper of this book is composed in part of post-consumer waste.

green press INITIATIVE

To him whose
"dominion is an everlasting dominion
that will not pass away,
and his kingdom . . . one that will never be destroyed."
Daniel 7:14

Contents

Part Four: **Is Jesus Really God's King?**

Part Five: **The Parables of the Kingdom**

Part Six: **The Withdrawal of the King**

Preface

What an extraordinary book Matthew is! It is the first of the Gospels, the longest, the most Jewish, the most evangelistic, and, in many ways, the most compelling. Nowhere does the Gospel name its author, but it has been ascribed to Matthew from the earliest days of church history, and for the first three or four centuries, it was the most highly regarded and most often quoted Gospel of the four. To some people, now as well as then, Matthew is the most important book ever written.

It is about Jesus of Nazareth, of course. That is what each of the Gospels is about. But each writer has his own way of handling the material regarding Jesus' life and has his own unique emphasis. In Matthew's case, the emphasis is on Jesus being the Messiah or King of Israel. Jesus is introduced this way at the beginning of the book: "Jesus Christ [Messiah] the son of David" (Matt. 1:1), and the theme is evident throughout.

I have tried to capture Matthew's emphasis by the titles given to the various sections of the Gospel: (1) "The Coming of the King" (chapters 1–4); (2) "The Sermon on the Mount" (chapters 5–7); (3) "The Power of the Kingdom" (chapters 8–10); (4) "Is Jesus Really God's King?" (chapters 11–12); (5) "The Parables of the Kingdom" (chapter 13); (6) "The Withdrawal of the King" (chapters 14–17); (7) "The Citizens of the Kingdom" (chapters 18–20); (8) "The King's Final Break with Judaism" (chapters 21–23); (9) "The Sermon on the Mount of Olives" (chapters 24–25); and (10) "The King's Death and Resurrection" (chapters 26–28).

The first six of these sections are covered in the present volume (chapters 1–17). The final four sections are covered in volume 2 (chapters 18–28).

Matthew begins with a genealogy proving the descent of Jesus not only from David, the greatest of the Jewish kings, but also from Abraham, the father of the Jewish people. He makes frequent references to the Old Testament, more than the other Gospel writers. The book contains at least forty quotations from the Old Testament, and the formal introductory formula "all this was done that it might be fulfilled which was spoken by the prophet, saying . . ." occurs no less than sixteen times. Matthew also contains more direct interaction between Jesus and the Jewish authorities than the other Gospels.

Yet Matthew also contains the strongest indictments of Jewish unbelief and shows a very strong interest in the Gentiles. Matthew traces Jesus' origins to David and Abraham, as I have indicated—a very Jewish beginning. But the genealogy also contains the names of four women, which is most un-Jewish, and three of these women were not Jews. Matthew also links the coming of the Gentile wise men to his account of Jesus' birth, and the book ends with Jesus' command to take the gospel to "all nations" (Matt. 28:19). The Great Commission is the Gospel's climax.

We could express Matthew's unique qualities this way: As the first of the Gospels, Matthew is a bridge book linking the Old Testament with its fervent anticipation of the Messiah to the realization of the Messiah's kingly rule over the new people of God, which is the church. Matthew is the only Gospel actually to use the word *church*. It occurs twice, in 16:18 and 18:17, the first having to do with Jesus building his church and the second with church discipline.

Matthew does not want us to forget that his message about this Jewish King and Savior is not only for Jews but for everyone. He is insisting, as much as did the author of the fourth Gospel, that Jesus Christ is "the Savior of the world" (John 4:42).

Is the Book of Matthew relevant today? It certainly is. In a largely secular age, as ours is, we need to know that Jesus is truly God's King. In a day of nominal Christianity, we need to hear Christ's call to "follow me." In a day of lax and lazy discipleship, we need to hear once again the command of Jesus to take the message of his death and resurrection to the world.

It has been thirty years since I first began to preach from the Gospels, starting with the Gospel of John in 1971, the third year of my ministry at Tenth Presbyterian Church in Philadelphia. Like most preachers I have returned to the Gospels again and again over the years, since they are the very heart of the Bible and tell of the life, death, and resurrection of Jesus Christ, who is the heart of Christianity. I have preached on the Sermon on the Mount, the parables, Jesus' teaching about discipleship, the cross, the resurrection, and other passages. But it is only in these studies that I have returned once again to explore an entire Gospel in detail.

May God bless this work by calling many to faith in Christ and deepening the discipleship of others, and to God be *all* the glory.

James Montgomery Boice
Philadelphia, Pennsylvania

Part One

The Coming of the King

1

Just a List of Names?

Matthew 1:1–17

A record of the genealogy of Jesus Christ the son of David, the son of Abraham. . . . Thus there were fourteen generations in all from Abraham to David, fourteen from David to the exile in Babylon, and fourteen from the exile to the Christ.

When C. Everett Koop, the former Surgeon General of the United States, was still living in Philadelphia and a regular attender at Tenth Presbyterian Church, he used to kid me about a blatant inconsistency in my handling of the Bible's genealogies. I had been preaching on Genesis and had made a serious point about the importance of the names found in Genesis 10, the so-called "table of the nations." I know I did, because my first volume on Genesis has three separate chapters on those verses. But then, when I came to a similar genealogy in the very next chapter, in Genesis 11, I calmly dismissed it as "just another list of names," according to Dr. Koop.

That is not exactly how I remember the story. But it is the question most people have as they come to the Bible's genealogies. Are genealogies important? Or are they "just a list of names"? Specifically, since Matthew begins with "a record of the genealogy of Jesus Christ the son of David, the son of Abraham," should this listing of names be studied seriously?

Matthew and His Very Jewish Book

Matthew was a Jew—his other name is Levi (compare Matt. 9:9–13 and Luke 5:27–32)—and his book was written chiefly to Jews about the Jewish Messiah whose name was Jesus. Matthew is the most Jewish of the Gospels.

The common starting point for each of the four Gospels is the ministry of John the Baptist, but each of the Gospels has a unique introduction that precedes its account of John's ministry. Mark begins with a simple one-line statement. Luke starts with a personal first-person account of his reasons for writing, directed to an influential friend whose name was Theophilus, followed by a detailed account of the miraculous births of John the Baptist and Jesus. His genealogy of Jesus does not appear until chapter 3. John has a poetical prologue that traces Jesus' origins to eternity past and speaks of the incarnation without any specific mention of Jesus' miraculous conception or birth. Matthew begins with a genealogy that traces Jesus' ancestry first to King David and then, further back, to Abraham.

Beginning a book with a genealogy seems strange to us, "just a listing of names," as I said. But knowing who a man was by knowing his ancestry was important to people in the ancient world, especially Jews, who needed to prove their Jewishness in order to take part in the temple worship. It is no accident, then, that Matthew begins with Jesus' genealogy or that his is the first of the Gospels to begin the New Testament. Matthew's genealogy proves that Jesus had descended from King David and was therefore qualified to be the Jews' Messiah ("Your house and your kingdom will endure forever before me," 2 Sam. 7:16). And his reference to Abraham is a first and early suggestion that Jesus is also the one through whom the blessings of God would be given, not only to Jews but to the Gentile nations as well ("All peoples on earth will be blessed through you," Gen. 12:3).

"During the first three centuries of the church, Matthew was the most highly revered and frequently quoted canonical Gospel," writes New Testament scholar D. A. Carson.[1]

Who was the author of this Gospel? The Gospel itself is anonymous; it makes no claims. But Matthew, the disciple of Jesus, was considered to be the author from the earliest days of church history. The earliest reference to him is by Papias, who is quoted by Eusebius in his *Ecclesiastical History* (3.39.16) as saying that "Matthew collected the oracles [of Jesus] in the Hebrew tongue,"[2] but there are also references to Matthew as the author of Matthew by other writers. Does this prove that Matthew wrote this book? Many modern scholars dispute it; they dispute nearly everything. But there is no good reason for rejecting this strong, early, and unanimous testimony.

We have already seen that Matthew was a Jew. The references to him in this Gospel (as well as in Mark and Luke) identify him as a tax collector. This was a despised occupation, as we can well imagine. But it also means that Matthew would have been well qualified to have compiled the Gospel. For one thing, he was probably literary and bilingual, even trilingual, dealing as he would have had to with Jews, Greeks, and Romans. He would have needed to keep records. He may even have become something like a scribe for the itinerant apostolic band. More than one writer suggests this possibility. Besides, there is this argument: Matthew was not a prominent disciple, like

Peter, James, or John. We know very little about him. Why should anyone have assigned the first of the four Gospels to Matthew if Matthew was not in fact the author?

Matthew's Jewishness and scribal interests emerge in another way as well: his frequent references to the Old Testament. Matthew contains at least forty formal quotations from the Old Testament,[3] and the formal introductory formula "all this was done that it might be fulfilled which was spoken by the prophet, saying . . ." occurs no less than sixteen times.

Matthew records more direct interaction between Jesus and the Jewish authorities than any other Gospel. Yet Matthew also contains the strongest indictments of Jewish unbelief. Matthew traces Jesus' origins to David and Abraham, as I have already indicated—a very Jewish beginning. But the genealogy also contains the names of four women, which is most un-Jewish, and three of these women were Gentiles. Moreover, the final words of the Gospel are the missionary commission in which Jesus instructs his disciples to "make disciples of all nations" (Matt. 28:19).

As the first of the Gospels, Matthew is a bridge book linking the Old Testament with its fervent anticipation of the Messiah to the realization of the Messiah's kingly rule over the new people of God, which is the church. Matthew is the only Gospel actually to use the word *church (ecclesia).*

Matthew's Genealogy of Jesus

Since Matthew's genealogy contains the names of women, Gentiles, and even noted sinners, the book shows that barriers between (1) men and women, (2) Jews and Gentiles, and (3) saints and sinners were falling through the work of Jesus Christ. Jesus' ancestry also provides a clue on this matter, showing that God chooses his servants from a wide spectrum of those from whom the respectably orthodox would turn away in horror.

But the genealogy is also notorious for problems, especially when it is compared with the corresponding genealogy in Luke 3. It does not require a New Testament scholar or even an astute reader of the New Testament to recognize that the genealogy of Matthew and the genealogy of Luke are not consistent with each other throughout. Matthew's genealogy begins with Abraham and moves forward in history to Christ. It traces Abraham's descendants through fourteen generations to David, David's descendants through fourteen generations to the Babylonian captivity, then the later descendants through fourteen more generations to "Jacob the father of Joseph, the husband of Mary, of whom was born Jesus, who is called Christ" (Matt. 1:16). Luke, on the other hand, moves backward. He begins with Joseph and goes back through David, to Abraham—and then even beyond Abraham to Adam, who, he says, was "the son of God" (Luke 3:37).

Two of Luke's sections present no problem. His final section—from Abraham to Adam—does not occur in Matthew's Gospel, so there is no basis for comparison. His second section—from David to Abraham—is also free of problems because it corresponds to Matthew's genealogy. The difficulty comes in Luke's first section, in which the names are different from those found in Matthew. This would be all right if we were dealing with the ancestries of two entirely different people, but these are both genealogies of Jesus. What is more, while both books trace Jesus' line through his adopted father Joseph, the husband of Mary, of whom our Lord was born, Matthew says that Joseph was the son of Jacob who descended from David through David's son and successor King Solomon (Matt. 1:16), and Luke states that Joseph was the son of Heli who had descended from David through Nathan, who was also David's son but Solomon's brother (Luke 3:23).

J. Gresham Machen's Solution

Several solutions have been offered to this genealogical problem. J. Gresham Machen, in his classic study *The Virgin Birth of Christ*,[4] analyzed this problem with customary thoroughness and presented the following solution. These are indeed both genealogies of Joseph, but whereas Matthew offers what Machen calls the "legal" descendants of David, that is, the line that actually sat upon the throne (or would have, had it continued down to Jesus' day without interruption), Luke presents the "paternal" line, that is, the line of literal father-to-son descent, which at last produced Joseph. Matthew's line does not necessarily indicate literal relationships but only a list of heirs to the throne, whatever their relationships to their immediate predecessors may have been. In this view, Heli was Joseph's literal father, but Jacob (who presumably had no sons to follow him) was Joseph's immediate predecessor in the "legal" line.

Machen says:

> Reconciliation might conceivably be effected in a number of different ways. But on the whole we are inclined to think that the true key to a solution to the problem (however the solution may run in detail) is to be found in the fact that Matthew, in an intentionally incomplete way, gives a list of incumbents (actual or potential) of the kingly Davidic throne, whereas Luke traces the descent of Joseph back through Nathan to David. Thus the genealogies cannot properly be used to exhibit contradiction between the Matthean and the Lukan accounts of the birth and infancy of our Lord.[5]

This makes good sense, for Matthew is certainly talking about heirs to the throne. His is a Jewish Gospel. Moreover, he constructs his genealogy from David onward, asking, "Who is the next heir?" By contrast, Luke is interested in actual paternity, so he constructs his genealogy from Joseph back to David, asking, "Who was so-and-so's father?"

My only reservation is this: According to Machen's theory, the loose or nonliteral genealogy is that of Matthew. It is the one that does not necessarily give a literal descent from father to son. By contrast, Luke's genealogy focuses on fatherhood and sonship. But it is striking, if that is indeed the case, that Matthew stresses the descent from father to son by use of the word *begat*—"Abraham begat Isaac, and Isaac begat Jacob" (KJV; the NIV says, "was the father of")—while Luke uses a looser form of speech to indicate the relationship, saying simply "of the" (NIV translates "son of"). If Luke is talking about strict paternity, as Machen argues, he is the one who should have used the more literal form.

Joseph's Line and Mary's Line

In my judgment, a better solution involves viewing the two lines as the lines of Joseph and Mary respectively, each thereby identified as a descendant of King David. This was the view of Bernhard Weiss and of Scotland's James Orr. It received classic expression in some of the early writings of Donald Grey Barnhouse, one of my predecessors as pastor of Tenth Presbyterian Church. According to this view, the distinction between the two lines of descent is not between the "legal" line and the "paternal" line, as Machen suggests, but between the "royal" line of those who actually sat on the throne and the "legal" line of descent from one oldest son to the next, even though these did not actually rule as kings.

Barnhouse begins by acknowledging that there are two genealogies.

> The lines run parallel from Abraham to David, but then Matthew comes down to Jesus by way of Solomon the son of David, while Luke comes down to Jesus by way of Nathan the son of David. In other words, the two genealogies are the lines of two brothers and the children become cousins. When I state that Luke's genealogy is that of the Virgin Mary and Matthew's genealogy is that of Joseph, I am not merely following the persistent tradition of the early church, as Dr. James Orr states it, but I am setting forth the only explanation that will fit the facts. The whole point of the difference is that Solomon's line was the royal line and Nathan's was the legal line.
>
> For example, the former king of England had an older brother, now the Duke of Windsor, who had a prior claim to the throne of Britain. Suppose that Windsor had been the father of a son by a real queen before he abdicated. It can readily be seen that such a child might be a strong pretender to the throne in case there was no other heir apparent. George VI is in the royal line for he has reigned; any children of Windsor might claim to be in a legal line. Nathan was the older brother of Solomon, but the younger brother took the throne. Nathan's line ran on through the years and ultimately produced the Virgin Mary. Solomon's line ran on through the years and ultimately produced Joseph. Matthew does not say that Joseph begat Jesus, but that he was the husband of Mary, of whom was born Jesus (Matt. 1:16). And Luke uses a word for son that includes what we should call a son-in-law.
>
> But the greatest proof of all lies in one of the names in the account of Matthew: the name Jechonias. It is that name that furnishes the reason for the inclusion of the genealogy of Jesus' step-father, for it proves that Joseph could not have been the father of Jesus, or if he had been, that Jesus could not have been the Messiah. In the use of that name is conclusive evidence that Jesus is

the son of Mary and not the son of Joseph. Jechonias was accursed of God with a curse that took the throne away from any of his descendants. "Thus saith the Lord," we read in Jeremiah 22:30, "write ye this man childless: a man that shall not prosper in his days; for no man of his seed shall prosper, sitting upon the throne of David, and ruling any more in Judah" (KJV). Not one of the seven sons of this man could have been king because of the curse of God. If Jesus had been the son of Joseph, he would have been accursed and could never have been the Messiah.

On the other hand, the line of Nathan was not the royal line. A son of Heli would have faced the fact that there was a regal line that would have contested any claim that came from the line of Nathan. How was the dilemma solved? It was solved in a manner that is so simple that it is the utter confusion of the agnostics who seek to tear the Bible to pieces. The answer is this: The line that had no curse upon it produced Heli and his daughter the Virgin Mary and her Son Jesus Christ. He is therefore eligible by the line of Nathan and exhausts that line. The line that had a curse on it produced Joseph and exhausts the line of Solomon, for Joseph's other children now have an elder brother who, legally, by adoption, is the royal heir. How can the title be free in any case? A curse on one line and the lack of reigning royalty in the other.

But when God the Holy Spirit begat the Lord Jesus in the womb of the Virgin without any use of a human father, the child that was born was the seed of David according to the flesh. And when Joseph married Mary and took the unborn child under his protecting care, giving him the title that had come down to him through his ancestor Solomon, the Lord Jesus became the legal Messiah, the royal Messiah, the uncursed Messiah, the true Messiah, the only possible Messiah. The lines are exhausted. Any man that ever comes into this world professing to fulfill the conditions will be a liar and the child of the devil.[6]

All Scripture Is Useful

We are only at the beginning of what will be a long study of Matthew, but already there are a few important conclusions to be drawn from our study. First, the problem with Matthew's and Luke's genealogies teaches us how to deal with difficulties in Scripture. When we come to a problem such as this on which sometimes even conservative scholars disagree, we tend to think the problem is unsolvable. But as we work on it and think about it, we often discover how the difficulties can be resolved. This encourages us to be patient when we deal with other difficulties.

Years ago a Bible teacher was riding through New York State on a train on his way to New England and went into the dining car for dinner. A man sat down across from him who, as it turned out, was an atheist. Finding that his companion was a Bible teacher, the atheist began to rehearse the difficulties he perceived to be in Scripture. He cited one difficulty after the other, but the man who was being attacked went right on eating. He was eating New England cod, a very bony fish, and as he ate he pushed the bones aside. Finally the atheist said, "Well, what do you do with all those difficulties in the Bible?"

The Bible teacher said, "I do with the difficulties just as I am doing with this cod. I eat the meat, and I put the bones aside for some fool to choke on."

A story such as this can be wrongly used if we suppose that we do not need to grapple with the problems we perceive. We do. We have to give the best possible answers we can give. But if we come to a problem we cannot resolve, it is not dishonesty but merely a mark of humility to lay it aside for a time until additional data comes in, as it tends to do.

The second lesson we can learn is patience in waiting for the second coming of Jesus. Through the years of Old Testament history, men and women looked forward to the coming of the Messiah. Every child of David was a potential Messiah, and the people kept their genealogies straight because they wanted to know who might possibly reign on the throne. Generation after generation went by, yet the Messiah did not come. It was only after a long wait that Jesus was at last born in Bethlehem, and those who had been waiting, people such as Simeon and Anna, saw him and rejoiced at his coming.

In a similar way, in our day the second coming of the Lord Jesus Christ seems delayed, and skeptics say, "Where is this 'coming' he promised? Ever since our fathers died, everything goes on as it has since the beginning of creation" (2 Peter 3:4). But all things have not continued unchanged from the beginning. There have been radical judgments of God in history. Moreover, Jesus came as promised, and he will soon come again. Knowing this, we should be patient and trust God to work in his own way and in his own time.

The final conclusion is the value of *all* Scripture. Second Timothy 3:16 says, "All Scripture is . . . useful." That includes even the genealogies! We sometimes say, "What possible value can these things have?" But they do have value, and even these problem genealogies have been used to bring people to faith in Christ.

Ron Blankley, a former area director for Campus Crusade for Christ, was walking through the student union of the University of Pennsylvania one day when he saw a student reading a Bible. He remembered Philip's approach to the Ethiopian, so he walked over to the student, introduced himself, and asked, "Do you understand what you're reading?"

The student replied, "No, as a matter of fact, I don't. I'm reading the genealogies of Jesus in Matthew and Luke, and I don't understand them because they seem to be different." Blankley had been at Tenth Presbyterian Church the Sunday immediately before this when, curiously enough, I had explained the genealogies exactly as I have just done here. He explained them to this student, and as a result of that explanation, the young man came to faith in Jesus Christ as his Savior.

The world has no use for Christ, so it is not surprising that it has no use for Christ's words. But we know the power of the Word and should not be afraid to proclaim it, allowing the Spirit of Christ to work even through the alleged problems to bring many to the Savior.[7]

2

Matthew's Witness to the Virgin Birth

Matthew 1:18–25

This is how the birth of Jesus Christ came about: His mother Mary was pledged to be married to Joseph, but before they came together, she was found to be with child through the Holy Spirit. Because Joseph her husband was a righteous man and did not want to expose her to public disgrace, he had in mind to divorce her quietly.

But after he had considered this, an angel of the Lord appeared to him in a dream and said, "Joseph son of David, do not be afraid to take Mary home as your wife, because what is conceived in her is from the Holy Spirit. She will give birth to a son, and you are to give him the name Jesus, because he will save his people from their sins."

Each year on Christmas Eve our church holds a candlelight and carol service, and at the end of this service, after we have read all the Christmas lessons and sung most of the great Christmas carols, we stand in the candle-lit sanctuary and sing "Silent Night" together.

> Silent night! Holy night!
> All is calm, all is bright
> Round yon virgin mother and Child . . .

In this way we profess belief in the virgin birth of Jesus as an important part of the Christmas story. And so do millions of others. Unfortunately, many do not believe it, and others who do, do not know why it is important.

In the early decades of this century, the virgin birth was a focal point for liberalism's many denials of Christian truth. Those who believed the Bible recognized that the virgin birth is indeed biblical and rose to the doctrine's defense, answering the liberal objections. They did such a good a job that eventually most liberals refused even to grapple with the arguments made on behalf of this truth. They just continued in their unbelief, as some people do, in spite of the fact that the Word of God clearly teaches the virgin birth and that the objections to it have been answered.

The Virgin Birth in Matthew

Much of this debate centered around the Old Testament text that Matthew cites as a prophecy of the virgin birth: Isaiah 7:14. "The virgin will be with child and will give birth to a son, and they will call him Immanuel" (Matt. 1:23).[1] It has been argued that Isaiah's word for the young woman, *bethulah,* does not necessarily mean "virgin," though it usually does. It can mean merely a young woman of marriageable age. But whatever Isaiah meant in his own context is a secondary matter here, since it is beyond doubt that Matthew at least meant to teach that Jesus was conceived by God apart from any human father. He makes this clear in Matthew 1:18, which reads, "This is how the birth of Jesus Christ came about: His mother Mary was pledged to be married to Joseph, but before they came together, she was found to be with child through the Holy Spirit."

The account then goes on to explain that Joseph was disturbed by Mary's pregnancy, as any man in his position would be. Being a righteous (that is, an upright) man, he did not think it proper to go through with the marriage and decided to break his engagement to Mary in a private manner. But while he was pondering this, an angel appeared to him to explain that Mary had not been unfaithful to him but that the child she was carrying had been conceived by God. The angel said, "Joseph son of David, do not be afraid to take Mary home as your wife, because what is conceived in her is from the Holy Spirit. She will give birth to a son, and you are to give him the name Jesus, because he will save his people from their sins" (vv. 20–21).

Joseph did as the angel had commanded, and the account concludes, "But he had no union with her until she gave birth to a son. And he gave him the name Jesus" (vv. 24–25).

Two Parallel Accounts

One thing we notice, as soon as we begin to compare Matthew's and Luke's accounts of Jesus' birth, is that they are both quite Jewish in character. Luke was a Greek who wrote in a polished Greek style. A good example is the long opening sentences (one sentence in the KJV) with which he began his Gospel (vv. 1–4). But as soon as we get past the prologue we find ourselves in one of the most Semitic sections of the New Testament (Luke 1:5–2:52). J. Gresham Machen said of Luke's prologue, "It would be difficult to imagine a more skillfully formed, and more typically Greek sentence than this." But he added, "This typically Greek sentence is followed by what is probably the most markedly Semitic section in the whole New Testament."[2]

This is so unlike Luke's other writing that we can only explain it by assuming that Luke got this material from an Aramaic or non-Greek source. He says in verse 3 that he had "carefully investigated everything [about the life of Jesus] from the beginning." So Luke must have talked with those who had been eyewitnesses of these events. In respect to Jesus' birth, Luke must have gotten his details from Mary, who would have been the original, best, and, at this late date, probably the only eyewitness of the nativity events left. Moreover, Luke must have received his material in some sort of written form, which may itself also go back to Mary.

When we turn from Luke to Matthew, we find that Matthew's account no less than Luke's is Jewish in character, evidenced, for example, in the matter of Joseph and Mary's betrothal and the problem it presented for Joseph. In Jewish culture at that time, a betrothal carried such a weight of personal commitment that something almost like a formal divorce was needed to dissolve the engagement. This circumstance did not prevail in the Greek or Roman cultures of the time.

As we read on, we discover that five times in the opening two chapters Matthew explains what was happening by a reference to the Old Testament. He employs a standard formula for Old Testament citations, saying, "All this took place to fulfill what the Lord had said through the prophet . . ." (Matt. 1:22; see 2:5, 15, 17, 23). Then he quotes the text that prophesied the event he recorded. I have already referred to Matthew 1:23, where he cites Isaiah 7:14 as proof of the virgin birth. He does the same thing in chapter 2, where he cites Micah 5:2 regarding Christ's birth in Bethlehem; Hosea 11:1, which speaks of God calling his "son" out of Egypt; Jeremiah 31:15, which deals with the people's weeping for the slain infants of Bethlehem; and an uncertain text prophesying that Jesus would "be called a Nazarene."

But there are differences between these chapters and the corresponding chapters in Luke. In Luke's Gospel, the Jewish chapters are clearly out of place. They are a Semitic island in a Greek literary sea. In Matthew's Gospel, they are not at all out of place, for the Gospel from beginning to end is Jewish, as I began to point out in the last chapter.

And there is this important difference too. When we study the specific content of Luke's chapters dealing with Jesus' birth, we find that the entire content and atmosphere are pre-Christian, which fits an early origin, such as a document going back to Mary. Everything that is spoken is in terms of God's fulfillment of his promises to Israel. There is not even a suggestion that the reason Jesus came to earth was that he might die for sin. On the other hand, when we turn to Matthew's Gospel, though it is clearly Jewish, it is also obviously post-Christian. That is, it was written after the death and resurrection of Jesus when the gospel of his atoning death was being proclaimed throughout the world. For example, it is said that the child's name would be "Jesus, because he will save his people from their sins" (v. 21). This reflects a later, gospel understanding. Similarly, in chapter 2, the significance of the Magi is that they were Gentiles and that Jesus was their king too.

True or False Accounts?

What is the relationship between these two accounts? When I consider parallel accounts (such as these or others in the Bible), I think of the way Reuben A. Torrey handled parallel accounts when he spoke of the resurrection. He pointed out that parallel accounts must have been produced by one of three methods: (1) They were invented in collusion, the people getting together to write their accounts, or (2) they were invented separately, that is, independently of each other, or (3) they were not invented at all but are factual records of observed events.[3]

Into which of these categories do Luke's and Matthew's accounts of the virgin birth fit?

1. *The accounts were invented in collusion.* On the surface this is a possibility. The writers could have gotten together in Jerusalem when Luke was there with Paul on Paul's last journey to the city. Luke could have said, "You know, Matthew, I'm writing a Gospel about Jesus, and I want to tell something about his birth. I wonder if you could help me with a few of the details." Matthew might have answered, "That's very interesting, Luke, because I'm doing the same thing. But I have to tell you that there's not much firsthand information about it anymore. We are going to have to make most of it up." So they would have put their heads together and begun to work out the details of their story.

Or there is another way it could have happened. We could suppose that Matthew had already written his Gospel and had passed from the scene. Perhaps he had died. But then Luke came to Jerusalem and, while researching the life of Jesus, came upon Matthew's papers and made use of them for his narrative. Or again, both authors might have made use of an entirely separate account of the birth of Jesus that had somehow been floating around the city.

Do these possibilities explain what we actually have in these two Gospels? If Matthew and Luke made up these accounts, would there be the kind of noticeable, apparent discrepancies we find? Luke talks about an angel appearing to Mary to announce the birth of Jesus. Matthew has an angelic announcement too, but Matthew's angel does not appear to Mary; he appears to Joseph. This is not a discrepancy. It might be expected that God explained what was happening to both Mary and Joseph. But this is not the kind of thing that would have been allowed to stand if these men had been creating their stories together. Luke would have said, "Matthew, that's a good story you've got about an angel appearing to Joseph, but in my account I have him appearing to Mary. We can't have both. We've got to decide who it's going to be." They would have picked one version only. Or if they had kept both, they would have included both versions in both narratives.

Here is another apparent contradiction. Luke tells about shepherds coming to worship the infant Christ. Matthew tells about wise men. I can imagine Matthew saying to Luke, "That is a very poignant and touching story you have there, but you have missed the point I am making. I want to present Jesus as Israel's king, and for that reason I need to show that even Gentile kings bowed before him." Luke might answer, "That's a good point, but we haven't seen many kings converted yet. Most Christians are simple people. Wouldn't it be better if we talked about humble shepherds and forgot about the kings?"

There are other examples. Luke says that Joseph and Mary came from Nazareth and went to Bethlehem because of the decree of Caesar Augustus that all the world should be taxed. But Matthew begins with Mary and Joseph in Bethlehem (Matt. 2:1). Matthew does not mention Nazareth until the end of chapter 2. Again, Luke indicates that after Jesus' birth the family returned to Nazareth from Bethlehem. But Matthew has an account of Herod's murder of the innocents and of the family's flight to Egypt, so that it was from Egypt rather than from Bethlehem that Mary, Joseph, and Jesus actually returned to Nazareth.

It is clear from these differences that the accounts of Matthew and Luke were not made up in collusion, for if they were, these seeming discrepancies would have been eliminated.

2. *The accounts were made up separately.* What about the second possibility, that Matthew and Luke invented their stories separately? Suppose Matthew was sitting in his little office in Jerusalem, and Luke was sitting in his little office somewhere else. They did not even know the other writer was working on a Gospel. They just decided on their own to make up stories about Jesus' birth. If that were the case, we could understand the existence of differences, but we could not explain the strong, underlying agreements, for there is no mistaking the fact that we are dealing with the same basic story in each Gospel. The central characters are the same, and the central event, the miraculous conception of Jesus by means of God's Holy Spirit, is identical.

When we put the accounts together, we have a long but consistent history. First, Zechariah was informed concerning the birth of John the Baptist (Luke 1:5–25). The annunciation to Zechariah was followed by the annunciation to Mary, an account parallel to the first (Luke 1:26–38). Understandably, Mary then went to visit Zechariah's wife, Elizabeth, Mary's relative (Luke 1:36), stayed with her for three months, and then returned to Nazareth (Luke 1:39–56). Luke's first chapter ends with the birth of John the Baptist (Luke 1:57–80).

Matthew picks up the story at this point. He says nothing of what has gone before, but what Luke has told is necessary to understand what happens. Matthew tells of the discovery of Mary's condition, of Joseph's puzzled indecision, and then the explanation of what was happening to Joseph by the angel (Matt. 1:18–25).

Luke continues by telling of the journey to Bethlehem, which explains how the couple got there (Luke 2:1–5). Matthew and Luke both record the birth, though Luke, who is writing from Mary's perspective, reports it at greater length (Matt. 1:25; Luke 2:6–7). Then Luke continues, telling of the visit of the shepherds to the manger (Luke 2:8–20), the circumcision of Jesus eight days after his birth (Luke 2:21), and the presentation of the child at the temple on the fortieth day, including several incidents linked to that presentation (Luke 2:22–40).

At last, Matthew records the visit of the Magi (Matt. 2:1–12), the flight to Egypt (Matt. 2:13–18), and finally the return to Nazareth, which is also told by Luke, though he does not relate the other instances (Matt. 2:19–23; Luke 2:39). It is impossible that there could have been this much harmony between the two accounts if they had been made up by Matthew and Luke working separately.

3. *The accounts were not made up at all; they are factual.* Where does that leave us? If we eliminate the possibility that the stories of the birth of Jesus were made up in collusion and the possibility that they were made up separately, the only other possibility is that they were not made up at all but rather are two, separate, accurate records of the events connected with Jesus' birth as their authors knew them. All we must add is that, although these events are fully historical, they are also supernatural, for this is the supreme moment in human history when the supernatural broke into the normal flow of historical events by the grace of our good God.

Call Him "Jesus"

Yet, how simply the story is told! "She will give birth to a son, and you are to give him the name Jesus, because he will save his people from their sins" (Matt. 1:21). The explanation of the meaning of Jesus' name is from the Old Testament, though Matthew does not draw attention to the fact. It is from Psalm 130, a psalm in which Israel is encouraged to "put your hope in the LORD" (v. 7). Why? Because, says the psalmist, "He himself will redeem Israel from all their sins" (v. 8). Even in the psalmist's day it was clear that these words pointed forward to a redeemer and an act of redemption yet to come. But in Matthew, as we begin the New Testament, we learn that the time of that redemption has come and that the one who is to perform the work is none other than God himself in the person of his one and only Son, Jesus Christ.

What a name this is! Jesus is the Greek form of the Hebrew name Jeshua or Joshua, and it means quite literally "Jehovah is salvation." This is the message that was conveyed to Joseph primarily, for he was told that the one who had been conceived in Mary by the Holy Spirit was a divine Messiah, the one who had been promised from the very beginning of Israel's history, and even before that, and that the work of this divine person would be a work of salvation, since "he will save his people from their sins." The prophesy from Isaiah reinforces this, for in addition to predicting that the Lord's conception would be supernatural ("the virgin will be with child"), the text also declares that he will be God incarnate, since his name will be Immanuel, which means "God with us" (Isa. 7:14).

This is what captured the sanctified imagination of Charles Wesley when he composed the second stanza of his great Christmas hymn "Hark! The Herald Angels Sing." Wesley must have had this passage in mind when he moved from the thought of Jesus' heavenly preexistence to his incarnation, ending with the powerful name Immanuel.

> Christ, by highest heaven adored,
> Christ, the everlasting Lord!
> Late in time behold him come,
> Offspring of the virgin's womb.
> Veiled in flesh the Godhead see;
> Hail the incarnate deity,
> Pleased as man with men to dwell.
> Jesus, our Emmanuel.
>
> Hark! The herald angels sing,
> "Glory to the newborn King."

Here is a point where, although we are still at the very beginning of Matthew's Gospel, we need to look forward to the end. For at the very end, in the very last sentence, the promise of this text returns again. Jesus has been crucified and raised from the dead. He has appeared to his disciples to commission them for the work he still has for them to do. They are to go into all the world and there make disciples of all nations. He tells them how this is to be done. They are to baptize in the name of the Father and of the Son and of the Holy Spirit, and they are to teach obedience to everything he has commanded. Then he concludes, "And surely I will be with you always, to the very end of the age" (Matt. 28:20).

Immanuel! God with us! And to the very end of this age!

At the beginning of the Gospel we find that Jesus is "God with us" by a supernatural conception in the womb of the Virgin Mary. But here at the end he is still with us, and will be with us always.

What a wonderful list of names we have for Jesus! The Bible is full of them. He is the First and the Last, the Beginning and the End, the Alpha and the Omega, the Ancient of Days. He is the King of Kings and the Lord of Lords. He is the Anointed One, the Messiah. He is our Prophet, Priest, and King. He is our Savior, the Only Wise God. He is our Wonderful Counselor, the

Mighty God, the Everlasting Father, the Prince of Peace. He is the Lord, the Almighty. He is the Door of the sheep, the Good Shepherd, the Great Shepherd, the Chief Shepherd, the Shepherd and Bishop of our souls. He is the Lamb Slain from before the foundation of the world. He is the Logos, the Light, the Light of the World, the Light of Life, the Tree of Life, the Word of Life, the Bread that came down from heaven, the Spring which, if a person drink of it, he will never thirst again. He is the Way and the Truth and the Life. He is the Resurrection and the Life. He is our Rock, our Bridegroom, our Beloved, and our Redeemer. He is the Head over all things, which is his body, the church.

But above all, he is "God with us," Immanuel, and he came from heaven to earth to save us from our sins.[4]

3

Wise Men Come to Jesus

Matthew 2:1–12

After Jesus was born in Bethlehem in Judea, during the time of King Herod, Magi from the east came to Jerusalem and asked, "Where is the one who has been born king of the Jews? We saw his star in the east and have come to worship him."

When King Herod heard this he was disturbed, and all Jerusalem with him. When he had called together all the people's chief priests and teachers of the law, he asked them where the Christ was to be born. "In Bethlehem in Judea," they replied, "for this is what the prophet has written:

"'But you, Bethlehem, in the land of Judah,
are by no means least among the rulers of Judah;
for out of you will come a ruler
who will be the shepherd of my people Israel.'" . . .

On coming to the house, they saw the child with his mother Mary, and they bowed down and worshiped him. Then they opened their treasures and presented him with gifts of gold and of incense and of myrrh.

In the first of his letters to the Christians at Corinth, the apostle Paul wrote that "not many . . . wise [men] by human standards, not many [who] were influential, not many . . . of noble birth" have been chosen by God to know Christ (1 Cor. 1:26). That is a true observation.

Yet the Christmas story tells us that from the beginning of the Christian era, there have been some who *were* wise, some who *were* of noble birth, some who *were* influential who came to worship Jesus. We call them the wise men, or Magi. They came from the distant East, probably Persia, and they were so distinguished even by the worldly standards of that day that their arrival in Jerusalem caused a stir. "King Herod was disturbed, and all Jerusalem with him" (v. 3). They came to Jerusalem asking, "Where is the one who has been born king of the Jews? We saw his star in the east and have come to worship him" (v. 2).

Persians Bearing Gifts

The Bible does not tell us very much about these ancient visitors to Jerusalem, and scholars have been puzzled about them and their journey ever since they made it. Millions of Christmas cards show three kings presenting gifts to a tiny child in a manger. People sing "We Three Kings of Orient Are." But we do not know for sure that *three* wise men brought gifts. There may have been many more than three. And we are not told that they were kings or even when they arrived in Bethlehem. It is likely, in view of their long journey and of Herod's command that all children under two years of age be killed, that they arrived after Jesus had already become a young child. The story contains a faint suggestion of this: When the Magi arrived in Bethlehem, Mary and her child were already settled in a house, no longer in the stable.

What about the star that seems to have guided them to that home? Many have attempted to explain it as an astronomical phenomenon. The earliest theorists viewed it as a comet. Such was the view of the great church father Origen of Alexandria. Later, Johannes Kepler, the father of modern astronomy, explained it as the conjunction of Jupiter and Saturn in the constellation of Pisces in the year 7 B.C. This view has been elaborated in various ways and is probably the favorite explanation of astronomers today.

More than likely, however, the "star" was a miraculous phenomenon, possibly an appearance of the Shekinah glory that had accompanied the people of Israel in their desert wanderings, signifying God's presence with them. Only something like the Shekinah could have led the wise men over the desert to Jerusalem, reappeared after their meeting with King Herod, guided them to Bethlehem, and then "stopped over the place where the child was" (v. 9), which is what the most straightforward reading of the story seems to indicate.[1]

The Bible shows little interest in these details. The fact that so little information of this kind is given shows that Matthew was not interested in how many wise men there were, the length of their journey, or the star. Rather, he was interested in the fact that from the very beginning of this story, Gentiles came to worship the Jewish Messiah. He was also interested in the significance of the gifts they bore.

Gold: The Metal of Kings

It is easy to see why gold was an appropriate gift for Jesus Christ. Gold is the metal of kings. When gold was presented to Jesus by the men of Persia, it was an acknowledgment of his right to rule.

In his commentary on Matthew, William Barclay notes that according to Seneca, the distinguished Roman orator and writer, it was the custom in Persia that no one could approach a king without a gift and that "gold, the king of metals," was the proper gift for "a king of men."[2] This is obvious from the discoveries of archaeologists. When a tomb is opened and is found to be filled with gold, it is usually proof that the deceased was a great person, most likely royalty. I have seen some of these gold relics. In Greece, in the ruins of the ancient city of Mycenae, dating from the time of the Trojan War, there is a cemetery in which the kings of the town were buried, and in the archeological museum at Athens, one can see the elaborate "death mask of Agamemnon," done in pure gold, which was discovered there. It is one of the greatest treasures of the ancient world. Similarly, in Cairo, the state museum contains the incredibly beautiful and literally priceless coffins and other tomb objects of King Tutankhamen, discovered in the Valley of the Kings at Thebes in 1922 by Howard Carter.

Some theologians have pointed out that when the wise men brought gold to the infant Jesus, they were being used by God to provide the funds necessary for Joseph to take the young child and his mother to Egypt to escape Herod's attempt on Jesus' life. This is probably true, but it is not as important as the significance of the gift itself. Jesus was a king, as the wise men knew and acknowledged (v. 2). He was the King of Kings. The wise men confessed his kingship when they presented their gift of gold.

Incense: The Worship of God

It is also easy to see why incense was a significant and symbolic gift. Incense was used in the temple worship. It was mixed with the oil used to anoint the priests of Israel, and it was blended into the meal offerings that were presented to the priests by the people to be offered as thanksgiving and praise gifts to God. Incense gave an offering its pleasant odor, and Paul was probably thinking of incense when he compared the gifts of the Philippians to such a sacrifice, calling them "a fragrant offering, an acceptable sacrifice, pleasing to God" (Phil. 4:18). In presenting incense, the wise men, either intentionally or unintentionally, pointed to Christ as our great High Priest, the one whose entire life was pleasing to his Father.

It is interesting to note that incense was never mixed with sin offerings, which were meat and wine offerings. Only the meal offerings, which were not for sin, contained incense. When we remember that, we think naturally of Jesus, to whom the incense was given. He was without sin. When his enemies came to him on one occasion, he challenged them with the question,

"Can any of you prove me guilty of sin?" (John 8:46). They were speechless. Earlier he had said of his Father, "I always do what pleases him" (John 8:29). None of us can say that. Since only the Lord Jesus Christ was sinless, it is fitting that incense was offered to him.

"We see from the symbolism of these gifts," wrote Donald Grey Barnhouse,

> that the eternal royalty and holiness of Christ were announced from his earliest years. He had come forth from heaven to perform the work of redemption, and he was prepared in every way to do the Father's will so that he might fulfill every demand and obligation of the law. Thus only would he become eligible to die on the cross; and by that cross alone redeem the world. That life could show that he was the fit candidate for the cross, and we cling with surety to the work that was accomplished there at Calvary, since we know that our sin-bearer was himself without sin.[3]

Myrrh: The Gift of Death

That observation leads naturally to the last and most significant of these gifts. Just as gold spoke of Christ's kingship and incense spoke of the perfection of his life, myrrh spoke of his death.

Myrrh was used in embalming. Because the trappings of death (although different) were as important then as today, myrrh was an important item of commerce in the ancient world. For instance, for Jesus' burial Nicodemus used one hundred pounds of myrrh and aloes to prepare the body. If one hundred pounds of that combination were used for just one body, a tremendous amount of myrrh must have been constantly bought and sold for funeral arrangements. Moreover, in Revelation 2 we read of a city of Asia Minor called Smyrna. The name is actually the Greek word for myrrh. The city was called Smyrna because its chief industry was the manufacture of myrrh.

By any human measure it would be odd, if not offensive, to present a spice used for embalming at the birth of a child. But it was not offensive in this case, nor was it odd. It was a gift of faith. Of course, we do not know exactly what the wise men may have surmised about Christ's future ministry or have intended by this gift, but we know from the Old Testament that Jesus' ministry was pictured again and again as one involving suffering. Psalm 22 describes Jesus' death by crucifixion; it was a verse from this psalm that Jesus quoted when he cried out from the cross, "My God, my God, why have you forsaken me?" (Ps. 22:1; see Matt. 27:46). Isaiah 53:4–5 says, "Surely he took up our infirmities and carried our sorrows, yet we considered him stricken by God, smitten by him, and afflicted. But he was pierced for our transgressions, he was crushed for our iniquities; the punishment that brought us peace was upon him, and by his wounds we are healed." Jesus came to suffer for our sin, and his suffering was symbolized by the Magi's gift of myrrh.

There was another use of myrrh in the ancient world that is important here; it was a use the Lord Jesus Christ refused. When he was about to be crucified and the soldiers offered him "wine mixed with myrrh," Jesus refused the offer (Mark 15:23). Myrrh was a crude anesthetic sometimes used to deaden pain, and Jesus wished to endure the full extent of suffering in his death for us. He was willing to bear all that the suffering and death entailed.[4]

William Barclay says rightly, "Gold for a king, frankincense for a priest, myrrh for one that was to die—these were the gifts of the wise men, and, even at the cradle of Christ, they foretold that he was to be the true King, the perfect High Priest, and in the end the supreme Savior of men."[5]

Wise, Wise Men

But enough about the wise men's gifts. Let's think about the Magi themselves. It is true that we do not know very much about these men, as I acknowledged earlier. We do not even know if they can properly be called wise men, since the word Matthew actually uses is *magoi,* rightly rendered "Magi" by the New International Version. *Magoi* actually means "great (or powerful) ones," and it indicates high position or influence. True enough! Nevertheless, these men were truly wise, and we would be wise to remember them and learn from them.

How were these men wise?

1. *They were wise enough to seek Jesus.* God had informed them of the birth of the new Jewish king, though we do not know exactly how. Realizing they were far from him, they did the wise thing. They prepared a traveling caravan and made their way to the capital city of the Jews. Moreover, when they got there and discovered that his birth was not a common topic of conversation, they asked people where he was. I notice that the story does not say the wise men asked their question of Herod first. In fact, they do not meet him until halfway through the story. They must have been asking everyone about Jesus and only came to Herod when their quest reached the monarch's ears.

Are you wise enough to seek Jesus? His birth has been announced well and widely. There is no mystery about it. Have you found him? If you have not yet found him, are you still seeking? A common contemporary saying asserts, "Wise men still seek him."

2. *They were wise enough to seek information.* There is another way in which the wise men were truly wise. They were wise enough to learn from others, even though there was little information to be had either from the people or their leaders. They were Magi, and in their own country, they were the ones from whom others sought information. They were the intellectuals of their culture. Some in their position would have been hindered by pride, but not these wise men. In this story they seek information, standing meekly as genuine disciples when the chief priests and teachers of the law opened the Scriptures and read to them from Micah 5:2: "But you, Bethlehem Ephrathah, though you are small among the clans of Judah, out of you will come for me one who will be ruler over Israel" (see Matt. 2:6).

What they learned when the Scriptures were opened to them was important. They learned that Christ was to be born in Bethlehem, a nearby town, and because they were wise, they must have understood that this was as significant for what it did not say as for what it did. We must suppose that the Magi were expecting to find the Lord Jesus Christ in Jerusalem, for that was the capital city and Jesus was the Jews' king. They probably expected to find Jesus in Herod's palace. But he was not there. In fact, the reigning king did not even know about his birth.

Not in the palace? Well, then, perhaps in the temple. Perhaps the new spiritual leader would be there. But Jesus was not to be found in the temple either. He had not emerged from the company of the priests or scribes. On the contrary, his birthplace was the little town of Bethlehem to the south of Jerusalem, an apparently insignificant spot, where the Scriptures had long ago indicated he would be born.

The wise men must have noticed that these teachers of the law were unspiritual and unworthy men, for they had so little interest in the birth of Israel's Messiah that they did not even accompany the Magi to Bethlehem to investigate his arrival for themselves. That did not bother the wise men. God was calling them to Christ, and his call would in time surely lead them to him. Their quest was so serious, their questions so earnest, that they were able to learn even from those who did not know where he was as well as from those, like the chief priests and teachers of the law, who knew but did not care. Above all, they were able to learn where Jesus was from the Bible.

Are you wise enough to find Jesus in the Bible? The wise men had to travel a long distance to find him, but no one has to travel a long distance today. The Bible says, "Do not say in your heart, 'Who will ascend into heaven?' (that is, to bring Christ down) or 'Who will descend into the deep?' (that is, to bring Christ up from the dead). But what does it say? 'The word is near you; it is in your mouth and in your heart,' that is, the word of faith we are proclaiming" (Rom. 10:6–8). Jesus is present in the gospel, and whoever calls on him will be saved.

3. *They were wise enough to worship him when they found him.* This point is very important, because some people seek even though they do not want to find the truth and embrace it. Paul spoke of these people when he warned Timothy of those who are "always learning but never able to acknowledge the truth" (2 Tim. 3:7). Some people love unbelief, and they use their accumulating knowledge as justification for it. The wise men were not like this. They wanted to know about Jesus, but they were not interested in this knowledge for its own sake. They knew when they found him that they would worship him and give him their gifts.

Our Worship and Our Gifts

Have you found Jesus? The point of the story, after all, is not that we might be entertained by the story of Jesus' birth but that we might find Christ, as the wise men did, and that we might worship him and offer him our gifts too.

What can you do to find Jesus? First, determine in advance that as soon as you find him you will worship him and give yourself to him, holding nothing back. The starting place is to pray: "Lord Jesus Christ, I do not yet know where you are or how I may find you. I have followed many false leads, some of which are in my own heart. I need help if I am to find you. God the Father must lead me to you. I admit that I do not even know what finding you may mean. But I do promise that if you reveal yourself to me, so that I discover you as my own personal God and Savior, I will be yours forever, and I will follow you wherever you lead me." If you are not yet a Christian, I urge you to follow after Jesus on those terms. If you seek him, you will find him.

What if you have already found him? What if you have already become a Christian? If that is the case, offer him your gifts, as the wise men did. Offer him your gold, your incense, and your myrrh.

Begin with your myrrh. Myrrh is not only a symbol of Christ's death, it is also a symbol of the spiritual death that should come to you for your sin. Lay it at Christ's feet, saying, "Lord Jesus Christ, I know that I am a sinner. I know that I should receive the consequence of my sin, which is to be barred from your holy presence forever. But I know that you took my sin, dying in my place. I believe that. I rejoice in that. Now I ask you to take me as your child forever. As a symbol, I now die to myself so I might live for you."

Next, come to Jesus with your incense. Incense symbolizes worship, and you need to worship him as your Savior and Lord. It also symbolizes the offering up of your life. When Jesus comes to live in you, he will do a good work in you so that the deeds produced in your life will become in turn "a fragrant offering, an acceptable sacrifice, pleasing to God."

Finally, bring your gold. When you offer your gold, you acknowledge the right of Christ to rule in your life. Say, "I am your servant. Direct my life and make me strong to serve you and others for your sake."

If you do these things, I think you will experience something we find at the very end of the story about the wise men. We are told that having been warned not to go back to Herod's palace because of his murderous intentions, "they returned to their country by another route" (v. 12). And so will you! Your life will follow a different path from the time you surrender it to Christ, and your path will be a good one.[6]

4

Out of Egypt

Matthew 2:13–23

When they had gone, an angel of the Lord appeared to Joseph in a dream. "Get up," he said, "take the child and his mother and escape to Egypt. Stay there until I tell you, for Herod is going to search for the child to kill him."

So he got up, took the child and his mother during the night and left for Egypt, where he stayed until the death of Herod. And so was fulfilled what the Lord had said through the prophet: "Out of Egypt I called my son."

One striking feature of Matthew's presentation of the birth and early childhood of Jesus in the first two chapters of his Gospel is the way he views each step as the fulfillment of Old Testament Scripture. He does this five times in these chapters, citing Isaiah 7:14 in 1:23; Micah 5:2 in 2:6; Hosea 11:1 in 2:15; Jeremiah 31:15 in 2:18; and an uncertain text in 2:23. These citations make an important point: Christianity is not a novelty but rather a religion founded by God long ago and now brought to fulfillment in Jesus Christ. These texts also document the link between the two testaments, for they demonstrate, as has sometimes been said, how "the New Testament is in the Old concealed, while the Old Testament is in the New revealed."

Prophecy and Its Fulfillment

Matthew's citations of the Old Testament also teach us something about how biblical prophecy should be understood. When most people today think of prophecy, they think of specific, clear predictions of some future event. And sometimes prophecy is exactly that. We have already seen one clear example in Matthew, and another example that is not quite as clear but is probably of the same kind.

The clear example is found in Matthew 2:6, where the religious leaders appeal to Micah 5:2 as a prediction of where the Messiah will be born:

> "In Bethlehem in Judea," they replied, "for this is what the prophet has written:
>
> "'But you, Bethlehem, in the land of Judah,
> are by no means least among the rulers of Judah;
> for out of you will come a ruler
> who will be the shepherd of my people Israel.'"

It is difficult to imagine a clearer, more specific prophecy. The Messiah would be born in Bethlehem.

The other prophecy is found in Isaiah 7:14, which is cited in Matthew 1:23. There is some uncertainty as to whether it is a prophecy about the birth of Jesus only, without reference to anything else, or is somehow linked to another, normal birth in Isaiah's own day,[1] but it is probably specific.

This is only one type of prophecy. The Old Testament sacrificial system is an example of another type. The author of Hebrews argues that the entire sacrificial system pointed forward to Jesus' death for sin and was fulfilled by him in the atonement. "Elsewhere in the New Testament," writes D. A. Carson,

> we learn how the law anticipated the gospel, how the levitical priesthood pointed to a new high priest who would effectively stand between God and humanity and never need replacing, how the ancient kingdom of David served as a model or "type" of the kingdom of God, how certain covenants had a built-in obsolescence that led believers to look forward to the dawning of the promised new covenant (Jer. 31:31–34) and much more.[2]

It is important to understand these general types of prophecy, because many of the links between the Old and New Testaments are general in nature, though no less significant than the specific predictions. More to the point, many of the Old Testament citations in Matthew must be understood in this broader way, as is the case with the three following examples.

The Flight to Egypt

Three Old Testament prophecies together cover the years between the coming of the wise men to worship Jesus (Matt. 2:1–12) and the appearance of John the Baptist as Jesus' forerunner (Matt. 3:1–17). These stories are about: (1) the family's flight to Egypt (Matt. 2:13–15); (2) Herod's murder of the children of Bethlehem (Matt. 2:16–18); and (3) the family's return to Nazareth (Matt. 2:19–23).

Herod must have thought he was being very clever when he asked the Magi to come back after they had found the child so that he could "go and worship him" too. He had no intention of doing that. Instead, he wanted to murder this apparent usurper to his throne. When he discovered that the wise men had outwitted him, he was furious and sought to eliminate the child by murdering all the young male children of the town.

Liberals have made much of the fact that this incident is not mentioned in any secular source, as if its absence proves it was invented to fulfill the verses Matthew cites from Hosea and Jeremiah. But Matthew was under no compulsion to invent such a story. Neither Hosea 11:1, which speaks of God bringing his son out of Egypt, nor Jeremiah 31:15, which refers to Rachel weeping for her children, requires a futuristic fulfillment. They are understandable in terms of past events alone. But aside from that fact, there is also no reason why the slaughter should have been mentioned in any other ancient writing. Herod would not have recorded it, for it did not paint him in a very good light. Further, Bethlehem was a small town, having no more than one thousand residents (perhaps as few as three hundred, according to some estimates). There would have been no more than a dozen or so young children. In an age of atrocities, the murder of these children would have been merely one additional cruelty and not a particularly striking one at that.

What we do know is that an action such as this perfectly suited Herod's character, especially in these last years of his life. Herod had always been ruthless, but in his later years, he was especially terrifying. He murdered his favorite wife, Mariamne, had her two sons strangled, and, as a last act of his long and violent career, had Antipater, another son, executed for promoting himself too precipitously as his heir. The slaughter of the young children would have been merely a minor offense for this great sinner.

In view of this danger, God warned Joseph to "take the child and his mother, and escape to Egypt" (v. 13), which they did (v. 14). Egypt was a natural place for the family's escape. It was not far away, and the border was only about seventy miles from Bethlehem. Besides, Egypt was a well-ordered Roman province well beyond Herod's jurisdiction, and it had a large Jewish population, roughly one million strong, according to Philo, who wrote about A.D. 40. Joseph would have had no trouble finding relatives and friends in Egypt or in securing work there.

It is at this point that Matthew brings in a text from Hosea: "And so was fulfilled what the Lord had said through the prophet: 'Out of Egypt I have called my son'" (v. 15). When we turn to this verse in Hosea, we find that it is not really about the Messiah who should come, but rather about Israel and God's deliverance of the people from Egypt at the time of the Exodus under Moses. William Barclay concluded of this and similar verses that Matthew was grasping for any possible prophecy he could find, even passages that are obviously not about Jesus at all.[3] But Matthew was not as foolish as that, or deceptive. Nor would his Jewish readers have been so gullible. Matthew would have known that Hosea 11:1 is about Israel. What Matthew understood (and wants us to understand) is something beyond a mere futuristic prophecy, namely, that Jesus is the ultimate embodiment of Israel, the one in whom is wrapped up the true character and destiny of the people. The fact that Jesus was taken to Egypt and returned from Egypt was one of God's ways of alerting us to how significant Christ's tie with his people really was.

Further, the context of the Hosea passage is not only the deliverance of the people from Egypt but also God's faithfulness to them in and beyond Egypt in spite of their disobedience. Israel was God's son, but a disobedient son. By contrast, Jesus is the beloved Son with whom the Father is "well pleased" (Matt. 3:17).

The Slaughter of the Children

The second of the three incidents in this section of the Gospel is the account of the slaughter of Bethlehem's young children, those "two years old and under" (v. 16). It is a brief account, for apart from the note that Herod determined the age span for the slaughter "in accordance with the time he had learned from the Magi," Matthew does not elaborate on the details. The wise men must have told Herod that the star had appeared more than a year before their arrival in Jerusalem, which would have been about right. They would have needed time to make preparations for their journey and cross the desert. Herod decided to kill all males under two years to insure that his murders would include this unidentified young usurper to the throne.

But Matthew's interest does not lie in the details of this story, as I said. He is interested in something said by Jeremiah in the thirty-first chapter of his prophecy (v. 15).

> Then what was said through the prophet Jeremiah was fulfilled:
>
> "A voice is heard in Ramah,
> weeping and great mourning,
> Rachel weeping for her children
> and refusing to be comforted,
> because they are no more."
>
> verses 17–18

If we check Jeremiah, we find that the tears of this verse are for those who are being carried into exile. In Matthew the tears are not even for the holy family, who, in a sense, went into exile in Egypt, but rather for those who remained behind and were slaughtered. That might be a reason for tears, but it is not a clear or obvious fulfillment of Jeremiah's prophecy.

What is Matthew doing? What is he thinking? Why does he quote this seemingly unrelated passage?

Some think the connection has to do with hope, for that is the actual message of Jeremiah 31. At the beginning of the chapter God says that he will continue to be the God of the exiled people (v. 1). He says that those who were not killed by the Babylonians will experience his "favor" (v. 2). He says that his love is "an everlasting love" (v. 3) and that he will "build you [the people] up" again (v. 4). Verse after verse speaks of Israel's future joy, referring to vineyards, flocks, herds, and dancing (vv. 4, 5, 7, 12, 13). God speaks of regathering the people "from the land of the north" and "from the ends of the earth" (v. 8). Then, after the verse that speaks of "Rachel weeping for her children" (v. 15), there is a promise that God will bring the people back to their own land (v. 17). In fact, the only reason for the reference to Rachel weeping for her children who have been taken into exile is the command to "restrain . . . from weeping" (v. 16). Instead of looking back in sorrow, the survivors were to look forward in hope.

There was hope for the exiles in Babylon because they would return to their own land, and there was hope for Israel because the Messiah escaped Herod's wrath and would return to his own land from Egypt. That may be what Matthew intends when he cites Jeremiah 31:15 as a prophecy.

Yet there may be even more to Matthew's use of Jeremiah. Matthew has already made the exile a significant turning point in Israel's history in his handling of the genealogy of Jesus in chapter 1. It is the break between the second and third sets of fourteen names in Christ's family tree (see vv. 11, 12, 17). The exile marked the end of the line of David's descendants who sat upon his throne and ruled from Jerusalem. Perhaps Matthew is saying that the true exile, with its lack of a Davidic king, is over now because the true King, the Messiah, has arrived.

This is how D. A. Carson sees it:

> Matthew has already made the Exile a turning point in his thought (1:11–12), for at that time the Davidic line was dethroned. The tears of the Exile are now being "fulfilled"—i.e., the tears begun in Jeremiah's day are climaxed and ended by the tears of the mothers of Bethlehem. The heir to David's throne has come, the Exile is over, the true Son of God has arrived, and he will introduce the new covenant (Matt. 26:28) promised by Jeremiah.[4]

The Return to Nazareth

The third of the historical episodes chosen to fill the gap between the time the wise men appeared to worship Jesus and the moment, years later, when John the Baptist announced his arrival to Israel, is the return of Joseph and his family to Nazareth. Matthew explains that after Herod died (in 4 B.C.), an angel appeared to Joseph in a dream telling him to go back to Israel. Joseph seems to have thought about returning to Bethlehem in

Judah, no doubt assuming that this was where Jesus, as a descendant of David and Israel's future king, should be raised. But he had doubts. Archelaus, a surviving son of Herod the Great, had come to the throne in Judah, and he was known to be as ruthless as his father. Would Jesus be safe in Bethlehem? While he was still considering what to do, God warned Joseph that this was a real danger. As a result, Joseph withdrew to Galilee, where Archelaus's somewhat milder brother, the tetrarch Herod Antipas, ruled.

At this point Matthew introduces the last of his references to the Old Testament: "So was fulfilled what was said through the prophets: 'He will be called a Nazarene'" (v. 23). This verse presents difficulty, however, because a specific verse referring to this prophecy does not exist in the Old Testament.

How should we handle this verse? First, we should note that Matthew introduces the verse by referring to prophets (plural, "through the prophets"), rather than saying, as he does in other instances, "This took place to fulfill what the Lord had said through the prophet" (Matt. 1:22) or "For this is what the prophet has written" (Matt. 2:5). This seems to indicate a general rather than specific Old Testament reference.

Further, he replaces the verb he usually uses in such introductory formulas ("said") with the conjunction *hoti,* which means "that."[5] This is the only place such a substitution occurs in the Gospel. Matthew is probably not citing a specific Old Testament text but instead is referring only to a general teaching of Scripture. A right rendering of his words might be, "This was to fulfill the teaching of the prophets that he would be called a Nazarene."

But the problem remains that nowhere in the Old Testament do the prophets say this about Jesus. Some have tried to explain the discrepancy by linking Nazareth to Nazirite, a person specially consecrated to God. But there is no real connection between these names, and Jesus was not a Nazirite, though he was fully consecrated to the Father.

A better explanation is probably found in the fact that Nazareth was a despised place, the kind of village we might refer to disparagingly as "Podunk" or "Endsville." It would have had that immediate ring to any Jew of that day who heard the name. What Matthew seems to be saying is that the prophets predicted the Messiah would be a despised person, the victim of slurs such as this. He would not be known as "Jesus of Bethlehem," with its many honorable Davidic overtones, though he had been born in Bethlehem. Instead, he would be called "Jesus the Nazarene." We remember how Nathanael responded when Philip told him that he, Andrew, and Peter had found the Messiah—"Jesus of Nazareth, the son of Joseph." Nathanael replied, "Nazareth! Can anything good come from there?" (John 1:46).

Matthew was right to remind his readers that the prophets foretold the Messiah would not be honored by his people but would be despised. One obvious passage is Isaiah 53:3:

> He was despised and rejected by men,
> a man of sorrows, and familiar with suffering.
> Like one from whom men hide their faces
> he was despised, and we esteemed him not.

Other texts exist as well (see Pss. 22:6–8, 13, 17; 69:9, 19–21; Isa. 49:7; 50:6; Dan. 9:26).

Be Wise and Be Warned

As we come to the end of this second chapter of Matthew, which tells of the wrath of Herod against the infant Christ and of God's preservation of his life through the flight to Egypt and the return to Nazareth, we need to step back and ask what the chapter as a whole has taught. There are two great lessons: first, the sovereignty of God, particularly in the details of the birth and life of Jesus the Messiah; and second, the need to confess Jesus as our King and Savior, rather than oppose him as Herod did.

We would do well to think here of Psalm 2, a prophecy of the Messiah, though not cited by Matthew, that explains what was happening in the events described in this chapter. Psalm 2 describes how the nations of the world conspire and the kings of the earth take their stand against the Lord and his Anointed One (in Hebrew "Anointed One" is Messiah). It is what Herod did and what all persons do apart from the supernatural working of the Holy Spirit in their lives. We do not want God's Messiah to reign over us. We want to rule ourselves.

But God is not troubled by this cosmic rebellion. God laughs at such folly. This is the only place in the Bible where God is said to laugh, and it is not a pleasant laugh. It is a scornful, scoffing laugh as God rebukes and terrifies his rebellious subjects saying, "I have installed my King on Zion, my holy hill" (v. 7). God assures his Messiah that he will give him the nations for his inheritance and the ends of the earth for his possession. "You will rule them with an iron scepter; you will dash them to pieces like pottery" (v. 9).

What, then, are we advised to do? The answer is clear. We are advised to "be wise" and "be warned" (v. 10), to "serve the LORD with fear" and to "rejoice with trembling" (v. 11). Above all, we are to "kiss the Son" in grateful, loving submission (v. 12). The ending says, "Blessed are all who take refuge in him." That is what these rulers will not do, of course. It is why they are in danger of a final, fierce destruction. But we are warned not to be among them.

The rulers of the world rage against Christ. But why should you? The hands he holds forth for you to kiss are hands that were pierced by nails when he was crucified in your place. One day he is coming as the great Judge of all. On that day the wicked will be punished, but today is the day of his grace. He invites you to come to him. Remember verse 12: "Blessed are all who take refuge in him." It is a reminder that the only refuge from the wrath of God is God's mercy unfolded at the cross of Jesus Christ.

5

A Voice in the Desert

Matthew 3:1–17

In those days John the Baptist came, preaching in the Desert of Judea and saying, "Repent, for the kingdom of heaven is near." This is he who was spoken of through the prophet Isaiah:

> *"A voice of one calling in the desert,*
> *'Prepare the way for the Lord,*
> *make straight paths for him.'"*

John's clothes were made of camel's hair, and he had a leather belt around his waist. His food was locusts and wild honey. People went out to him from Jerusalem and all Judea and the whole region of the Jordan. Confessing their sins, they were baptized by him in the Jordan River.

It does not take a very careful reading of the Gospels to notice that although each of them begins in a manner significantly different from the others, they come together at the point of recording the appearance and work of John the Baptist. This is no accident, of course, because John's words pointed to the coming of Christ, and his baptism of Jesus marked the official commencement of Christ's ministry.

We know Jesus' baptism was the official starting point of his ministry based on the words of Peter to the disciples after the ascension of Jesus following his resurrection. Peter wanted the disciples to choose another witness to take the place of Judas, who had betrayed Jesus, listing as a requirement for this replacement that he be "one of the men who have been with us the whole time the Lord Jesus went in and out among us, *beginning from John's baptism*" (Acts 1:21–22). Since John's baptism of Jesus marked the beginning of Jesus' work, the witness had to be chosen from those who had been present from that defining moment forward.

The appearance of John as the necessary forerunner of the Messiah had also been prophesied in the Old Testament, most clearly in Isaiah 40:3 and in Malachi 3:1 and 4:5–6. The first of these texts is the one cited by Matthew himself in verse 3.

> "A voice of one calling in the desert,
> 'Prepare the way for the Lord,
> make straight paths for him.'"

As for the other verses, Malachi 3:1 reads, "See, I will send my messenger, who will prepare the way before me," and Malachi 4:5–6, the very last verses of the Old Testament say, "See, I will send you the prophet Elijah before that great and dreadful day of the LORD comes. He will turn the hearts of the fathers to their children, and the hearts of the children to their fathers; or else I will come and strike the land with a curse." An angel had told John's father, Zechariah, that John would fulfill this last prophecy (see Luke 1:17), and Jesus subsequently identified John as the "Elijah" Malachi had foretold (Matt. 17:10–13).

The fulfillment of these prophecies could hardly have been left out, and by introducing John as their exact fulfillment, Matthew rightly ties together the end of the Old Testament and the beginning of the New Testament. There had not been a prophet in Israel for four hundred years, since Malachi. But after four hundred silent years, the flow of God's revelation starts again as Matthew picks up precisely where Malachi had left off.

William Barclay said the coming of John was like "a light which lit up the dark places" and "a wind which swept from God throughout the country."[1]

The Ministry of John

John the Baptist was a great man, whose greatness is overshadowed only because Christians rightly focus on the life and work of Jesus, whom he preceded and announced. John said of Jesus, "He must become greater; I must become less" (John 3:30). But Jesus said of John, "Among those born of women there has not risen anyone greater than John the Baptist" (Matt. 11:11). If Jesus had not come when he did, we would undoubtedly think of John in company with such other outstanding Old Testament figures as Elijah and Elisha.

In Luke's Gospel, the ministry of John is dated to the fifteenth year of the reign of Tiberius Caesar, which would have been sometime in the year A.D.

26 (Luke 3:1). In that year both John and Jesus would have been about thirty years old. John dressed like his great predecessor Elijah, wearing a rough camel's hair coat bound with a leather belt (see 2 Kings 1:8), and he preached in the Jordan Valley, calling Israel to repentance in preparation for the coming of the Messiah. His message is summarized by Matthew in verse 2: "Repent, for the kingdom of heaven is near."

Harry Ironside wrote that "such a ministry is needed greatly today when men have lost, in large measure, the sense of the sinfulness of sin," adding, "It is useless to preach the gospel of the grace of God to men who have no realization of their need of that grace."[2]

The Message of John the Baptist

Although Matthew, Mark, Luke, and John each mention John the Baptist, what they tell about him varies significantly. Mark is the most direct. He introduces John as the messenger who was sent ahead of Jesus, using words that are the same as some of those used by Matthew. Luke is most extensive. He offers a lengthy account of John's birth (forty-five verses in chapter 1) and a substantial record of John's teaching (twenty verses in chapter 3). The author of the fourth Gospel introduces John as early as the prologue (John 1:6–8), records his denial that he was the Messiah or Christ (vv. 19–28), and highlights his testimony that Jesus is "the Lamb of God, who takes away the sin of the world" (vv. 29–34). John also mentions John the Baptist later in his Gospel (John 3:22–36; 5:33–36).

As does Luke, Matthew emphasizes John's teaching. But it is not the ethical teaching he emphasizes: "The man with two tunics should share with him who has none" (Luke 3:11); tax collectors should not "collect any more than [they] are required to" (v. 13); soldiers should not "extort money" or "accuse people falsely—be content with your pay" (v. 14). In Matthew, John's teaching concerns the coming of the kingdom of heaven and the need to prepare for it by repentance and a forward-looking faith in the Messiah.

John's message contained three parts, according to Matthew: (1) a warning, (2) a promise, and (3) a demand.

1. *A warning: "The kingdom of heaven is near" (v. 2).* The most unusual feature of John's preaching was his announcement that the kingdom of heaven was at hand. This phrase, the "kingdom of heaven," is used thirty-two times in Matthew's Gospel, and this is its first occurrence. It has its roots in the Old Testament prophecies of a coming messianic king and points to a place or time in which God will specifically reign or rule.

Because Matthew uses the words "kingdom of heaven" while Mark and Luke refer to the "kingdom of God," some commentators (dispensationalists have led the way in this distinction) have understood Mark's and Luke's words to refer to a distinctly spiritual kingdom consisting of true believers in Christ and Matthew's words to refer to the messianic kingdom that is to be set up on earth when Jesus returns a second time in glory. As a result of this distinction, dispensationalists treat Matthew as a uniquely Jewish Gospel in which an earthly millennial kingdom was first offered to the Jewish people and rejected by them. Therefore, the "kingdom of heaven" was postponed, and the gospel of salvation through Christ replaced it for this current church age.[3]

This is a false distinction, as most commentators recognize. Jesus did not offer a millennial kingdom (plan A) and then move to the gospel of grace (plan B) when the first plan was rejected. Nor are the ethics of the kingdom for an age other than our own. The kingdom of heaven and the kingdom of God are the same reality. Why then does Matthew prefer "kingdom of heaven" to "kingdom of God" as his characteristic phrase? The answer is surely because (1) this was a Jewish way of speaking (the word *heaven* was often substituted for the word *God,* which the Jews were reluctant to pronounce), and (2) the phrase "kingdom of heaven" suggests that the kingdom is also of Jesus the Son, rather than only the reign of God the Father.

Both these phrases are broad terms, having to do with the reign or rule of God. In one sense the entire universe is God's kingdom, because God is everywhere the sovereign God. In a more restricted sense, the kingdom of heaven (or God) is the place at which God rules in the lives of his redeemed people. The ethics of the kingdom are for these elect and redeemed people. In the situation presented in Matthew 3, the kingdom of heaven is at hand because Jesus Christ, the King of kings, was on earth and was about to be revealed to humankind.

But why was the announcement of the nearness of the kingdom a warning? Because one of the King's roles would be that of judge. Just as the Old Testament prophets warned that "the day of the Lord" would be a time of judgment as well as blessing, John also warned that the coming of the kingdom would be a revelation of God's wrath against the ungodly. John said to the Pharisees and Sadducees, "You brood of vipers! Who warned you to flee from the coming wrath? . . . The ax is already at the root of the trees, and every tree that does not produce good fruit will be cut down and thrown into the fire" (vv. 7, 10).

It is true that Jesus did not come as the judge on this occasion. The final judgment will occur when he appears the second time. But his coming was nevertheless a true judgment, because it compels men and women to take sides either with or against him. John said, "His winnowing fork is in his hand, and he will clear his threshing floor, gathering his wheat into his barn and burning up the chaff with unquenchable fire" (v. 12).

2. *A promise: "After me will come one who is more powerful than I" (v. 11).* The second important part of John's teaching is what we have already anticipated in speaking of the coming of the kingdom of heaven: The King himself was coming. In fact, he was already on earth.

John did not know who the Messiah was at this point, because he had not received the sign that would identify him. He said, "I would not have known him, except that the one who sent me to baptize with water told me, 'The man on whom you see the Spirit come down and remain is he who will baptize with the Holy Spirit'" (John 1:33). But when Jesus was pointed out to John as the one expected, John identified him first as to his person ("the Son of God," John 1:34) and second as to his saving work ("the Lamb of God, who takes away the sin of the world," John 1:29). This is exactly what we have to proclaim about Jesus Christ today: who he is and what he has done. It is the essence of the Christian gospel.

3. *A demand: "Repent" (v. 2).* The last main point of John's message according to Matthew (as well as Mark and Luke, but not John) was repentance: "Repent, for the kingdom of heaven is near" (v. 2). This is a powerful demand. The Hebrew word for repentance (*teshubah,* the noun of the verb *shuv,* meaning "to turn") means more than simply having a change of mind or even being sorry for one's sins. The Greek word *metanoeo* means "to have a change of mind," and the Hebrew word *naham* means chiefly "to be sorry." But John's call for repentance meant more than this, which he showed by accusing the Pharisees and Sadducees of an outward and thus inadequate repentance only. John was demanding a radical change of life.

On one occasion a group of children were asked about repentance. One said that it meant being sorry for your sins. But a little girl defined it better, saying, "It's being sorry enough to quit."

D. A. Carson writes, "What is meant is not a merely intellectual change of mind or mere grief, still less doing penance . . . , but a radical transformation of the entire person, a fundamental turnaround involving mind and action and including overtones of grief, which results in 'fruit in keeping with repentance.'"[4] Repentance presupposes that our lives are off course and we need to turn them around. But it also points us in the direction of the Savior, who alone is able to make atonement for our sins.

The Baptism of John

The second important thing about the work given to John, in addition to his message, was his practice of baptizing people as a sign that they had done what he demanded. They had repented of their sins and were looking forward to the coming Messiah.

Many commentators suggest that John copied his practice of baptizing from Jewish proselyte baptism or from the ritual purification of the Essenes, who had centers not far from the lower Jordan River where John was. But the comparison does not adequately recognize the uniqueness of John's practice. Essene baptisms were not really baptisms; they were purifications. And proselyte baptisms signified the admission of Gentiles into the Jewish community and were never administered to Jews. John's baptism was a once-for-all baptism, and it was primarily for Jews, though John would not have excluded Gentiles. This is why John's practice was so striking and effective. Matthew says, "People went out to him from Jerusalem and all Judea and the whole region of the Jordan. Confessing their sins, they were baptized by him in the Jordan River" (vv. 5–6).

Something of the surprise in John's unprecedented calling of Jews to make public repentance of their sins by being baptized is seen in his rebuke of the religious leaders who would have been excusing themselves from John's demand on the ground that they were Jews. "We have Abraham as our father," they were thinking (v. 9). John rejected that claim in exactly the way Jesus and then Paul did after him. Jesus told the leaders, "If you were Abraham's [true] children, . . . you would do the things Abraham did. As it is, you are determined to kill me, a man who has told you the truth that I heard from God" (John 8:39–40). He called them children of their true father the devil (vv. 41, 44). In another place he said that Gentiles would take their places with Abraham in the kingdom of heaven while Jews themselves would be cast out (Matt. 8:10–12). As for Paul, he wrote that "not all who are descended from Israel are Israel" (Rom. 9:6). In other words, not all who are physically descended from Abraham or the other Jewish patriarchs are God's spiritual or regenerated children.

The situation is exactly the same for us today as it was for Jews then. No one is saved by his or her ancestry. You will not be accepted by God because your mother was a Christian or because some other godly relative has prayed for you. You yourself must repent of your sin and put your trust in Jesus, who alone is God's beloved Son and the Savior.

John's Baptism of Jesus

While John was engaged in this important preparatory ministry, Jesus suddenly stood before him requesting to be baptized. John did not want to do it. "I need to be baptized by you, and do you come to me?" he protested (v. 14). This does not mean that John recognized Jesus as the Messiah at this point; he said later that he did not know him until after he had received the sign from heaven (see John 1:31–33). It only means that John recognized him as one morally superior to himself. John probably knew Jesus personally or at least knew about him because of the relationship between their mothers, Mary and Elizabeth, who were cousins. John knew that it would be more fitting for Jesus to baptize him than for him to baptize Jesus.

But that is a minor problem. A much bigger problem is the meaning of Jesus' response to John: "Let it be so now; it is proper for us to do this to fulfill all righteousness" (v. 15). Since John's baptism was a baptism unto repentance and Jesus had no sin of which to repent, how is it that he sought baptism by John in the first place? And why did he seek this, as he said to John, "to fulfill all righteousness"? How could baptism add anything to the already perfect righteousness of Jesus Christ?

There have been many attempts to explain this, and they vary greatly because, as William Hendriksen admits, "The answer has not been specifically revealed to us."[5] Some see it as an anticipation of Jesus' own death by which he was to secure righteousness for all. Others see it as obedience to God's command through John that all devout Jews be baptized.[6]

In my opinion the best way to understand Jesus' words is by understanding what I see as the primary significance of baptism, which is not immersion or sprinkling (that has only to do with the mode or form of baptism) but the idea of identification, which is what I think the word *baptizo* primarily means.[7] In Christian baptism we are identified with Jesus in his death and resurrection so that his death becomes our death and his resurrection our resurrection. In Jesus' baptism by John, Jesus identified himself with us in our humanity, thereby taking on himself the obligation to fulfill all righteousness so that he might be a perfect Savior and substitute for us. This was the beginning of what theologians call Christ's active obedience. His passive obedience was his submitting to death on the cross in our place. His active obedience was his perfect obedience to all God's commandments and decrees.

I think Harry Ironside expresses the idea rightly when he says, "He who was to take the sinner's place came to be baptized of John, that he might thereby be identified with sinners for whom he was to lay down his life."[8]

God's Seal on John's Sign

The last two verses of chapter 3 record the testimony of God the Father to Jesus. We might call it God's authenticating seal on the outward sign of John's water baptism of Jesus. This was an impressive testimony for two reasons. First, the entire Trinity was present: the Father who spoke from heaven, the Son of God who was baptized, and the Spirit of God who was seen descending like a dove on Jesus. It is difficult to think of any testimony more impressive than one in which the entire Godhead is involved.

The second reason involves the words that were spoken. "A voice from heaven [that is, God's voice] said, 'This is my Son, whom I love; with him I am well pleased'" (v. 17). Any Jew who knew the Old Testament would immediately have a setting for these words. The first part of the sentence ("This is my Son") comes from Psalm 2:7, where God declares of his Messiah, "You are my Son. . . . Ask of me, and I will make the nations your inheritance. . . . You will rule them with an iron scepter; you will dash them to pieces like pottery" (vv. 7–9). The second part of the sentence ("with him I am well pleased") comes from Isaiah 42:1, at the beginning of the prophecies of God's suffering servant who would atone for Israel's sin (Isa. 42:1–9; 49:1–7; 50:1–11; and 52:13–53:12). So here, in the words of God himself, we have verification of the essential message of John the Baptist and Christianity itself, described earlier, namely, that Jesus is the Son of God, the Messiah, and that his work was to save his people from their sins.

I end with these questions: Do you love Jesus? And are you well pleased with him? The Father certainly is; that is what these words state clearly. If the Father is pleased with Jesus, shouldn't you be? If you are not, you are far from being a true Christian. If you are, surely you will want to follow Jesus in faithful obedience and point others to him, as John the Baptist did.

6

Jesus and the Devil

Matthew 4:1–11

Then Jesus was led by the Spirit into the desert to be tempted by the devil. After fasting forty days and forty nights, he was hungry. The tempter came to him and said, "If you are the Son of God, tell these stones to become bread."

Jesus answered, "It is written: 'Man does not live on bread alone, but on every word that comes from the mouth of God.'"

Then the devil took him to the holy city and had him stand on the highest point of the temple. "If you are the Son of God," he said, "throw yourself down. For it is written:

"'He will command his angels concerning you,
and they will lift you up in their hands,
so that you will not strike your foot against a stone.'"

Jesus answered him, "It is also written: 'Do not put the Lord your God to the test.'"

Again, the devil took him to a very high mountain and showed him all the kingdoms of the world and their splendor. "All this I will give you," he said, "if you will bow down and worship me."

Jesus said to him, "Away from me, Satan! For it is written: 'Worship the Lord your God, and serve him only.'"

Then the devil left him, and angels came and attended him.

Who is Jesus Christ? We should have a fairly complete answer to that question by now, because we have been given several clear answers to it in the first three chapters of this Gospel.

The first verse of Matthew's Gospel presents Jesus as "the son of David, the son of Abraham," and the verses that follow prove that combination of titles from Jesus' genealogy. The account of Jesus' birth reveals him as the one who will "save his people from their sins" (Matt. 1:21) and as "Immanuel," which means "God with us" (v. 23). In the second chapter, Gentile Magi seek Jesus as the "king of the Jews" (Matt. 2:2) and then worship him as God (v. 11). In chapter 3 John the Baptist identifies Jesus as the messianic King. Most impressive of all, at Jesus' baptism the voice of God is heard from heaven declaring boldly, "This is my Son, whom I love; with him I am well pleased" (Matt. 3:17).

Son of David. Son of Abraham. Immanuel. God with us. King of the Jews. Messiah. Son of God. What an impressive list of titles! Ah, but is Jesus *really* God's Son? Is he *really* the Messiah? Those are questions worth asking, because not too long after this even John the Baptist will have doubts. He will send his disciples to Jesus, asking him, "Are you the one who was to come, or should we expect someone else?" (Matt. 11:3). Is Jesus really God's Son? That is the question answered in this section of the Gospel, where we read of Jesus' temptation by Satan.

The chapter begins by saying, "Then Jesus was led by the Spirit into the desert to be tempted by the devil" (Matt. 4:1). Since the initiative in this account is with God—the verse says, "Jesus was led *by the Spirit* into the desert to be tempted"—the necessary starting place for this study must be the nature of the "temptation." In English the word *tempt* has come to mean almost without exception "tempt to do evil." But the word for tempt in Hebrew and Greek means "to test or prove." This can include a tempting to do evil, but it often means only a "testing to prove the value or good quality of," just as a person might test gold by submersing it in acid. If the gold is pure, nothing happens. If it is not, the impurity is burned off.

It was in this sense that Abraham was "tested" by God when he was called to sacrifice his son Isaac, and Job was tested by the things that happened to him. When the Spirit led Jesus into the desert to be tempted by Satan, the act was a test designed to show that Jesus really was God's Son and that he would follow the path God had laid out for him.

Our Great Enemy the Devil

But that is only from God's point of view! It was God's purpose. From the point of view of the devil and his purpose, the temptation *was* evil, for it was an attempt to get Jesus to question God's word, misuse God's promises in Scripture, and try to win the world for himself by linking up with Satan rather than by going to the cross.

How did Satan go about it? Was it an internal struggle within the mind of Jesus only? Or was there an actual appearance of Satan in some form? This is not an easy question to answer. Aspects of the temptation seem to be physical, such as the suggestion to turn the stones on the ground to bread. In fact, when Satan says, "Tell *these* stones to become bread," he seems to be pointing to them. Similarly, when he tempts Jesus to throw himself down from the temple, part of the temptation at least seems to include a spectacular public display. On the other hand, there is no mountain anywhere in the world, let alone in Palestine, from which the tempter and Jesus could literally see all the kingdoms of the world. That temptation seems to have been visionary. Therefore, it is difficult to say exactly how these temptations were expressed or what physical form, if any, Satan took.

What is clear from the account is that the temptations came to Jesus from outside of himself, for we are told that the devil "came to" Jesus, "took him" to the holy city, and "took him" to a very high mountain. This is not unimportant, for the only way Jesus could have been tempted was from an outside force and not internally. When we are tempted, we are assailed by an enemy within as well as by temptations from without. In fact, as James says, "Each one is tempted when, by his own evil desire, he is dragged away and enticed" (James 1:14). We are tempted by our fleshly natures, as well as by the world and the devil. Jesus, who had no sinful nature, could only be tempted from something outside himself, which is what happens in this account.

But what a setting for it! We cannot miss comparing the circumstances of Jesus with those of Adam and Eve in Eden when they were similarly tempted. Adam and Eve were in paradise; Jesus was in the vast, desolate wilderness of Judah. Adam and Eve were physically content and satisfied. They were free to eat from any of the trees of the garden, save the tree of the knowledge of good and evil; Jesus was hungry, having fasted for forty days and forty nights. Adam and Eve were together. They had each other for company and mutual support; Jesus was alone. Yet Adam and Eve rapidly succumbed to Satan's wiles, carrying the entire human race into sin, misery, destruction, and both physical and spiritual death, while Jesus stood firm as the Savior who was to bring life and salvation to the race.

Satan's Three Temptations

Satan used three temptations: the temptation to turn stones into bread, the temptation to test God by jumping from the temple, and the temptation to escape the cross by falling down and worshiping Satan. Each of these temptations is related to what Jesus had heard from heaven at his baptism, namely, that he was God's "Son" with whom God the Father was "well pleased." We saw in the last study that the first part of that endorsement came from Psalm 2, where Jesus is identified as the divine Messiah to whom the rulers of the world should bow. The second part comes from the Suffering Servant songs of Isaiah, which speak of suffering as the only possible pathway to that triumph.

As R. V. G. Tasker so nicely put it, "His [Christ's] temptations in the wilderness were temptations to rely upon the first part of the message spoken by the heavenly voice at his baptism ['This is my Son, whom I love'] to such an extent that he might be able to avoid treading the way marked out for him in the second part [the way of suffering]."[1]

1. *"If you are the Son of God, tell these stones to become bread" (v. 3)*. Most of the commentators on Matthew understand these words to be an admission that Jesus really was God's Son (meaning, "*Since* you are the Son of God . . .") and thus merely a temptation to abuse his status by a misuse of his divine power.[2] This would have been a genuine temptation, of course; it would have been a temptation to doubt God's willingness or ability to care for Jesus as a Son and perhaps also to misuse his divine power to avoid the sufferings inherent in his having assumed human nature. Yet I think R. C. Sproul is right when he suggests that the emphasis is on the word *if* ("*If* you are the Son of God . . ."). In this case, the temptation's focus lies in questioning God's earlier statement.[3]

Back in Eden, to which this account is certainly connected, Adam and Eve were tempted to doubt the word of God. God had told them that they would die if they ate from the fruit of the forbidden tree, but Satan countered, "You will not surely die" (Gen. 3:4). Here, in a similar manner, Satan suggests that Jesus may not actually be God's Son, or, if he is, he should settle any doubts on the matter once and for all by a miracle. Thus, it was a temptation to question the express word of God hidden under what seemed to be a concern for Jesus' physical hunger.

Jesus had no trouble answering Satan. He did it by quoting a verse from Deuteronomy: "It is written: 'Man does not live on bread alone, but on every word that comes from the mouth of God'" (Matt. 4:4; see Deut. 8:3). If the temptation were only to misuse his supernatural power, Jesus' reply would not be directly to the point. But if the temptation were to doubt the word of God by testing it, Jesus' answer would mean, "It does not really matter much whether I have physical bread to eat, since God will preserve my life as long as he wants so I can do what he wants. I trust him in that. What does matter is whether I believe God's word implicitly or not. If I should doubt his word, even for a moment, all is lost."

2. *"If you are the Son of God, . . . throw yourself down" (v. 6)*. The truth of God's word lies behind the next temptation too.[4] Jesus had rejected the devil's first temptation by quoting Scripture. So the devil got into the act himself, saying something like this: "Well, I see you are a student of the Bible, since you've memorized that verse from Deuteronomy. But, of course, I am a Bible student myself, and not long ago, when I was reading Psalms, I came across Psalm 91:11–12, which says, 'He will command his angels concerning you, . . . and they will lift you up in their hands, so that you will not strike your foot against a stone.' Do you believe that? I believe it. In fact, I believe it so much that I am going to make this suggestion. Let's go up to the highest point of the temple, and then you can jump off. God will save you, and the people who see the miracle will realize that you are the Messiah and follow you immediately. It will make a great impression and will get your ministry off to a rip-roaring start."

Satan tempted Christ to advance the work of God by spectacular and obviously worldly means, which is exactly what many evangelicals are doing today when they try to impress people with so-called "signs and wonders" or by entertainment reminiscent of television. We cannot accomplish invisible spiritual work by outward worldly means. At the same time, the devil's suggestion was also a temptation to spiritual presumption, to demand a supernatural sign from God in response to an action he had neither encouraged nor commanded. Jesus replied to this suggestion by another quotation from Deuteronomy: "It is also written: 'Do not put the Lord your God to the test'" (Matt. 4:7; see Deut. 6:16). He meant, "Satan, you want me to test God, but you have to understand that God is not the one who is to be tested. I am the one being tested, and that means my responsibility is not to challenge my Father but to trust him."

In this reply, Jesus introduced an important principle of sound Bible study, which is not only to trust the Word of God implicitly and absolutely (that is what the first temptation was about) but to interpret Scripture with Scripture, never taking a verse out of context but rather interpreting it by use of other verses or the Bible as a whole. This is what the Protestant reformers called "the analogy of faith," meaning that Scripture interprets itself *(Scriptura sui interpres)*. The Westminster divines expressed it well when they said, "The infallible rule of interpretation of Scripture is the Scripture itself: and therefore, when there is a question about the true and full sense of any Scripture (which is not manifold, but one), it must be searched and known by other places that speak more clearly" (*The Westminster Confession of Faith,* 1, xi).

This does not mean we will not encounter passages of the Bible that are difficult for us to understand. On the contrary, it suggests we will encounter such passages. But at the same time it says that God is the author of Scripture, and for that reason, the statements of Scripture will always complement and reinforce each other when rightly understood. If they do not do this, God is speaking with a forked tongue, which is impossible for him to do. Jesus knew this, which was why he appealed to Deuteronomy 6:16 to reject the devil's temptation. When taken as a whole, the Bible will always provide for a consistent and God-trusting way of life.

3. *"All this I will give you . . . if you will bow down and worship me" (v. 9).* In the third temptation Satan threw off all subtlety and asked for Jesus' worship. Satan showed Jesus the kingdoms of the world and their glory and offered them in exchange for Christ's worship. This is the only temptation that does not refer directly to the words "You are my Son." They are still in the background, however, since they come from Psalm 2:7–8, where the Father promises his Son precisely these kingdoms as his inheritance:

> He said to me, "You are my Son;
> today I have become your Father.
> Ask of me,
> and I will make the nations your inheritance,
> the ends of the earth your possession."

This is what Satan was offering to Jesus—but in the world's way, that is, by an alliance with Satan and evil rather than by the cross.

Jesus has been appointed by God to rule the world. Revelation 11:15 says, "The kingdom of the world has become the kingdom of our Lord and of his Christ, and he will reign forever and ever." But the path to this triumph was through suffering. Henry IV of Navarre (1553–1610) compromised his Protestant faith in order to be crowned King of France. "Paris is well worth a mass," Henry chuckled. For Jesus, the entire world was not worth a single genuflection. Jesus replied to Satan using another verse from Deuteronomy: "Away from me, Satan! For it is written: 'Worship the Lord your God, and serve him only'" (Matt. 4:10; see Deut. 6:13).

In all Scripture there is no better example of the power of specific sayings of the Word of God to turn Satan away and save the one being tempted.

Our Battle and Our Strong Weapon

It should be obvious from everything I have said about the temptations of Jesus and how he overcame them that there is direct application for our lives when we are tempted and must stand against Satan's wiles. Let me summarize by these three statements.

1. *We face the same battle.* I sometimes point out when I am writing about Satan that the devil is not omnipresent as God is. Satan cannot be everywhere tempting everyone at all times. He is only a creature. This means that he has probably never tempted you or anyone you know directly. In the entire Bible we know of only a few people—Eve (but not Adam), Job, Jesus, Judas, and Ananias (but not Sapphira)—who were tempted by Satan directly. But this does not mean we do not face spiritual battles every day. We do. Paul wrote about these battles in his letter to the Ephesians, saying, "For our struggle is not against flesh and blood, but against the rulers, against the authorities, against the powers of this dark world and against the spiritual forces of evil in the heavenly realms" (Eph. 6:12).

These battles are so fierce that Paul warned us to be ready for them by arming ourselves with God's armor. We are to put on "the belt of truth," "the breastplate of righteousness," "the shield of faith" and "the helmet of salvation" and have our "feet fitted with the readiness that comes from the gospel of peace" (vv. 14–17). We must be fully equipped for the struggle.

2. *We have the same choice.* As Jesus did, we have the choice of trusting God and sticking to the path he sets before us or distrusting God and seeking to win victories for God or ourselves in the world's way. What will it be? Will we go God's way? Or will we follow the world, the flesh, or the devil? Joshua challenged the people of his generation, saying, "Choose for yourselves this day whom you will serve, whether the gods your forefathers served beyond the River, or the gods of the Amorites, in whose land you are living. But as for me and my household, we will serve the LORD" (Josh. 24:15).

3. *We can have the same victory.* The Bible says, "No temptation has seized you except what is common to man. And God is faithful; he will not let you be tempted beyond what you can bear. But when you are tempted, he will also provide a way out so that you can stand up under it" (1 Cor. 10:13). True. But what is that path to victory? The temptation of our Lord points the way: "It is written! . . . It is written! . . . It is written!" As Paul told the Ephesians, the only offensive weapon we have is "the sword of the Spirit, which is the word of God" (Eph. 6:17).

Remember Christ's example. Here is Jesus—the holy Son of the almighty God, the one in whom neither Satan nor man could find any wrong or gain even the tiniest foothold. Jesus' eyes were always on the glory of his Father. He lived in the closest possible communion with him. But if Jesus, your Lord and Savior, needed to know Scripture in order to resist Satan and win the victory over him, how much more do you and I need it to win a corresponding victory! We must know it word for word. You say, "Well, I have a general idea of what the Bible is about." That is a start, but it is not enough. You must know the Bible well and have key parts of it memorized if you are to overcome temptation.

Years ago, when I was writing a sermon on chapter 6 of Ephesians and was considering "the sword of the Spirit" and how it must be used, I recalled how many swords I had seen in my day, particularly in the British Isles. Some were ornate. Some were historically significant, having belonged to kings or other influential people. Some were large, some small. I enjoyed looking at them, but they had never done me any good, nor will they. They are not mine. I cannot hold them. They are locked away in great museums, and they will remain there. For a sword to do me any good, it would have to be mine. I would have to take it up and use it.

So also with the words of God. God's words are wonderful words. They speak to every need of the human mind and heart. But to be useful to us, the Bible's words must be yours and mine specifically. We must study them and memorize them, for only the words of God that we actually know will be useful to us in living for God and overcoming temptation.[5]

7

The Dawning of God's Kingdom

Matthew 4:12–25

When Jesus heard that John had been put in prison, he returned to Galilee. Leaving Nazareth, he went and lived in Capernaum, which was by the lake in the area of Zebulun and Naphtali—to fulfill what was said through the prophet Isaiah:

"Land of Zebulun and land of Naphtali,
the way to the sea, along the Jordan,
Galilee of the Gentiles—
the people living in darkness
have seen a great light;
on those living in the land of the shadow of death
a light has dawned."

From that time on Jesus began to preach, "Repent, for the kingdom of heaven is near."

At the end of John 20, two verses serve as an important clue for understanding the unique nature of the accounts of the life of Jesus Christ that we call the Gospels (John 20:30–31). They say Jesus did many things that are not recorded in John's Gospel, but that these were included so that people reading the Gospel might believe Jesus is the Christ and through believing might have life in his name. John included what he did because he had a specific objective in mind. Therefore, he also left out much that might otherwise have been recorded.

What is true for John is true for the other Gospels as well, though the principle of selection is not so deliberately stated. We find an example of this in the second half of Matthew 4. At this point Matthew begins to write about Jesus' ministry (from v. 12). Everything prior to this has been an introduction. But in starting where he does, Matthew passes over many things from the earlier work of Jesus in Judea and Galilee that could have been included.

We are told about some of these things in John. Before returning to Galilee (which John records in 4:43), Jesus met and called the first of his disciples, turned the water to wine at Cana, resided for a short while in Capernaum, returned to Jerusalem for an early Passover, drove the money changers from the temple, talked to Nicodemus, conducted an early teaching ministry in the Judean countryside, and had his encounter with the woman of Samaria on his way north again (see John 1:19–4:42). It is at this point that Matthew seems to pick up the story (Matt. 4:12–25).

Matthew does not say that the ministry of Jesus overlapped with that of John the Baptist, as John indicates (John 3:22–23), but Matthew's language allows for that possibility. In verse 11, Jesus was in the desert near the Jordan. Now Matthew says only that "when Jesus heard that John had been put in prison, he returned to Galilee" (v. 12). This would have been about a year later. He does not tell how John came to be imprisoned at this point, but he does tell about it later on (see chap. 14:1–12).

Galilee of the Gentiles

What Matthew is concerned about and emphasizes—this is what governs his selection, at least of this early material—is that Jesus began his work in *Galilee,* which he identifies by a quotation from Isaiah 9:1–2 as "Galilee of the Gentiles." In other words, Jesus, the Jewish Messiah and King, began his ministry in a predominantly Gentile area and did so in fulfillment of an important Old Testament prophecy:

> "Land of Zebulun and land of Naphtali,
> the way to the sea, along the Jordan,
> Galilee of the Gentiles—
> the people living in darkness
> have seen a great light;
> on those living in the land of the shadow of death
> a light has dawned."
>
> Matthew 4:15–16

What makes this emphasis especially striking is that verses 13–16, the heart of the section, are unique to Matthew. They do not occur in Mark, Luke, or John. This seems strange at first, since Matthew is the most Jewish of the Gospels. Yet we may remember that Matthew also links the coming of the

Gentile wise men to his account of Jesus' birth and that the book ends with Christ's command to take the gospel to "all nations" (Matt. 28:19).

Matthew does not want us to forget, at the start of the Gospel, at the end, or anywhere in between, that his message about this Jewish King and Savior is not only for Jews but for everyone. He is insisting, as much as did the author of the fourth Gospel, that Jesus Christ is "the Savior of the world" (John 4:42).

What about "Galilee of the Gentiles"? Where was it? What was it like? *Galil* means a "circuit." So Galilee of the Gentiles probably refers to the circuit of twenty Gentile cities given to King Solomon by Hiram, king of Tyre (see 1 Kings 9:11). Galilee was known as the area to the west of the Sea of Galilee at least from the time of Joshua (see Josh. 20:7). At the time of the conquest, Galilee was settled by the tribes of Zebulun and Naphtali. But there were many Gentile cities there and in the larger surrounding area, and Galilee became even more Gentile after the Assyrian conquest of the northern kingdom in 721 B.C.

Galilee was not large. It was about fifty miles from north to south and about twenty-five miles across. Yet it was densely populated and was much more prosperous than the mountainous area of Judah to the south. Writing about a generation after the time of Jesus, the Jewish historian Josephus said there were 204 cities in Galilee that had more than 15,000 inhabitants. He should have known; he had been a military commander in the region.

We are not told why Jesus left Nazareth and adopted Capernaum as "his own town" (Matt. 9:1), but if the incident with which Luke begins his account of Christ's ministry occurred before this move—the attempt to throw Jesus off a cliff at Nazareth as a result of his first preaching (Luke 4:14–30)—that violent response would have been a very good reason. Matthew does not mention this, however. From Matthew's account we can only suppose that Jesus relocated because Capernaum's central location made it a fit base for the developing Galilean ministry. Today Capernaum is only a collection of ruins, including a partially rebuilt synagogue. But we know it was an important center in Jesus' day because it had a tax office, which Matthew had once managed, and a military garrison. From this base Jesus moved "throughout Galilee" for the greater part of his formal, three-year ministry (v. 23).

Light for the Gentiles

In verse 23, Matthew tells what Jesus did in these months: "Jesus went throughout Galilee, teaching in their synagogues, preaching the good news of the kingdom, and healing every disease and sickness among the people." But in verse 17 he begins with the matter of chief importance, indicating that "Jesus began to preach, 'Repent, for the kingdom of heaven is near.'"

Although these are only brief statements of what Jesus was proclaiming in those days, they still tell us a great deal, especially when we put them together. They tell us that the heart of Jesus' message was the dawning of "the kingdom of heaven." The kingdom of heaven had come near because

Jesus had come near. As to the message of that kingdom, which Jesus was now preaching, it was "the good news" (the gospel), namely, that Jesus was himself the promised Messiah or Savior. John had prepared for his coming, and now he had come. If we should then ask, "But how do we get to have a share in that kingdom or become part of it?" the answer is clear: "Repent and believe the good news," exactly the message ministers of the gospel have been given to preach to people everywhere today.

The message was the same before Christ's coming too, though the Old Testament faith included an anticipation of Christ's coming. It is also important to note that the message preached by Jesus was exactly the message that had been preached by John the Baptist. John said, "Repent, for the kingdom of heaven is near" (Matt. 3:1). In the same way, Jesus preached, "Repent, for the kingdom of heaven is near" (Matt. 4:17). This indicates that there are no contradictions in Scripture and that the gospel is always one gospel. Jesus will add more to it later, of course, in fact, in the very next chapters. But even here it is the full gospel. It is the gospel you and I are also called on to believe and teach to others.

The Calling of the Four

We have been introduced to the first important location for Jesus' ministry: "Galilee of the Gentiles" (v. 15). We have been introduced to his message: "Repent, for the kingdom of heaven is near" (v. 17). Now we are to be introduced to an important part of his methodology: to call disciples he would teach and who would then teach and preach to other people.

According to the fourth Gospel, Jesus was already acquainted with some of these men. Andrew had been a follower of John the Baptist and was one of two who followed Jesus when John identified him as "the Lamb of God, who takes away the sin of the world" (John 1:29). The other disciple is unnamed but was probably John himself. The chapter also tells how Andrew brought his brother Peter to Jesus, and then how Jesus called Philip, who called Nathanael (vv. 40–51). Thus, two of these brothers, Andrew and Peter (and probably John also), were already known to Jesus and had been called by him earlier.

So what is Matthew describing in verses 18–22? He seems to be referring to a specific further call to ministry, that is, to leave everything and begin to follow Jesus. Jesus had invited the disciples to follow him on the earlier occasion (John 1:43), but this was different, which Matthew indicates by reporting that they immediately "left their nets" (in the case of Peter and Andrew), "the boat and their father" (in the case of James and John), and followed Jesus.

Later in the Gospel, Matthew will tell how Jesus called him (Matt. 9:9–13) and will introduce the others too (Matt. 10:2–4). But here he tells about the call of these four, probably because they were with Jesus from the earliest stages and were active in the Galilean ministry. The calling of the disciples shows that Jesus does not work without means and that his chief way of advancing his kingdom is by preaching.

These are the first four disciples:

1. *Simon Peter.* Peter became the natural leader of the Twelve and is mentioned in every list of the apostles (Matt. 10:2–4; Mark 3:16–19; Luke 6:13–16; Acts 1:13). There are major stories about Peter in Matthew 16:13–23 (and parallels); 26:69–75 (and parallels); and John 21:15–22.

2. *Andrew.* Andrew is not as prominent as the other three disciples, but he is important. He is always seen bringing other people to Jesus (John 1:40–42; 6:8–9; 12:20–22).

3. *James.* James was the first of the apostles to be martyred. He was killed by King Herod, who, when he saw that James' execution pleased the Jews, arrested Peter, intending to kill him also (Acts 12:1–2).

4. *John.* John called himself the apostle whom Jesus loved (John 13:23; 19:26). He wrote the fourth Gospel as well as the three Johannine letters and Revelation. It is worth noting here that although John's brother James was the first of the apostles to be martyred, John seems to have lived longer than any of the others, dying on the island of Patmos at an advanced age. This reminds us that we cannot predict God's ways. God does one thing with one of his disciples and something quite different with another.

"Follow Me"

In many texts, Jesus explains in greater detail and with other images what it means to be his disciple, but the command to follow him, which occurs in the middle of Matthew's account of Jesus' calling these first four disciples, is most basic.

We find it in many of these stories. It is here, in Jesus' calling of Peter, Andrew, James, and John. But several chapters later, in Matthew 9:9–13 (parallels in Mark 2:13–17 and Luke 5:27–31), it appears in Jesus' call of Matthew. Matthew was a tax-collector; he was despised by the people for his collaboration with the Roman authorities. But he obeyed Jesus and followed him. When the people protested Jesus' involvement with this "sinner," Jesus replied, "It is not the healthy who need a doctor, but the sick. But go and learn what this means: 'I desire mercy, not sacrifice.' For I have not come to call the righteous, but sinners" (Matt. 9:12–13). His explanation shows that the command to follow Jesus was not only a physical following or even, as it were, an invitation to learn more about him to see if one wanted to be a permanent disciple. It was a turning from sin for salvation, to be healed by God.

The Gospel of John does things differently from the Synoptics, but the call to follow Jesus is no less prominent there. Indeed, there is a sense in which it provides a framework for the Gospel. Chapter 1 contains a long narrative in which John the Baptist bears witness to Jesus as the Son of God and the Lamb of God, and, as a result, two of John's disciples begin to follow Jesus, as I indicated earlier. Then, at the end of the Gospel Jesus tells Peter, whom he has just recommissioned to service, "Follow me!" (John 21:19). When Peter shifts attention from himself to the beloved disciple, Jesus replies,

"If I want him to remain alive until I return, what is that to you? You must follow me" (v. 22). Coming at the end of the Gospel, as they do, these words are a statement to all would-be Christians that discipleship means following Jesus in a personal and costly way.

In all, the words "follow me" occur thirteen times in the Gospels. But in addition, there are scores of references in which one person or another is said to have followed Christ. Why are these two words so important? They are important because they teach important truths about what it means to be one of Christ's disciples.

1. *Obedience.* Obedience is an unpopular concept today, which is why we use phrases such as "blind obedience" or "mindless adherence" to authority. We think of it as enemy soldiers blindly carrying out the inhuman orders of an evil commander. When we see a phrase like "follow me," we interpret it as a mere invitation and match our evangelism to that pattern. We ask people to follow Jesus, promising that he will make them happy if they do. There may be an element of invitation in Christ's call to sinners, of course, but it can hardly escape any thoughtful student that the words "follow me" are an imperative, a command—which is why those commanded to follow Jesus did in fact immediately leave their nets, boats, counting tables, or whatever else was occupying them and follow Jesus.

Without obedience there is no genuine Christianity. It is not that people cannot "follow" Jesus in some lesser sense and then perhaps fall away when the demands of genuine discipleship become clear to them. Many persons in the Gospels seem to have done just that. The rich young ruler is one example. But that is not the same thing as a sheep of Christ's flock hearing his call and responding to his voice as he recognizes Jesus to be his rightful Lord and Master. Those who are truly Christ's sheep both hear and obey his call from the beginning and thus enter a life in which obedience is a chief characteristic.

2. *Repentance.* When Jesus called Matthew, he called one who knew he was a "sinner." Jesus emphasized repentance (Matt. 9:13), but the need for repentance is no less evident in the calls of the other disciples. In both Matthew and Mark the calling of the first disciples is preceded by a record of Christ's first preaching, focusing on the word "Repent" (Matt. 4:17). In Luke the equivalent account is embedded in the story of Jesus' miraculous intervention as the disciples fished. As a result, they caught so many fish their net began to break. That story ends with Peter's awe at Christ's holiness, which led him to cry out, "Go away from me, Lord; I am a sinful man" (Luke 5:8). The point is that it is impossible to follow Christ without repentance.

How could it be otherwise? Jesus is the holy, sinless Son of God. He has never taken one step in any sinful direction. He has never had a single sinful thought. Anyone who is following him, therefore, must by definition turn his back to sin and set his face toward righteousness. Christians do sin, but when they do, they must confess their sin and turn from it, being restored to fellowship again. Anyone who thinks he or she can follow Christ without renouncing sin is at best badly confused. At the worst, this person is not a true Christian.

3. *Submission.* Following Jesus also involves submission. In one of his most important sayings about discipleship, Jesus describes submission as putting on a yoke. This suggests a number of things, but chiefly it suggests submission to Christ for work assigned. It is the picture of an animal yoked to others as well as to a farm implement for labor. *Submit* comes from the Latin words *sub* (meaning "under") and *mitto* (meaning "to put" or "place"). Therefore, submission means being placed under the authority of another. Again, how could it be otherwise if the one we are following is our true King and Lord, and we are truly his disciples?

4. *Trust.* The fourth element involved in following Christ is trust. It is impossible to follow Christ without trusting him, for a lack of trust will cause us to deviate from the path he takes or cause us to choose to leave him. By contrast, it is impossible to genuinely trust Christ and not follow him, since a failure to follow means a person is committed to some other goal or is trusting some other thing or person.

5. *Perseverance.* Following Christ also involves perseverance because following is not an isolated act, done once and for all and never to be repeated. Rather, it is a lifetime commitment that is not fulfilled until the race is won, the final barrier crossed, the crown received, and all rewards laid gratefully at the feet of Jesus. Following Jesus is not only a door to be entered but a path to be followed, and the true disciple proves the reality of his discipleship by following that path to the end. David wrote about it in Psalm 119. The section of the psalm that begins, "Your word is a lamp to my feet and a light for my path" (v. 105), ends with the words, "My heart is set on keeping your decrees *to the very end*" (v. 112). That is it! A true disciple is one who follows Christ to the end of everything.

Charles Haddon Spurgeon wrote that Jesus' call of these early disciples, like his call of every disciple, was (1) imperial, (2) appropriate, (3) full of promise, (4) instructive, and (5) effectual. "They come straightway; they come at all cost; they come without a question; they come to quit old haunts; they come to follow their leader without stipulation or reserve," he noted.[1]

Two Thrusts: Teaching and Healing

The last verses of Matthew 4 record the two main thrusts of Christ's ministry: "teaching in their synagogues," including preaching, and "healing every disease and sickness among the people." They give us an outline for what follows since the next chapters contain material grouped under these two heads: first teaching (chaps. 5–7); then healing (chaps. 8–9). Matthew contains six main sections of teaching: chapters 5–7, 10, 13, 18, 23, 24–25.

The last thing Matthew tells us in this chapter is that as a result of Jesus' teaching and healing, the good news about him spread throughout Syria,

Galilee, the Decapolis, Jerusalem, Judea, and the region across the Jordan (vv. 24–25), covering all the major regions of the country, especially those to the north. These were spiritually dark regions, but the Light had come and the Holy Spirit was drawing people from these diverse dark places to Jesus.

The world is equally dark today. The light of the gospel has been unveiled by God's grace, but men and women continue to prefer the darkness to God's light. If you are one of them, now is the time to repent of your sin, take up your cross, and begin to follow Jesus Christ daily.

Where is Christ's kingdom? The kingdom is here, but judgment is just around the corner. You will not escape judgment in that coming day if you turn your back on the King now.

Part Two

The Sermon on the Mount

8

The New Humanity

Matthew 5:1–16

Now when he saw the crowds, he went up on a mountainside and sat down. His disciples came to him, and he began to teach them, saying:

"Blessed are the poor in spirit,
for theirs is the kingdom of heaven.
Blessed are those who mourn,
for they will be comforted.
Blessed are the meek,
for they will inherit the earth.
Blessed are those who hunger and thirst for righteousness,
for they will be filled.
Blessed are the merciful,
for they will be shown mercy.
Blessed are the pure in heart,
for they will see God.
Blessed are those who are persecuted because of righteousness,
for theirs is the kingdom of heaven."

On one of my library shelves I have a volume titled *Great Sermons of the World,* compiled by a man who was a great preacher himself, Dr. Clarence E. Macartney. The book contains sermons by such well-known preachers as the apostle Peter, John Chrysostom, Martin Luther, John Wesley, Jonathan Edwards, George Whitefield, and many others. But the first sermon in the book is the Sermon on the Mount by Jesus Christ.

The Sermon on the Mount is found in Matthew 5–7, and it is the best-known and most extensively studied discourse in the world. It has been the subject of thousands of books and articles, so many that there are now books about the books, volumes written merely to survey this voluminous material so a student can get a handle on the various approaches to the sermon.

Matthew's account is a shortened report of many things Jesus must have been teaching in these days. It can be read in ten minutes, and we cannot suppose that the crowds Matthew mentions walked to some remote area to hear Jesus and then he merely talked to them for ten minutes. Quite the contrary. On one occasion a teaching session like this turned into a three-day conference (see Matt. 15:32), and we may suppose that something similar happened here. The teaching may have been spread over days. Matthew offers the sermon as an actual teaching session on an actual occasion, as does Luke in his parallel version.[1] But it is also a sample of the kind of teaching Jesus was presenting throughout Galilee at this stage of his ministry. It is the first of six similar collections of teaching in the Gospel: chapters 5–7, 10, 13, 18, 23, and 24–25.

Is the Sermon for Today?

The theme of the Sermon on the Mount is the nature of the kingdom of heaven and the kind of life required of those who desire to become a part of it. This is clear from the repetition of the words "kingdom of heaven" and from the way they are used. Reference to the kingdom is found in the first of the beatitudes ("Blessed are the poor in spirit, for theirs is the kingdom of heaven," Matt. 5:3); it closes the beatitudes ("Blessed are those who are persecuted because of righteousness, for theirs is the kingdom of heaven," Matt. 5:10); it is given as the reason for the place of the Old Testament law in the kingdom ("Unless your righteousness surpasses that of the Pharisees and the teachers of the law, you will certainly not enter the kingdom of heaven," Matt. 5:20); it appears at the start of the Lord's Prayer ("Your kingdom come," Matt. 6:10); and it is at the sermon's climax ("Not everyone who says to me, 'Lord, Lord,' will enter the kingdom of heaven," Matt. 7:21). The Sermon on the Mount also follows Matthew's statement about Jesus preaching the "good news of the kingdom" throughout Galilee (Matt. 4:23–25), which clearly means he was teaching about the nature of that kingdom.

But here is a problem. The standards Jesus erects in this sermon are so high, the morality so difficult, that numerous attempts have been made to explain why it is not to be taken seriously as a way of living demanded of God's people by Jesus. Here are two of the most important.

1. *Dispensationalism.* According to this popular approach, the Sermon on the Mount is a statement of the principles on which the coming messianic kingdom would be founded. If Israel had repented of its sin and welcomed

Christ, Jesus would have established this kind of righteousness on earth. But Jesus was rejected, and as a result, the kingdom of heaven was postponed. I. M. Haldeman wrote, "This sermon . . . cannot be taken in its plain import and be applied to Christians universally. . . . It has been tried in spots . . . but it has always been like planting a beautiful flower in stony ground or in a dry and withering atmosphere."[2] Along the same lines, the earliest edition of the Scofield Reference Bible says, "The Sermon on the Mount in its primary application gives neither the privilege nor the duty of the church."

But it does, of course! In fact, it is precisely a world such as ours with its manifold evil and injustice that the sermon has in mind, not a millennial kingdom in which only righteousness will exist. This is so obvious that some later dispensationalists have modified their earlier teaching by speaking of the sermon's timeless ethics, while nevertheless continuing to drive a wedge between it and authentic Christianity.[3]

2. *Lutheran orthodoxy*. Lutherans take the Sermon on the Mount seriously, as they do the whole of Scripture. But in line with their characteristic emphasis on law and gospel, they view it as an exposition of the Old Testament law designed to drive men and women to grace. There is something to this, of course. Law must drive us to grace, because none of us can please God by achieving the law's standards. But this is not all the Sermon on the Mount is about. The sermon does point us to God's grace, but it also tells how we are to live as God's people. Lutherans think of the righteousness referred to in the sermon as Christ's imputed righteousness, but it is an actual righteousness that must characterize the lives of all who are truly a part of God's kingdom (see Matt. 5:6, 10, 20; 6:1, 33).

At the other extreme from these two inadequate approaches to the Sermon on the Mount is its use by the Social Gospel movement, which flourished at the beginning of the twentieth century. In those years, social reformers such as Washington Gladden and Walter Rauschenbusch offered the sermon as a sort of road map to social progress, believing that the kingdom of God could be actualized if people would only take Christ's ethical teaching seriously. These men should be commended for their sensitivity to social ills and their desire for an improved society, but their vision was destroyed by two world wars, repeated recessions, mass genocides, and many types of social and economic oppression. The problem with the Social Gospel movement is that it tried to urge Jesus' ethics on those who did not possess Jesus' life, and they could not do it.

Which points us to the right way to view Christ's sermon! The nature of the kingdom (1) drives us to despair of ourselves and our morality in order that (2) we might turn in faith to Jesus Christ and that, as a result of finding new life in him, we might (3) live as Jesus himself lived when he was in this world. In other words, the sermon is about how we are to become and also live as God's new humanity.

What Does *Blessed* Mean?

God's new humanity! It must be new, because the standards set in the opening verses of the sermon are unlike anything that is known or can even be dreamed of by the old humanity. Left to ourselves, our natural beatitudes would go something like this: Blessed are the rich, for they have it all and have it all now; blessed are the happy, for they are content with themselves and don't need others; blessed are the arrogant, for people defer to them; blessed are those who fight for the good things in life, for they will get them; blessed are the sophisticated, for they will have a good time.

By contrast, Jesus calls those "blessed" who are poor in spirit, who mourn for sin, who are meek, who hunger and thirst after righteousness, who are merciful, who are pure in heart, who make peace and are persecuted.

What does *blessed* mean? The Greek word is sometimes rendered "happy," but that is not good enough in our day since "happy" has become so debased. The Greek word for *blessed* is *makarios,* and it is used to describe a person who is especially favored by God and who is therefore in some sense happy or fortunate because of it. Our use of the word *happy* has to do with how we feel about something, and that is not the idea here at all. Besides, *happy* is based on the old Anglo Saxon word *hap,* which means chance, as in "whatever happens" or "happenstance." Happiness is circumstantial; therefore, it is uncertain, temporary, and insecure. The blessedness of the Christian is not temporary or uncertain. It is unshakable.

The Beatitudes

What are the characteristics of those who are blessed by God? This version of Jesus' sermon reveals eight characteristics, expressed as eight beatitudes.[4]

1. *"Blessed are the poor in spirit" (v. 3).* This has nothing to do with poverty, because poverty in itself is not good. Jesus is not endorsing social exploitation, squalor, slums, or starvation. To be poor in spirit is to be poor in the inward man, not in outward circumstances, and (which is even more important) to know it. In other words, to be poor in spirit is to know one's deep spiritual poverty before God.

The first great principle of the Sermon on the Mount, therefore, is to know that we cannot meet its standards by ourselves. It is not a list of high but attainable goals, as if we could motivate each other by saying, "Come on now, you can do it! Just keep trying!" D. A. Carson gets it right when he says:

> To be poor in spirit is not to lack courage but to acknowledge spiritual bankruptcy. . . . The kingdom of heaven is not given on the basis of race, . . . earned merits, the military zeal and prowess of Zealots, or the wealth of a Zacchaeus. It is given to the poor, the despised publicans, the prostitutes, those who are so "poor" they know they can offer nothing and do not try. They cry for mercy, and they alone are heard.[5]

2. *"Blessed are those who mourn" (v. 4).* Mourn for what? If the first beatitude has to do with spiritual poverty and the hopeless state of a human being before God apart from grace, the second must refer to mourning for sin. And if that is correct, then the comfort promised is the comfort of the gospel. "Comfort, comfort my people," wrote Isaiah. Why? Because "her sin has been paid for," the prophet answers (Isa. 40:2). That is the only true, effective, and lasting comfort for anyone, and it is just what is promised in Christ's sermon. We often weep in this life, for our own sin and for the sin around us that harms so many people. But there is comfort in the gospel, and we look forward to the day when sin will be removed forever and God "will wipe away every tear from [our] eyes" (Rev. 21:4).

It is worth noting that these first two beatitudes echo the language of Isaiah 61:1–2 ("the Lord has anointed me to preach good news to the poor . . . to comfort all who mourn"), the messianic prophecy Jesus used to introduce his ministry at Nazareth, according to Luke 4:18–19.

3. *"Blessed are the meek" (v. 5).* To most people today, *meek* means weak or lacking spirit, perhaps even cowardly. But that is not what Jesus is commending. Moses was the meekest man of his day (Num. 12:3), but he was anything but cowardly. A better word for *meek* would be *gentle,* but even this has to be explained. It is the gentleness of love, good manners, self-discipline, and, above all, quietly trusting and submitting oneself to God.

Many of the beatitudes are based on Old Testament texts; this one is taken directly from the Old Testament. It comes from Psalm 37:11, which says, "The meek will inherit the land and enjoy great peace." What is important about the psalm is that it explains what these meek people are like. In a series of powerful statements, it says that they "do not fret because of evil men"; they "trust in the Lord and do good"; they "delight" in the Lord, are "still before" him, and "refrain from anger" (vv. 1, 3–5, 7–8). People like this are genuinely blessed by God. They also possess the earth because they take what God spreads before them and enjoy it, while others fight for more and fail to enjoy even what they have.

4. *"Blessed are those who hunger and thirst for righteousness" (v. 6).* At this point it is natural to think of righteousness as the divine, imputed righteousness that those who have humbled themselves before God and mourn for sin desire. But this is probably not what Jesus is saying. The problem with this view is that righteousness is not used this way in Matthew; the idea of imputed righteousness is Pauline. In Matthew's Gospel, righteousness refers to actual righteousness, expressing itself in right deeds (see Matt. 6:1, for instance). The people described in this verse are those who want to be righteous, to do what is right, and also long to see upright actions by other people and in other places. Jesus says they will experience this upright way of life through himself and the power of his gospel.

5. *"Blessed are the merciful" (v. 7).* The fifth, sixth, and seventh of the beatitudes, beginning with "blessed are the merciful," describe the inner char-

acter of the Christian. He is merciful, pure in heart, and always ready and anxious to make peace. Mercy is first, because it is what we experience first when we are saved by Jesus Christ. It is like grace in that it comes to those who don't deserve it. But mercy has the additional quality of grace being poured out on those who apart from it are miserable and pitied. Christ had mercy on us and saved us. Therefore, we are to be merciful in our dealings with others. Jesus promises that if we do, we will receive mercy upon mercy, constant mercy. We certainly need it!

6. *"Blessed are the pure in heart" (v. 8).* This is another beatitude extracted from Psalms, in this case Psalm 24:3–4, which asks, "Who may ascend the hill of the Lord?" and answers, "He who has clean hands and a pure heart." To see God (sometimes referred to as the beatific vision) was the great desire of the Old Testament saints. But only those who are utterly pure can see God. What Jesus promises here, a very great promise, is that those who are brought into his kingdom and who experience his grace will be purified of all sin and will see God one day. Referring to Jesus himself, the apostle John later wrote, "We know that when he appears, we shall be like him, for we shall see him as he is" (1 John 3:2).

7. *"Blessed are the peacemakers" (v. 9).* This beatitude calls people not just to be peaceful persons but to be peacemakers, that is, to work actively for peace among antagonistic persons. Can followers of Christ do this? They not only can, they must, for they have experienced the peace between themselves and God that God himself made possible through the cross of Jesus Christ. Christian peacemaking includes witnessing to the gospel, but it also extends to all kinds of human reconciliation.

8. *"Blessed are those who are persecuted because of righteousness" (v. 10).* This last beatitude is stated briefly in verse 10, but then verses 11 and 12 also elaborate on it, changing the pronouns from the third to the second person (from "those who" to "you"). This change shifts the focus of persecution from something that is being thought of in a general way to something that will affect Christ's followers personally. The matter is made personal in another way too, since persecution "because of righteousness" (v. 10) now becomes persecution "because of me" (v. 11), that is, because of their relationship with Christ.

The persecution Jesus is talking about and for which believers are to "rejoice and be glad" is not the hostility that will come to them from the world because they have made themselves a nuisance, insulted people they are trying to influence, or been rude, crude, or fanatical. It is because they have become like Christ in his righteousness and are therefore being hated for righteousness' sake, as Jesus was.

When Jesus came into the world, he exposed the evil in the world simply by being righteous, and the world hated him for it. Before he came, people could get away with hypocrisy, lying, dishonesty, and pride, because others acted the same way. But when Jesus came, those dark vices were exposed for what they are, just as light always illuminates the darkness. If a Christian lives like Jesus Christ, he or she will be persecuted. But Jesus says that we are to rejoice when that happens. Why? First, persecution shows that we are in the company of those who have been faithful before us, for they too were persecuted: "in the same way they persecuted the prophets who were before you" (v. 12). Second, we have a "great . . . reward in heaven" (v. 12).

We do not experience much real persecution for the sake of Christ today, at least not in the Western world. But this is something the early Christians understood very well and believers in many countries that are hostile to Christianity also understand today. Peter understood it, for he refers to this beatitude twice in his first epistle, where he deals with persecution: "If you should suffer for what is right, you are blessed" (1 Peter 3:14) and "If you are insulted because of the name of Christ, you are blessed" (1 Peter 4:14). Persecution is a common experience for Christians, but it is proof that we belong to Jesus here as well as evidence of those heavenly blessings we will enjoy hereafter.

Salt and Light in the World

So much has been written about these next verses (vv. 13–16) that it is difficult to say anything new about them. Jesus uses two images to illustrate how his disciples are to function in the world. They are to be like salt, which does three things: It flavors food, it preserves some foods from decaying, and it makes a person thirsty. We are to do similar things, especially make others thirsty for the life that is to be found in Jesus Christ. We are also to be like light that cannot be hidden. Christians are to be like a city on a hill or a lamp that is placed on a stand to provide illumination for a household.

Salt is of value. Light is something that is noticed or stands out. Those who are citizens of the kingdom of heaven will be both. They must be both. But the only reason they will be able to function as salt is that they will be joined to Jesus Christ and so receive their "saltiness" from him. And the only reason they will be like light is that they will have received their light from Jesus.

One of my favorite illustrations makes this point. Donald Barnhouse used to say that when Christ was in the world, he was a bit like the sun, which is here by day and gone by night. The sun gives light, but when the sun goes down, the moon comes up. The moon is a bit like the church. The moon shines too, but it only shines because it reflects the sun's light. Jesus said, "I am the light of the world" (John 8:12; 9:5). But when he was thinking that he would soon be taken out of the world, he told his disciples, "You are the light of the world" (Matt. 5:14).

In this age the world is illuminated by the church, sometimes brightly, as in the full moon of revival, sometimes only dimly, as today when there is only a thin sliver of genuine Christianity and we do not even know if it is a waxing or a waning quarter. But full moon or waning quarter, we are always to reflect the light of Jesus Christ as brightly as we can.

9

The Fulfilling of the Law

Matthew 5:17–20

"Do not think that I have come to abolish the Law or the Prophets; I have not come to abolish them but to fulfill them. I tell you the truth, until heaven and earth disappear, not the smallest letter, not the least stroke of a pen, will by any means disappear from the Law until everything is accomplished. Anyone who breaks one of the least of these commandments and teaches others to do the same will be called least in the kingdom of heaven, but whoever practices and teaches these commands will be called great in the kingdom of heaven. For I tell you that unless your righteousness surpasses that of the Pharisees and the teachers of the law, you will certainly not enter the kingdom of heaven."

The eight beatitudes that begin the Sermon on the Mount are probably its best-known portion, with the possible exception of the Golden Rule found in Matthew 7:12. But in a sense they are only the introduction, describing the kind of people the rest of the sermon is for. The main body of the sermon actually begins with verse 17 of chapter 5, and it continues to verse 12 of chapter 7, the verses marked off by what scholars call an *inclusio,* meaning a repetition of words that both begin and end a section, serving a bit like an envelope or a wrap for what comes in between.

The words "the Law and the Prophets" are the *inclusio* for this section. They introduce it in 5:17 ("Do not think that I have come to abolish the Law or the Prophets"), and they end it in 7:12, the statement of the Golden Rule I just referred to ("So in everything, do to others what you would have them do to you, for this sums up the Law and the Prophets").

Jesus and the Old Testament

When Jesus starts by saying, "Do not think that I have come to abolish the Law or the Prophets" (v. 17), he is referring to misunderstandings concerning his teaching that had developed in the early days of his Galilean ministry. D. A. Carson does not want to make too much of this beginning. He says that the words are not to be understood "as the refutation of some well-entrenched and clearly defined position," only "as a teaching device Jesus used to clarify certain aspects of the kingdom."[1] But the Gospel does contain suggestions of some things that might have led to misunderstandings and criticisms in this area.

For example, a few chapters after the conclusion of the Sermon on the Mount, the disciples of John the Baptist come to Jesus with a question that indicates he was perceived as less demanding in his piety than either John or the Pharisees: "How is it that we and the Pharisees fast, but your disciples do not fast?" (Matt. 9:14). Again, an implied criticism seems to exist in the contrast people were making between Jesus and John the Baptist: "John came neither eating nor drinking. . . . The Son of Man came eating and drinking, and they say, 'Here is a glutton and a drunkard, a friend of tax collectors and "sinners"'" (Matt. 11:18–19). Tax collectors and "sinners" were judged as breakers of God's law.

Most significantly, Jesus was thought to favor sinning on the Sabbath. When the disciples picked heads of grain on the Sabbath and ate them, the observing Pharisees said, "Look! Your disciples are doing what is unlawful on the Sabbath" (Matt. 12:2). At other times they objected to his healing on the Sabbath (Mark 3:1–6; Luke 6:1–11; 13:10–17; John 5:1–18). In one way or another, each of the Gospels indicates that controversy over the Sabbath was the initial reason for the hostility of the leaders toward Jesus that led at last to his arrest and crucifixion.

What Jesus insists on here is that he had not come to "abolish" the Law or the Prophets but to "fulfill" them (v. 17). In what sense was this true? What did Jesus actually mean? If we look at the big picture, we have to acknowledge that his death certainly abolished the Old Testament sacrificial system. And there were other things Jesus set aside, such as the Jews' strict laws of kosher. In what sense did Jesus come not to abolish but to fulfill the Old Testament? There have been a number of answers.

1. *Jesus came to fulfill the law's moral demands.* Some understand verse 17 as Christ's claim that he came to fulfill the law's moral demands. Jesus did this perfectly, of course. He was sinless. He could even ask his enemies, "Can any of you prove me guilty of sin?" and leave them speechless (John 8:46). But while it is true that Jesus fulfilled the moral demands of God's law, to understand "fulfill" in this way is out of place in this context. The issue in this paragraph is not how Jesus lived but what he was teaching. Were his teachings contrary to the Old Testament? John A. Broadus raises this exact objection, citing the authority of no less a scholar than John Calvin in support.[2]

2. *Jesus completed the law's inadequate teaching with his teaching.* Some who understand that this verse is about the teachings of Jesus take it to mean that Jesus was fulfilling the law by completing it, that is, by adding to or rounding out what was already found in the Old Testament. The problem with this view is that Jesus seems to be doing the exact opposite in this paragraph, not for a moment suggesting anything about the incompleteness or inadequacy of the law but rather insisting on its perfection and abiding validity (v. 18). Jesus added to the Old Testament writings, of course. We have a New Testament now also. But that is not what Jesus is dealing with in these verses.

3. *Christ himself is the fulfillment of the law.* The best explanation is that we should understand "fulfill" in the same sense it had earlier, when it was used of Old Testament prophecies that were fulfilled by Jesus' coming: Matthew 1:22; 2:15, 17; 4:14, for example. This means that the Bible is about Jesus and that he is its fulfillment in all ways. He fulfills the moral law by his obedience, the prophecies by the specifics of life, and the sacrificial system by his once-and-for-all atonement. This is a part of what Paul means in Romans 10:4 when he calls Christ "the end of the law."

This is how D. A. Carson sees it: "The best interpretation of these . . . verses says that Jesus fulfills the Law and the Prophets in that they point to him, and he is their fulfillment. The antithesis is not between 'abolish' and 'keep' but between 'abolish' and 'fulfill.'"[3] Jesus is thus "not primarily engaged . . . in extending, annulling or intensifying the OT law, but in showing the direction in which it points."[4]

The Authority of the Bible

This establishes the lasting validity of the Old Testament, of course. It concerns the Messiah and his work. But this is also what the next verse teaches, though in a different way. In this verse, Jesus establishes the authority of the Old Testament by insisting that not even the smallest part of it will be lost until it is perfectly fulfilled (v. 18).

The more literal translation of the King James Version reads, "not one jot or one tittle." Knowing how obscure that must sound to most people today, the New International Version reads, "not the smallest letter, not the least stroke of a pen." This is because the jot (Hebrew, *yodh*) is the smallest letter of the Hebrew alphabet. It resembles a comma, though it is written near the top of the letters rather than near the bottom. The tittle is a serif, the small projection on letters that distinguishes a Roman typeface from a more modern one. In many Bibles, Psalm 119 is divided into twenty-two sections, each preceded by a Hebrew letter. The reader of such a Bible can discover what a tittle is by comparing the letter before verse 9 with the letter before verse 81. The first is a *beth.* The second is a *kaph.* The only difference between them is a tittle. The same feature distinguishes *daleth* from *resh* and *waw* from *zayin* (the letters before verses 25 and 153, and 41 and 49).

Jesus gives particular weight to his assertion of the Old Testament's truth, extent, and duration by prefacing the statement with the words, "I tell you the truth" (in Greek, "Amen, I say to you"), or "I affirm this for a fact." R. T. France calls this phrase "Jesus' own signature," since no other teacher is known to have used it. It occurs thirty-one times in Matthew and twenty-five times in John (in John's case with a double "Amen").[5]

Why should this be so greatly emphasized? Obviously because the utter truthfulness and abiding authority of the Bible is critical to everything we are to know and believe as Christ's followers. If God has spoken to us in the Bible, if the Bible is his Word, then the Bible must be truthful, because God is a God of truth; it must be reliable in all its parts, because God is utterly reliable; it must be lastingly authoritative, because God is the only ultimate and eternally abiding authority. If the Bible is not truthful, in even one of its very small parts, then it is not from God and it has no more authority over us than any other merely human document.

This is why the fiercest attacks on Christianity have always focused on this point, just as a hostile army concentrates its attack against the critical point in the opposing army's line. Here are three ways people have tried to undermine the Bible's authority.

1. *By appealing to tradition.* This was the chief problem in Jesus' day. His opponents were the Pharisees, the most formally upright of the various sects of Judaism and the chief defenders of the law. But the law they were defending was the law as they understood it, which meant that it had been filtered through their rabbinical traditions. Unable to keep the law (as we all are) but unwilling to come to Jesus as their Savior, they did what many people do. They trimmed the law to fit their traditions. It was still difficult to keep, but it seemed manageable. Jesus told them, "You diligently study the Scriptures because you think that by them you possess eternal life. These are the Scriptures that testify about me, yet you refuse to come to me to have life" (John 5:39–40). A little later he said, "Your accuser is Moses on whom your hopes are set" (v. 45). The next section of the Sermon on the Mount explains how some had distorted the law and how it ought to be interpreted.

The Pharisees were not the only ones who did this. Distorting the Bible by man-made traditions also marked the church of the Middle Ages and is what the Protestant reformers protested by the slogan *sola Scriptura. Sola Scriptura* means "Scripture alone" as the believer's ultimate authority. The reformers knew that Christians will always have traditions, some of them right and valuable and others not. But by *sola Scriptura* they meant to say that whenever our traditions and the Bible are in conflict, the Bible must be given preeminence. If we can be shown from Scripture that our traditions are wrong, then we must change our traditions if we are truly Christians.

2. *By elevating reason above revelation.* The second assault on the Bible's authority was to measure it by mere reason and judge it by scientific or historical assumptions. This assault emerged with the eighteenth-century Enlightenment,

and it is still with us in the form of liberal Christianity. Liberalism judges the Bible by the measure of human reasoning alone, assuming that if what the Bible says disagrees with what we consider right or think we have discovered, then it is the Bible and not ourselves that is mistaken.

We need our minds, of course. God has given us the ability to reason, and we should use it, especially when studying the Bible. But if our reason and the Bible are in conflict, our reason must bow to the Bible's authority. This is the only reasonable thing to do if the Bible has actually been given to us by God, as Christians maintain. God knows everything we do not know and he knows it to perfection. When God tells us something, we can be sure that what he is saying can be trusted.

3. *By rejecting the Bible's sufficiency.* The first of these three assaults on the Bible was the ancient one practiced by the Pharisees and by the medieval church. The second came from the Enlightenment and liberalism. The third hits closer to home because it is the error of evangelicals who agree with everything Jesus taught in this sermon, even arguing for the inerrancy of the Bible's jots and tittles, but who still undermine the Bible's authority by supposing that somehow the Bible is just not adequate for the work demanded of Christians today.

Is the Bible sufficient for *the church's evangelistic task?* Many do not seem to think so since they abandon Bible teaching for "signs and wonders," sociological techniques, and entertainment. Many attract large congregations by such methods, often on television. But trying to do God's work in secular ways only produces secular results, and the rapid turnover in many of these ministries shows this to be the case.

Is the Bible sufficient for *growth in Christian character or godliness?* Many do not believe it. So they offer self-help programs or recommend counseling instead. I am not saying these offerings have no value at all. They do in some cases. But we have more of this kind of Christianity than at any time in the long history of the church, and for many sectors of the church, true Christian character and godliness have never been more lacking.

Is the Bible sufficient for *making an impact on society?* Again, many do not think so. Instead of teaching the Bible, they put their effort into political action groups, lobby for changes on the Supreme Court, or try to elect increasing numbers of Christian legislators. Some of these efforts have some value, but they are not God's way of changing either people or society. Christians need to stand on the sure foundation of God's Word and expect God to bless it in transforming human lives. It is a matter of simple faith in God rather than unbelief.

The Measure of a Disciple

Not only do Christians need to believe the Bible and stand on it as a matter of principle, they need to obey it and act on it too, which is the ultimate test of whether any of us actually believe God's Word or not. This is what

Jesus addresses in the next verse when he says, "Anyone who breaks one of the least of these commandments and teaches others to do the same will be called least in the kingdom of heaven, but whoever practices and teaches these commands will be called great in the kingdom of heaven" (v. 19).

One thing this verse teaches is the existence of gradations in God's kingdom, that is, degrees of rewards. Some disciples will rate high, others low. Moreover, this evaluation will be according to a two-pronged scale: (1) It will take note of whoever keeps the law and does not break it, and (2) it will take note of whoever teaches the law to others and does not lead them to break it. So the standard is both personal adherence and obedience to God's Word and also the communication or teaching of that Word to others.

Teachers of the Bible have a particularly high obligation in this area. The disciples themselves were among them. They were learning from Jesus, but before long the disciples would be teaching others in Christ's name. When that day came, they would need to be sure they were teaching God's Word and not their own ideas or anything that might lead others to break God's law. They would be judged on whether they lived and taught what God had commanded. All Christians will be judged by this measure. Jesus suggested this when he spoke about anyone who might mislead God's children: "It would be better for [such a person] to be thrown into the sea with a millstone tied around his neck than for him to cause one of these little ones to sin" (Luke 17:2).

Faith, Justification, and Good Works

Verse 19 is mostly negative, addressing the failure to practice and teach what is right. In the last verse of this section, we come to what is positive. But strikingly, the positive is no more encouraging than the negative. It is stunning, sobering, even frightening in its rigor. "For I tell you that unless your righteousness surpasses that of the Pharisees and the teachers of the law, you will certainly not enter the kingdom of heaven" (v. 20). More even than the Pharisees and teachers of the law? Aren't they the most upright and moral of all people? Aren't they known everywhere for their good works?

Jesus' statement is especially sobering in contrast to what he has just said. In the preceding verse he said that failing to practice the law or teaching others to break it would result in a dishonorable place in God's kingdom. But here he says that without a righteousness surpassing even that of the Pharisees and teachers of the law, the alleged disciple will have no place in God's kingdom at all.

Here I have to correct the way I wrote about this verse a quarter of a century ago. When I handled this verse for the first time in a series of messages that eventually appeared in my book *The Sermon on the Mount: An Exposition,* I taught that the righteousness referred to in verse 20 is the divine righteousness that comes to us by God imputing it to us on the basis of Jesus' death.[6] Nothing I said about the need for imputed righteousness was wrong in itself. We do need that righteousness. Without it we are lost. But as I have indicated several times earlier in this series, this is not the way "righteousness" is used in Matthew's Gospel.

In Matthew, "righteousness" means an actual conformity to God's demands in Scripture, both externally and also internally, as the next verses in the Sermon on the Mount will show. But how are we to match that to what we have heard about justification through Christ's work on our behalf?

The answer is that although justification by the imputed righteousness of Christ is the core of the gospel and utterly essential—Luther called it "the doctrine by which the church stands or falls"—it is not the whole of the gospel, and it is not what Jesus is talking about here. It is true that God justifies the ungodly on the basis of Christ's work, but that is not all God does. God also regenerates the one who is being justified. Thus, there is no justification without regeneration, just as there is no regeneration without justification. The important point is that the re-created person will actually live a moral life superior to that of the Pharisees.

Regeneration is what Jesus was talking about when he told Nicodemus, "You must be born again" (John 3:7). It is what Paul was writing about when he told the Ephesians, "God . . . made us alive with Christ even when we were dead in transgressions" (Eph. 2:4–5). On the basis of this distinction, Paul then speaks of two kinds of works, those we are capable of by ourselves (like the righteousness of the Pharisees) and those that are produced in us by the new life of Christ within. Paul wrote, "For it is by grace you have been saved, through faith—and this not from yourselves, it is the gift of God—not by works, so that no one can boast. For we are God's workmanship, created in Christ Jesus to do good works, which God prepared in advance for us to do" (Eph. 2:8–10). As D. A. Carson rightly observes, "Verse 20 does not establish how the righteousness is to be gained, developed or empowered; it simply lays out the demand."[7]

How then is this superior, practical righteousness to be gained, developed, and empowered? It is by coming to Christ, finding both justification and new life in him, and then by obeying and serving God by God's own power. We are not capable of obeying and serving God by our own strength. We will be able to do it only because "it is God who works in you to will and to act according to his good purpose" (Phil. 2:13).

The wonderful thing about this is that when we find ourselves doing good works, we will not take credit for ourselves (which is what the Pharisees did, judging themselves to be persons who were morally superior to other people). Instead, we will give all the glory to God by whom this righteousness is attained and by whose power alone these good works can be done. Moreover, we will marvel at the wisdom of God, which made such a great salvation possible, and we will say, as Paul did in Romans, "To him be the glory forever! Amen" (Rom. 11:36).[8]

10

Ethics of the Heart

Matthew 5:21–47

"You have heard that it was said to the people long ago, 'Do not murder, and anyone who murders will be subject to judgment.' But I tell you that anyone who is angry with his brother will be subject to judgment. . . .

"You have heard that it was said, 'Do not commit adultery.' But I tell you that anyone who looks at a woman lustfully has already committed adultery with her in his heart. . . .

"It has been said, 'Anyone who divorces his wife must give her a certificate of divorce.' But I tell you that anyone who divorces his wife, except for marital unfaithfulness, causes her to become an adulteress, and anyone who marries the divorced woman commits adultery. . . .

"Again, you have heard that it was said to the people long ago, 'Do not break your oath, but keep the oaths you have made to the Lord.' But I tell you, Do not swear at all. . . .

"You have heard that it was said, 'Eye for eye, and tooth for tooth.' But I tell you, Do not resist an evil person. If someone strikes you on the right cheek, turn to him the other also. . . .

"You have heard that it was said, 'Love your neighbor and hate your enemy.' But I tell you: Love your enemies and pray for those who persecute you, that you may be sons of your Father in heaven."

John H. Gerstner, a former professor at Pittsburgh Theological Seminary, observed on one occasion that modern authors write as if they had never met a righteous man or a virtuous woman.

If that is correct, it presents a serious problem for us: What, then, is righteousness? And where can righteousness be found?

We might ask the same questions at this point in our study of the Sermon on the Mount. The acknowledged moral giants of Jesus' day were the Pharisees and the teachers of the law. They made it their lifetime goal to study and obey the Scriptures. But Jesus has just said that the only people who can enter the kingdom of heaven are those who possess a righteousness surpassing the righteousness of these teachers. Where, then, shall we turn to discover what true righteousness is like? We must turn to Jesus, of course. But in addition to that, we can turn to what Jesus talks about in the next section of the Sermon on the Mount. He has called for a righteousness surpassing that of the Pharisees in verse 20. Now, from verse 21 to the end of chapter 5, he explains what a righteousness that "surpasses that of the Pharisees and the teachers of the law" is like. We need to think about these verses carefully, because there is no better treatment of the differences between these two kinds of righteousness anywhere else in the Bible, and we must have this better righteousness.

Our starting place is to understand that the contrasts in this section are not between Moses' teaching and Jesus' teaching, for Jesus has already stated his intention to uphold the Old Testament law. William Barclay is entirely wrong when he writes that "Jesus quotes the Law, only to contradict it, and to substitute a teaching of his own."[1] Rather, the contrasts are between the way the law had been mishandled by the Pharisees and how it should be handled. When Jesus quotes from the Old Testament, he says, "It is written" (see Matt. 4:4, 7, 10). But in these verses, when he introduces the Pharisees' and others' mistaken teaching, he begins, "It was said" or "It has been said" (vv. 21, 27, 31, 33, 38, 43), indicating that what he is rejecting is not the Old Testament teaching but those human interpretations that had distorted it.

Murder: The Sixth Commandment

The way Jesus handles this material is by contrasts ("You have heard that it was said . . . but I tell you . . ."), and the point at which these contrasts begin is the sixth commandment. Ever since Sinai, the Jews had known "you shall not murder"; it was part of God's law. But the leaders of the people had joined that commandment (found in Exod. 20:13) to Numbers 35:30, which demanded death for murderers, implying that the sixth commandment referred only to the specific act of killing.

Is that all murder is? asked Jesus. Is it nothing but killing? Suppose a man wants to kill his enemy but is stopped by some unexpected circumstance. Is he innocent just because he didn't get a chance to follow through on his desire? Suppose he is too cowardly to kill but would like to do it. Or suppose he is just afraid of getting caught. What if he only hates his enemy? Or insults him? Is he still innocent of breaking this commandment?

No, says Jesus. In a human court the only acts that can be judged and punished are external acts, because human beings can look only on outward things. They cannot see the heart. But in God's court "anyone who is angry with his brother will be subject to judgment," and anyone who merely says, "'You fool!' will be in danger of the fire of hell" (v. 22).

This is not earth-shatteringly new, of course. The Pharisees and other teachers of the law should have discovered this deeper meaning of the sixth commandment by themselves. William Hendriksen observed rightly,

> There was no excuse for the fact that in their interpretation of the sixth commandment the scribes and Pharisees of Jesus' day, in agreement with the men of long ago, were omitting the main lesson. Moses had emphasized love for God (Deut. 6:5) and for man (Lev. 19:18). Not only that but the very first domestic quarrel narrative, the story of Cain and Abel, had in a very impressive manner pointed up the evil of jealous anger, as being the root of murder (Gen. 4:1–16). . . . Accordingly Jesus, in interpreting the sixth commandment as he does, far from annulling it, is showing what it had meant from the very beginning.[2]

There is something else in these verses. It is true that they interpret the sixth commandment definitively. We now know exactly what the words "you shall not murder" mean. But in addition to that, Jesus also tells us what to do when we do become angry or when we know we have done something wrong to someone else. (1) We must make the wrong right, being reconciled to our brother (vv. 24–25); and (2) we must make things right immediately, even before we worship God (vv. 23–24).

The reason God comes into the picture is because the sin of anger, like all sins, is ultimately against God and must be made right before him. This is why Jesus talks about being "thrown into prison" until "you have paid the last penny" (vv. 25–26). It is not just a human prison he is thinking of. It is hell, which brings the end of the section (v. 26) back to what Jesus warned his hearers of at the beginning (v. 22).

Adultery: The Seventh Commandment

What Jesus taught about murder in verses 21–26 he now teaches in a directly parallel way about adultery, in verses 27–30. He defines it first, teaching that lust or any other impure sexual thoughts are the equivalent of adultery, just as anger or scornful talk is the equivalent of murder. Then he teaches what can be done about it, saying that whatever causes a person trouble in this area should be dealt with radically.

Is adultery wrong? Yes, that is what Jesus teaches. Is sex outside of marriage wrong? Yes, that is clear too. But Jesus is not just picking on people who have fallen into open sexual sins, as so many in our day have. He is probing deeper into the meaning of this commandment, and what he is saying is that the root of the problem is in the impure desires of the heart. It is there, in the heart, that something is radically wrong.

I recall the section of *Mere Christianity* in which the great Christian apologist C. S. Lewis is discussing ethics and comes to the Bible's teaching about sex. He says that the appetite is in ludicrous excess of its function. Then he illustrates.

> You can get a large audience together for a strip-tease act—that is, to watch a girl undress on the stage. Now suppose you came to a country where you could fill a theatre by simply bringing a covered plate onto the stage and then slowly lifting the cover so as to let everyone see, just before the lights went out, that it contained a mutton chop or a bit of bacon, would you not think that in that country something had gone wrong with the appetite for food? And would not anyone who had grown up in a different world think there was something equally queer about the state of the sex instinct among us?[3]

The common argument against this idea is that sex is a problem but that it has become so only because it has been hushed up, as the Victorians are supposed to have done. But that was a century ago. In our day sex and sex-related matters are not hushed up. Nor have they been hushed up for decades. They are discussed without end in magazines and on radio and television, not to mention their treatment in movies. Yet we have more outright perversions, more adultery, more divorce, more illegitimacy, and more downright misery and confusion in this area than at any time in our history. Hushed up? As Lewis says, it is probably the other way around. People hushed up sex originally because it had become such a cesspool, and it may happen again as our present promiscuous age gives rise to a new Victorian temperament.

In the meantime, what should be done? I suppose Jesus was thinking of people living in an age such as ours when he prescribed the radical treatment described in verses 29 and 30. As many people know, these verses led the early church father Origen to obey them literally by having himself castrated. This is not what Jesus is teaching here since he explains himself in Matthew 18:7–9, where hands and eyes stand for "things that cause people to sin" (v. 7). So the meaning is this: Get rid of whatever is tempting you to sin. Suggestive movies, especially the kind you can rent at video stores and bring home to watch privately? Pornography? Even the daily talk shows that wallow in sexual dirt almost endlessly? Yes, indeed. All of the above. Get rid of the poison. Shut the shows off. Protect your mind from such defilement.

Of course, in the final analysis, the answer to the problem is not merely to escape the temptation, especially today when it is nearly impossible to avoid all perverse sexual stimulation by our culture. The real answer is a biblical understanding of marriage and of joyful sexual experience within it. But that is something developed elsewhere in the New Testament.

Divorce: Deuteronomy 24:1–4

The great problem with marriage among the Jews in Jesus' day was the ease with which so many men divorced their wives. How could this happen in a culture so deliberately based on the Bible and its standards? Or among a people known for being so centered on the family? The answer is what we have been noting all along: the perversion of the heart. In the case of divorce it worked like this.

The only passage in the Old Testament to deal explicity with divorce was Deuteronomy 24:1–4, which reads:

> If a man marries a woman who becomes displeasing to him because he finds something indecent about her, and he writes her a certificate of divorce, gives it to her and sends her from his house, and if after she leaves his house she becomes the wife of another man, and her second husband dislikes her and writes her a certificate of divorce, gives it to her and sends her from his house, or if he dies, then her first husband, who divorced her, is not allowed to marry her again after she has been defiled.

That passage does not teach divorce, though it recognizes that it happens, noting that husbands should give their wives formal divorce certificates to indicate they had renounced all claim to them. The point of the passage is that if a woman has been divorced by her husband, marries another man, and is then released from that marriage either by another divorce or by the second husband's death, then she is not allowed to return to the first husband on the grounds that "she has been defiled."

But here is what happened. In exactly the way people often function in moral areas today, the teachers of Christ's time had become legalistic about the "certificate of divorce" but excessively liberal about what the husband was allowed to find "displeasing" or "indecent" in his wife. They ignored the matter of remarrying the first husband entirely.

Defining what was displeasing led to a well-known disagreement between the Rabbis Shammai and Hillel. Shammai was a conservative, and he interpreted the grounds of offense as adultery or sexual impurity in the woman. Hillel was a liberal, and he broadened the woman's offense to include even so trivial matters as spoiling dinner, being troublesome or given to quarrels, or speaking disrespectfully of her husband's parents. Given the nature of the human heart, it is easy to see which interpretation prevailed. Divorce was allowed for nearly anything.

This issue will come up again later when we get to Matthew 19:3–12, where it is discussed in greater detail. But already we see the answer. What Jesus says is that God doesn't like divorce at all—something the Pharisees could have discovered themselves from such texts as Malachi 2:16 ("'I hate divorce,' says the Lord God of Israel")—and that whoever divorces his wife for whatever cause at all (excepting "marital unfaithfulness") causes her to commit adultery, presumably because she would find it necessary to remarry, and that whoever married her would also be guilty of adultery. According to Jesus, the Old Testament is on the side of upholding and preserving marriages rather than encouraging divorce.

Hendriksen says,

> The more we study Christ's teaching as presented to us in this passage the more we begin to appreciate it. Here, by means of a few simple words, Jesus discourages divorce, refutes the rabbinical misinterpretation of the law, reaffirms the law's true meaning (cf. Matt. 5:17–18), censures the guilty party, defends the innocent, and throughout it all upholds the sacredness and inviolability of the marriage bond as ordained by God![4]

Taking Oaths: Numbers 30:2

What about telling the truth? According to surveys, Americans lie all the time, often with no apparent reason.[5] But in most other societies, both past and present, telling the truth has always been judged an important personal virtue. What was the problem in Jesus' day then? It was exactly what we have been seeing all along: the corruption of the heart.

People knew they were to keep their word, as we do. Above all, they knew if they had taken an oath they were to keep it.[6] But the rabbis focused on the specific wording of the oath, distinguishing between those that were binding and those that were not. If the Bible said, "Keep the oaths you have made to the Lord," such oaths were clearly binding. But what about oaths that were made only "to heaven" or "by the temple" or "by one's life"? Were such oaths binding? An entire tractate of the Mishnah *(Shebuoth)* is given to distinguishing between oaths that had to be kept and those that did not. We see a reflection of this thinking in Matthew 23:16–22, where Jesus elaborates on some of these distinctions, but his point in chapter 23 is the same as here: Any failure to keep one's word is a sin before God. Hence, for the righteous man there should be no need for oaths at all. On the contrary, a righteous man's yes should be yes, and his no should be no.

These verses do not forbid oaths under formal occasions, as in a court of law, since the Bible contains examples of such oaths (see Rom. 1:9; 2 Cor. 1:23; Phil. 1:8; 1 Thess. 2:5, 10). Even God takes oaths (Heb. 6:17–19).

Retaliation: The *Lex Talionis*

What about the law of retaliation, the so-called *lex talionis?* Various forms of this law date back to the ancient law code of Hammurabi (2285–2242 B.C.), but it is also expressly stated in the Old Testament in at least three places: Exodus 21:23–25; Leviticus 24:19–20; Deuteronomy 19:21. It limits recovery to the actual damage done. However, the Old Testament also forbids an individual from seeking revenge or bearing grudges: Leviticus 19:18; Proverbs

20:22; 24:29. Jesus told the people they were wrong to focus on verses that refer to revenge (though limited) and ignore those that call for a forgiving heart. The right attitude was not to insist on their rights and even to bear cheerfully many types of wrongs (vv. 40–42).

Love for Enemies: Leviticus 19:18

The examples that conclude Jesus' words about the *lex talionis* lead to the last of his six antitheses, the command to love our enemies. Again, the people knew that they were to love their neighbors, for that was stated clearly in Leviticus 19:18. Jesus calls it the second great commandment in Matthew 22:39, after the first, which is to "love the LORD your God with all your heart and with all your soul and with all your strength" (Deut. 6:5). But if the law said, "Love your neighbor," did that not allow hatred of our enemies by contrast? That is what some were teaching, even though the words "and hate your enemies" are found nowhere in the Bible.

Jesus teaches that the citizens of the kingdom are to love their enemies as well as their friends, because that is the way the heavenly King treats them. It is only as they display kindness to those who are evil as well as to those who are good that they will be able to demonstrate that they are the true sons and daughters of God.

The Summary: "Be Perfect"

Jesus' summary is in verse 48: "Be perfect, therefore, as your heavenly Father is perfect." This verse does not teach perfectionism, since none of us are or can be perfect in this world. But what does it teach?

William Barclay explains it by use of the meaning of the Greek word *teleios* ("perfect"), which describes something perfectly suited to the end for which it was created, like a full-grown adult as opposed to a person who is still a child, or a tool perfectly suited to a task. "The Greek idea of perfection is functional," Barclay says.[7] R. V. G. Tasker sees it differently. He thinks Torrey is right "in supposing that the underlying Aramaic word was active in sense, and that the meaning here is 'all-including (in your good will) even as your Father includes all.'"[8] Harry Ironside also sees the verse as a call for impartiality, arguing, "This is perfection in the sense of the complete absence of partiality, thus imitating him who is no respecter of persons (Acts 10:34), but who lavishes his favors upon just and unjust alike."[9]

Those interpretations could be on the right track, but I think D. A. Carson is wiser when he refuses to drop the idea of perfection so easily. It is true that we will never be perfect in this life, but the perfections outlined in this sermon are still those for which we should aim and that we should increasingly attain by God's grace and power in our lives. Carson notes that the form of this verse is exactly the same as Leviticus 19:2, with "holy" merely being displaced by "perfect" ("Be holy because I, the Lord your God, am holy"), and that Leviticus 19:2 is likewise urged on God's people in the Bible.[10]

What Jesus is saying is that the "direction in which the law has always pointed is not toward mere judicial restraints, concessions arising out of the hardness of men's hearts, still less casuistical perversions, nor even to the 'law of love.' . . . No, it pointed rather to all the perfection of God, exemplified by the authoritative interpretation of the law bound up in the preceding antitheses. This perfection Jesus' disciples must emulate if they are truly followers of him who fulfills the Law and the Prophets."[11]

Barclay is not entirely wrong when he says that we should be perfectly fitted to that for which we were created. But this is not some low standard, as if it meant only to be a well-rounded person. We were created to be like God, to aim at Christ-like character. The only way we will be able to aim at that character and achieve it is if God gives us a transformed heart.

11

The Practice of True Religion

Matthew 6:1–18

"Be careful not to do your 'acts of righteousness' before men, to be seen by them. If you do, you will have no reward from your Father in heaven. . . . But when you give to the needy, do not let your left hand know what your right hand is doing, so that your giving may be in secret. Then your Father, who sees what is done in secret, will reward you.

"And when you pray, do not be like the hypocrites, for they love to pray standing in the synagogues and on the street corners to be seen by men. I tell you the truth, they have received their reward in full. But when you pray, go into your room, close the door and pray to your Father, who is unseen. Then your Father, who sees what is done in secret, will reward you. . . .

"When you fast, do not look somber as the hypocrites do, for they disfigure their faces to show men they are fasting. I tell you the truth, they have received their reward in full. But when you fast, put oil on your head and wash your face, so that it will not be obvious to men that you are fasting, but only to your Father, who is unseen; and your Father, who sees what is done in secret, will reward you."

There is a wonderful wholeness as well as a compelling organization to Jesus' Sermon on the Mount, and we come to appreciate it more and more as we move carefully through Christ's teaching.

Jesus has described the incredibly high standard of righteousness required of those who would be his disciples: (1) explaining that it must be superior to that of the Pharisees and teachers of the law, (2) describing it in six representative areas, and (3) insisting that his disciples pursue perfection, since

God is perfect. But now he moves to those outward "acts of righteousness" (Matt. 6:1), which we would call the actual practice of religion, and he warns of a great danger: hypocrisy. In order to be his disciples, to be citizens of his kingdom, those who are his must practice their religion from the heart and not for the notice, approbation, and reward of men. In this section of the sermon, Jesus develops what he had already taught about our need for a transformed heart.

Righteousnesses (dikaiosunen) in verse 1 is not easy to translate. The New International Version translates it as "acts of righteousness," which is probably the best that can be done in contemporary English, though the term has to do with the practice of religion and not mere good works. We might say *piety*, but piety usually refers to what we call a pious attitude. *Devotions* is a possibility, but we usually limit devotions to such matters as Bible reading and prayer. *Religion* might work if what we mean is, "Do not make public displays of your religion in order to attract other people's attention."

What Jesus has in mind are the three chief acts of Jewish piety that he discusses in verses 1–18: almsgiving, prayer, and fasting. These form a unit of their own, and Jesus follows the same outline in discussing them: (1) a *warning* not to seek man's praise, (2) an *assurance* that those who do will get only an earthly reward, (3) a *command* to perform such acts privately, and (4) a *promise* that God, who sees in secret, will reward the disciple openly.

Giving to the Poor

Jesus' first example of religious practice is almsgiving, or giving to the poor (vv. 1–4). The law declared, "There will always be poor people in the land. Therefore I command you to be openhanded toward your brothers and toward the poor and needy in your land" (Deut. 15:11; see vv. 7–11; also Exod. 23:10–11; Lev. 19:10; and Ps. 112:9). The rabbis said, "Greater is he who gives alms than he who offers sacrifices" and "He who gives in secret is greater than Moses."[1] Jesus agreed that this is a religious duty, for he is not *telling* us to give alms in these verses; he is assuming we will do it.

What Jesus is concerned about is how the giving will be done. Will it be done to win approval from other men and women? Most giving is for that reason. It is why the world publishes lists of donors to its publicly supported institutions, listing lifetime members, president's clubs, century clubs, patrons, friends, and so on. Unfortunately, this sometimes erupts in religious circles too, when people want their giving to be noticed. Jesus called it announcing one's gifts "with trumpets," meaning, as we might say, that such people are "blowing their own horn."

People call attention to their giving because they want to be praised by other people. And they will be! Jesus says. They will get their reward on earth, but only on earth. The piety Jesus seeks is one that drives people to give because of the need of the receiving person and not for the praise of other people. How do we avoid hypocrisy? By keeping our giving quiet, Jesus teaches. D. A. Carson says, "The way to avoid hypocrisy is not to cease giving but to do so with such secrecy that we scarcely know what we have given."[2]

Praying to Be Heard

The second of Jesus' examples of religious piety and the one he deals with at greatest length is prayer. He teaches about prayer generally, gives an example of what true prayer should be, and then elaborates on one of the items he teaches us to pray for. This is treated in roughly the same manner as charitable giving. He assumes his disciples will pray, but he is concerned about how prayer is done. Using the same outline as in the previous example, Jesus warns us not to seek man's praise, assures us that those who do will get only an earthly answer, commands us to perform such acts privately, and promises that God, who hears in secret, will reward us openly.

In the first paragraph, Jesus speaks of two wrong types of prayer.

1. *Ostentatious prayer (vv. 5–6).* This is prayer uttered in the most visible places with the goal of being heard and seen by other people. We have an example of this in Christ's parable of the Pharisee and the tax collector. The Pharisee "stood up and prayed about himself" (Luke 18:11). He had his reward; he was noticed by the people standing by. They must have said, "Look at that Pharisee! How pious he is!" Yet Jesus said that it was the tax collector who was justified. He did not call attention to himself but rather "stood at a distance," praying, "God, have mercy on me, a sinner" (v. 13). He had his reward in heaven.

2. *Repetitious prayer (vv. 7–8).* The second kind of badly conceived prayer is repetitious prayer, which Jesus identifies as characteristic of Gentiles or pagans. The prayers of the priests of Baal in the days of Elijah are an example. They called on Baal "from morning till noon," calling louder and louder and even "slashed themselves with swords and spears" (see 1 Kings 18:25–29). But Baal did not hear them.

Jesus is not condemning long prayers in these verses since he himself spent long nights and many hours in prayer. What he is condemning is "vain repetition," a phrase that came into the King James Version by way of Theodore Beza's commentary. The Greek word is *battalogeo* (v. 7), probably from the Aramaic word *battal,* meaning "idle." It is a warning against vain words in praying. Sadly, many religious prayers are like this. Indeed, we can even be idle in our repetition of the so-called Lord's Prayer, which follows these verses. We should remember that the slang term "pitter-patter" in English comes from the Latin words that begin the Lord's Prayer *(Pater Noster)* and are an observation on how meaningless the empty repetition of even these famous words has sometimes seemed to unbelievers. Augustine was on the right track when he properly distinguished between much speaking in prayer and much praying.

The Lord's Prayer

In contrast with ostentatious and repetitive prayers, Jesus now gives his disciples a model of what real prayer should be (vv. 9–13). We call it the Lord's Prayer, but it is actually the disciples' prayer, since Jesus could never have prayed for the forgiveness of sins as he instructs us to do in verse 12. The true "Lord's Prayer" is in John 17.

I have called this a model prayer, for that is what it is. It is not a prayer to be memorized and repeated mechanically, though it is not wrong to repeat these words thoughtfully in a liturgical service. Jesus did not say, "This is *what* you should pray." He said, "This is *how* you should pray," meaning that our requests should be along these lines. The prayer is a brief prayer; Jesus has told us to avoid vain repetitions, after all. But more than this, it is a pointed summary of what we should pray for.

There are six petitions, following the initial address to God as Father. The first three concern God's honor, God's kingdom, and God's will; the last three concern human needs. This places God's concerns first, just as with the Ten Commandments the first table concerns the duties we owe to God and the second table concerns the duties we owe to our neighbors. In our day the order is usually reversed. We begin with human needs and unfortunately often never even get around to God and God's glory at all.[3]

1. *"Hallowed be your name."* The first petition of the Lord's Prayer is that the name of God might be honored. God's name (actually names) stands for God himself, as he is revealed in nature and Scripture. Hence, to honor the name is to honor God, to hold him in the highest reverence and exalt him above all others.

What is the "name" of God we should honor? There are many names for God. He is *Elohim,* the creator of the heavens and the earth (Gen. 1:1). He is *El Elyon,* the Most High God (Gen. 14:18–19). He is *Jehovah,* "I AM WHO I AM," the name by which he revealed himself to Moses at the burning bush (Exod. 3:14). He is *Jehovah Jireh,* the God who provides (Gen. 22:14). He is *Adonai,* the Lord. In this prayer, Jesus introduces God as "Our *Father* in heaven" (v. 9).

It is a nearly unbelievable privilege for us to call God Father. Before the coming of Jesus Christ, this was an unknown name in most prayers. Pagans did not pray this way. Even in the Old Testament the word *father* appears in reference to God only fourteen times, and never once does any individual Israelite address God directly as "my Father." It would have been considered much too intimate. In fact, the Jews of Jesus' day did not even like to use the name "God." They spoke of "heaven" or "the Most High" or merely "Lord" instead. All this was completely overturned by Jesus. Jesus always referred to God as his Father, and here in the Sermon on the Mount he authorizes his followers to do likewise.

But what a delicate balance of truth. On the one hand, we are permitted to call God Father, even using the most personal of all words, *abba,* the best translation of which is "daddy." It is the word Jesus seemed to have used in all his prayers (see Matt. 11:25; 26:39, 42; Mark 14:36; Luke 23:34; John 11:41; 12:27; 17:1, 5, 11, 21, 24, 25). The God to whom we pray is personal (no mere being) and caring ("our Father"). But he is also the holy and sovereign God, who is "in heaven." Moreover, his name must be honored by everyone ("hallowed be your name") and his rule acknowledged ("your kingdom come"). The God to whom we pray must never be treated lightly.

2. *"Your kingdom come."* We have already given some thought to the meaning of God's kingdom (in studying Matthew 3:1), and we will come back to it again (particularly in the parables of the kingdom in chapter 13). It has to do with God's reign or rule, which, in one sense, involves God's sovereign ordering of all things at all times, but, in another sense, concerns his direction of the lives of his people. Here the prayer is for God's rule in two senses. First, may you rule increasingly in the lives of your people; and second, may your final messianic kingdom come soon.

3. *"Your will be done."* In this petition, much like the previous one, the disciple asks that he and others might live in growing obedience to God's declared desires as they are found in Scripture, and that the day may quickly come when sin will be judged and the whole universe be willingly subject to God's will, even as believers desire to be subject now (Rom. 12:2). This should be our desire, and we should always be careful to examine the attitudes of our hearts and our day-by-day actions in accordance with it. As D. A. Carson says, "These first three petitions, though they focus on God's name, God's kingdom, and God's will, are nevertheless prayers that he may act in such a way that his people will hallow his name, submit to his reign, and do his will. It is therefore impossible to pray this prayer in sincerity without humbly committing oneself to such a course."[4]

4. *"Give us today our daily bread."* Halfway through the prayer, as we come to the fourth of these representative petitions, we turn from prayer for the advancement of God's name, God's kingdom, and God's will to prayer for our personal needs: (1) life's necessities, (2) forgiveness of sins, and (3) deliverance from temptation and the devil.

It should be obvious that prayer for "daily bread" is not for mere bread alone, still less the bread of the Lord's Supper, which is what Jerome suggested. It is prayer for real food and for whatever else we need to sustain ourselves physically. There has been much uncertainty about the word translated "daily," as in "daily bread," since until very recently the word it translates *(epiousios)* was unknown in any ancient text except for the two versions of this prayer in Matthew and Luke. What did it mean? Origen was aware of this uncertainty and suggested that Matthew made the word up. However, as Barclay reports in his commentary on Matthew, not long ago a papyrus was uncovered in which *epiousios* appeared on a woman's shopping list, as an obvious reminder to buy a necessary food item for the next day. Therefore, the meaning of the fourth petition is what has been assumed by most people all along, namely, give us the necessities of life for this day (or the day immediately ahead).[5] We need to pray this day by day, of course. But then, when we receive what we need for our daily living, we also need to thank God from whom these and all other good gifts come (James 1:17).

5. *"Forgive us our debts."* It is not only provision for daily living that we need, of course. We are not only creatures, we are sinful creatures. Hence, we also need forgiveness for our many sins, which God provides on the basis of the substitutionary death of Jesus Christ. It is why Jesus came. This petition of the Lord's Prayer says, "Forgive us our debts, as we also have forgiven our debtors" (v. 12).

What is the connection between the two parts of this petition? We do not earn God's forgiveness by forgiving others. We know that because of the Bible's teaching elsewhere. But if that is not the right interpretation, what does the verse mean? Some have explained it by distinguishing between forgiveness for our sins on the basis of Christ's death, which gives us a permanent right standing before God, and forgiveness for sins committed day by day, which break our fellowship with God and for which we need to make constant confession and seek cleansing (see 1 John 1:9). But that involves a secondary and dependent experience of forgiveness that seems out of place here. This prayer is so brief that the prayer "forgive us our debts" should embrace the forgiveness of all sin in all relationships, and it is this that is somehow linked to our own forgiving attitude or lack of it.

A better explanation of the connection between these two parts of the petition is that we must have a profound change of heart, expressing itself, among other ways, in a willingness to forgive others if we have experienced God's forgiveness ourselves. It is similar to having saving faith. We are not saved by our faith; salvation is by grace. But faith must be present if we are to be saved. In the same way, forgiveness in us must be present if we are to receive forgiveness. Moreover, both the power to believe and the ability to forgive are from God. H. N. Ridderbos rightly asserts, "By forgiving his debtors the believer shows himself to be a child of God."[6] R. T. France expressed the same idea when he wrote, "The point is not so much that forgiving is a prior condition of being forgiven, but that forgiveness cannot be a one-way process."[7]

This is not something to be taken lightly, for we cannot help but notice that this is the only one of the six petitions in this prayer that is picked up again and amplified by Jesus (in vv. 14–15). "If you forgive men when they sin against you, your heavenly Father will also forgive you. But if you do not forgive men their sins, your heavenly Father will not forgive your sins." This should impress us with the importance—even more, the necessity—of forgiving others. This point is also made strongly in Christ's parable of the unforgiving steward (in Matt. 18:21–35).

6. *"Lead us not into temptation."* Last of all, we should pray for deliverance: first, that we might be kept from trials or temptation ("lead us not into temp-

tation") and second, that we might be delivered from the devil ("but deliver us from the evil one").

The last three petitions are joined by the word *and,* showing that they are three constant needs of God's people: provision for our daily needs *and* forgiveness of sins *and* deliverance from evil. The petitions for deliverance from temptation and from the evil one are not linked by *and,* which means that they belong together as parts of one request, that is, deliverance from temptation and from the evil (or evil one) that stands behind it. The word for "evil one" can be translated as "evil" only because the Greek word is either masculine or neuter, but the difference is slight. Obviously we need God's deliverance from evil from any source or in any form.[8]

Fasting as a Spiritual Discipline

The final "act of righteousness" Jesus discusses is fasting (vv. 16–18). In the Old Testament, fasting had been commanded only on the Day of Atonement, but during the Babylonian exile, regular fast days for remembrance of past disasters had been instituted and had become a major part of Jewish religion. A question about whether these fasts should continue after the return to the land of Israel was raised and answered in Zechariah 7 and 8. Significantly, Jesus answers it the same way here! The issue is not how often we should fast, he implies. It is how we fast and why.

As far as the "how" is concerned, we are to do it privately before God and not to seek attention from men, exactly what Jesus said about giving to the poor and prayer. If we fast before other people, we will have a reward, but it will be from them only. There will be no reward in heaven.

For most of us, the greater issue about fasting is why we should fast. Or should we? Here we are assisted by examples found in the New Testament. Two are conspicuous. First, Peter was fasting in Joppa prior to receiving the vision of the great sheet let down from heaven, which led to the opening of the gospel to the Gentiles (see Acts 10:11). Second, the Christians at Antioch were fasting when the Holy Spirit directed them to send Paul and Barnabas on the first great missionary journey (see Acts 13:2–3). Those were probably the two most significant moments in the history of the early Christian church, and in each case, the believers involved were seeking God and his will and were answered by strong, unmistakable, and historically significant directions.

I do not know how this applies to your situation, but I assume there will be occasions when you will want to set aside time to fast and seek God. I am fairly confident that God will answer directly.

12

Christians and the World

Matthew 6:19–7:12

"Do not store up for yourselves treasures on earth, where moth and rust destroy, and where thieves break in and steal. But store up for yourselves treasures in heaven, where moth and rust do not destroy, and where thieves do not break in and steal. . . .

"Therefore I tell you, do not worry about your life, what you will eat or drink; or about your body, what you will wear. Is not life more important than food, and the body more important than clothes? . . . For the pagans run after all these things, and your heavenly Father knows that you need them. But seek first his kingdom and his righteousness, and all these things will be given to you as well. . . .

"So in everything, do to others what you would have them do to you, for this sums up the Law and the Prophets."

Up to this point in the Sermon on the Mount, Jesus has spoken almost entirely about the spiritual character of those who would be his disciples and of the relationship they must have with God. But Christianity is not just a vertical relationship between us and God. It also has horizontal dimensions because we are material as well as spiritual creatures and live in a space-time, physical universe populated by other people.

What should our lives be like on this level? How should we regard material things such as food, clothing, and money? How should we think about the future, which we view in terms of having possessions or lacking them? How should we relate to people who are different from us and do not act as we think they should act? And what do these matters have to do with the fact that we belong to God and should be learning to trust him? Jesus addresses these matters (from 6:19 to 7:12), and his point is this: What he has said about our relationship with God must govern how we think about earthly matters too. In these verses he talks about wealth, worry, judging others, and our constant need for prayer. He ends this section with the best-known saying in the entire Sermon on the Mount, the Golden Rule.

Storing Up Heavenly Treasure

What about storing up treasure on earth? More than likely we all know people who have ruined their lives by putting the pursuit of wealth above their families or other worthwhile things. If you do not know such people, there are ample illustrations in the Bible. Achan caused the defeat of the armies of Israel at Ai and suffered death himself, along with his family, because he coveted a beautiful Babylonian garment, two hundred pieces of silver, and an ingot of gold, items that God told the people not to take from Jericho during their conquest of the city. Solomon allowed the love of money and women to ruin his spiritual life. Ananias and Sapphira lied about money, pretending they had given the full price of a piece of land to the church while they were actually keeping back part of it.

Yet it is not money itself that is the problem, though the Bible hints at the danger often associated with having a great deal of it. The Bible contains examples of people who were wealthy but who handled their wealth rightly. Abraham was a rich man. So were Job and David. The problem lies with how we think about money and whether it or the love of God and his glory is our priority.

This is Jesus' concern in verses 19–24. He is not speaking against possessions, only a ruinous preoccupation with them. And he is giving sound reasons why we should make it our priority to store up spiritual treasure in heaven rather than material treasure on earth. He gives four reasons, and each is worth our most serious consideration.

1. *Material things do not last (vv. 19–20).* Moths destroy clothing. The word translated "rust" *(brosis)* means "an eating away" and probably refers to the destruction of stored grain by rodents. Rust destroys things. It will ruin even an expensive Ferrari in time. What the moths and rust do not ruin, thieves can steal—or the government can take through excessive taxation. And even if we are able to escape the moths, rust, and the IRS—even if the value of our stocks just continues to rise—eventually even "heaven and earth will pass away" (Matt. 24:35), and everything that is material will be gone. Where will you be then if you have not laid up lasting spiritual treasure in heaven? On another occasion Jesus said, "What good will it be for a man if he gains the whole world, yet forfeits his soul?" (Matt. 16:26).

2. *Focusing on money will bind us to this earth (v. 21).* We are creatures of the earth, which is why possessions are not bad in and of themselves. But we are also made for heaven, and our highest and most noble thoughts concern not what we have in common with the animals but that we are made in God's

image and for fellowship with God. If we concentrate on wealth alone, we strangle what is best about us and become only empty shells of what God created us to be.

3. *Concentrating on things clouds our vision (vv. 22–23).* This is what Jesus has in mind in his illustration of a clear or a clouded-over eye. William Barclay explains:

> The idea behind this passage is one of childlike simplicity. The eye is regarded as the window by which the light gets into the whole body. The color and state of a window decide what light gets into a room. If the window is clear, clean and undistorted, the light will come flooding into the room and will illuminate every corner of it. If the glass of the window is colored or frosted, distorted, dirty or obscure, the light will be hindered, and the room will not be lit up. . . . So then, says Jesus, the light which gets into any man's heart and soul and being depends on the spiritual state of the eye through which it has to pass, for the eye is the window of the whole body.[1]

If you are absorbed with money, you will miss everything else in life that really matters.

4. *No one can serve God and Money at the same time (v. 24).* In the original text of this verse, the word translated "Money" is *Mammon* (KJV). *Mammon* came from a Hebrew verb meaning "to entrust" or "to place in someone's keeping." The noun, therefore, referred to the wealth one entrusted to another for safekeeping. At this stage the word did not have any bad connotations. If something bad was meant, it was necessary to put another word with it, as in "mammon of unrighteousness." Yet as time went by, the meaning of mammon shifted from the passive sense of "that which is entrusted" to the active sense of "that in which one trusts." When that happened, the word originally spelled with a small "m" came to be spelled with a capital "M," as designating a god, which is why the New International Version capitalizes the word *Money!*

"You cannot serve both God and Money," says Jesus. We like to think we can; we are great compromisers. Or we think we are serving God by making money. True, we can use our money to serve God. Some do. But if our hearts are set on our possessions, which is probably an accurate description of most of us, we are not actually serving God whatever we may suppose we are doing.

D. Martyn Lloyd-Jones tells of a farmer who reported happily to his wife that his best cow had given birth to twin calves, one red and one white. He said, "You know, I have been led of the Lord to dedicate one of the calves to him. We will raise them together. Then when the time comes to sell them, we will keep the money from the one calf and give the money from the other to the Lord."

His wife asked which one he was going to dedicate to the Lord, but he answered that there was no need to decide that now since he was going to treat both of them alike. Several months later he came into the kitchen looking very sad. When his wife asked what was troubling him he answered, "I have bad news. The Lord's calf is dead."

"But you had not decided which was to be the Lord's calf," she objected.

"Oh, yes," he said. "I had always determined that it was to be the white one, and it is the white one that has died."[2]

Sadly, it is always that way with us—it is always the Lord's calf that dies—unless we decide from the beginning that we are here to serve God above everything else and that everything we possess has been given to us by God and is to be held in stewardship for him. If we make such a decision, we will find when we die that we have actually been laying up eternal spiritual treasure in heaven and that nothing has destroyed it.

Three Reasons Not to Worry

The chief reason we are so preoccupied with our possessions and with acquiring more of them is that we worry about the future and do not trust God to care for us. This is why Jesus goes on to discuss worry in the next section (vv. 25–34). "Therefore I tell you, do not worry about your life, what you will eat or drink; or about your body, what you will wear. . . . For the pagans run after all these things, and your heavenly Father knows that you need them. But seek first his kingdom and his righteousness, and all these things will be given to you as well" (vv. 25, 32, 33). As Herman Ridderbos notes, "In telling his listeners not to worry, Jesus basically was warning against the very same sin he had spoken of in the previous verses: dependence on earthly goods."[3]

Why shouldn't we worry? Jesus gives three reasons, marked by a three-fold repetition of the word *therefore* or *so* (the same word in Greek) in verses 25, 31, and 34. In each case, the "therefore" points back to what came immediately before. In other words, because of the truth in verse 24, we should not worry; because of the truth in verses 26–30, we should not worry; and because of the truth in verses 32 and 33, we should not worry.

1. *You cannot serve God and worry too.* Jesus' first "therefore" (v. 25) picks up on the contrast between God and Money that he developed in verse 24: "You cannot serve both God and Money." To serve God you must trust God, and you are not trusting God if you are worrying. Do you remember the first answer of the Westminster Shorter Catechism? "Man's chief end is to glorify God and to enjoy him forever." If that is an accurate description of what life is about and what our service to God means, it is clear that we cannot either serve or glorify God while questioning his ability to take care of us. We will be working hard to augment our possessions, and if we are doing that, we will not be serving God. Therefore, stop worrying.

Kenneth S. Wuest wrote wisely, "We commit sin when we worry. We do not trust God when we worry. We do not receive answers to prayer when we worry, because we are not trusting."[4]

2. *If you are worrying, you are overlooking God's care of the rest of his creation.* You do not have to be a great theologian or even a great Bible student to see

that God cares for his creation—for the birds, the flowers, even the common grass of the field. But if he provides for the rest of his creation, don't you suppose he will also care for you? He will, of course. So don't worry. If you do, you are really slandering God in regard to his wisdom, knowledge, power, goodness, and providential care.

3. *It is only by putting God first that we can be sure of anything.* If we are created to know God and serve God, then the only ultimately successful course in life is to trust God and not worry. If God has created us and has redeemed us through the work of Jesus Christ, are we to suppose that he will fail to care for us? Of course not. He will take care of us. Therefore, make it your goal to seek God's interests first and see if your physical needs do not come to you naturally and without any concern on your part.

You can't do anything about the future anyway. The future is in God's hands and will be managed perfectly by God whether you worry about it or not. "Therefore do not worry about tomorrow," says Jesus, "for tomorrow will worry about itself. Each day has enough trouble of its own" (v. 34).

Right Judging and Wrong Judging

Whenever Christians say that something is either right or wrong, or whenever they speak out against immoral or destructive behavior in another person, they are frequently told that they are not to judge, meaning that any behavior is right and that any attempt to deny that it is right is itself wrong. In fact, in our postmodern environment, the only acknowledged evil is claiming that someone else is mistaken.

Is that what Jesus meant when he said, "Do not judge, or you too will be judged" (Matt. 7:1)? Obviously not, because the last verse of the section in which he speaks of a false kind of judging requires judging, rather extreme judging, in fact. In order not to "give dogs what is sacred" or "throw your pearls to pigs" you must distinguish between what is sacred, and therefore of great value, and what is not. And you must even be able to identify the dogs and pigs! No, it is not the necessity of making proper judgments that Jesus is concerned about, but rather what we would call censoriousness, that is, judging the minor faults of other people without acknowledging and correcting our own perhaps even greater failures.

Is there a connection between this matter and what has gone before in Christ's sermon? There may be. For one thing, the image of an eye with a plank sticking out of it is a particular example of the clouded eye Jesus spoke about in chapter 6. Again, there may be a connection by contrast. In the first two items Jesus mentions—the love of money, rather than the love of God, and worry—we are dealing with a disciple for whom material things are more important than spiritual things. But in the case developed here, we have one who has gone to the opposite extreme and has become fanatical or overly zealous about religious matters. This person has become judgmental of others without perceiving his own deep faults.

The verb for "judge" in this passage is *krino,* and it has exactly the same force here as it does in Romans 14:10–12, where Paul writes, "You, then, why do you judge your brother? Or why do you look down on your brother? For we will all stand before God's judgment seat. It is written: 'As surely as I live,' says the Lord, 'every knee will bow before me; every tongue will confess to God.' So then, each of us will give an account of himself to God." If we believe what Paul said, we will turn from hypocrisy, enabling us to build others up rather than tearing them down.

Prayer to the Father

But how are we to do that, especially when we are usually blind to our faults and so inclined to hypocrisy? We will never be able to overcome this failure by ourselves. As a matter of fact, there is nothing in this entire sermon that we can achieve rightly or wholly by ourselves. The only way we can live out the Sermon on the Mount is by appropriating the new life of God, which we receive as we come to faith in Jesus Christ and as we learn to ask God for the right inclinations and the power we must have to pursue them.

This must be why Jesus begins to talk about prayer again at this point, especially after he has already discussed it extensively in chapter 6. What he is saying here is that we need God's power to do right in all areas: to work for spiritual treasure, to trust God rather than worry about the future, and to stop looking down on those we think are inferior to us. These verses (vv. 7–11) are an immensely important passage about prayer.

First, they teach that if we are Christ's disciples, having entered by faith into the kingdom of heaven, then we have God as our Father, and the God who is our Father is generous and giving. If a child wants to ask his father for something, the child will pattern his request on what he knows of his father's temperament. If the father is ill-tempered and stingy, the child will ask for a little only, carefully and at a well-chosen moment. If the father is good-natured and generous, the child will present his need openly and with freedom. It is the same spiritually, says Jesus. If God were like the pagans imagined him to be—capricious, selfish, even vengeful—the one who prays would be on guard and would even try to bribe God or win him over. But if God is gracious, as Jesus taught, then we need not be afraid to ask him for whatever we need at any time.

Yet we must ask. That is the second important truth. God cares for us even if we do not ask, as an earthly father cares for even unresponsive children. But God wants us to have a personal relationship with him, and for that to happen, we must communicate with God in prayer. God gives, but he gives even more when we ask. James says, "You do not have, because you do not ask God" (James 4:2). Jesus gives the positive side of that sentence when he says, "Ask and it will be given to you; seek and you will find; knock and the door will be opened to you" (v. 7).

The third important truth in these verses is that we are to keep praying. The verbs in verse 7 are present imperatives. This does not mean we are to practice vain repetitions; Jesus has already dismissed that in chapter 6. We do not get more from God by repeating our requests over and over. But it does mean we are never to grow weary of asking, seeking, and knocking since we know that God is always hearing and always answering.

The Golden Rule

At last we come to the Golden Rule: "So in everything, do to others what you would have them do to you, for this sums up the Law and the Prophets" (v. 12). This is Jesus' summary, and not only of the Law and the Prophets. It is also a summary of the entire body of the sermon, for the phrase "the Law and the Prophets" is the *inclusio* that both introduces the main section of the sermon (at Matt. 5:17) and now concludes it.

What is important and unique about this verse, the best-known of all Christ's sayings, is that it is expressed in a positive form. It is not difficult to find parallels to Christ's rule in its negative form. The great Rabbi Hillel said, "What is hateful to yourself, do to no other; that is the whole Law; the rest is commentary" *(Shabbath* 31a). In the apocryphal book of Tobit, composed several centuries before the time of Jesus, the hero tells his young son, "What thou hatest, do to no man." William Barclay, who lists these examples among many others, cites close parallels from Confucius, Epictetus, the Stoics, and the *Hymns of the Faith* of Buddhism.[5] But these are negative. They say, "Do not do to others what you would not want them to do to you." By contrast, Jesus turned the saying completely around, saying positively, "So in everything, do to others what you would have them do to you."

It has always been possible for people to keep the negative version of this rule, for it is essentially a sound and necessary legal principle. If we are to get along in a civilized society, we must discipline ourselves so we do not injure other people. We must obey the law, stop at stop signs, pay our bills, avoid overt acts of prejudice, and many such things. It is a bit like an honest man paying taxes. We do it because we must, while hoping we will have enough left over for ourselves after we have paid them.

How different when we look at our obligations positively. Now it is no longer a matter of legal principle, doing what needs to be done to get along or stay out of trouble. What is needed now is a transformed life, which is why we cannot keep the Golden Rule or any other standard of this sermon by ourselves. If we are operating by the law, our minds are on ourselves. To fix our attention on the needs, cares, loves, joys, hopes, and dreams of other people, we must be transformed people. In other words, we must turn from the demands of the law entirely to receive a new, spiritual life from God.

Christian faith begins with a confession of our failure, followed by faith in Jesus Christ as Savior. But it continues as we learn to put the needs and wants of other people first. In other words, it is only when we have learned to love God with all our heart, soul, mind, and strength that we can begin to love our neighbors as ourselves (Matt. 22:37–39; Mark 12:28–31).

13

Two Ways Only

Matthew 7:13–29

"Enter through the narrow gate. For wide is the gate and broad is the road that leads to destruction, and many enter through it. But small is the gate and narrow the road that leads to life, and only a few find it.

"Watch out for false prophets. . . .

"Not every one who says to me, 'Lord, Lord,' will enter the kingdom of heaven, but only he who does the will of my Father who is in heaven. . . .

"Therefore everyone who hears these words of mine and puts them into practice is like a wise man who built his house on the rock. The rain came down, the streams rose, and the winds blew and beat against that house; yet it did not fall, because it had its foundation on the rock. But everyone who hears these words of mine and does not put them into practice is like a foolish man who built his house on sand. The rain came down, the streams rose, and the winds blew and beat against that house, and it fell with a great crash."

When Jesus had finished saying these things, the crowds were amazed at his teaching, because he taught them as one who had authority, and not as their teachers of the law.

One of the worst things that can be taught in religion is that all roads eventually lead to heaven. It is not true, of course, which is bad enough in itself, for all lies are harmful. But in addition to being false, the idea that all ways are equally good is damnable since the one who follows any way other than that laid out by Jesus Christ will perish in the life to come.

This is what Jesus stresses in the concluding section of the Sermon on the Mount (Matt. 7:13–27). He has instructed his followers in the way to blessedness before God. He has reaffirmed the abiding importance of the Old Testament, explaining that it demands a true internal righteousness and not merely an outward conformity to certain regulations. He has examined the chief areas of religious piety and has even talked about the relationship of the believer to the world. He has summarized his teaching by the Golden Rule. Now he wraps up his sermon by insisting that the only way to heaven is by obeying or building on his words. All other ways, however wise, plausible, or attractive they may seem, lead to condemnation.

We can put it another way. Having shown what God requires of those who would belong to his kingdom, Jesus now warns his listeners about falling by the wayside through apathy, the deceit of false teachers, hypocrisy, or sheer folly, and thus failing to enter the kingdom.

What Jesus says in these last verses is that everyone must choose either one or the other of two ways, exactly what Jeremiah said when he wrote of "the way of life and the way of death" (Jer. 21:8), or what the first psalm urges when it contrasts those who "walk in the counsel of the wicked" with those whose "delight is in the law of the Lord" (vv. 1–2). Here Jesus presses his points by a series of four contrasting images. He speaks of two gates (and two paths), two trees (or teachers), two claims (or professions), and two builders (or foundations). In each case the choice of the one way leads to heaven; the choice of the other leads to hell.

A Broad or Narrow Gate

What does Jesus mean when he says, "Enter through the narrow gate. For wide is the gate and broad is the road that leads to destruction, and many enter through it. But small is the gate and narrow the road that leads to life, and only a few find it" (vv. 13–14)? Do we go through the gate to get onto the road? In that case, the gate would be conversion and the road would be the Christian life. Do we enter the path in order to reach the gate and pass through it either to hell or heaven? In that case, the gate would be death. Or is the path continuing in Christ's teachings until we come to the point of regeneration or conversion?

There have been strong defenders of each option, of course. I thought in terms of the last of these when I wrote *The Sermon on the Mount* some years ago.[1] But each position is probably guilty of making false distinctions. These verses treat the gate and the road alike, which means they are probably two images for the same thing. In other words, there are only two ways, whether you think of them as gates to be entered or roads to be pursued. The important point is that you make sure you enter the gate and travel on the road that leads to life.

Still, "making sure" is probably too weak a way of capturing what Jesus is saying by this first set of contrasts. Jesus is speaking of a narrow gate and a narrow road as contrasted with a wide gate and a wide road, and he is warning us against taking the easy as opposed to the difficult way. At this point the two images work together, which is why he combines them as he does. Both teach the comparative ease of drifting along through life to damnation as opposed to the difficulty of pursuing and gaining eternal life.

Many who preach the gospel today are out of step with Jesus in this matter. They may preach a gospel, but they make it sound easy to become a Christian and be saved. Jesus did not. William Hendriksen had it right when he wrote, "Our Lord does not follow the method that is used by certain self-styled revivalists, who speak as if 'getting saved' is one of the easiest things in the world. Jesus, on the contrary, pictures entrance into the kingdom as being, on the one hand, most desirable; yet, on the other, not at all easy. The entrance-gate is narrow. It must be 'found.'"[2]

This is an important word for you if you are drifting along in your religion, even if your religion is Christianity. Do not assume you are on the way to life unless you are actually pursuing it in obedience to Christ. Jesus did not teach that it would be easy either to become or be a Christian. He said it would be difficult. Anything worthwhile is.

Fruitful or Barren Trees

In the next paragraph (vv. 15–20), Jesus warns about false teachers, for apathy is not the only enemy would-be Christians must face if they are going to get to heaven. They will also encounter people who teach destructive doctrines. Jesus calls these false prophets "wolves" in "sheep's clothing" because they will pretend to be harmless members of Christ's flock even though their intent is to plunder and destroy it. But they will not be just members of the flock, mere sheep among others! They will be teachers too, or as we would say, ministers of the gospel. We remember how Paul predicted that after his departure from Ephesus "savage wolves" of precisely this kind would emerge to harm the flock there (Acts 20:29).

Do we have false prophets today? We certainly do. Moreover, they are not only in pews and pulpits. They are in denominational structures, in seminaries, and in church-related colleges. And they hold prominent and influential positions, like many who are heading up the counterfeit revivals of our day or who have large followings because of their television programs. I find it amusing, in light of our text, that we sometimes call an academic diploma a sheepskin. Some professors and ministers cover their intentions with the sheepskins of higher learning while using their knowledge of the Bible and church history to damage the budding faith of those who hear them. We must be warned against such teachers.

How are we to detect false teachers, especially if they know more than we do and their credentials surpass our own? The answer Jesus gives is good works.

He says it twice, once at the start of this section ("By their fruit you will recognize them," v. 16) and again at the end ("Thus, by their fruit you will recognize them," v. 20). In between, Jesus compares teachers in the church to trees. Good ones produce only good fruit; bad ones produce bad.

This can be applied in two ways. First, a genuine Christian life will show evidence of good works. Salvation is not by works. Anyone who trusts in his or her works for salvation is not saved, because that person is not trusting in the work of Jesus Christ alone (Eph. 2:8–9). But, on the other hand, it is also an error to suppose that a person can be a genuine Christian without doing good works since a Christian has the life of Christ within, and Christ's life will always express itself in doing good. This is especially true of teachers. Progress in the Christian life is often slow, and new believers may be far from producing much that is unmistakably good fruit. But teachers must! If teachers are not living a high level of Christianity and are not producing good fruit, they are false teachers and wolves.

These words are an example of what we have already studied in chapter 5, where Jesus warned his disciples, "Unless your righteousness surpasses that of the Pharisees and the teachers of the law, you will certainly not enter the kingdom of heaven" (v. 20).

The second way in which we can understand Jesus' demand for good fruit in teachers is to say that their teaching must be spiritually satisfying, for that is what the fruit of good trees is meant to be. There were bushes in Israel that had little berries that resembled grapes and certain thistles whose flowers resembled figs. But the berries were bitter, unfit to eat, and the flowers were deceptions. So also with the teaching of false prophets. William Barclay says,

> There may be a superficial resemblance between the true and the false prophet. The false prophet may wear the right clothes and use the right language; but you cannot sustain life with the berries of a buckthorn or the flowers of a thistle; and the life of the soul can never be sustained with the food which a false prophet offers. The real test of any teaching is: Does it strengthen a man to bear the burdens of life, and to walk in the way wherein he ought to go?[3]

Let me put it this way. Does the teaching you are receiving satisfy your soul? Does it bring you closer to God? Does it equip you to live for Jesus Christ at home and in your place of work? Does it make you less selfish? Does it prompt you to help and serve other people when you have an opportunity to do so? If it does not, find teaching that does. Find a place where the teaching takes root and flourishes in growth and spiritual satisfaction. The only instruction that will ever satisfy you in this way is accurate Bible teaching.

True or Empty Claims

In the third example, Jesus contrasts those who profess to follow Jesus—they call him "Lord, Lord"—yet do not do what God requires, and those (the contrast is implied, though it is not explicitly stated) who do the will of God and thereby prove that their discipleship is genuine (vv. 21–23). If the contrast between the two gates or paths describes apathy and the contrast between the true and false teachers describes deceit, this contrast describes hypocrisy. It is professing faith in Jesus Christ while actually rejecting or disobeying him.

At this point in Christ's applications we sense an intensifying evil. Adherence to the teaching of false prophets in Jesus' second example is worse than the apathy of the first, and the hypocrisy of the third example is worse than the deception of the second. In the second case, the potential disciple has been led astray by others. In the illustration we are looking at now, the disciple is false himself since he is professing one thing while practicing another. Two important matters are worth noting.

1. *This person has the right doctrines.* He calls Jesus "Lord, Lord," confessing Jesus' deity and professing that he is his master. But he is not following Jesus as his master. There were times in Jesus' ministry when people called him Lord, meaning perhaps no more than "Sir." Lord was a title of respect. But here a great deal more is involved, for it is Jesus who is speaking, and he is using the word with the richest possible meaning. In the Old Testament, *Lord* is usually translated "Jehovah," a name for God. In New Testament settings the equivalent word is *kyrios,* the title by which citizens of the Roman Empire addressed the emperor as a god. What Jesus is saying is that there will be people in the church who will confess his divinity but who will not be saved. They will be on the expansive road to hell.

Can that really be? Certainly, it can! A person can sit in the pews of a church for years, firmly believing that Jesus is God, that he died on the cross for sin, and even that he is returning one day to judge the world, yet never have come to the point of actually trusting that same Jesus Christ as his Savior. This was the case with Martin Luther. Luther left secular life to enter the monastery of the Augustinian hermits in Erfurt, Germany. He was ordained to the priesthood and made rapid progress as a monk. He studied the Bible and even lectured on Psalms, Romans, Galatians, Hebrews, and Titus. If someone had asked him in those days if he believed in the deity of Jesus Christ, he would have replied, "Of course, I do. I have always believed it." He would have confessed that Jesus died for sinners. He would have professed belief in Christ's eventual return in judgment, though he would have added, "I tremble at the thought."

Luther believed the right doctrines, but he did not understand the gospel and did not trust Jesus Christ fully and only as his Savior. It was only after God revealed the truth of justification to him from his study of Romans that he trusted Christ and, as he later said, "passed through that gate to Paradise."

2. *This person has prophesied and done miracles.* It is more difficult to understand how this can be, but it is what Jesus declares: "Many will say to me on that day, 'Lord, Lord, did we not prophesy in your name, and in your name drive out demons and perform many miracles?'" (v. 22). Jesus does not deny

they did miracles. He accepts their profession as a fact. But he also does not deny their self-deception. Their hypocrisy has escalated to a point at which they have actually fooled themselves. They believe their deceptions. But neither eloquent teaching nor miracles prove one to be a true disciple, and these persons are exposed as "evildoers."

The people spoken of here have the right doctrine; they profess Jesus as "Lord." They have prophesied; they have exorcised demons; they have done miracles. Moreover, they have done this "in [Jesus'] name." Jesus does not deny any of these facts, but these apparent Christians are still condemned. They are condemned not because their teaching was wrong or their miracles spurious but because they did not practice what they preached. They were bearing bad fruit, even when they were professing to be good.

So beware, especially if you sense you are a nominal Christian only. There are many paths to hell, many of them religious, but there is only one way to heaven, and that is through trusting in Jesus Christ.

Wise and Foolish Builders

The last of Jesus' illustrations contrasts two builders, a wise builder and one who is foolish.

> Therefore everyone who hears these words of mine and puts them into practice is like a wise man who built his house on the rock. The rain came down, the streams rose, and the winds blew and beat against that house; yet it did not fall, because it had its foundation on the rock. But everyone who hears these words of mine and does not put them into practice is like a foolish man who built his house on sand. The rain came down, the streams rose, and the winds blew and beat against that house, and it fell with a great crash.
>
> Matthew 7:24–27

The important thing to notice about this illustration is that the foundation Jesus is talking about is not Jesus himself but his teaching. We teach children to sing, "So build your house on the Lord Jesus Christ." But this is not a matter of merely giving our hearts to Jesus; it is a matter of building on what Jesus says. Rippon's hymn states it correctly: "How firm a foundation, ye saints of the Lord, is laid for your faith *in his excellent Word.*"

This is the point we have been dealing with in one way or another from the very first words of the sermon. When we studied the beatitudes, we saw how they were built on Scripture, the first two coming from Isaiah 61:1–2, the third from Psalm 37:11, the sixth from Psalm 24:3–4, and so on. The next section of the sermon dealt with the Bible directly, teaching that Jesus did not come to abolish the Bible's teachings but to fulfill them. The next three sections explained the meaning of several Old Testament commands and practices and taught how Christians are to relate to the world and its concerns. The Golden Rule summed up "the Law and the Prophets." Now, at the very end, Jesus teaches that the one who would be his disciple must build his or her entire life on the Bible. Building on Jesus' words will save you both in life and in death.

Dr. Joseph Parker was a popular English preacher. He tells in his autobiography how at one time he placed too much weight on the destructive theories of his day and found himself undervaluing the Bible. At this point a great sorrow entered his life. His wife of many years became sick and died within a few hours. Parker was unable to share his grief with anyone else, and walking through the empty rooms of his house, he felt for some footing in the theories of his day and found none. "But then," he said, addressing a company of his fellow pastors, "in those dark hours of my soul's anguish, when filled with doubt and trembling in fear, I [recalled] the old gospel of redemption alone through the blood of Christ, the gospel I had preached in those earlier days, and I put my foot down on that, and . . . I found firm standing. I stand there today, and I shall die resting upon that blessed glorious truth of salvation alone through the precious blood of Christ."[4]

Building on Christ's words will also save you in death, for that is what escaping the storm's destruction actually refers to. This is not merely a matter of finding something that will get you through life, fit to stand against "the slings and arrows of outrageous fortune," as it were. It is a matter of standing upright at the final judgment and not being carried off to hell by God's verdict and command.

A Time to Decide

At the end of this chapter we read that the people were amazed at Jesus' teaching. And rightly so! He had presented himself as "the Lord," the unique Son of God (calling God "my Father"), and the judge at the final day. He had spoken with absolute authority, and what he was requiring was radical submission to his rule as Lord of God's kingdom.

What does this mean to you personally? The people who heard the Lord Jesus Christ that day in Galilee, when he preached the Sermon on the Mount, were "amazed at his teaching, because he taught as one who had authority, and not as their teachers of the law" (vv. 28–29). Yet the text does not say that any who heard him then believed in his doctrine or committed themselves to him. I am sure some did. Some do today. But sadly, in our hectic, more sophisticated century, it is even more possible to do what the majority must have done in that day: let the hour of salvation pass by.

What is the most important message of this sermon? It is the person of Jesus of Nazareth himself. He is the Son of God. He spoke as no man has ever spoken. He lived as he preached, and then he died and rose again that those who believe him and trust him might pass from death to life and enter heaven to be with him forever. Do you believe that? Have you committed your life here and your future hereafter to Christ's care?

If you make that commitment, Jesus will do for you what he has promised. He will bless you in the sense given to that word in the beatitudes. He will make you salt to benefit others, and light to this dark world. He will enable you to understand and obey the Bible. He will teach you to pray. Then he will bear you through all the cares, dangers, and frustrations of this life to an eternity of unbroken fellowship with him in heaven.

Do you believe that? Listen, he is speaking to you now. He is saying, "Come to me, all you who are weary and burdened, and I will give you rest" (see Matt. 11:28). He is saying, "Believe on me." Let your heart say, "Yes, Lord, I am coming to you. I want you to be my Savior."[5] But be warned! It is easier to prefer what is wide and broad and attractive. It is natural to drift along to perdition with the crowd.

Part Three

The Power of the Kingdom

14

Jesus and Disease

Matthew 8:1–17

When he came down from the mountainside, large crowds followed him. A man with leprosy came and knelt before him and said, "Lord, if you are willing, you can make me clean."

Jesus reached out his hand and touched the man. "I am willing," he said. "Be clean!" Immediately he was cured of his leprosy. . . .

When Jesus had entered Capernaum, a centurion came to him, asking for help. "Lord," he said, "my servant lies at home paralyzed and in terrible suffering." . . .

Then Jesus said to the centurion, "Go! It will be done just as you believed it would." And his servant was healed at that very hour.

When Jesus came into Peter's house, he saw Peter's mother-in-law lying in bed with a fever. He touched her hand and the fever left her, and she got up and began to wait on him.

When evening came, many who were demon-possessed were brought to him, and he drove out the spirits with a word and healed all the sick. This was to fulfill what was spoken through the prophet Isaiah:

> *"He took up our infirmities*
> *and carried our diseases."*

Anyone who takes time to compare the four Gospels, especially the first three, the so-called Synoptic Gospels, will notice two things about their arrangement of material. First, there is a rough chronological order. Each tells about Jesus' baptism by John somewhere at the beginning; proceeds with accounts of Christ's public teaching and miracles; continues with his arrest by the Jerusalem authorities, his trial, and crucifixion; and ends with an account of Jesus' resurrection. Second, in what seems to be a contradiction to the chronology, the ordering of material varies at places. In these sections the accounts seem to be arranged by topics.

This is what we find in Matthew 5–9. The Sermon on the Mount (chaps. 5–7) is a collection of the kind of teaching Jesus was doing in Galilee during these early days of ministry. Now, in chapters 8 and 9, we have a collection of miracle stories in which Matthew records evidence of Jesus' authority over disease from this same period. The section ends with Jesus imparting some of his authority to the apostles (Matt. 10:1–4), after which they are dispersed to teach others as he has taught them (vv. 5–42).

This pattern was announced at the end of chapter 4, where we are told that "Jesus went throughout Galilee, *teaching* in their synagogues, *preaching* the good news of the kingdom, and *healing* every disease and sickness among the people" (v. 23).

The Pattern of Chapters 8 and 9

In these chapters, Matthew records nine works of Jesus, broken up by two stories about the calling of disciples. In the first group of miracles, Jesus heals: (1) a leper, (2) a centurion's servant, and (3) Peter's mother-in-law (Matt. 8:1–17). This is followed by a discussion of discipleship in verses 18–22. The second group of miracles contains: (4) the calming of a storm, (5) the healing of two demon-possessed men, and (6) the healing of a paralytic (Matt. 8:23–9:8). In the break following these miracles, Matthew records his own call to discipleship followed by a discussion about fasting (vv. 9–17). Then there are three final miracles: (7) a composite story about the healing of a sick woman and the raising of a dead girl, (8) the healing of two blind men, and (9) the deliverance of a third demon-possessed man—followed by Jesus' teaching about the need for Christian workers (vv. 35–38).

This arrangement encourages us to look for the spiritual meanings that led Matthew to include the stories he did and order them as he has, rather than be content merely with their narrative value.

The First Three Healings

Starting with the first group, we have: (1) the healing of a man who had leprosy, (2) the healing of the servant of a Roman centurion, and (3) the healing of Peter's mother-in-law, who was sick with a fever. The last account adds that many more were healed at this time, which itself suggests the stories we have are selective.

1. *A man with leprosy (vv. 1–4).* In the ancient world, leprosy was the most terrible of all diseases. There was no medical treatment, and the disease

caused the body to rot away, leading to an inevitable death. Most people considered lepers virtually dead already. Moreover, leprosy had social implications. It separated the victim from other human beings since he or she had to go about calling out, "Unclean! Unclean!" to warn any who were near to keep away. No one dared to touch a leper. In Israel it was illegal even to greet a leper. Lepers were not allowed to share in the services of the synagogue or worship at the temple in Jerusalem. In fact, lepers were barred from Jerusalem, as from all walled towns. William Barclay, who supplies these and other facts about lepers, says, "There never has been any disease which so separated a man from his fellow-men as leprosy did."[1]

Separated from other human beings, yes, but not from God! For here, in this first of the miracle stories in Matthew's Gospel, Jesus not only heals the leper but does so by reaching out and touching him, as no one in that day would have done. Verse 3 says, "Jesus reached out his hand and touched the man. 'I am willing,' he said. 'Be clean!'" This was so striking an action that each of the Synoptic Gospels records that Jesus touched him.

What is the point of this miracle then, assuming, as I have suggested, that the miracles are grouped together to make theological points and not merely for their narrative value? The first thing to understand, as any Jewish reader would have understood instinctively, is that leprosy rendered a person "spiritually unclean" and therefore cursed by God. The clearest biblical example is the judgment on Miriam, Moses' sister, who was stricken with leprosy for speaking against Moses when he married a woman from Ethiopia and who had to remain outside the camp until God healed her (see Num. 12:1–15). The reason the law did not allow a person to touch a leper was not only because leprosy was thought to be spread by contact but also because the touch made the one who touched the leper unclean and therefore cursed by God also.

But notice this! When Jesus touched the leper, his touch, rather than contaminating Jesus, cured the leper. It is a spectacular demonstration of what Jesus' coming does in respect to human sin. Jesus did not become sinful by becoming one of us; rather, he made it possible for us to be cleansed from sin by his contact.

Why did Jesus instruct the healed man to tell no one? The answer to that question, while a bit aside from our main purpose, is that Jesus probably did not want to draw attention to himself as a miracle worker. Mark 1, which provides further information about what was going on at this stage of Jesus' ministry, gives us an idea of what might have happened if Jesus had received more attention. It tells us that Jesus was healing many people, but he did not want a desire for healings to hinder his more important work of preaching the gospel, which is why he says he had come (Mark 1:38).

2. *A centurion's servant (vv. 5–13).* The second miracle in chapter 8 is another story of a healing, but it adds two elements not present in the first story. First, it is about a Roman centurion, which means it is about a Gentile. This indicates that the gospel Jesus was preaching is for the entire world and

not for Jewish people only. We have already noticed this as a recurring emphasis in Matthew, even though Matthew is the most Jewish of the Gospels. It begins with Gentile Magi coming to Jesus, and it ends with the command to "make disciples of *all* nations" (Matt. 28:19). Here a Gentile approaches Jesus and is not turned away.

This point is clear from the mere specifics of the story, but lest we miss it, Matthew adds Jesus' unexpected teaching about the heavenly banquet to be held at the end of the age. He says, "I say to you that many will come from the east and the west, and will take their places at the feast with Abraham, Isaac, and Jacob in the kingdom of heaven. But the subjects of the kingdom will be thrown outside, into the darkness, where there will be weeping and gnashing of teeth" (vv. 11–12). Those "from the east and the west" are Gentiles. Jesus is teaching that Gentiles will sit down with Jews at the messianic banquet—that is, Gentiles will be saved—while many of the privileged children of the kingdom, the Jews, will perish.

Second, the healing takes place through the channel of the centurion's faith, and what a great faith it is! The centurion tells Jesus about the sad condition of his servant: "Lord, my servant lies at home paralyzed and in terrible suffering" (v. 6). Jesus says that he will heal him (v. 7). But in a most surprising response, instead of merely saying, "Thank you," and waiting for Jesus to come and perform the healing, the centurion replies, "Lord, I do not deserve to have you come under my roof. But just say the word, and my servant will be healed. For I myself am a man under authority, with soldiers under me. I tell this one, 'Go,' and he goes; and that one, 'Come,' and he comes. I say to my servant, 'Do this,' and he does it" (vv. 8–9). Jesus was so impressed with this answer that he observed he had not found any person in Israel with such faith.

Why did the centurion speak about authority? And why does Matthew include these comments? D. A. Carson explains the man's thinking like this:

> All "authority" (*exousia,* as in 7:29) belonged to the emperor and was delegated. Therefore, because he was under the emperor's authority, when the centurion spoke, he spoke with the emperor's authority, and so his command was obeyed. . . . This self-understanding the centurion applied to Jesus. Precisely because Jesus was under God's authority, he was vested with God's authority, so that when Jesus spoke, God spoke. To defy Jesus was to defy God; and Jesus' word must therefore be vested with God's authority that is able to heal sickness.[2]

The greatness of this man's faith was not merely that he believed Jesus could heal from a distance, but it was in the degree to which he had understood that Jesus spoke with God's authority and as God. In linking faith to the matter of Jesus' authority, as the centurion did, we see how the stories of healing carry forward the theme found at the end of chapter 7: "He taught as one who had authority, and not as their teachers of the law" (v. 29). In chapters 5–7 Jesus taught with authority; now he is healing with authority as well.[3]

3. *Peter's mother-in-law (vv. 14–17).* The third miracle story in this section of Matthew is the healing of Peter's mother-in-law, joined to the healing of many demon-possessed and other sick people at this time. It lets us know, as an unrelated point, that Peter was married and that he had moved from Bethsaida to Capernaum with his wife, presumably to be close to Jesus.

This healing is told briefly in Matthew but at greater length in Mark and Luke (Mark 1:29–34 and Luke 4:38–44). In the second and third Gospels, attention is given to the people's attempts to get Jesus to carry on an extensive ministry of healing and to Jesus' rejection of their suggestion in order to keep preaching instead (Mark 1:38; Luke 4:43). Matthew replaces Mark and Luke's emphasis with a reference to Isaiah 53:4, which Jesus is said to have fulfilled: "He took up our infirmities and carried our sorrows."

Matthew did not need to show that Jesus came to preach. He had already done that by the extensive example of his teaching in chapters 5–7. No similar account of Jesus' teaching is found before this incident in either Mark or Luke. What Matthew is stressing is that Jesus healed people as well as taught and that he did it in fulfillment of the Bible's prophecies.

A Summary Text from Isaiah

But there is more to Matthew's citation of Isaiah 53:4. To begin with, we should note that the verse Matthew cites is from the Suffering Servant sections of that prophecy, to which there has already been one subtle reference. When God spoke from heaven at the time of Jesus' baptism he said, "This is my Son, whom I love; with him I am well pleased" (Matt. 3:17). The first part of those words comes from Psalm 2:7, which identifies the Messiah as the divine "Son" of God. The second part, from Isaiah 42:1, indicates the type of work assigned to God's servant, namely, to die for sin. The text quoted by Matthew in chapter 8, Isaiah 53:4, comes from the most explicit of the Suffering Servant passages, immediately before the words "he was pierced for our transgressions, he was crushed for our iniquities" (Isa. 53:5).

Some unperceptive critics suggest that Matthew habitually misuses Old Testament texts for his own limited purposes, but all this shows is how thoroughly these scholars misunderstand Matthew. Matthew knows that Isaiah 53 is about Christ's suffering for sin. When he supplies his own translation of the Hebrew text ("he bore our griefs and carried our sorrows," rendered "infirmities" and "diseases") rather than the Septuagint ("he bears our sins and is grieved for us"), he is making the point that Jesus' healing of our sicknesses is evidence of a far more important healing of our sins, which is what these stories are actually about.

We may miss seeing this in chapter 8, but we can hardly miss it in the next chapter, where Jesus tells a paralyzed man, "Your sins are forgiven" (Matt. 9:2). When the teachers of the law complain that this is blasphemy, since only God can forgive sins, Jesus replies, "Which is easier: to say, 'Your sins are forgiven,' or to say, 'Get up and walk'?" (v. 5). Then, so they would know that "the Son of Man has authority on earth to forgive sins," he healed the paralytic (vv. 6–7). The linkage between healing sickness and forgiving sins is carried into the next section as well. In verses 12 and 13 Jesus tells the Pharisees and everyone else who may have been complaining about his association with tax collectors and sinners, "It is not the healthy who need a doctor, but the sick. . . . I have not come to call the righteous, but sinners" (vv. 12–13).

In each of these stories, sickness is used as an illustration of sin—we might call the disease "sin-sickness"—and Jesus' healing of those who are physically sick becomes an outward demonstration of the Lord's more important authority over sin and his ability to forgive it.

Some Lessons about Sin

With this in mind, we need to go back to the miracle stories and look at them not as simple stories about Jesus' ability to make sick people well—people who have viewed the stories in this way have sometimes mistakenly believed that the New Testament teaches all Christians have the right to perfect health—but for what these stories teach us about sin and its cure. When we do this, we find four unmistakable lessons.

1. *We are spiritually sick.* Even worse, we are dying because of sin. This is why Matthew begins with the leper's healing; lepers were considered as good as dead. Yet the same point is made in each of the other stories. The centurion's servant was dying, and as far as Peter's mother-in-law is concerned, we should remember that in ancient times, before antibiotics and aspirin, more people died from fever than from any other single cause.

The point is that we are all perishing in sin, and there is no human remedy that will save us. True, the problem is worse than being merely sick. Paul told the Ephesians that we are actually dead already as far as being able to do anything to help ourselves is concerned. We need something much like a resurrection. That is why Paul wrote, "As for you, you were dead in your transgressions and sins. . . . But because of his great love for us, God, who is rich in mercy, made us alive with Christ even when we were dead in transgressions" (Eph. 2:1, 4). But Matthew is not recording a resurrection story at this point. He is telling how Jesus healed the sick early in his ministry. He is presenting our desperate condition as a terminal disease. Without God and the power God alone has to heal us, we will perish eternally.

2. *We need a Savior.* This is the next point. We need a Savior, and Jesus is that Savior. This is probably a second reason why the author of the Gospel summarizes his account of the first three healings by citing Isaiah 53:4. That verse expresses a link between the healing of disease and the healing of sin's sickness, but it also comes from a passage that prophesies the coming messianic Savior. Jesus is that Savior, and his authority both to heal and to forgive human sin is proof of it. There is no other Savior, because no other speaks or heals with such power.

3. *Faith is necessary.* A moment ago I referred to Ephesians 2 to show that in God's sight we are not merely sick with sin but actually dead in sin and need a resurrection. However, that passage also teaches that faith is the channel by which the salvation of God comes to us. Faith is not a good work of ours for which we can take credit; God makes it possible. But faith is still something we do, and it is necessary. We must believe. God does not believe for us. Ephesians 2:8–9 says, "For it is by grace you have been saved, through faith—and this not from yourselves, it is the gift of God—not by works, so that no one can boast." We see the need for faith in two of these three stories.

Did the leper have faith? He did, and it was of a remarkable sort. As Howard Vos points out in his commentary on Matthew, the leper did not say, "If you can" but "If you will."[4] That is, he began by believing that Jesus could heal him. The only question was whether Jesus would choose to do so. As for the Roman centurion, we have already seen how exceptional his faith was and how Jesus praised it as exceeding anything to be found in Israel. He understood that Jesus spoke with the authority and power of God. Therefore, it was not even necessary that Jesus enter his house to heal his servant. He could do it by a word and from a distance. This is what you and I need too, if we are to be saved from sin. Our condition is desperate. Jesus is the physician who alone can save us, but we must have faith in him. Do you? Faith is the one thing we need, the one thing that really matters.

Bishop John Ryle asks pointedly,

> What do we each know of this faith? . . . Our learning may be small: but do we believe?—Our opportunities of giving and working for Christ's cause may be few: but do we believe?—We may neither be able to preach, nor write, nor argue for the gospel: but do we believe?—May we never rest till we can answer this inquiry. . . . Faith in Christ is most precious in God's sight, and like most precious things is rare. By it true Christians live; by it they stand; by it they overcome the world. Without this faith no one can be saved.[5]

4. *The stakes are life or death.* This is the most important matter you will ever be asked to consider, for at stake is your life or your death: the life of God to be enjoyed in part now, though more fully later and forever, or the way of death that is bad enough now but will become indescribably tragic and inescapable when you pass from this phase of your existence to eternity. In this very passage, Jesus describes spiritual death as being "thrown outside, into the darkness, where there will be weeping and gnashing of teeth" (v. 12). Those are frightening words. I would not dare to utter them myself, if I did not have Christ's teaching. But I think Jesus knew what he was talking about. Don't you?

If you do, why don't you turn from your sin and believe on him now as your Savior? The people in these three stories did.

15

The Cost of Discipleship

Matthew 8:18–22

When Jesus saw the crowd around him, he gave orders to cross to the other side of the lake. Then a teacher of the law came to him and said, "Teacher, I will follow you wherever you go."

Jesus replied, "Foxes have holes and birds of the air have nests, but the Son of Man has no place to lay his head."

Another disciple said to him, "Lord, first let me go and bury my father."

But Jesus told him, "Follow me, and let the dead bury their own dead."

It is not unusual to hear Christians talk about Jesus as Lord and that this title should be acknowledged by his followers. But many otherwise well-intentioned but erring Christians believe it is possible to have Jesus as Savior without having him as Lord and even go so far as to maintain that "lordship salvation," as they call it, is a false gospel. Teachers like myself who oppose this error say that there is only one *Lord* Jesus Christ and that anyone who believes in a Savior who is not the Lord does not believe in the true Christ. We call for commitment to the true Lord Jesus Christ and challenge the presumption of those who claim to be Christians while at the same time disregard or disobey Christ's commands.

If we could reject all lesser views of what it means to be a Christian and produce a generation of those who are genuinely committed to Christ and obeying him, by the power of God's Spirit, that generation of believers could radically change the world.

Jesus' Understanding of Discipleship

Jesus' understanding of discipleship was different from our own. If an unchurched person should come to us and indicate that he or she wanted to be a Christian and follow Jesus, most of us would be delighted. We would invite the person to give a testimony and receive him or her into our church. But at this point in Matthew's Gospel, we read stories in which Jesus rejected such enthusiasm and actually seems to have turned two would-be disciples away, as he did with others on other occasions. As Jesus evaluated them, the first person was too quick to promise and the second was too slow to perform. Jesus told the first that following him meant being homeless. He told the second that loyalty to him came before loyalty even to the closest members of one's family. As far as we know, both turned away.

Since these stories come in the middle of a section documenting the authority of Jesus over sickness, we might ask why Matthew has included them here, especially since Mark leaves these conversations out entirely and Luke, although he includes similar material, inserts it at a much later point in Christ's ministry, about six months before the crucifixion (Luke 9:57–62). The obvious answer is that Matthew wants to show that the same Jesus, who has authority over sickness, nature, and demons, also has authority over the lives of his disciples. Jesus determines what following him will involve, not us. Therefore, if you are going to follow Jesus, it must be on his terms rather than your own.

The First Would-Be Disciple

Matthew begins by saying that when Jesus saw the large crowds that had been attracted by his healings, he gave orders to cross to the other side of the Sea of Galilee in a boat. But before he could get in, a teacher of the law came to him with a promise to follow wherever he might go. That is precisely what is required of a disciple, of course. It is what the apostles themselves were doing. But this man had apparently failed to think through what following Jesus might involve, and Jesus, who did not want anyone to follow him under false apprehensions, replied, "Foxes have holes and birds of the air have nests, but the Son of Man has no place to lay his head" (v. 20).

Jesus did have places to sleep, of course. He had friends like Mary and Martha and their brother, Lazarus, who invited him in and even provided meals for him and his disciples. But he had no possessions. He never owned a home. When he was arrested and crucified, he owned nothing but the clothes on his back. Even more, his life was one long series of rejections by his own people and by the Gentiles. William Hendriksen wrote accurately, "As the story develops, Judea rejects him (John 5:18), Galilee casts him out (John 6:66), Gadara begs him to leave its district (Matt. 8:34), Samaria refuses him lodging (Luke 9:53), earth will not have him (Matt. 27:23), and finally even heaven forsakes him (Matt. 27:46)."[1]

Had this would-be follower seriously considered that? Or more to the point, have we? The fact that Jesus never owned a home does not mean we can never own homes. Most people do, including Christians. But it does remind us that we may be called to give up homes or any other possessions in Jesus' service. So consider the cost before you begin to build the tower.

Still, we can miss the point if all we are thinking about are homes and other material possessions. The issue is actually discipleship and that of the most demanding sort. In days of hardship, particularly in periods of persecution, those who are in the process of becoming Christians count the cost carefully before taking up Christ's cross, and preachers do not beguile them with false promises of an easy life or indulgence of sins. But in good times, prosperous times, the cost does not seem so high, and people take the name of Christ without undergoing the radical transformation that true conversion implies.

Dietrich Bonhoeffer, the German churchman of the Nazi era who eventually suffered martyrdom for his opposition to Hitler's policies, called this erroneous theology "cheap grace." He said, "Cheap grace is the preaching of forgiveness without requiring repentance, baptism without church discipline, communion without confession, absolution without personal confession. Cheap grace is grace without discipleship, grace without the cross, grace without Jesus Christ living and incarnate."[2]

The contrast is "costly" grace. "Costly grace is the treasure hidden in the field; for the sake of it a man will gladly go and sell all that he has. It is the pearl of great price, to buy which the merchant will sell all his goods. It is the kingly rule of Christ, for whose sake a man will pluck out the eye which causes him to stumble; it is the call of Jesus Christ at which the disciple leaves his nets and follows him. . . . Such grace is *costly* because it calls us to follow, and it is *grace* because it calls us to follow *Jesus Christ.*"[3]

Most of us live in a rather mindless environment. Life is too fast, and our contact with other persons too impersonal for much serious reflection. Even in church we are more often encouraged to join this committee, back that project, or serve on this church board than we are counseled to examine our relationship with God and Jesus Christ. As long as we are performing for the church, few will question whether our profession is genuine or spurious. How many sermons suggest that members of a church may not actually be saved, although they are members? How many teachers stress that a personal, self-denying, costly, and persistent following of Christ is necessary if a person is to be acknowledged by Jesus at the final day?

In the absence of such teaching, millions drift on, assuming that because they have made some verbal acknowledgment of Jesus Christ ten, twenty, or even thirty years ago and have not done anything terribly bad since, they are Christians, when actually they may be far from Christ, devoid of grace, and in danger of perishing forever. Jesus never permitted anyone to harbor such a damaging delusion. He challenged prospective followers to count the cost before deciding to join him.

The Second Would-Be Disciple

The second of these two would-be disciples was a man who said he wanted to follow Jesus, but only after he had first met his family obligations. He wanted to bury his father. Jesus' answer was, "Follow me, and let the dead bury their own dead" (v. 22).

At first glance this seems to be a terribly insensitive reply, as if the man's father had just died and Jesus would not even let him arrange for or attend the funeral. But that is probably not what was involved. For one thing, in Israel the dead were required to be buried on the same day they died. If the man's father had died, he wouldn't even have been in the crowd surrounding Jesus. He would have been at home. However, since he is asking permission to bury his father before following Jesus, what he probably means is that he wants to remain at home during his father's last years and follow Jesus only after that phase of his life is over. When Jesus told him to forget about waiting for his father to die, he was saying that the time to believe on him and become his disciple is right now. Discipleship is always a present obligation. We can never put it off. Indeed, we do not know whether an opportunity to follow Jesus tomorrow or another day will come.

This is not just a pragmatic or practical matter either, as if Jesus were merely crying, "*Carpe diem*" ("Seize the day" of opportunity). When Jesus talks about the dead burying their dead, he is speaking in spiritual terms since it is obvious that physically dead people can't do anything to anyone, including bury other dead people. The dead who are to bury the dead are spiritually dead people, those who are awake to the issues of this world but who are dead to spiritual realities. They will attend to this world's obligations, Jesus says. It is different for those who have been awakened to spiritual matters. They perceive realities the spiritually dead cannot fathom and will drop everything to follow Jesus.

A little further on, in Matthew 10, which we will come to later, Jesus intensifies this command, saying that he has come to turn

> "a man against his father,
>   a daughter against her mother,
> a daughter-in-law against her mother-in-law—
>   a man's enemies will be the members of his own household."
>
> Matthew 10:35–36

These and similar warnings teach that we must chose between Christ and other persons (even members of our families) and declare that we cannot be Christ's followers without rejecting anyone who is opposing him or who would exercise a higher position of affection in our lives.

This teaching challenges us with four shocking truths.

1. *The radical demands of Christ's kingdom.* Over the years I have been asked to serve on various boards of Christian organizations, and to the extent that

I have had the time, I have been happy to do so. I have done everything I have been able to do for these organizations, but I have not left my parents or family to assume these responsibilities. In fact, I have not surrendered any legitimate responsibility to serve on boards. Christ's statements about the demands of his kingdom are not like that. We think of most jobs as something that can be taken on and then later dropped (if it pleases us to drop it) with no great issues involved. But when Jesus presented the demands of his kingdom, he explained them as callings that demanded the most radical commitment from his followers. Following Jesus was never to be a part-time occupation.

2. *The unique authority of Jesus Christ.* Jesus' statements also challenge us by his unique authority. Who would dare say such things unless he possessed unique authority? Who but God could make such demands?

This is the great question in these chapters, and it confronted everyone who came in contact with the Lord. When Jesus began to teach, they marveled "because he taught as one who had authority and not as their teachers of the law" (Matt. 7:29). When he quieted the storm on the Sea of Galilee, those who were with him were amazed, asking, "What kind of man is this? Even the winds and the waves obey him!" (Matt. 8:27). When he forgave the sins of the paralytic, the teachers of the law said, "This fellow is blaspheming!" because no one is able to forgive sins but God (Matt. 9:3). It became evident to everyone who met him that Jesus was speaking and acting with more than human authority. Was he the Son of God? That was the question they were asking. Some rejected that answer and eventually crucified him as a deceiver, but those who recognized his authority (validated by his numerous miracles) drew the inevitable conclusions and worshiped him as God.

If Jesus is God, then the demands of his kingdom become even more radical than we have imagined. When we hear Jesus saying that we must hate our fathers and mothers, wives and children, in order to be his disciples, it seems shockingly extreme. But if he is God, it is not extreme at all. If he is God, nothing he could possibly demand is outrageous. If he is God, we owe him total obedience and total self-surrender.

On the other hand, the fact that Jesus is God makes our total surrender all right. He is not an arbitrary god who has no concern for us and, so we might imagine, has a passion only for his own self-aggrandizement and glory. God made us. He has given us life and families and homes and a reasonable portion of this world's goods to enjoy. These things are good precisely because they are made by God and are God's gifts. It follows that if God requires us to give up one or more of these things in a specific situation—as a pioneer missionary might have to do to take the gospel to some remote area of the world—it is because the demand, difficult as it may appear, is nevertheless good in that particular situation.

3. *The priorities of true discipleship.* As soon as we talk about good in every situation or personal sacrifice in a specific situation, we tend to relax, assum-

ing that we are therefore off the hook and that the disturbing radical nature of true Christian discipleship need not affect us. But this is a false conclusion. It is true that Jesus may never ask us to break with our families for his sake or sell all we have and give to the poor in order to follow him. Indeed, in the great majority of cases, this is not required at all. But *we must be willing* to obey in these or any other areas if Jesus asks it, and we must actually do it, if he does. This is to say, we must get our priorities straight. Following Jesus must be the most important thing in our lives, yes, even more important than our lives. We must not do anything to subtract from that high commitment. We must do everything to strengthen it.

George Eldon Ladd comments on discipleship this way:

> The most radical form of . . . renunciation includes a man's very life; unless he hates his own life he cannot be a disciple (Luke 14:26). Obviously, this does not mean that every disciple must die; he must, however, be ready to do so. He no longer lives for himself but for the Kingdom of God. What happens to him is unimportant; for the fate of the Kingdom is all important. . . . In the place of selfish attainment, however altruistic and noble, one is to desire alone the rule of God.[4]

Some will think of this as a burden, but those who follow Jesus find it a liberating force. Indecision is inhibiting. The one who knows what he is committed to can move forward.

4. *The dangers of this hedonistic world.* Christ's statement about putting him before family responsibilities also reveals the shocking truth about the dangers of this world, even in the areas of normal relations and affections. We must say to ourselves, "If I can be kept from Christ by the normal and proper love that I should have for parents, spouse, children, or siblings, as Christ obviously teaches I can be, then how dangerous must the many other snares of this world be!"

Bishop John Ryle wrote wisely:

> It is not open sin, or open unbelief, which robs Christ of his professing servants, so much as the love of the world, the fear of the world, the cares of the world, the business of the world, the money of the world, the pleasures of the world, and the desire to keep in touch with the world. This is the great rock on which thousands of young people are continually making shipwreck. They do not object to any article of the Christian faith. They do not deliberately choose evil and openly rebel against God. They hope somehow to get to heaven at last, and they think it proper to have some religion. But they cannot give up their idol: they must have the world. And so after running well and bidding fair for heaven while boys and girls, they turn aside when they become men and women and go down the broad way which leads to destruction. They begin with Abraham and Moses and end with Demas and Lot's wife.[5]

How can a person resist the world's temptations if they can come to us even through the proper affection and loyalty we feel for our families? The best way is by being bold in confessing Jesus Christ.[6]

The "Son of Man"

There is one more thing we need to notice in this study: the title "Son of Man," used in verse 20 for the first time in the Gospel. It occurs eighty-one times in the Gospels, including sixty-nine times in the Synoptics. In each case, it is found either on the lips of Jesus or (in two cases only) on the lips of those who are quoting Jesus.

What does the title "Son of Man" mean? On the surface the words only mean "a man," and they are actually used this way in the Old Testament, as in Psalm 8:4, which asks, "What is man that you are mindful of him, the son of man that you care for him?" The addition of *son* particularizes the word *man,* just as the phrase "son of wealth" means a particular rich man or the words "son of sin" mean a particular sinner.

But there is more to the title than this, since Jesus did not refer to himself merely as "*a* son of man," which would have highlighted his humanity only. He referred to himself as "*the* Son of Man," and this specific "Son of Man" must be the individual referred to in the seventh chapter of Daniel. In that chapter Daniel records a vision in which he saw "one like a son of man, coming with the clouds of heaven. He approached the Ancient of Days and was led into his presence. He was given authority, glory and sovereign power; all peoples, nations and men of every language worshiped him. His dominion is an everlasting dominion that will not pass away, and his kingdom is one that will never be destroyed" (vv. 13–14). This individual is "like a son of man," but he is also invested with the authority, glory, and sovereign power of almighty God. Jesus unveiled this meaning of the title when he told the high priest who was presiding at his trial, "In the future you will see the Son of Man sitting at the right hand of the Mighty One and coming on the clouds of heaven" (Matt. 26:64).

Why did Jesus call himself "Son of Man" and not a more obvious messianic title? Presumably because it was the most ambiguous of the messianic titles, and by it he could avoid many misunderstandings of his mission while pouring into these words all the meanings he desired them to have. In Matthew alone he uses "Son of Man" to affirm his full deity (Matt. 16:13–17), to teach that he has authority on earth to forgive sin (Matt. 9:6), that he would ransom his people from their sins (Matt. 20:28), that he would die on the cross and rise from the dead on the third day (Matt. 17:22–23; 20:18–19), and that he will return one day in judgment (Matt. 24:27–31). That combination of ideas was puzzling to his Jewish contemporaries. They asked, "Who is this 'Son of Man'?" (John 12:34). But the answer to that searching question is the very essence of Christian theology: the person of Christ and the gospel.[7]

One day every knee will bow before Jesus Christ. It is what Daniel 7:14 says. *You* will bow, either in grateful adoration or in bitter defeat and crushed capitulation. If you are to bow in adoration and not in defeat, the time for it is now. Do not let the demand for absolute loyalty or the difficulties of following Jesus keep you back, as they seem to have done in the case of the would-be disciples we have been studying. Run to Jesus, cast yourself before him, worship him as God and Savior, and get on with the task of living for him in every moment of your life.

16

Jesus, Storms, and Demons

Matthew 8:23–34

Then he got into the boat and his disciples followed him. Without warning, a furious storm came up on the lake, so that the waves swept over the boat. But Jesus was sleeping. The disciples went and woke him, saying, "Lord, save us! We're going to drown!"

He replied, "You of little faith, why are you so afraid?" Then he got up and rebuked the winds and the waves, and it was completely calm.

The men were amazed and asked, "What kind of man is this? Even the winds and the waves obey him!"

When he arrived at the other side in the region of the Gadarenes, two demon-possessed men coming from the tombs met him. They were so violent that no one could pass that way. "What do you want with us, Son of God?" they shouted. "Have you come here to torture us before the appointed time?"

Some distance from them a large herd of pigs was feeding. The demons begged Jesus, "If you drive us out, send us into the herd of pigs."

He said to them, "Go!" So they came out and went into the pigs, and the whole herd rushed down the steep bank into the lake and died in the water.

Not many people are amazed anymore—by anything. It wasn't always this way. In the Middle Ages people were amazed by power, wealth, and pageantry. In the early days of the Industrial Revolution and well into our own lifetimes, people were amazed by science and its achievements. People marveled at discoveries that prolong life, the speed with which cars and airplanes travel, the ease of telephone communication. For a time we were amazed at space travel. We were amazed by computers. But not much amazes us anymore. The accelerating flow of inventions and their rapid dissemination throughout the world have numbed us and made even the most amazing things seem commonplace.

Christianity too! The most amazing thing about Christianity is God's grace. We used to speak of it as "amazing grace," but amazing grace is no longer amazing to most people. Yet one reality continues to amaze us if we give it a chance, and that is the person of Jesus Christ. Jesus amazes us because he is infinitely engaging. He never exhausts our interest. I read some time ago that the two people about whom more books have been written than any others are Napoleon, the French general and emperor, and Abraham Lincoln, the sixteenth president of the United States. But that is not quite accurate. Beyond any question, more books have been written about Jesus of Nazareth than any other person. The Gospels were first: Matthew, Mark, Luke, and John. But hundreds, thousands, and eventually hundreds of thousands of books followed them. And they continue to be written. I am writing one myself as I pursue this exposition of Matthew's Gospel.

Most people do not want to acknowledge Jesus as the Son of God or bow to him as their personal Lord and Savior, but somehow most people who actually have heard of Jesus can't quite banish Jesus from their minds. The person of Jesus broods over our discordant secular times, and who he is and what he was about remains a current question.

The Disciples Were Amazed

It was a question for Jesus' disciples too, and in the first of the two miracle stories we are looking at in this study we find them expressing their amazement at his authority. Their amazement had probably been growing for some time. At the end of the Sermon on the Mount we read that when Jesus had finished speaking, "the crowds were amazed at his teaching, because he taught as one who had authority, and not as their teachers of the law" (Matt. 7:28–29). The disciples were a part of the crowds, and they, like the others, must have been amazed at the authority of Jesus' words. When Jesus began to express his authority by healing people, their amazement grew.

The disciples had observed Jesus' authority over sickness in his healing of the leper, the servant of the Roman centurion, and Peter's mother-in-law, as well as unnamed others (Matt. 8:16). Now they are to witness two more areas in which Jesus displays his authority: over nature and over demons. In the first case, Jesus calms a terrifying storm on the Sea of Galilee. In the second case, he drives demons out of two men who were living on the other side of the lake in the region of the Gadarenes.

It is in connection with the first of those stories that we read of the disciples' amazement specifically: "The men were amazed and asked, 'What kind of man is this? Even the winds and the waves obey him!'" (Matt. 8:27).

Discipleship: Following Jesus

The story of Jesus calming the storm on the Sea of Galilee is more than a miracle intended to amaze his followers, however. It is about discipleship and faith. Without faith there can be no discipleship. Yet at this stage of their lives the disciples' faith was rudimentary at best.

There is a connection between the first line of this account and the two stories about would-be disciples that come immediately before it (in vv. 18–22). Both of those men expressed a wish to follow Jesus. The first said, "I will follow you wherever you go." But after Jesus explained that he had "no place to lay his head" (v. 20), this man apparently did not follow. The second disciple wanted to attend to family duties first. He wanted to stay at home until his father died and he could bury him, but Jesus said, "Follow me, and let the dead bury their own dead" (v. 22). According to Jesus, nothing can come before a deliberate, active, practical following for one who wants to be his disciple.

Now, in the first line of this new story, we read, "Then he got into the boat *and his disciples followed him*" (v. 23). That is certainly significant. We will see very shortly that the disciples had little idea whom it was they were following. Their faith was small, but they were following and had actually left their houses, family, land, and occupations to be with Jesus. In chapter 4 we were told that Peter and Andrew "left their nets and followed him" (v. 20) and that James and John "left the boat and their father and followed him" (v. 22). In chapter 9 we will be told that Matthew abandoned his "tax collector's booth . . . and followed him" (v. 9). There was a great deal more following to come, of course. The disciples had much to learn about what being a disciple meant, but they had heard Jesus' call, trusted him, and obeyed his summons. They had passed through the small gate and were on the narrow path that leads to life with Jesus Christ.

Which leads to this question: Are you on that path? Have you left all lesser loyalties to follow Jesus? It is not enough merely to be impressed with Jesus' person and teachings or even to be amazed at his miracles. The vital thing is actually to follow him.

Weak Faith Growing Stronger

How about their faith? The disciples had some faith, or they would not have been following Jesus at all, nor would they have turned to him in their fear, as they do in this story. However, their faith was weak at best. It needed to become strong.

The story is told in each of the Synoptic Gospels (in Matt. 8:23–27; Mark 4:35–41; and Luke 8:22–25). Pressed by the crowds who wanted healings more than teaching, Jesus got into a boat to cross to the other side of the Sea of Galilee. The sea is about thirteen miles long from north to south and about eight miles wide. Crossing from Capernaum to the Decapolis, therefore, was not a great journey. But Galilee is also 680 feet below sea level, and it is not uncommon for the cold winds of the western mountains to rush down the gullies and whip the waters of the lake into raging violence. This was what happened as the boat carrying Jesus and the disciples crossed the sea. One moment Galilee was calm. The next a furious storm came up, the waves threatened to engulf the vessel, and the disciples were sure they would drown.

Where was Jesus? Surprisingly, Jesus was asleep in the stern, resting on a cushion, as Mark records (Mark 4:38). Jesus must have been exhausted from teaching the crowds, and his fatigue explains why he needed to escape from their selfish clamoring. No matter! Waking him up, the disciples cried fearfully, "Teacher, don't you care if we drown?" (v. 38). Jesus did, of course. He spoke to the storm, subduing it, and saved them.

It was right for the disciples to turn to Jesus in their peril. So should we. The problem was not that they turned to Jesus. The problem was that their faith was so small. They were afraid of dying when they should have known Jesus would care for them and preserve them even from the storm. They should have known, as a songwriter said, "No water can swallow the ship where lies the Master of ocean, and earth, and skies."

John Ryle wrote wisely, "How many have faith and love enough to forsake all for Christ's sake, and to follow him whithersoever he goes, and yet are full of fears in the hour of trial! How many have grace enough to turn to Jesus in every trouble, crying, 'Lord, save us,' and yet not grace enough to lie still, and believe in the darkest hour that all is well!"[1]

Faith Centered on Jesus Christ

Yet the point of the story is not so much that the disciples' faith was weak, though it was. Faith must be centered on Jesus, and if it is, even if it is weak, it will be met by Christ's power. We have already witnessed an example of *great* faith. The Roman centurion had faith that Jesus could heal his paralyzed servant even without going to his house, and Jesus praised him for it. But there are other people with weak faith who are nevertheless also helped by Jesus. One man cried weakly, "I do believe; help me to overcome my unbelief!" (Mark 9:24). He was concerned about his son who had a demon. He was desperate. Jesus took him at his word, rebuked the evil spirit, and healed the boy. What was important was that he came to Jesus and trusted him as much as he was able.

In the story we are studying, Jesus rebuked the winds and the waves, and in a moment the sea was calm. Even the waves stopped rolling. That provoked the disciples' utter amazement, and they reacted quickly, asking, "What kind of man is this? Even the winds and the waves obey him!" (v. 27).

"Much that is wrong on earth can be corrected. . . . But it takes deity to change the weather," observed William Hendriksen,[2] and he was right. The psalmist wrote of God, "You rule over the surging sea; when its waves mount up, you still them" (Ps. 89:9; see Pss. 29:3–4, 10; 65:5–7; 107:23–32). God pointed to such power himself in his interrogation of Job.

> Who shut up the sea behind doors
> when it burst forth from the womb,
> When I made the clouds its garment
> and wrapped it in thick darkness,
> When I fixed limits for it
> and set its doors and bars in place,
> when I said, "This far you may come and no farther;
> here is where your proud waves halt"?
>
> Job 38:8–11

Since the story ends with the disciples' question, it is clear that its main point is christological, that is, it is mostly about Jesus and not merely a story about faith or a lack of it. And what a revealing story! One moment Jesus is asleep in the storm, overcome with exhaustion. He is clearly a normal man. The next moment he is calming the wind and waves, which only God can do. In this story, discipleship, faith, and the person of Jesus come together. The calling of Jesus leads to faith, faith leads those who believe to discipleship, and those who follow Jesus as disciples grow in the knowledge of who he is and all that he can do.

Jesus and the Hosts of Hell

It must have been in sober silence on a calm sea that this subdued bunch of men returned to their oars and resumed rowing their small craft across the lake to the land of the Gadarenes.[3] This was the western border of an area known as the Decapolis (a Greek word meaning "ten cities"), and most of its inhabitants were Gentile. The people Jesus and the disciples met in the region were obviously Gentiles, because they kept pigs, and no Jew would have kept such unclean and greatly detested animals.

We know what the disciples were thinking as they crossed the lake because it was stated at the end of the preceding story. They were asking themselves, "What kind of a man is this?" If we keep that in mind, it is amusing to discover in this story that while they were asking themselves this question, the demons came out of the tombs to tell them.[4] The demons had possessed two men, according to Matthew's account,[5] and they addressed Jesus boldly, crying, "What do you want with us, Son of God? . . . Have you come here to torture us before the appointed time?" (v. 29). Mark and Luke add that they called Jesus "Son of the Most High God" (Mark 5:7; Luke 8:28), and Luke says "they begged him repeatedly not to order them to go into the Abyss" (Luke 8:31).

It is worth reflecting on what the demons knew and were not afraid to announce, since their words reveal that they knew and believed more about Jesus than most human beings either know or acknowledge today. The demons recognized the following:

1. *Jesus is the Son of God.* The disciples were only beginning to get a glimpse of this truth and will not actually articulate it fully until Peter's great confession of faith in chapter 16: "You are the Christ, the Son of the living God" (Matt. 16:16). Jesus explained that it required a special revelation from God to make that truth clear to Peter (v. 17), but here the devils instinctively address Jesus as the unique "Son of God" and the "Son of the Most High God." James wrote that "the demons believe [in God]—and shudder" (James 2:19). Yet they exceed that minimal confession in this story since here they also acknowledge Jesus as God's Son.

2. *There is a final judgment, and they will suffer torment when the time comes.* Human beings cherish many dangerous illusions at this point: (1) there will be no final judgment; or (2) if there is, they will be spared the judgment; or (3) they are without any serious shortcoming in God's sight; or (4) if they are to be blamed for anything, God will be too kind to judge them for it; or (5) if there is a judgment, the place to which they are sent will be pleasant—just a matter of spending some quality time with old friends. The demons do not have such illusions. They know there is a hell, and they know they will be sent there at the proper moment. In this story their greatest fear is that they will be sent to hell before the final judgment.

3. *Jesus has authority to dispose of them as he wishes.* The third thing the demons knew and that most human beings either do not know or deliberately reject is that Jesus has authority to do with them as he wishes and when he wishes. This is an acknowledgment of the utter sovereignty of God and that Jesus, being the Son of God, has that sovereignty. The second psalm speaks of Jesus' sovereignty and warns us about it, saying,

> Kiss the Son, lest he be angry
>   and you be destroyed in your way,
> for his wrath can flare up in a moment.
>   Blessed are all who take refuge in him.
>
> Psalm 2:12

The demons did not do that, of course. They did not kiss the Son in submission, nor did they take refuge in his coming sacrifice for sin. But we can, and must, if we are to be saved from hell. Have you done it? To bow before the sovereign authority of Jesus Christ is another expression of what it actually means to be a Christian.

We do not know a great deal about demons, only what the Bible tells us about them, and that is not much. Yet it is clear from this story that the demons are spirit beings that abhor a disembodied state. This seems to be why they try to possess the bodies of human beings. Here, when Jesus is about to drive them from the demon-possessed men, the demons beg him at least to send them into a herd of pigs feeding nearby. Jesus sends them into the pigs, and when he does, the entire herd rushes down the steep bank at the side of the lake and perishes in the water that he and his disciples had just safely crossed (v. 32).

Why did Jesus allow the demons to go into the pigs and let the pigs perish? Some have complained that Jesus was inconsiderate in regard to those who owned the pigs. Others say the pigs were probably owned by Jews and that Jesus was punishing them for raising these forbidden animals. The actual reason is probably the same as the reason Jesus healed the paralyzed man in the next story, that is, as a visible proof of what had happened. In that story the healing is an outward proof that Jesus had indeed been able to forgive the man's sins, which would have been an unverifiable claim without it. In this story the destruction of the pigs showed that the demons had indeed left the two demon-possessed men and that the men were completely healed. There was no question of whether the demons would trouble the two men again.

Our Great Salvation

All this is actually about faith in Christ, salvation, and discipleship, of course. When we read about the possession of the men by demons, we are to understand that we are like them apart from the work of Jesus Christ. We may not be possessed by demons literally, but we are possessed by an evil spirit of sin, that is, by our own evil natures. Our sin leads us to various acts of violence, as the demons did in the case of these poor men, and it drives us from the company of other human beings. It is even right to say that we are dying people living among dead people, for life apart from Jesus Christ is a graveyard. There is no natural hope of being saved.

Unless Jesus comes! Which is exactly what he does. We do not ask him to come. He comes uninvited, and even then the evil spirits within us are hostile to him and want him to go. Salvation comes when Jesus addresses our evil spirit of sin and drives it out, leaving us "sitting there" quietly, "dressed and in [our] right mind" (Mark 5:15).

What about the people of Gadara? This is the sad part of the story, for instead of welcoming Jesus to their country, the people "pleaded with him to leave their region" (v. 34). They didn't drive him away or stone him, which shows they were afraid of his power, but they didn't welcome him either, obviously preferring their pigs to healthy people.

So Jesus left. But he also did something that Matthew does not tell us but that Mark and Luke record. He left the men who had been delivered to be witnesses to their countrymen, saying, "Go home to your family and tell them how much the Lord has done for you, and how he has had mercy on you" (Mark 5:19; see Luke 8:39). They did, and again we are told that "the people were amazed" (Mark 5:20). If people are not amazed at Jesus today, might it be because you and I have not witnessed adequately to his wonderful power and great grace? If you have been saved from sin, that is an amazing act of God. Don't you think you should tell other people about it?

17

Who Can Forgive Sin?

Matthew 9:1–17

Jesus stepped into a boat, crossed over and came to his own town. Some men brought to him a paralytic, lying on a mat. When Jesus saw their faith, he said to the paralytic, "Take heart, son; your sins are forgiven."

At this, some of the teachers of the law said to themselves, "This fellow is blaspheming!"

Knowing their thoughts, Jesus said, "Why do you entertain evil thoughts in your hearts? Which is easier: to say, 'Your sins are forgiven,' or to say, 'Get up and walk'? But so that you may know that the Son of Man has authority on earth to forgive sins. . . ." Then he said to the paralytic, "Get up, take your mat and go home." And the man got up and went home. When the crowd saw this, they were filled with awe; and they praised God, who had given such authority to men.

As Jesus went on from there, he saw a man named Matthew sitting at the tax collector's booth. "Follow me," he told him, and Matthew got up and followed him.

While Jesus was having dinner at Matthew's house, many tax collectors and "sinners" came and ate with him and his disciples. When the Pharisees saw this, they asked his disciples, "Why does your teacher eat with tax collectors and 'sinners'?"

On hearing this, Jesus said, "It is not the healthy who need a doctor, but the sick. But go and learn what this means: 'I desire mercy, not sacrifice.' For I have not come to call the righteous, but sinners."

People who read Matthew for the first time may think the arrangement of material is haphazard or at best merely topical. It is not haphazard, as I have indicated before. It *is* topical. But it is more than topical. The material in Matthew moves forward to a climax in chapters 9 and 10. First of all, we see a progression in the nine miracles. They start with simple physical healings: the man with leprosy, the sick servant of the centurion, Peter's mother-in-law. Then they advance to Jesus' power over nature, as he quiets a storm on the Sea of Galilee, and even over demons when he casts many of them out of the demon-possessed men from Gadara. In chapter 9, Jesus raises the dead and restores sight and speech to people who are blind and mute.

This escalating development is also seen in the careful arrangement of the interjected material (Matt. 8:18–22; 9:9–17). It concerns: (1) what it means to follow Jesus, (2) the authority of Jesus to forgive sins, and (3) the commissioning of those who have followed Jesus to take part in the missionary enterprise (Matt. 10:5–42). The obligation to tell others about Jesus is introduced in chapter 9 and forms the whole of chapter 10.

In the chapter we come to now, we discover opposition from the Jewish leaders for the first time, an opposition that will grow to the point at which they will scheme to have Jesus crucified by the Gospel's end. In these verses, Jesus' opponents accuse him of (1) blasphemy, (2) living with tax collectors and "sinners," and (3) a lack of piety. In the next study we will see how they accuse him of working his cures by the devil's power.

The Sixth Miracle: Healing a Paralyzed Man

The sixth miracle in this important sequence of nine early miracles is well known. It is the story of how a paralyzed man was brought to Jesus by four of his friends and how Jesus not only healed him of his paralysis but forgave him his sin (Matt. 9:1–8).

The story is also found in Mark 2:1–12 and Luke 5:17–26, both of which add details that Matthew omits in order to concentrate on his chief point, namely, Jesus' authority to forgive sin. Jesus had recrossed the Sea of Galilee, after having been asked to leave Gadara by the people who lived there, and he had come to Capernaum once more, a city now called "his own town" (v. 1). The other Gospels say that he was teaching in a house and so many people had gathered around him that there was no room for anyone else to get in. Some men came carrying their paralyzed friend, and when they found they were unable to get in to see Jesus, they went onto the roof, removed some of the tiles, and lowered the paralyzed man on a mat directly in front of Jesus. Jesus stopped teaching, and everyone waited breathlessly to see what he would do. It was a dramatic moment.

I suppose the man on the mat was looking apprehensive and perhaps even afraid, because Jesus' first words were a helpful encouragement: "Take heart, son." That meant, "Don't be afraid. I don't mind. Something good is going to happen." Then, with hardly a pause, Jesus continues boldly, "Your sins are forgiven" (v. 2).

"What did we just hear?" the teachers of the law asked themselves at once. "Did we hear him say, 'Your sins are forgiven'? How dare he say that? No one has authority to forgive sins but God. Claiming to be able to forgive sins is a claim to be God. This man is guilty of the vilest blasphemy. He should be stoned."

They were entirely right in their facts, of course. Matthew expects his readers to understand the point. It is clear that only God can forgive sin. There is no disputing that. But it follows from this starting point that if Jesus can forgive sin, as he is about to show he can, then Jesus is God or at the very least speaks and acts with God's authority. This is precisely the way Jesus handles their unspoken question. Knowing their thoughts, which he calls evil, Jesus asks them, "Which is easier: to say, 'Your sins are forgiven,' or to say, 'Get up and walk'? But so that you may know that the Son of Man has authority on earth to forgive sins . . ." (vv. 5–6). He then tells the paralyzed man, "Get up, take your mat and go home" (v. 6). And the man does, completely cured! The people are astonished. We are told that "they praised God, who had given such authority to men" (v. 8).

They didn't go far enough—it would be a while before anyone confessed Jesus' full deity (Matt. 16:16)—but they went as far as they could go.

Lessons from the Story

This story contains two important lessons.

1. *The root problem of the human race is sin.* Jesus raised this issue. Does this mean the paralyzed man was a sinner in some special sense and that his sin was the reason for his paralysis? Does it mean instead that all sickness is somehow linked to sin so that dealing with the one always has some bearing on the other? Matthew doesn't answer these questions because he is telling the story to show that Jesus has power both to heal and to forgive. Other chapters teach that not all illness is directly linked to sin. The story of the healing of the blind man in John 9 proves it. But some sickness is, and, in any case, in the final analysis all human ills flow from the fall and our resulting sinful condition.

Here is another question that requires a yes and no answer: Is there healing in the atonement? That is, does the forgiveness of sin by Jesus because of his atonement always lead to physical healing or good health? The answer is yes in the ultimate sense. All who are saved from sin by Jesus will one day be delivered from all physical manifestations of sin. Our resurrection bodies will be free of sin's effects. But the answer is no, if what we mean by this connection is the right of believers to have perfect health now. Not all do, and ultimately all of us die.

D. A. Carson answers the question like this:

> It is . . . quite correct to say, for instance, that there is healing in the atonement—a slogan in many Christian circles. But in the same sense, there is also a resur-

rection body and a new heaven and a new earth in the atonement. That does not mean I can expect to claim my resurrection body now, simply because it has been paid for. Though secured by Christ's cross and resurrection, our resurrection bodies come to us, according to the New Testament, only when Christ returns. And the same may be true, in many instances, of healing. God may bestow healing now, but he has certainly not pledged himself to do so. But one day, all true believers will be perfectly healed.[1]

Matthew's point is that Jesus raised the sin question because the final purpose of his coming was to deal with it, not to ignore it or treat it lightly. How different from people today, or even some of the people in this story! Today we do any of three things, or all of them: (1) we ignore sin, as if it does not exist, (2) we blame it on someone else, either our genes or our environment, or (3) we pretend that it does not matter. But sin does matter! It is the source of all our problems, and Jesus takes it seriously.

2. *Jesus' authority to forgive sin proves his deity.* After seeing the miracle, the people understood that God had given Jesus some astonishing authority. But Matthew points out more than this. The Pharisees accused Jesus of blaspheming, since only God can forgive sin, and since Jesus forgave the sin, his as-yet-unspoken claim to deity was upheld.

This is why this example of healing is so important. The issue was the ability of Jesus to forgive sin. Anyone can claim such authority. You or I or anyone else can say to someone, "I forgive your sin," meaning not merely that we are not going to dwell on the offense but that we actually have authority to absolve the sin or deliver the one who is forgiven from its punishment. We can *say* it, but who would take it seriously, except a few individuals like the Pharisees who are scandalized by blasphemy? But if someone couples the forgiveness of sins, which is invisible and unseen, to physical healing, which is both visible and verifiable, and then actually performs the healing, the claim is substantiated. And when that occurs, we had better be "filled with awe," as the onlookers were, for it means that somehow God himself is among us.

The Calling of Matthew

Everything I have been saying about Jesus' authority to forgive sin carries over into the next story also, which is why Matthew has included the account of his own calling to be a disciple here. He told about the calling of some of the first disciples earlier (in Matt. 4:18–22). He will provide a full list of the Twelve in chapter 10 (vv. 2–4). Here he includes his own calling to indicate that, like the paralyzed man, he too needed to be healed by Jesus and that the malady he most needed to have cured was his sin. The account shows that his friends needed the same healing as well.

There are several obvious verbal links between the two stories that make these points explicit, and one of them is that just as the paralyzed man was a sinner, so too are the people appearing in this story. In the opinion of the Pharisees, Matthew and his friends were mere "tax collectors and 'sinners,'" the kind of people with whom they would not associate. But it is precisely sinners that Jesus came to save, and Matthew is happy to put himself in their company as merely another sinner saved by grace.[2]

Matthew is doing in his narrative what the great Dutch painter Rembrandt van Rijn did in one of his most famous paintings of the crucifixion. He portrayed all the characters one would expect in such a scene: Jesus, the two thieves, the soldiers, and a large crowd of onlookers. But down in the corner of the painting, as one who shared in the guilt of the crucifixion and is not afraid to admit it, Rembrandt has painted a portrait of himself. Thus, as Matthew, he has testified to the fact that he too was a sinner and that he trusted in Jesus as the one who died to save him from his sin.

Rejected by Others but Not by God

One of the remarkable incidents in the last chapter was how Jesus helped a Roman centurion, a Gentile whom most Jews would have called unclean and with whom they would have had no social contact. But Matthew himself, though a Jew, was even worse than the centurion in their eyes. He was unacceptable in at least three ways.

1. *He was politically unacceptable.* As a collector of taxes he was one who had collaborated with the occupying authorities. That was enough to ostracize him. But in addition, tax collectors often grew rich by extorting more than was owed, and they were hated for it. William Barclay reports the existence of three main statutory taxes: (1) a ground tax of one-tenth of the grain and one-fifth of fruit and grapes, (2) an income tax of 1 percent of a person's income, and (3) a poll tax imposed on all males fourteen to sixty-five, and every female twelve to sixty-five. In addition, however, the collectors grew rich by overcharging on many other taxes. A duty tax of 2.5 percent to 12.5 percent was levied on all imported and exported goods. There were taxes for using main roads and for crossing bridges, for entering market towns or using harbors. Pack animals were taxed, as were the wheels and axles of carts.[3]

Capernaum was a town where major roads came together. Therefore, Matthew was at the junction to levy taxes on goods that passed by.

2. *He was religiously unacceptable.* He was considered unclean. Jewish law barred tax collectors from all synagogue services on the basis of Leviticus 20:5, which required orthodox Jews to cut off anyone who was guilty of "prostituting [himself] to Moloch." Tax collectors were not even allowed to witness in a court of law.

3. *He was socially unacceptable.* Religious people spoke of those who failed to keep every petty detail of the law as the *'am ha'arets* ("people of the land"). The orthodox were forbidden to go on a journey with them, do business with them, give them anything, receive anything from them, have them as guests or be guests in their homes. Matthew was one of these.

But here is the wonderful thing. Though politically, religiously, and socially unacceptable to the self-righteous leading Jews of his day, Matthew was not unacceptable to Jesus and therefore not unacceptable to God, which is what really mattered. Jesus called him to "Follow me," just as he had called the earlier disciples. When he did, Matthew did exactly what the paralyzed man had done when Jesus forgave his sins and healed him; he "got up" (compare vv. 7, 9) and followed Jesus, being as thoroughly healed of his deep-rooted sin as the paralyzed man was. Matthew does not mention this, but Luke adds that he "left everything"—that means his position, job, and income—to follow Jesus (Luke 5:28).

Was Matthew truly converted? He certainly was, and he showed it in at least three ways, two of which we have just noted.

1. *He "got up" and followed Jesus.* An inactive faith is no faith at all. Saving faith shows in one's actions.

2. *He left everything to do it.* Nothing is ever allowed to stand in the way of one who is a genuine disciple. Truly converted people leave houses, land, family, and everything else to follow Jesus.

3. *He arranged to have his friends meet Jesus.* This is another link between the story of Matthew's calling and the story of the healing of the paralyzed man in verses 1–8. In the first story, the friends of the paralyzed man brought him to Jesus to be healed. Here, in verse 10, Matthew tries to do the same thing with his unconverted friends. This is a natural act for those Jesus has saved, and it makes us ask, Are we in that great company of witnesses? Are we introducing our friends to Jesus? We cannot make people Christians; it is something only God can do. But we must do everything possible to tell them about Jesus and have them meet him.

The Opposition Grows

Yet at the same time people are bringing their friends to Jesus, others are trying to keep people from him. We have already seen the beginning of this opposition in the story of the healing of the paralytic. The teachers of the law objected when Jesus forgave the paralyzed man of his sins, claiming that only God can forgive sins. They accused him of blasphemy. In the continuation of the story of Matthew's conversion and in the discussion about fasting that follows in verses 14–17, two more criticisms emerge.

1. *Jesus was associating with "tax collectors and 'sinners.'"* This was an attack on his morals, for the obvious implication was that if he associated with low types, he must be like them. He was with "sinners" because he liked and wished to share in their sin.

Jesus responded to this criticism with an illustration and a quotation from the Old Testament. The illustration was drawn from medicine. "It is not the healthy who need a doctor," he said, "but the sick." Today when people are sick, they usually go to a doctor or to a hospital. In Jesus' day there were no hospitals or doctors' offices. Doctors went to the patients. They actually made house calls. Jesus drew on this common pattern to explain that he was a doctor of the soul and that, if he were to help those who were sick in soul, he had to go where they were. This does not mean his critics were spiritually healthy, as the continuing conversation shows. They were actually as paralyzed by their sin as the paralytic and as unclean as the despised tax collector. But it does mean that Jesus was correct to act as he was acting. In fact, if the Pharisees were the spiritual leaders of the people as they claimed they were, they should have been trying to reach and save the lost, as he was.

Jesus also challenged them to reexamine their actions by looking at Hosea 6:6. Hosea had been attacking the false, formal religion of his day, saying that the people professed to follow God because they were going through the outward acts of religion, while actually their hearts were far from him. He quotes God as saying, "For I desire mercy, not sacrifice, and acknowledgment of God rather than burnt offerings" (Hosea 6:6).

This verse must have been a favorite with Jesus, for he cites it again in 12:7. In that passage, as well as here, Jesus is saying that if the leaders of the people were really right with God, they would show mercy to the lost and seek to call them to repentance and faith, as Jesus was.

This is where this conversation ends, for Jesus concludes by saying, "I have not come to call the righteous, but sinners" (v. 13). The "call" in this verse is to repentance and faith in Jesus as the Savior, of course, which Luke makes clear by mentioning repentance explicitly in his telling of the story (Luke 5:32).

2. *Jesus was failing to be properly pious.* The next conversation was initiated by the disciples of John the Baptist and probably occurred at a later time rather than at Matthew's dinner. Matthew includes it here because it is another example of the charges that were being lodged at Jesus by his enemies. It had to do with fasting. "We fast, and so do the Pharisees," they objected. "Why don't you?"[4]

The question gains special poignancy by being placed next to the account of Matthew's dinner. At the very time when Matthew, his friends, and Jesus were feasting in Matthew's house, the Pharisees and the disciples of John the Baptist were fasting—and seemed to be unhappy about it. Jesus replied that he had come to his own as a bridegroom coming to his bride and that it was not right to practice fasting at a wedding. Besides, he said, what I am bringing is quite new, like a piece of new cloth or new wine, and anything as new as this simply cannot be imposed on old forms. New cloth stitched to old cloth will tear it when the new cloth shrinks, and new, fermenting wine will burst old wineskins.

The picture of a bridegroom coming to his bride looks forward ultimately to the great marriage supper in heaven. But first Jesus will go to the cross and die, which is what the mention of future fasting in verse 15 predicts and the rest of the Gospel carefully records.

18

Three More Healings

Matthew 9:18–34

While he was saying this, a ruler came and knelt before him and said, "My daughter has just died. But come and put your hand on her, and she will live." Jesus got up and went with him, and so did his disciples.

Just then a woman who had been subject to bleeding for twelve years came up behind him and touched the edge of his cloak. She said to herself, "If I only touch his cloak, I will be healed."

Jesus turned and saw her. "Take heart, daughter," he said, "your faith has healed you." And the woman was healed from that moment.

When Jesus entered the ruler's house and saw the flute players and the noisy crowd, he said, "Go away. The girl is not dead but asleep." But they laughed at him. After the crowd had been put outside, he went in and took the girl by the hand, and she got up. News of this spread through all that region. . . .

While they were going out, a man who was demon-possessed and could not talk was brought to Jesus. And when the demon was driven out, the man who had been mute spoke. The crowd was amazed and said, "Nothing like this has ever been seen in Israel."

But the Pharisees said, "It is by the prince of demons that he drives out demons."

In this study we come to the last set of miracles in Matthew 8 and 9. The first set of three is in Matthew 8:1–17: (1) the healing of a leper, (2) the healing of the sick servant of a Roman centurion, and (3) the healing of Peter's mother-in-law. The second set includes: (4) the quieting of the wind and waves on Galilee, (5) the deliverance of two demon-possessed men from Gadara, and (6) the healing of a paralyzed man. This second set of miracles is in Matthew 8:18–9:8. In Matthew 9:18–34, the miracles include: (7) a double miracle involving the raising of a dead girl to life coupled with the healing of a woman who suffered from a flow of blood, (8) the healing of two blind men, and (9) the healing of a demon-possessed man who had been unable to speak.

Understanding the Accounts

At the beginning we looked at these accounts largely as stories showing Jesus' authority over sickness, just as chapters 5–7 focused on his authority as a teacher. But as we have progressed through these accounts, we have begun to see that they concern much more than physical healing.

For one thing, the calming of the wind and waves on the Sea of Galilee showed Jesus' astonishing authority over nature. The next story showed his authority over demons, which is much more a spiritual than a physical matter. Most suggestive of all was the link between the forgiveness of sins and the healing of the paralyzed man in chapter 9. Matthew selected these specific stories to show that Jesus came not so much to heal us of our physical diseases but to cure us of our sin, our far more serious malady, and to set us on the path of useful service for him.

This insight gives us a helpful clue for interpreting everything else in chapters 8–10. The first three healing stories were not given particularly weighty meanings. The emphasis seemed to be mostly on the faith possessed by those who were healed, particularly the faith of the centurion who believed that Jesus could heal his servant even from a distance. But now we can see that even these first narratives held additional meaning. Matthew revealed what he was actually writing about when he quoted Isaiah 53:4: "He took up our infirmities and carried our diseases."

Critics have claimed that Matthew misused this text since it is about the Messiah bearing sin rather than about healing diseases and that Matthew has been recording healing stories. But Matthew knew what Isaiah 53 is about as well as anyone. When he quotes Isaiah, he is saying that what is really disclosed in these healing stories is Jesus' ability to take away our sin and restore us to spiritual health.

Understanding this underlying meaning also explains the parenthetical material and why it was placed where it was. The first had to do with discipleship, with those who said they wanted to follow Jesus but who were concerned about other things and therefore did not follow. They did not follow Jesus for healing, so they remained in their sins. The second passage concerned the calling of Matthew himself and Jesus' statement that he had come not to call the righteous but sinners. Like the paralytic in the preceding story, Matthew was healed, but he was healed of sin. Moreover, when Matthew was healed, he showed it immediately by seeking to introduce his many friends to the Savior.

Significantly, chapters 8–10 end with Jesus commissioning the disciples to the task of world evangelism, which is a way of saying that this is the work to which true discipleship leads. If we have left everything to follow Jesus, as the disciples did, and if we have been truly received by Jesus and have been forgiven our sin, as Matthew was, then we will tell others about Jesus. We will not be content until the entire world has been told that Jesus is the King of Kings and the Savior.

A Double Healing

Now that we have the overall framework for these chapters, we are ready to look at the three final healings. The first involves the raising of the dead daughter of a synagogue ruler and the healing of the bleeding woman that is joined to it (Matt. 9:18–26). These stories are also told in Mark and Luke, but Matthew's account is the most condensed version. Matthew tells the incidents in nine verses, whereas Mark uses twenty-three verses (Mark 5:21–43) and Luke uses seventeen (Luke 8:40–56).

1. *The case of Jairus.* Matthew says that while Jesus was teaching about fasting (vv. 14–17) a ruler asked him to come and raise his daughter from the dead. In the Gospels, "ruler" almost always means a ruler of the synagogue, but in any case, Mark makes this clear in his account, where we also learn that this man's name is Jairus (Mark 5:22). Mark says that at the time the ruler first approached Jesus, his daughter had not yet died but that she died before Jesus reached her: "While Jesus was still speaking, some men came from the house of Jairus, the synagogue ruler. 'Your daughter is dead,' they said. 'Why bother the teacher any more?'" (v. 35).

Earlier in this series of miracles, when we were studying the healing of the Roman centurion's servant, we remarked on the extraordinary faith of the centurion. He believed that Jesus could heal his servant even without coming to his house. The faith of the synagogue ruler is also striking. True, he asked Jesus to "come and put your hand on her" (Matt. 9:18), which falls short of the centurion's perception, but at some point in the story, later if not at the beginning, knowing that his daughter had died he still trusted Jesus. Besides, he was from among those religious leaders who were jealous of Jesus and very quickly became hostile to him and tried to destroy him.

What made Jairus appeal to a man most of his peers rejected? No doubt, it was utter desperation! His daughter was dying or was already dead, and he had nowhere else to turn. Desperation may not have been the best of motives, but it drove him to Jesus and that was all that really mattered. It has been the case for many people. They may not have come to Jesus for any other reason but that something in their lives made them desperate. So they came to Jesus and discovered that he did not scorn them for their inadequate or poor motives but met their needs instead.

I commend Jairus as an example. If you have a need that no one else is able to meet, turn to Jesus. Above all, turn to him if you feel the burden of your sin and seek forgiveness. There is no one who can forgive sin and free you from sin's burden but Jesus Christ.

2. *The case of the bleeding woman.* Wasn't it desperation that drove this woman to Jesus too? The woman is nameless, but she is introduced as a desperate case since she "had been subject to bleeding for twelve years" (v. 20), to which Luke also adds, "No one could heal her" (Luke 8:43). It is important to think about her condition since it so obviously illustrates our own desperate condition due to sin.

First, she was *unclean.* The words the Gospel writers use are carefully chosen, as we might expect from men who are describing the health problems of a woman. But what we surmise from their accounts is that the woman was suffering from excessive menstrual bleeding. Whatever the source, the bleeding would have weakened her—she would have been anemic as well as subject to further diseases—and she would have been considered ceremonially unclean by the Jews, as was the leper whom Jesus healed in chapter 8. The condition of a woman subject to such bleeding and how she was to be treated is described in Leviticus 15:25–33.

Second, she was *isolated.* People could not come into contact with a menstruating woman without being made unclean by that contact. In fact, they could not even lie on a bed where she had lain or sit on a chair where she had sat. No one could touch her, and she was not allowed to touch other people. Sadly, her bleeding would have destroyed her chances for marriage, or, if she were married, it would have precluded all sexual relations with her husband. She must have been very, very lonely.

Third, she was *incurable.* Luke makes this clearer than the other two writers when he explains that "no one could heal her" (Luke 8:43), but it is obvious from the other Gospels as well. All three Synoptic Gospels say that she had been ill for "twelve years" (v. 20), and Mark adds that, in spite of her having seen many doctors, "instead of getting better she grew worse" (Mark 5:26).[1]

When we put the story of the synagogue ruler's daughter and the woman who suffered from bleeding together, we have an apt picture of everyone apart from the healing grace of Jesus Christ. I am sure these stories are linked in the Gospels because the circumstances of the cures are intertwined; that is, they actually happened at the same time and were remembered together by the writers. But the stories also reinforce one another (and belong together for that reason) since what was true of the woman was true of the girl too, and vice versa. The dead were as unclean as menstruating women and lepers. They could not be touched. That is why Matthew points out that Jesus overthrew the taboo by taking the dead girl by the hand (v. 25). Again, there is no isolation so utterly complete as death, either for the dead person or for those who have lost the one loved. As far as the woman was concerned, she was bleeding to death even if she was not dead yet. As for being incurable, the condition of the dead girl and the condition of the woman were both clearly beyond hope.

But not for Jesus. What we are told is that the woman's contact with Jesus healed her "from that moment" (v. 22) and that as soon as Jesus had taken the dead girl by the hand she got up, being raised from the death that held her.[2] None are too unclean, too isolated, or too hopeless for Jesus to save. He can even raise the dead.

Hope for the Hopeless

The point of these stories is that this is exactly what Jesus does in the case of everyone who is saved from sin. It is what he has done for you if you are a Christian. What does sin do to us after all? Obviously, it makes us *unclean.* It contaminates us, and none of us can come before the purity of God's presence until our sin is dealt with. When Isaiah saw the Lord seated upon his throne in heaven he cried out, "I am ruined! For I am a man of unclean lips, and I live among a people of unclean lips" (Isa. 6:5). He trembled before God until an angel touched his lips with a coal from the altar, saying, "Your guilt is taken away and your sin atoned for" (v. 7).

Sin also *isolates.* It keeps us from God, which is the worst thing about sin, but it also isolates us from other people, creating hurts, hard feelings, and misunderstandings between races, individuals, and even members of one's own family. Isaiah also wrote of our isolation from God: "Your iniquities have separated you from your God; your sins have hidden his face from you, so that he will not hear" (Isa. 59:2).

Then, too, our condition is *hopeless* apart from grace. Nothing could be more hopeless than death, and we are described as being "dead" in our sins (Eph. 2:1). But the same chapter of the Bible that says we were dead in our sins also says, "But because of his great love for us, God, who is rich in mercy, made us alive with Christ even when we were dead in transgressions—it is by grace you have been saved. And God raised us up with Christ and seated us with him in the heavenly realms in Christ Jesus, in order that in the coming ages he might show the incomparable riches of his grace, expressed in his kindness to us in Christ Jesus" (Eph. 2:4–7). There is no finer picture of that love, grace, resurrection power, and salvation than Matthew's account of the healings of the ruler's dead daughter and the bleeding woman.

A Healing of Two Blind Men

We come next to the last part of chapter 9, which contains two more healing stories. The first, which is the eighth in the overall series, is about the healing of two blind men (vv. 27–31). If we look at them in the same context in which we have been looking at the other miracles, we see that they are concerned with what Jesus does when he saves sinners.

These two men came after him, crying out, "Have mercy on us, Son of David" (v. 27). This is the first use of the title "Son of David" in Matthew, and there can be little doubt that it is used here as in other places with strong messianic expectations. Can it actually be the case that these blind men were confessing Jesus as the Messiah? That is exactly what they were doing! In fact, it was their faith in Jesus as the Messiah that led them to cry out as they did. The messianic age was understood to be a time when "the eyes of the blind [would be] opened and the ears of the deaf unstopped," when "the lame [would] leap like a deer, and the mute tongue shout for joy" (Isa. 35:5–6). "If Jesus was really the Messiah, the blind reasoned, then he would have mercy on them; and they would have their sight," writes D. A. Carson.[3] They may not have been certain that their faith was rightly placed before they cried out, but it was their only chance. Their condition was as hopeless as that of the people in the preceding story. Yet once Jesus turned to them, called them inside, questioned them, and healed them, they knew he was indeed the Savior and the King of Israel.

"Do you believe that I am able to do this?" he asked.

"Yes, Lord," they replied. Then he touched their eyes, and their sight was restored completely.

This story and the following one about the man who could not talk are unique to Matthew, though Mark and Luke include stories of the healing of blind men later on in their Gospels (see Mark 8:22–26; 10:46–52; parallels in Matt. 20:29–34; Luke 18:35–43). Why does Matthew include such a story here? The reason is his understanding of what these healing stories teach. If we have been right in our study thus far, they teach what is involved when Jesus saves men and women from their sin. They portray our spiritual condition—we are all unclean, isolated, hopeless, even dead in our sins—and they show that to be saved from sin we need the powerful, forgiving, saving grace of God, which is to be found in Jesus Christ alone.

What follows then? Clearly, what follows is the opening of our eyes to see Jesus even better than we did before. Before their healing, the blind men saw Jesus in their mind's eye, enough to identify him as the Messiah. But when their eyes were opened, they saw him as he is, and they began to "spread the news about him all over that region" (v. 31).

What happened here reminds us of what happened when Jesus appeared to the two Emmaus disciples when they were making their way back home after the resurrection. They had heard about Christ's resurrection, but they did not believe it. Dead men do not rise. When Jesus appeared to them, they failed to recognize him. This was a spiritual blindness, illustrated by their inability to see who he was. But he began to teach them from the Old Testament, and when he did, "their eyes were opened and they recognized him" (Luke 24:31).

There are three great "openings" in Luke 24: first, the Scriptures (vv. 27, 32); then, their eyes (v. 31); finally, their minds, as they came to understand even the Scriptures in new ways (v. 45).

A Demon-Possessed Man

The last story is also unique to Matthew's Gospel. So why does Matthew include the healing of a demon-possessed man at this point (vv. 32–33), especially since he already told the story of two demon-possessed men earlier and in detail (Matt. 8:28–34)? Matthew probably included this unique story because due to the man's demon-possession he "could not talk," but after the demon was driven out he could (vv. 32–33).[4] In other words, Matthew included this healing because it fits his pattern of explaining what salvation is and where it leads. In this case, it leads to speaking for Jesus, which is exactly what Jesus commissions his disciples to do in the next chapter.

Matthew's point is that people who have been saved from sin will see Jesus in new ways and will tell others about him. Having been lost sheep themselves, they will have compassion on other sheep who also belong to Jesus but have not yet been brought into his fold (see v. 36).

And speaking of speaking, we should note that there are three kinds of speaking in these final verses. First, the crowds are amazed and speak *about* Jesus. They say, "Nothing like this has ever been seen in Israel" (v. 33). True, but not good enough. At the very least, the miracles should have led them to faith in Jesus as the Messiah. These miracles prepare for the defense of Jesus' messiahship to the disciples of John the Baptist in chapter 11. "The blind receive sight, the lame walk, those who have leprosy are cured, the deaf hear, the dead are raised, and the good news is preached to the poor" (v. 5).

Second, the Pharisees speak *against* Jesus. We saw the sad beginning of their opposition earlier when they called his claim to forgive sin blasphemy. Then they criticized him for eating with "sinners." In the story of the raising of Jairus's daughter, they laughed at him. Here they do the worst thing of all. Being helpless to deny the miracle, they attribute it to Satan's power, thereby showing themselves to be closer to Satan than to Jesus. They say, "It is by the prince of demons that he drives out demons" (v. 34).[5]

The third kind of speaking is speaking *for* Jesus, and it is illustrated by the testimonies of those who were healed. They had experienced a wonderful deliverance, and they were unable to keep silent about it. All who have been saved by Jesus will want to talk about it. Don't you?

19

Prayer for Christian Workers

Matthew 9:35–10:4

Jesus went through all the towns and villages, teaching in their synagogues, preaching the good news of the kingdom and healing every disease and sickness. When he saw the crowds, he had compassion on them, because they were harassed and helpless, like sheep without a shepherd. Then he said to his disciples, "The harvest is plentiful but the workers are few. Ask the Lord of the harvest, therefore, to send out workers into his harvest field."

He called the twelve disciples to him and gave them authority to drive out evil spirits and to heal every disease and sickness.

These are the names of the twelve apostles: first, Simon (who is called Peter) and his brother Andrew; James the son of Zebedee, and his brother John; Philip and Bartholomew; Thomas and Matthew the tax collector; James son of Alphaeus, and Thaddaeus; Simon the Zealot and Judas Iscariot, who betrayed him.

A true church is a missionary church. But why should the followers of Jesus Christ be involved in missions? There are at least four reasons: (1) the lost condition of the world, (2) the Great Commission, (3) the love of God working in us, and (4) the many opportunities for advancing Christ's kingdom. Strikingly, all four are in the passage before us.

The starting point is the terrible accusation the Pharisees made against Jesus. They said, "He casts out demons by the ruler of demons"; that is, he gets his power from the devil (v. 34). But notice how Jesus answers them.

Three chapters later he gives a reasoned answer, explaining that if his power to cast out demons is from the devil, then Satan would be working against himself, like a kingdom divided into warring factions, and a divided kingdom cannot stand (Matt. 12:25–32). In these verses he answers his critics simply by continuing to do good. The text says, "Jesus went through all the towns and villages, teaching in their synagogues, preaching the good news of the kingdom and healing every disease and sickness" (Matt. 9:35).

This is an important lesson for us. There are many lessons in these short verses, as we will see, but if we get nothing else from this passage, we should learn that our best and most effective response to those who hate, criticize, or slander us is merely to keep doing the right thing. We can always answer our enemies by doing good.

Or we can make this connection. The Pharisees were speaking *against* Jesus. Now Jesus teaches those who know him and have benefited from his teaching to speak *for* him. The discourse that follows these opening verses is the second of six large teaching sections in the Gospel (chaps. 5–7, 10, 13, 18, 23, and 24–25), and it is part of a pattern in which Jesus trains the apostles for their mission in the world. It was for the disciples, yes, but it is for us too! The first part applies to their first missionary tour (Matt. 10:5–16), but this part is followed by a section for days farther off, a part describing what Christ's followers would experience between his death and his return a second time for judgment (Matt. 10:17–42).

The verses that conclude Matthew 9 (vv. 35–38) and begin Matthew 10 (vv. 1–4) are an introduction to this important training passage. These verses tell us four important things about Jesus: (1) what he was doing at this time, (2) what Jesus saw as he moved among the people, (3) what he instructed his disciples to do about the need he perceived, and (4) the action he took.

What Jesus Was Doing

What was Jesus doing at this time? The first verse tells us that Jesus was doing exactly what he had been doing all along. To see this we need to compare Matthew 9:35 with Matthew 4:23. Matthew 9:35 is a deliberate echo of the earlier verse, which is repeated almost word for word. Matthew 4:23 says, "Jesus went throughout Galilee, teaching in their synagogues, preaching the good news of the kingdom, and healing every disease and sickness among the people." Here, in Matthew 9:35, we read again, "Jesus went through all the towns and villages, teaching in their synagogues, preaching the good news of the kingdom and healing every disease and sickness." So Jesus not only had work to do, he had done it, and he was continuing to do it.

1. *Jesus taught in their synagogues.* This is the point at which Jesus always began, and it is where we must start if we are to model our ministry after his. The people he saw were "harassed and helpless, like sheep without a shep-

herd" (v. 36), and the reason they were helpless is that they did not know the Bible. They should have known it; they had possessed the Old Testament for centuries, and their teachers should have been teaching it to them. But they were like people today. They had not been taught, and they did not have the inclination to seek out Bible truths themselves. What they needed to know and what Jesus certainly taught them was who God is, what God has made us to be, how we have fallen short of God's righteousness and corrupted his image within us, and how we need a Savior who can save us from sin and from ourselves.

2. *Jesus preached the good news.* That leads to the "good news," of course, which is what Jesus "preached" to them. Preaching is not the same thing as teaching. Teaching is instruction; it has to do with content, and it is primary. Preaching contains instruction, but it is more than instruction. It is also proclamation, an announcement of what the listeners must hear and to which they must respond. Preaching is the point at which teaching becomes personal. The word that is used for "preaching" in this passage is *kerusso,* which is what a king's herald does. A herald speaks for the king, making his decrees known. In this case, the proclamation was about the kingdom of God and his anointed King, Jesus, who is the Christ. This decree was good news, and the good news was that the awaited King, who is also the Savior whom we need to save us from our sins, had now come.

3. *Jesus healed their diseases.* These were literal diseases, of course. His power to heal disease was one evidence that he was the Messiah. As he told the disciples of John the Baptist later, "The blind receive sight, the lame walk, those who have leprosy are cured, the deaf hear, the dead are raised, and the good news is preached to the poor" (Matt. 11:5). But we have also seen that the healing of physical disease is linked to and illustrates the far more important healing that has to do with sin. What we need most is forgiveness of our sins and reconciliation with God, which is what Jesus accomplishes. This is the *really* good news of the kingdom.

Today we have the power of the Holy Spirit to bless our words about Christ and bring those who hear our message to repentance and faith in him. In that sense our work is like that of Jesus. We teach the Bible, preach the gospel, and heal sin-sickness, as the Holy Spirit blesses our words and brings people to Christ.

The Need Jesus Saw

As Jesus moved throughout Galilee teaching and healing the people, he was moved by their pitiful condition. Verse 36 says that he had compassion for them, because they were like shepherdless sheep, uncared for and completely helpless. "They were harassed and helpless, like sheep without a shepherd" (v. 36).

The image of shepherdless sheep has strong Old Testament roots and is fully developed in the New Testament. Numbers 27:17 tells how Moses, who was once a shepherd himself, prayed for a successor (who turned out to be Joshua) so that the people would "not be like sheep without a shepherd." In 1 Kings 22:17, Micaiah predicted the death of King Ahab at Ramoth Gilead, saying, "I saw all Israel scattered on the hills like sheep without a shepherd" (see 2 Chron. 18:16). Ezekiel wrote an entire chapter against the false shepherds of Israel because they "only take care of themselves" (Ezek. 34:2) and "do not take care of the flock" (v. 3), as a result of which the sheep "were scattered over the whole earth, and no one searched or looked for them" (v. 6; see vv. 1–31).

Most extensive of all are the later chapters of Zechariah in which he denounced the wicked shepherds of Israel (see Zech. 10:2–3; 11:4–17; 13:7–9) and even predicted the killing of the good shepherd who would come (Zech. 13:7). On the last night before his arrest, Jesus applied Zechariah's prophecy to himself, telling his distressed disciples, "This very night you will all fall away on account of me, for it is written: 'Strike the shepherd, and the sheep will be scattered'" (Matt. 26:31, quoting Zech. 13:7).

The interesting thing about these Old Testament passages is that in nearly every case the image is negative. The shepherds are false, selfish, or negligent, and the sheep are neglected. In the New Testament and the words of Jesus, however, we find the positive side of the image. In his parable of the lost sheep, Jesus compared the Father to a shepherd who searches until the lost sheep is found, even though ninety-nine are already safe (Matt. 18:10–14).

Best known of all are Jesus' words about himself in John 10. After an exposure of men who pretended to be shepherds but were not and a description of the true nature of the sheep, Jesus reveals himself as the shepherd whom the sheep will follow:

> I am the good shepherd. The good shepherd lays down his life for the sheep. The hired hand is not the shepherd who owns the sheep. So when he sees the wolf coming, he abandons the sheep and runs away. Then the wolf attacks the flock and scatters it. The man runs away because he is a hired hand and cares nothing for the sheep. I am the good shepherd; I know my sheep and my sheep know me—just as the Father knows me and I know the Father—and I lay down my life for the sheep. I have other sheep that are not of this sheep pen. I must bring them also. They too will listen to my voice, and there shall be one flock and one shepherd.
>
> verses 11–16

In Jesus' day, as in many subsequent periods of church history, the religious leaders were burdening the people with legalistic niceties instead of seeking them out and wooing them with the gospel of God's grace. They were encumbering the people with laws about the Sabbath, fasts, clothing, and tithes. They looked down on them too! The Pharisees regarded the common people as hardly worthy of their attention, even as chaff to be destroyed.

They called them the *'am ha'arets* (the "people of the land"). By contrast, Jesus saw them as helpless sheep and a harvest to be gathered in.

The Prayer Jesus Asked For

Jesus had been going about among the common people, preaching the gospel and healing their diseases. He was moved with compassion because they were like sheep without a shepherd, harassed and helpless. He was aware of the volume of work to be done, the great harvest to be reaped. But there was a problem: The harvest was indeed great, but there were few workers. Therefore, in the third great statement of these verses, Jesus tells his disciples what they are to do about it. They are to pray. "The harvest is plentiful," he said, "but the workers are few. Ask the Lord of the harvest, therefore, to send out workers into his harvest field" (Matt. 9:37–38).

That is a command for us also, of course, a command to pray for missionaries and other Christian workers. We need to take it seriously and obey it. Yet it is not just numbers that matter. If we look closely at this verse, we will see that it is also important that workers are the right kind. They must be people sent by God, not people who are self-appointed, because the harvest is God's harvest, and God is its Lord.

We need workers who have been sent into the harvest fields by God. If God does not send them, they may respond to some missionary appeal and go out, but when the heat of the day comes and the work becomes difficult, they will abandon the harvest and go home just as the false shepherds abandon the flock when wolves or other dangers threaten. Indeed, one way we can know the workers who are sent by God is that they do not abandon the harvest or shrink from battle when the fighting gets fierce. May God give us that kind of leader, especially in our day, when the battle lines are poorly drawn and people want peace more than truth and popularity more than the approval of Jesus Christ.

The Action Jesus Took

At this point we might think we have reached the end of the lessons in the passage, since a need has been perceived and described, and we have been told to pray for a solution: "Ask the Lord of the harvest, therefore, to send out workers into his harvest field" (v. 38). What more can we do? We have been told to pray, so we pray. That is the end of it. Ah, but it is not. What strikes us at this point is that having instructed his disciples to pray and undoubtedly having prayed himself, Jesus also took action. He placed "the very men who had been urged to pray that the Lord of the harvest might thrust out laborers into his harvest . . . in the forefront of these laborers."[1]

Matthew 10:1 says, "He called his twelve disciples to him and gave them authority to drive out evil spirits and to heal every disease and sickness." This is the first time Matthew has specifically mentioned "the Twelve" ("twelve disciples" in verse 1 and "twelve apostles" in verse 2), but he has already introduced four of these men in chapter 4: Peter and Andrew, James and John (vv. 18–22), and himself in chapter 9 (v. 9). Here, in verses 2–4, he lists them all. A list of the twelve apostles is found (with slight changes of order and some variation of names) three other places in the New Testament: Mark 3:16–19; Luke 6:13–16; and Acts 1:13. Matthew is unique in that he is the only one to introduce the twelve apostles in six pairs—(1) Peter and Andrew, (2) James and John, (3) Philip and Bartholomew, (4) Thomas and Matthew, (5) James and Thaddaeus, and (6) Simon and Judas. This may reflect the fact that, according to Mark, the twelve were originally sent out in pairs to do their work (Mark 6:7).

These are the twelve apostles:

1. *Simon (who is called Peter) and his brother Andrew.* Peter is always placed first in the lists of apostles, which must reflect that he was a true leader. He was not over the others; they only had one master, who was Jesus. But Peter was *primus inter pares* ("a first among equals"). Peter and his brother Andrew were fishermen. They came from Bethsaida (John 1:44), and they were both probably followers of John the Baptist before Jesus called them (see John 1:35–42). Jesus gave Simon the name Cephas (an Aramaic word that is the equivalent of "Peter" in Greek), meaning "rock." We are told more about Peter in the New Testament than about any other apostle.[2]

Andrew is not as prominent as his outspoken and impetuous brother, but he is important. He is often seen bringing others to Jesus, including Peter himself (John 1:40–42; 6:8–9; 12:20–22).

2. *James son of Zebedee, and his brother John.* James and John were a second set of prominent brothers, and, like the first two brothers, they also were fishermen. Their father was Zebedee, and the family was wealthy enough to employ other workers (Mark 1:20) and to help support Jesus and his disciples (Matt. 27:56). It was Zebedee's wife who did this, and her name was probably Salome (compare Matt. 27:56; Mark 15:40; 16:1). She was concerned about her sons' future roles and did not hesitate to ask that they might have the two most prominent places in Jesus' kingdom (Matt. 20:20–21). Jesus called James and John "Boanerges" (sons of "thunder") probably because of their intense and vehement personalities. On one occasion they wanted to destroy a Samaritan city that had rejected Jesus (Luke 9:51–56).

James was probably the older of the two, since he is always mentioned first. He was the first of the apostles to be martyred. He was killed by King Herod, who also arrested Peter when he saw that James' execution pleased the Jews (Acts 12:1–2). John is more prominent. He appears frequently in the New Testament and was responsible for five of the New Testament books.[3] Since James was the first of the apostles to be martyred and John seems to have lived longer than any of the others, dying on the island of Patmos at an advanced age, we are reminded that we cannot predict or explain God's ways. God does one thing with one of his disciples and something quite different with another, for his own wise ends.

3. *Philip and Bartholomew.* Philip is a Greek name meaning "lover of horses." He was from Bethsaida, as were Peter and Andrew, and is mentioned mostly in John (see John 1:43–48; 6:5–7; 12:21–22; 14:8). Bartholomew is an Aramaic name meaning "son of Tolmai." He seems to be the same person as Nathanael, who came from Cana (John 21:2) and is remembered most for Jesus' tribute to him in John 1:47.

4. *Thomas and Matthew the tax collector.* Thomas is also called Didymus, which means a "twin" (John 11:16; 21:2). He appears only in John (John 11:16; 14:5; 20:24–29). He is called "doubting Thomas" because of the incident in John 20, but he was also courageous (John 11:16), and it is his bright confession of faith that John uses to climax his Gospel (John 20:28). Matthew describes himself as "the tax collector," thereby calling attention to the dishonorable business that had occupied him before Jesus' call. His words are probably a humble acknowledgment of God's grace to him. The other Gospels contain no such allusion.

5. *James son of Alphaeus, and Thaddaeus.* The words "of Alphaeus" distinguish this James from James the son of Zebedee, who was the brother of John. We do not know much about him. However, Matthew's father was also called Alphaeus (Mark 2:14), and if this is the same Alphaeus, Matthew and James would have been a third set of brothers. By elimination, Thaddaeus is probably Jude (called "Judas, not Iscariot" in John 14:22). He may be the author of the book by that name. "Thaddaeus" means "beloved." Only John 14:22 tells us anything about him.

6. *Simon the Zealot and Judas Iscariot, who betrayed him.* The first of these names is actually "Simon the Cananaean," the latter being an Aramaic word for "zealot," which is what he is called explicitly by Luke (Luke 6:15; Acts 1:13). The Zealots were a party of nationalists, and therefore, "Simon the Zealot" is probably a reference to Simon's past political associations. The epithet also distinguishes him from Simon Peter.

Last in every one of these four lists of apostles is Judas, the disciple who betrayed Jesus. His second name, Iscariot, has been explained in various ways, some of them fanciful. But Iscariot was probably a place name, meaning one from Kerioth, a town in Judah. Judas was the treasurer of the band, but he was not honest (see John 12:6; 13:29), and he objected to Mary's use of her valuable perfume to anoint Jesus (John 12:4–6). The account of Judas' betrayal of Jesus is told in Matthew 26:14–56 (also Mark 14:10–50; Luke 22:3–53; John 13:2–30; 18:2–3), his suicide in Matthew 27:3–10 and Acts 1:15–19.

E Pluribus Unum

What strikes us most about these apostles is Jesus' success at welding such widely diverse people into an amazingly influential band that he used to change the world profoundly, pervasively, and forever.

Hendriksen writes:

> We cannot fail to be impressed with the majesty of the Savior, whose drawing power, incomparable wisdom, and matchless love were so astounding that he was able to gather round himself and to unite into one family men of entirely different, at times even opposite, backgrounds and temperaments. Included in this little band was Peter the optimist (Matt. 14:28; 26:33, 35), but also Thomas the pessimist (John 11:16; 20:24, 25); Simon the one-time Zealot, hating taxes and eager to overthrow the Roman government, but also Matthew, who had voluntarily offered his tax collecting services to that same Roman government; Peter, John, and Matthew, destined to become renowned through their writings, but also James the Less, who remains obscure but must have fulfilled his mission.[4]

If Jesus used disciples such as these, he can use you. He can draw you into that remarkably diverse band of people called the church. But remember, *these* disciples trusted Jesus and obeyed him. You must do that too.

20

The Christian Mission: Phase One

Matthew 10:5–16

These twelve Jesus sent out with the following instructions: "Do not go among the Gentiles or enter any town of the Samaritans. Go rather to the lost sheep of Israel. As you go, preach this message: 'The kingdom of heaven is near.' Heal the sick, raise the dead, cleanse those who have leprosy, drive out demons. Freely you have received, freely give. Do not take along any gold or silver or copper in your belts; take no bag for the journey, or extra tunic, or sandals or a staff; for the worker is worth his keep.

"Whatever town or village you enter, search for some worthy person there and stay at his house until you leave. As you enter the home, give it your greeting. If the home is deserving, let your peace rest on it; if it is not, let your peace return to you. If anyone will not welcome you or listen to your words, shake the dust off your feet when you leave that home or town. I tell you the truth, it will be more bearable for Sodom and Gomorrah on the day of judgment than for that town. I am sending you out like sheep among wolves. Therefore be as shrewd as snakes and as innocent as doves."

There is something very significant about the ordination of a Christian to the ministry, at least if that person has been called to the work by God and takes the call seriously. My own ordination took place in the First Presbyterian Church of Pittsburgh, Pennsylvania. Pastor Dr. Robert Lamont presided, and Dr. Carl F. H. Henry, who had been my mentor at *Christianity Today*, delivered the sermon. When Henry had completed his sermon, he gave me a short charge, which he had written down and which I still have in the drawer of my desk in Philadelphia. It reads:

> James Boice, you bear the name of a brother of our Lord. You cherish the message of all the apostles. May you share the momentum of the apostle to the Gentiles in matching the myths of our age with the timeless truth of the revelation of God's Word.

In Matthew 10:5–42, we have a record of the first Christian ordination ever to take place. It is a particularly important and solemn one, for in this chapter we read about the Lord commissioning the twelve apostles to preach in Galilee. As John Ryle notes, "Never was there so important an ordination! Never was there so solemn a charge!"[1]

These words are the second of six collections of Jesus' teachings in the Gospel, beginning with the Sermon on the Mount. They are in Matthew 5–7, 10, 13, 18, 23, and 24–25.

A Discourse in Two Parts

Jesus' words to the apostles are not a mere historical account, a relic of the past. They have present significance. At first glance the instructions all seem to have been given to the disciples when Jesus sent them out on their first missionary tour, and they can be understood in this way. Still, a careful reading uncovers significant differences between the first twelve verses (vv. 5–16) and verses 17–42, which suggest that something more may be involved. The first section pictures an immediate mission in which the men are to go to Israel only (vv. 5–6) and quickly, not even taking supplies for their journey (vv. 9–10). The second section seems to look farther into the future when the gospel will be preached to Gentiles too (v. 18). In that day the messengers of Christ will need supplies, and they will be able to expect an increasing degree of opposition, even to the point of being flogged for their profession (v. 17), something that did not happen to any of the disciples during Jesus' lifetime, to our knowledge.

It is possible that all these instructions could have been given to the disciples at the same time, telling them what they were to do in the immediate future (on this particular tour) and what they could expect to be doing and experiencing farther down the road. But we have already seen that Matthew combines material from different settings into sustained discourses—he did it in the case of the Sermon on the Mount—and there are reasons to think he is also doing that here.

One indication is the way this same material is used in Mark and Luke. Verses 5–8 of Matthew 10 are unique to Matthew. Verses 9–16 have parallels in Mark 6, in the account of the sending out of the Twelve, and in two places in Luke: Luke 9, where the Twelve are commissioned, and Luke 10, where the Seventy-two are sent out. Verses 17–25 of Matthew 10, where the most obvious differences occur, have parallels in Mark and Luke too, but they are in the discourses that concern the end times: Mark 13 and Luke 21. Verses 26–39 have no parallels in Mark, but they are found scattered in four different places in Luke (Luke 12:2–9, 51–53; 14:26–27; and 17:33). The last verses of Matthew 10, verses 40–42, are again unique to Matthew.

The best explanation of this puzzling combination of material is that Matthew was writing his Gospel after the Lord's resurrection when the first Christians were already beginning to preach throughout the Gentile world and that his chief concern would have been for how they were to do it and what they could expect. He is writing about Jesus' commissioning of these very first missionaries, so he describes that mission carefully. He shows among other things that the Jews were not neglected in the gospel proclamation. On the contrary, the gospel was preached to them first. Matthew is the most Jewish of the Gospels. Yet that was past history when he was writing. Therefore, he also picks up material from Jesus' later teaching and inserts it here to show that those who were doing the preaching in his day were part of the same great missionary enterprise and that Jesus had instructions for them too. In the second section of chapter 10 (vv. 17–42) we find conditions that will prevail until Jesus' second coming.

In these first verses (vv. 5–16) Jesus tells his disciples: (1) where they should go, (2) the message they should preach, (3) how they should think about money, (4) what they should expect, and finally (5) the character they should show.

Where They Should Go

The detail that most restricts the first section of the chapter (vv. 5–16) to this initial missionary tour is the limitation set for the sphere of the apostles' labors: "Do not go among the Gentiles or enter any town of the Samaritans. Go rather to the lost sheep of Israel" (vv. 5–6).

Why this restriction? Some commentators take a great deal of space at this point to explain who the Samaritans were, pointing out that they were a mixed breed of half-Jewish, half-Gentile people and that they had established their own center for worship on Mount Gerazim. They were despised by most Jews, who would actually take long detours around Samaria when traveling from Galilee in the north to Judah in the south, and vice versa, rather than go through their country. John A. Broadus, in his *Commentary on Matthew,* explains at length the origin and history of the Samaritans.[2] Yet this does not go very far to explain Jesus' restriction on the disciples' ministry. For one thing, Jesus had been warmly received by some Samaritans early in his ministry (John 4:39–42), and he went through Samaria several times after that (see Luke 9:52; 17:11). For another, we can't overlook the fact that the restriction was not only against Samaria but against Gentile lands too.

A better, reasonable explanation is that no one can do everything at once and that the obvious starting place for their work was Galilee, where the disciples already were. The restriction would have kept them from wandering either into the Gentile territories to the north and east or into Samaria to the south. It would be like Jesus saying, as he later did, "You will be my witnesses in Jerusalem [first], and [only after you have done that] in all Judea and Samaria, and to the ends of the earth" (Acts 1:8).

But this is still not enough of an explanation. The best explanation is found in Christ's words to the woman of Samaria, when he said, "Salvation is from the Jews" (John 4:22). It was a statement that the Jewish heritage, and not the Samaritan imitation, was the true and only source of God's revelation in past days and that it was proper that the work of calling fallen men and women to Jesus should begin there. It is significant that Jesus confined his work almost entirely to Jews himself, saying that he was sent "only to the lost sheep of Israel" (Matt. 15:24), the very words used in Matthew 10.

Later, the apostle Paul adopted the same priority, explaining that the gospel is "the power of God for the salvation of everyone who believes: first for the Jew, then for the Gentile" (Rom. 1:16).

The Message They Should Preach

But the message is the same! That is what the next verses teach. One teaching says that an earthly messianic kingdom was offered to the Jews first and that only after it was rejected was a quite different gospel, the gospel of salvation through the death of Christ, offered to the world at large, embracing both Jews and Gentiles. But that is not the way we should read Matthew. Matthew knows nothing of two gospels. There is only one gospel of God's rule in Jesus Christ, and he takes pains to show that it was preached from the beginning.

It was the message of John the Baptist, introduced for the first time in Matthew 3: "Repent, for the kingdom of heaven is near" (v. 2). It was the message preached by Jesus himself in Matthew 4: "Repent, for the kingdom of heaven is near" (v. 17). It is what the disciples are told to preach here: "The kingdom of heaven is near" (Matt. 10:7). Later, in chapter 24, Jesus will prophesy that this same "gospel of the kingdom will be preached in the whole world as a testimony to all nations, and then the end will come" (v. 14).[3] The only difference between the early preaching and our preaching today is that then the kingdom of God was just "near." Jesus was on earth, but he had not yet died for sin, nor had he risen from the dead. Today the kingdom is not only near, it is realized, and we proclaim a crucified, risen, and returning Christ, who is both our Lord and Savior.

According to this teaching, the gospel is the good news of the kingly rule of Jesus Christ. And if we should ask, How do we get a share in this kingdom? the answer is exactly what the disciples would have said: "Repent of your sin and believe on Jesus Christ." That is what the apostles were sent to preach and what we must continue to preach until Jesus returns.

How They Should Think about Money

What about practical matters? Like taking offerings? Or paying for the trip? Interestingly, Jesus is quite specific in this area. He indicates that the disciples are not to set a fee for their services: "Freely you have received, freely give" (v. 8). They are not to worry about provisions, not even to the point of taking money or extra clothing: "Do not take along any gold or silver or copper in your belts; take no bag for the journey, or extra tunic, or sandals or a staff" (vv. 9–10). But neither are they to refuse support since "the worker is worth his keep" (v. 10). As far as lodging is concerned, they are to accept whatever hospitality the upright people of the place might give them: "Whatever town or village you enter, search for some worthy person there and stay at his house until you leave" (v. 11).

This is obviously balanced counsel, and although not all of it applies to our day, most does. The part that does not seem to apply directly or at all times is the prohibition against taking along money or other provisions. Some Christians have taken this literally, neglecting to make sensible provisions for their work. But they forget that Jesus later changed these instructions. Luke tells us that at the Last Supper Jesus referred to this first mission tour, asking, "When I sent you without purse, bag or sandals, did you lack anything?" (Luke 22:35).

"Nothing," they answered.

Then he said, "But now if you have a purse, take it, and also a bag; and if you don't have a sword, sell your cloak and buy one" (v. 36). Jesus was saying that the conditions following his crucifixion would be different from those that prevailed early in his earthly ministry.

But there is continuity too. Three important principles should guide our work even today.

1. *The gospel must be offered without price.* Everyone knows there are costs associated even with preaching the gospel; if nothing else, the preacher has to eat. But the gospel is the message of God's free grace to us in Jesus Christ, and it is always jarring, contradictory, and sometimes blatantly sinful when a price is placed upon the preaching. In some cases fixing a price on preaching has destroyed both ministers and their ministries.

How do we uphold this principle today? Ministers can do it in various ways. Some, such as Billy Graham, receive a fixed salary from their governing organizations and accept no honorariums. Others accept honorariums but do not ask for them. For my part, I never ask a fee for anything I do, and sometimes I do not accept money at all—as when I preside at weddings or take part in presbytery events. I often say that it is good for ministers to do some of their work for nothing to remind them that preaching the gospel is different from running a business and that they have been sent by Jesus not to make money but to offer the gospel freely as God himself offers it, "without money and without cost" (Isa. 55:1).

2. *God's people should support God's ministers.* On the other hand, ministers do need support, just like everyone else. They too need places to live and have families to support and feed. Who will support them? We can hardly

expect the ungodly to do it. Ministers will be rejected, even persecuted by them. If ministers are to receive support, it must come from God's people, described in these verses as those who are "worthy" (v. 11). Worthy people will see to it that God's workers are supported, and when they give their support, the ministers are not to refuse it. Paul operated like this, never asking for money but gratefully acknowledging the provision he received from those who had responded to the gospel (Phil. 1:4–5; 4:10–20).

3. *Ministers need to trust God for their support.* What if God's people are negligent of their duty, as they sometimes are? In that case, the Christian worker has an opportunity to show that ultimately his trust is in God, who cares for his workers more than anyone else could. This is the main point Jesus made when he told the disciples not to take money or extra clothing or shoes for the journey. The disciples needed these things. They were not to refuse replacements for these necessary items when they were offered. But they were not to take extras in order to show that they were God's messengers and were genuinely trusting him for their needs. God would see that what they needed would be given to them along the way.

What They Should Expect

Fourth, these verses deal with what the first preachers of the gospel were to expect as they copied Jesus, going out among all the towns and villages preaching the good news and healing the people's diseases. Our first reaction is to suppose that they should have been well received. Who is more welcome than bearers of good news? Or those who are able to drive out demons and heal diseases? But when we remember the way people received Jesus, we know that presuming a good reception is too facile. Jesus did all these things, but he was "despised and rejected . . . a man of sorrows, and familiar with suffering" (Isa. 53:3).

What the disciples were to expect is made clear in verses 11–15. Some people would receive them; they were to stay with such "worthy" people. But others would reject them and their message. If they were rejected, they were to shake off the dust from their feet and leave that house or village. At this period Jews would do this when they departed Gentile lands to reenter Jewish territory. What Jesus is saying is that if a Jewish home refused to receive his apostles and believe the gospel, the disciples should consider them Gentiles, that is, beyond the covenant blessings belonging to the chosen nation. We find Paul doing this at Pisidian Antioch in Acts 13:51 and at Corinth in Acts 18:6.

This section is not only a warning to workers about what to expect as a response to their preaching and what to do about it but also a warning to unbelievers that rejecting the gospel is a serious matter. It is similar to perishing as did the cities of Sodom and Gomorrah, which were destroyed for their wickedness in the days of Abraham. Jesus said, "I tell you the truth, it will be more bearable for Sodom and Gomorrah on the day of judgment than for that town" (v. 15).

Sodom and Gomorrah were notorious for their corruption, but the cities that would reject Christ's messengers would not be guilty of the same sins. The citizens would consider themselves quite godly. John Ryle wrote, "Men are apt to forget that it does not require great open sins to be sinned in order to ruin a soul forever. They have only to go on hearing without believing, listening without repenting, going to church without going to Christ, and by and by they will find themselves in hell!"[4] This a difficult thing to have to say, but sadly it is true.

The Character They Should Show

The last verse of this section says, "I am sending you out like sheep among wolves. Therefore be shrewd as snakes and as innocent as doves" (v. 16). Luke puts this verse at the beginning of Jesus' charge to the Seventy. Matthew uses it as a summary of the instructions to the Twelve as well as a transition into the verses that describe the later ministry. Three images suggest the appropriate character of Christ's messengers.

1. *Sheep among wolves.* The world is a dangerous place, and Christians are vulnerable, like sheep among wolves. Yet in spite of the danger they are to remain sheep. It is always a problem when ministers of the gospel resort to power or savage behavior to accomplish spiritual ends, for then they are like wolves themselves. We cannot forget that we are sent not to overpower the wolves or destroy them but to convert them. Charles Spurgeon argued that the only weapons of Christians "are that they are weaponless."[5]

2. *Shrewd as snakes.* This is the same language as Genesis 3:1, where the word *shrewd (phronimos)* is used of Satan. But the word *innocent* that follows shows that this is a sanctified shrewdness and not a cunning one. The King James Version may be better: "wise as serpents." William Hendriksen wrote, "The keenness here recommended . . . involves insight into the nature of one's surroundings, . . . circumspection, sanctified common sense, wisdom to do the right thing at the right time and place and in the right manner, [and] a serious attempt always to discover the best means to achieve the highest goal."[6]

3. *Innocent as doves.* Finally, the messengers of Christ are to be "innocent as doves." This refers not so much to moral purity as to a purity of manners. They are to be straightforward, without guile, like Nathanael, whom Jesus called "a true Israelite, in whom there is nothing false" (John 1:47). With Christians, what you see should be what you get. Unfortunately, Christians are not always like this. Therefore, we need to keep especially close to Jesus Christ. It is only by keeping close to Jesus that we will become like him.

Could anyone ever embark on a greater enterprise than the one Jesus has given to us: to go into the entire world with the gospel, summoning men and women to repentance and faith in Jesus Christ? Nothing we can do will ever be greater or more important than that. If this is so, however, we need to take care how we go about our witnessing. We must do it carefully and be sure we are actually serving Jesus Christ.

21

The Christian Mission: Phase Two

Matthew 10:17–42

"Do not suppose that I have come to bring peace to the earth. I did not come to bring peace, but a sword. For I have come to turn

> *"'a man against his father,*
> *a daughter against her mother,*
> *a daughter-in-law against her mother-in-law—*
> *a man's enemies will be the members of his own household.'*

"Anyone who loves his father or mother more than me is not worthy of me; anyone who loves his son or daughter more than me is not worthy of me; and anyone who does not take his cross and follow me is not worthy of me. Whoever finds his life will lose it, and whoever loses his life for my sake will find it.

"He who receives you receives me, and he who receives me receives the one who sent me. Anyone who receives a prophet because he is a prophet will receive a prophet's reward, and anyone who receives a righteous man because he is a righteous man will receive a righteous man's reward. And if anyone gives even a cup of cold water to one of these little ones because he is my disciple, I tell you the truth, he will certainly not lose his reward."

Comparing the first three Gospels raises problems, but sometimes the comparisons are helpful, as is the case here. In Mark's and Luke's accounts, Jesus' instructions to the Twelve end with the material Matthew reported in the first half of chapter 8 (vv. 1–16). Instead of stopping at this point, however, as Mark and Luke do, Matthew continues by adding Jesus' words found in verses 17–42. These words are not inappropriate for these first disciples, though they are different in some respects from what Jesus told them earlier. But their real application—and the reason Matthew has appended the material—is for the mission of the disciples and others following Jesus' death and resurrection. In other words, the addition is for us specifically.

Three chief differences exist between this and the earlier section.

1. *There will be severe persecution (vv. 17, 21–23).* No evidence exists that the disciples experienced persecution until after Jesus' death, resurrection, and ascension.

2. *The disciples will witness before Gentiles (v. 18).* In the first discourse, Jesus told them to avoid Gentile territory, to limit their mission "to the lost sheep of Israel" (v. 6).

3. *There is a reference to the "coming" of the Son of Man (v. 23).* This seems to refer to a judgment at the end of history. When we put these points together, they tell us that Jesus anticipated a significant time of witnessing in the midst of persecution. "In short," as D. A. Carson writes, "a witnessing and suffering church."[1]

But First a Problem

There are problems, however. One of them is verse 23, a verse that many scholars consider among the most difficult in the New Testament to understand. In it Jesus says to the disciples, "You will not finish going through the cities of Israel before the Son of Man comes." How can that be? Jesus has not come again, and are we to think that the cities of Israel, either then or now, have not been evangelized? Or to look at it another way, Jesus is speaking to the original twelve disciples. Does his instruction not infer that he will come again in judgment in their lifetimes?

It should surprise no one to hear that scholars have offered many possible solutions. D. A. Carson lists seven of them.[2]

1. *The "coming" of Jesus refers to a coming of the historical Jesus to the Twelve, following their mission.* He was telling the Twelve to get going, because they will not have finished going throughout all Israel before he catches up with them. This is the most mundane solution, but it doesn't fit the setting very well. The chief problem is that there is no evidence that the disciples suffered persecution during this early period. Even if we suppose they did, the language of this verse is too solemn for so simple an idea. This is a "verily, verily" saying ("I tell you the truth," NIV), and the reference to the Son of Man suggests a sober final judgment.

2. *The "coming" of Jesus refers to Jesus' public identification of himself as Messiah after the resurrection.* Some of the earlier commentators, such as Chrysostom, Calvin, and Beza, saw this as the coming of Christ by the Holy Spirit at Pentecost. This explanation fails to account for a time of persecution or for the haste Jesus is urging.

3. *The "coming" of Jesus is the second coming referred to in Matthew 24:30; 25:31; and 26:64.* It refers to his coming in judgment "with the holy angels." This is the most obvious meaning of the verse, and it has the advantage of interpreting the word *coming* in the same way throughout the Gospel. Yet it creates a problem with the words "of Israel." How can these cities not have been evangelized in all the many centuries since Jesus spoke this prophecy? To escape this difficulty, some commentators identify Israel as the world, but this is foreign to Matthew's use of both words.

4. *Albert Schweitzer argued that Jesus expected the end of time to arrive so quickly that he did not expect to see the disciples return before the end came.* In this interpretation, Jesus would have been mistaken. This is not acceptable to anyone who believes that Jesus is the divine and thus inerrant Son of God.

5. *Some have linked interpretations three and four to teach that Jesus expected the end of history within a single generation.* There are hints, however, of a much longer delay, both here and elsewhere in Matthew, particularly in chapters 24 and 25. Even more important, Jesus would have been mistaken according to this view also.

6. *Dispensationalists see this as a distant second coming but bring in their view of the present church as something of a parenthesis in the unfolding of prophetic history and so as something entirely overlooked here.* According to the dispensationalist system, verse 23 refers to Jewish witnessing among Jews after the largely Gentile church has been taken up to heaven. Unfortunately, this understanding detaches verse 23 from its context and provides a meaning that would have been incomprehensible to the disciples as well as to the first readers of the Gospel.

7. *The "coming" of the Son of Man refers to his coming in judgment against Israel at the time of the Roman destruction of Jerusalem in* A.D. *70.* This explanation seems a bit far-fetched, but D. A. Carson favors it, arguing that "the coming of the Son of Man in verse 23 marks that stage in the coming of the kingdom in which the judgment repeatedly foretold falls on the Jews. With it the temple cultus disappears, and the new wine necessarily takes to new wineskins. . . . The age of the kingdom comes into its own, precisely because so many of the structured foreshadowings of the Old Testament, bound up with the cultus and nation, now disappear."[3] According to Carson, what Jesus means is that the disciples "will not have finished evangelizing the cities of Israel before the Son of Man comes in judgment on Israel."[4]

This is a difficult matter to solve. Although I have respect for Carson's critical judgment, I find it difficult to believe this verse refers only to work done before the fall of Jerusalem, which seems to me to be extraneous to the context. I think it is better to see verse 23 as stating a general principle: We will always have work to do and we will never get to all the places we ought to go before Christ's second coming. Reference to "Israel" here would be an application of the principle to this particular setting. The disciples would not get to all the cities of Israel, just as we will not get to all the world's cities in our day, but we should get on with the Great Commission anyway. We need to keep moving.

The second half of chapter 10 contains instructions about what we can expect while we wait for the Lord to come. We need to think about these words carefully.

We Are to Expect Opposition

The first thing these verses say is that we can expect opposition. As far as the disciples were concerned, they could expect that in time they would be "hand[ed] . . . over to the local councils and flog[ged] . . . in their synagogues" (v. 17). This is what happened to Peter and other apostles in Acts 5:40 and to Paul on five separate occasions (see 2 Cor. 11:24). As far as we are concerned, we can expect to be hated even by members of our own families (vv. 21, 34–36) and to be severely persecuted (vv. 17, 23), even to the point of being put to death (v. 28).

We should expect persecution because Jesus was treated this way and "a student is not above his teacher" (v. 24). "If the head of the house has been called Beelzebub, how much more the members of his household!" (v. 25).[5] Should we be different? We belong to Jesus, after all.

There will be good results, however. For one thing, persecution in one place will cause us to move to other places that also need the gospel (v. 23). This happened to the Christians in Jerusalem as a result of the persecution that followed the killing of Stephen. It was how the gospel spread from Jerusalem to Judea and Samaria (Acts 8:1). Again, persecution brought the disciples before governors and kings before whom they bore important testimony. We can think of governors such as Felix and Festus, and kings such as Herod Agrippa I and Agrippa II. Acts documents the disciples' testimony before these rulers, and testimony such as theirs has continued through the ages as believers have been privileged to testify before local magistrates, justices, despots, tyrants, presidents, and even kings.

Speaking before the powerful people of this world might be intimidating to normal Christians like ourselves. But Jesus tells us not to worry about what we should say since the Holy Spirit will enable us to testify well and wisely when the proper time comes. "When they arrest you, do not worry about what to say or how to say it. At that time you will be given what to say, for it will not be you speaking, but the Spirit of your Father speaking through you" (vv. 19–20).

It is worth observing that this is an instruction for martyrs, not for preachers, who *should* give thought to what they will say and how to say it!

We Are Not to Be Afraid

The second major theme of Matthew 8:17–42 is that Christ's followers are not to be afraid as they pursue their evangelistic work, in spite of the hatred and persecution they will face. This is the most emphasized part of Jesus' instructions; the words "do not be afraid" are repeated three times (vv. 26, 28, 31). Why should we not be afraid? In this section of the address, Jesus gives three reasons.

1. *The truth will triumph (vv. 26–27).* At the final judgment those who have persecuted Christ's followers will be exposed as the wicked persons they are, and those who have been faithful to Christ will be exonerated. The good they have done will be noted. This theme appears again in Matthew 25, where Christ's faithful servants are rewarded with Jesus' commendation: "Well done, good and faithful servant! You have been faithful with a few things; I will put you in charge of many things. Come and share your master's happiness" (vv. 21, 23), and where those who have done good to others for Christ's sake are praised for it: "I tell you the truth, whatever you did for one of the least of these brothers of mine, you did for me" (v. 40).

If that is the case, then Jesus' disciples should not be afraid of those who are in powerful positions but should be bold in their public testimony. What Jesus was telling them in private now—things they did not understand fully but would understand after the resurrection—they should proclaim fully and widely then (v. 27). This is a word for every Christian, but it is a special instruction for preachers, for it tells those who would preach the gospel three things. First, they must listen to Jesus, for no one can speak for Jesus until Jesus has first spoken to him. Second, they must speak only what they have heard from Jesus and not something that comes out of their own minds or imaginations. Third, they must speak Christ's words even if their speaking gains them the hatred of the world.

William Barclay, who makes these points in his commentary on Matthew,[6] tells about an occasion when Hugh Latimer, one of the most outstanding figures of the English Reformation, was preaching before King Henry VIII. He was about to say something he knew the king would dislike, so he held an audible dialogue with himself in the pulpit, calling out, "Latimer! Latimer! Be careful what you say. The king is here." Then he paused and went on: "Latimer! Latimer! Be careful what you say. The King of kings is here."[7] Such knowledge gives boldness to Christ's preachers. They know that one day they will give an accounting to the King of all kings. This is what gave such boldness to John Knox. They said as they buried Knox, "Here lies one who feared God so much that he never feared the face of any man."

2. *The soul matters more than the body (v. 28).* The second reason the followers of Christ are not to fear the powerful people of this world is that the soul matters more than the body and that, at the worst, the rulers of this world can take only our lives. If we are going to be afraid of anyone, it should be God, who alone will determine our final destinies. Jesus said it like this: "Do not be afraid of those who kill the body but cannot kill the soul. Rather, be afraid of the One who can destroy both soul and body in hell" (v. 28).

What else but such a transcendent, eternal perspective enabled Martin Luther to declare before the mighty of his day, "Here I stand. I can do no other. May God help me. Amen."[8] Or to say to other Christians,

> Let goods and kindred go, this mortal life also;
> The body they may kill: God's truth abideth still;
> His kingdom is forever.

We should remember that it is not in an earthly body but in a spiritual body that we will share that kingdom with him.

3. *God is sovereign (vv. 29–31).* The final reason we are not to be afraid as we testify for Christ is that God is sovereign in this, as in all things. Nothing will happen to us that is not fully known by God and ordered by God for his own glory and ultimately for our good and the good of others. Here Jesus compares us to sparrows, one of the smallest and least significant of birds, saying that if God cares for them, he will certainly care for us since we are "worth more than many sparrows" (v. 31).

We Must Confess Christ Openly

The last verses of this discourse focus on a person's relationship with Jesus, but they do so in two ways. First, they focus on the disciple himself and whether he remains true to Jesus or not. Second, they focus on people who receive or reject his followers.

Jesus says that a person who would be his disciple must value him more than: (1) a favorable judgment by this world's rulers: "Whoever acknowledges me before men, I will also acknowledge him before my Father in heaven. But whoever disowns me before men, I will disown him before my Father in heaven" (vv. 32–33); (2) the love of one's own family: "Anyone who loves his father or mother more than me is not worthy of me; anyone who loves his son or daughter more than me is not worthy of me" (v. 37); and (3) even life itself: "Anyone who does not take his cross and follow me is not worthy of me. Whoever finds his life will lose it, and whoever loses his life for my sake will find it" (vv. 38–39). There is no higher demand or more exalted calling.

The reference to divisions among one's family members is a fairly close quotation of Micah 7:6, but it is not saying that what will happen because of Christian testimony is a fulfillment of that text. Micah describes an unfortunate situation that existed because of wickedness in Israel during the reign of King Ahaz. Jesus is only saying that a similar situation will exist in future days because of the preaching of the gospel.

The point of all these verses is the necessity of deciding for Christ and remaining faithful to Christ until the end. We cannot drift along and expect that everything will turn out all right. To fail to decide for Christ and live for Christ is to be against him. It is to perish.

What extraordinary teachings these are! They show Jesus' amazing self-understanding, for who but a man who knew himself to be God could make such statements? If Jesus is not God come in the flesh, this is either an example of an incredible insanity or else a hideous attempt to deceive other persons. Which is it? If Jesus was insane, ignore him. It is the only rational thing to do. If he was attempting to deceive other people, expose him. Fight his lies for the sake of those who might be taken in and harmed by them. On the other hand, if Jesus is who he claimed to be—if he is the true Son of God—then Jesus speaks the words of God and must be both believed and obeyed. If Jesus is the Son of God, these are the most important words you will ever hear since your eternal destiny hangs on your acceptance or rejection of them.

We Will Not Lack Rewards

The last paragraph of this section strikes a positive note. Jesus reflects on a person's relationship to him in terms of the person's reception or rejection of his messengers. It is the second of the two relationships I mentioned earlier.

What is surprising about these last sentences is that they speak of spiritual rewards. They develop a sequence, a descending progression. First, the one who receives Jesus receives the one who sent him. Second, the one who receives Jesus' prophets, because they are prophets—that is, because they speak the truth about Jesus—will have a spiritual reward, because the prophet will lead him to Jesus. Third, the one who receives a righteous man, because he is a righteous man, will be in the same position. Finally, the one who receives even the least of Christ's disciples will be rewarded also and in the same way.

This means every Christian's testimony is important—the testimony of the least of Christ's disciples as well as the testimony of one of the twelve apostles—and the critical matter in every case, now as then, is a person's relationship to Jesus Christ. To receive Christ as he is presented by the messengers of Christ is to experience God and salvation. To turn from Christ is to perish.

These words were spoken nearly two thousand years ago, and it is through obedience to them that Christ's followers have taken the gospel of salvation from sin by his death throughout the world. It is because of these words that the gospel is being presented to you now. In Christ's name and by his authority, I say to you, "Believe in the Lord Jesus, and you will be saved" (Acts 16:31). In Christ's name and by the same authority, I also say, "Reject Jesus Christ, and you will perish forever." I cannot make the matter any clearer than that.

Part Four

Is Jesus Really God's King?

22

Jesus and John the Baptist

Matthew 11:1–19

When John heard in prison what Christ was doing, he sent his disciples to ask him, "Are you the one who was to come, or should we expect someone else?"

Jesus replied, "Go back and report to John what you hear and see: The blind receive sight, the lame walk, those who have leprosy are cured, the deaf hear, the dead are raised, and the good news is preached to the poor. Blessed is the man who does not fall away on account of me."

As John's disciples were leaving, Jesus began to speak to the crowd about John: "What did you go out into the desert to see? A reed swayed by the wind? If not, what did you go out to see? A man dressed in fine clothes? No, those who wear fine clothes are in kings' palaces. Then what did you go out to see? A prophet? Yes, I tell you, and more than a prophet. This is the one about whom it is written:

"'I will send my messenger ahead of you,
who will prepare your way before you.'

"I tell you the truth: Among those born of women there has not risen anyone greater than John the Baptist; yet he who is least in the kingdom of heaven is greater than he. From the days of John the Baptist until now, the kingdom of heaven has been forcefully advancing, and forceful men lay hold of it. For all the Prophets and the Law prophesied until John. And if you are willing to accept it, he is the Elijah who was to come."

Each of the Gospels shows that after a few months of initial enthusiasm for Jesus and his ministry, opposition began to grow so that at last Jesus was rejected by both the leaders and the people and was crucified. This was a complex period historically, and a variety of factors were at work, which makes outlining these middle sections of the Gospels difficult. In Luke the opposition begins with Jesus' first teaching in Nazareth, his home town (Luke 4:16–30). Matthew records objections to Jesus' healing of the paralytic and later two blind men (Matt. 9:3, 34). Each of the Gospels unites in saying that much of the opposition came from the Pharisees and others who objected to Jesus' disregard of their tight rules for observing the Sabbath (see Matt. 12:1–14; Mark 2:23–3:6; Luke 6:1–11; John 5:1–16).

In chapters 11 and 12, Matthew begins to describe this rising opposition. What holds these chapters together? The best way to hold them together is by asking the critical question: "Is Jesus really God's king?" The kingdom of God has been Matthew's theme from the beginning: "Repent, for the kingdom of heaven is near" (Matt. 3:2; 4:17). He is presenting Jesus as the king of that kingdom. But is Jesus really God's king? In these chapters we find three varying assessments of him.

1. *John the Baptist had doubts (Matt. 11:1–19).* John had identified Jesus as the Messiah. He had received an identifying sign from heaven (Matt. 3:16–17). But now he sends disciples to ask Jesus, "Are you the one who was to come, or should we expect someone else?" (v. 3).

2. *The masses would not believe (Matt. 11:20–30).* The masses had been exposed to John, and now they were being exposed to Jesus. But they were critical of both teachers. Jesus compared them to pouting children who would not take part either in a happy game or a sad one. Here he foretells a final terrible judgment on the cities of Korazin, Bethsaida, and Capernaum because the people would not repent of their sin and believe on him.

3. *The leaders launched a formal opposition (Matt. 12:1–50).* Earlier the Pharisees had slandered Jesus by saying that he drove out demons "by the prince of demons" (Matt. 9:34; repeated in 12:24). In this section they go beyond mere slander and begin to plot "how they might kill" him (v. 14).

In chapters 11 and 12, Jesus deals with each of these objections in turn and in appropriately different ways. We will examine his responses in detail as we go along. But we can note at the start that Jesus' overall response seems to have been a change in tactics since from this point on he restricts his most serious teaching to the disciples only while speaking to the rest of the people in parables or mysteries. Jesus' parables are introduced for the first time in chapter 13, following Matthew's account of the beginning of the people's opposition.

John the Baptist's Doubts

Matthew starts with John the Baptist and his doubts. There is a link to the previous verses, particularly to Matthew 10:41, since the story about John is an illustration of Jesus' words about receiving a prophet because he is a prophet. It happens in two ways. Some would not receive John, who came as a prophet (see Matt. 11:7–19). But also, John needed to receive Jesus by faith himself even though Jesus did not seem to be living up to what John had expected him to do.

An old interpretation of these verses considers doubt to be inconsistent with John's role as Christ's forerunner. Noted commentators such as Chrysostom, Augustine, Jerome, Luther, Calvin, Beza, and, more recently, John Ryle have argued that John's question was asked not for his benefit but for the sake of the disciples.[1] But Matthew says the question was John's, and it is not strange that John should have had doubts about Jesus. The greatest characters of the Bible all had weak moments, and there is no reason to think that John was any less subject to human weaknesses than figures such as Abraham, Moses, Elijah, David, and others.

There are several reasons why John the Baptist may have doubted.

1. *He was in prison (v. 2).* He was cut off from what was happening. According to Josephus, who writes about John in his *Antiquities,* Herod had imprisoned John in the fortress of Machaerus (modern Khirbet Mukawer), about five miles east of the Dead Sea, a particularly hot and desolate environment (xviii, 19). So although John must have had contact with his disciples, he was still sidelined, and this must have been excessively difficult for a man of his free temperament. Many a leader has languished in isolation who was at one time fearless in public speech and action.

2. *John must have been drained emotionally.* It is difficult not to compare John to Elijah, whom he resembled in many ways. Elijah had denounced the sins of King Ahab and Queen Jezebel, just as John had denounced the sins of Herod and his stolen paramour Herodias. Drained from his encounter, Elijah had fled to the desert wanting to die (1 Kings 19). Would John have been any less exhausted after his demanding ministry?

3. *Jesus was not living up to what John had expected or prophesied.* This is the most important reason. John may have been emotionally drained, but he was no weakling, and he knew what he had been sent to do. He had announced the coming of the Messiah and had rightly pointed out that he would exercise a ministry of judgment. John had said, "His winnowing fork is in his hand, and he will clear his threshing floor, gathering his wheat into the barn and burning up the chaff with unquenchable fire" (Matt. 3:12). That is what the Messiah was expected to do. It was written down that way in the Bible. But what did John observe? On the one hand, Jesus was clearly doing good, apparently empowered by the Holy Spirit, but where was the prophesied ministry of judgment?

D. A. Carson asks:

> It was all right to heal the sick, raise the dead, cast out demons, still storms, preach righteousness, and announce the kingdom; but where was the judgment? Had the corruptions and cruelties of Caesar been abruptly shut down? Had the hypocritical temple leaders been banished? Had the disgusting corruptions of Herod Antipas been confronted? Why was he, John the Baptist, languishing in the stifling heat of the prison at Machaerus fortress for chal-

lenging the morals of Herod, while Jesus the alleged Messiah did nothing about this injustice?[2]

As far as John could see, the world was as wicked as it was before Jesus began his ministry.

Isn't that a reasonable objection even now? Jews tell the story of a New York City rabbi who was told by a witnessing Christian that Jesus was the Messiah. The rabbi walked to his window, looked out at the city, unchanged in all its corruption, and returned, shaking his head. "No," he said, "when the Messiah comes there will be justice."

Jesus' Words for John the Baptist

It is worth noting that Jesus did not condemn John the Baptist for his doubt, any more than God condemned Elijah for his breakdown after the victory on Mount Carmel. The reason, of course, is that doubt is not unbelief. It is something midway between faith and unbelief. Author Os Guinness called it being "in two minds," the title he gave to a perceptive book on this subject years ago. Besides, doubt is a common, natural state for human beings, who never see the whole picture and whose thinking is often clouded by their physical condition or circumstances. Instead of condemning John, Jesus ministered to him from the Bible, reminding him of the messianic passages that had been fulfilled. Then, when John's disciples were on their way back to the prison, Jesus praised John to the people.

Jesus' answer to John in verses 5 and 6 is not presented as a specific quotation from the Old Testament, but it was a reference to Isaiah 35:5–6 and 61:1–2, with possible allusions to Isaiah 26:19 and 29:18–19. The best known of these four texts is Isaiah 61:1–2, because it is the passage Jesus took as the basis for his first sermon in the synagogue at Nazareth:

> "The Spirit of the Sovereign LORD is on me,
> because the LORD has anointed me
> to preach good news to the poor.
> He sent me to bind up the brokenhearted,
> to proclaim freedom for the captives
> and release from darkness for the prisoners,
> to proclaim the year of the Lord's favor."
>
> Isaiah 61:1–2; see Luke 4:18–19

All these passages describe physical miracles such as giving sight to the blind, hearing to the deaf, movement to people who are paralyzed (Isa. 35:5–6), restoring the dead to life (Isa. 26:19), and helping the poor (Isa. 29:18–19). They are all explicitly messianic texts. But the interesting thing is that all four of these passages also go on to speak of a work of messianic judgment, the very thing John had been proclaiming, but which Jesus pointedly leaves out. This was most obvious in Nazareth where Jesus stopped his reading of Isaiah 61 just before the words "and the day of vengeance of our God" (v. 2).

Why did Jesus stop at this point? Obviously, because this was not the object of his ministry at this time. One day he *would* come in judgment and the second half of the prophecies *would* be fulfilled. But for now, his goal was to teach the Bible, preach the gospel, and heal the sick. In other words, the days in which we live are to be days of God's favor, days of grace.

We had better be glad they are! Because if it is judgment we want, it is judgment we will get, and judgment will destroy us. It is not justice we need, it is salvation. We need grace. We need grace to believe on Jesus as the Savior he is and to cling to him in spite of the evil we see around us and the things we cannot fully understand. This is the point of Jesus' last words to John, a blessing that was a warning at the same time: "Blessed is the man who does not fall away on account of me" (v. 6). These words acknowledge John's good start; he was indeed one who had faith in Jesus. But he must persist to the end, as must all Christ's followers (Matt. 10:22). The day of God's judgment will come. We can wait for that. But while we wait we must get on with the job of proclaiming Jesus Christ as Savior. This is a word for us as well as for John the Baptist.

Jesus' Words about John the Baptist

After John's disciples had begun to return to their imprisoned teacher, Jesus praised John to the people. He praised him as a prophet, exactly what the people had gone out into the desert to see. But, said Jesus, John was even "more than a prophet" (v. 9). How so? John not only prophesied about Christ's coming but was himself a fulfillment of prophecies about the Messiah's forerunner. Jesus cites Malachi 3:1 with slight changes to make it a direct address of God the Father to himself. "I will send my messenger ahead of you, who will prepare your way before you."

What made John so special is that he had the privilege of actually pointing out the Messiah, which none of his predecessors had done. John did no miracles (John 10:41), but he was greater than any of the earlier prophets (or anyone else who had come before him) simply because he had the job of announcing and then actually identifying Jesus as the Christ.

This must have been a startling statement to people who knew of such Old Testament giants as Abraham, Moses, and David, not to mention Elijah, whom John resembled, who did great miracles. However, in the next breath Jesus says something even more startling than this. He said that in spite of John's greatness, "he who is least in the kingdom of heaven is greater than he" (v. 11). How can that be? How can the least gifted, least significant, least prominent, least outspoken of today's believers be greater than this greatest of Old Testament figures, and therefore greater also than all the others? For this reason: because they can point to Jesus and witness to his work more clearly than even John could.

Do you understand what a great position and privilege that is? And how highly valued you are in God's sight because of that privilege? If you really did understand it, wouldn't you be more active in telling others about the Lord Jesus Christ than you are?

But remember: Your greatness is because of Christ and your opportunity to point to him, not because of what you are yourself. D. A. Carson wrote:

> So often Christians want to establish their "greatness" with reference to their work, their giving, their intelligence, their preaching, their gifts, their courage, their discernment. But Jesus unhesitatingly affirmed that even the least believer is greater than Moses or John the Baptist, simply because of his or her ability, living on this side of the coming of Jesus the Messiah, to point him out with greater clarity and understanding than all his forerunners ever could. If we really believe this truth, it will dissipate all cheap vying for position and force us to recognize that our true significance lies in our witness to the Lord Jesus Christ.[3]

How about verse 12? This has been understood in two ways since the key verb *(biazetai)* can be rendered either "has been forcefully advancing" or "is being attacked." People who do not want to associate force with a spiritual kingdom choose the latter. But the first translation is appropriate to the context and has been rightly selected by many Bible versions. In Matthew 1–10, the kingdom *has* been advancing forcefully. Jesus has expelled demons and defeated illnesses. The parallel text in Luke 16:16 replaces the forceful advancing of the kingdom by the preaching of the gospel. As for forceful men laying hold of the kingdom, this is exactly what is required. The disciples of Jesus must not be like the indecisive persons of Matthew 8:18–22. Instead they must be bold, resolute, forceful, and determined.

We have already read suggestions of how this works, as I have indicated. But we are going to see it developed further in chapter 13, where Jesus shows how the kingdom advances and how those who perceive its superlative value will sell everything they have to possess it.[4]

What about John being Elijah "if you are willing to accept it" (v. 14)? This is not a great problem. John was not literally Elijah (see John 1:21), but we are told that he came "in the spirit and power of Elijah" (see Luke 1:17) and was therefore called Elijah by Jesus: "I tell you, Elijah has already come, and they did not recognize him, but have done to him everything they wished" (Matt. 17:12). Matthew then says that "the disciples understood that he was talking to them about John the Baptist" (v. 13). Accepting John as Elijah would have meant accepting him as the forerunner of the Messiah and thus accepting Jesus as the Messiah, which is what the generation Jesus refers to next did not do.

Jesus' Words to the Crowd

Jesus had spoken of blessing for those who received a prophet because he is a prophet, and a righteous man because he is a righteous man (Matt.

10:41). Here he applies those words to the crowd in respect to both John the Baptist and himself. A prophet had indeed come, and a righteous man too. But they had received neither, preferring their own errors to the truth and their own wicked ways to righteousness.

The analogy of the children can be read in two ways. There can be two groups of children, one representing Jesus (who played the flute), the other John (who sang a dirge). Each group was dissatisfied with the other. This preserves a strict analogy, but it suggests that the disciples of Jesus were dissatisfied with the disciples of John, and vice versa. On the other hand, the people can be identified as these spoiled children who will not play regardless of the game that is proposed. They will neither dance nor mourn. They don't like John's way of teaching, but neither do they like what Jesus does. This is not as perfect an analogy, but it does a better job of leading into the point of verses 18 and 19: "For John came neither eating nor drinking, and they say, 'He has a demon.' The Son of Man came eating and drinking, and they say, 'Here is a glutton and a drunkard, a friend of tax collectors and "sinners."'"

It is no different today, of course. God has many messengers with many varying gifts. Some are powerful speakers who can move a crowd to tears. Others are intellectual; they make a careful case for Christianity and present many powerful proofs of the gospel. Some teachers are outgoing, talkative, people-oriented. Others are retiring and thoughtful. Some write books. Others lead movements. Still others speak on radio or appear on television. Some are old and teach with the wisdom of their years. Some are young and proclaim the truth with youthful vigor. Some are prophetic. Some are analytic. None of this matters to a generation of determined sinners who say in opposition, "This one is too loud. That one is too quiet. This one is too intellectual. That one is too superficial."

So it is that we play the flute for those of our time, and they will not dance. We sing a dirge, and they will not mourn. What is to happen to such people? They will perish at the judgment, as Jesus explains (vv. 20–24).

Don't let that happen in your case. If you are rejecting Jesus Christ as your Savior, it is not because the gospel has not been taught or because thoughtful preachers have not defended it. It is because you do not want to repent of your sin and trust Christ instead of clinging to your own faulty character and weak works. You excuse yourself by pretending you are wise to do as you are doing, too wise to be taken in by any cheap religious claims. But you are not wise. If you think you are, you are the greatest of fools. The only wise course is to abandon any attempts to save yourself and repent of your sin and commit yourself to Jesus.

Jesus says in the last verse of this section, "Wisdom is proved right by her actions."[5] That is as true today as it ever was, and it is as true in spiritual matters as in the mundane matters of daily life. If you are a wise person, you will act rightly, and acting rightly means to turn from sin and follow Jesus.

23

Unbelief and a Wonderful Invitation

Matthew 11:20–30

Then Jesus began to denounce the cities in which most of his miracles had been performed, because they did not repent. "Woe to you, Korazin! Woe to you, Bethsaida! If the miracles that were performed in you had been performed in Tyre and Sidon, they would have repented long ago in sackcloth and ashes. But I tell you, it will be more bearable for Tyre and Sidon on the day of judgment than for you. And you, Capernaum, will you be lifted up to the skies? No, you will go down to the depths. If the miracles that were performed in you had been performed in Sodom, it would have remained to this day. But I tell you that it will be more bearable for Sodom on the day of judgment than for you. . . .

"Come to me, all you who are weary and burdened, and I will give you rest. Take my yoke upon you and learn from me, for I am gentle and humble in heart, and you will find rest for your souls. For my yoke is easy and my burden is light."

Where did schools come from? Most people would answer by referring to the school established by Plato in Athens. Plato had studied with Socrates, but Plato was the first to offer a fixed course of study in one location extending over three or four years. Since Plato recruited his students from a public playing field on the outskirts of Athens, called Academus from the name of an athletic hero, Plato's school became known as the Academy. The school passed from teacher to teacher and lasted for about nine hundred years.

Aristotle, who studied under Plato for twenty years, set up a school of his own, choosing as his site another public playing field called the Lyceum. The

Greek word for these playing fields was *gymnasium.* It is interesting that from these two Greek institutions numerous countries have derived their names for a school. The Germanic nations call their primary schools gymnasiums, Frenchmen call their schools lycees, after the Lyceum, while English-speaking nations call many of their schools academies. The educational establishments of the Western world can be traced to these Greek schools, and millions of today's students are the successors of those first Greek pupils.

Yet not nearly as many are in the school of Plato as are in the school of Jesus Christ. Jesus founded his school when he told those of his day, "Come to me, all you who are weary and burdened, and I will give you rest. Take my yoke upon you and learn from me, for I am gentle and humble in heart, and you will find rest for your souls. For my yoke is easy and my burden is light" (Matt. 11:28–30).

Refusing to Learn

Sadly, not all are willing to matriculate in Christ's school. One of the problems with education today is that many students flatly refuse to learn. If we can carry the analogy this far, it might be said that this was true in the days of Jesus Christ, since the verses in which Jesus invites people to learn of him are in the middle of two chapters in which Matthew records three negative assessments of Jesus by such persons.

The first example of an at-least-partially negative assessment was that of John the Baptist. We looked at John in the last study. Jesus failed to fulfill John's expectations of what he thought the Messiah should do, which was to bring judgment on the wicked of that day. So John sent disciples to Jesus to ask, "Are you the one who was to come, or should we expect someone else?" (Matt. 11:3). Jesus was the one, of course. He was not indifferent to evil. In the verses we are studying now he predicts a final judgment for those who refuse to receive his message (Matt. 11:20–24). Still, the time for that judgment had not yet arrived. Instead, it was the day for God's grace, which Jesus proved by reporting how the sick were being healed and the poor were hearing the gospel.

The third example, which we will come to in the next study, was the hostile reaction of the Pharisees and other religious leaders, who thought Jesus was undermining their teaching, particularly about Sabbath observance. Theirs was a professional jealousy, and the bottom line of their jealous rejection was that they "went out and plotted how they might kill Jesus" (Matt. 12:14).

In the verses we are looking at now (Matt. 11:20–30), Jesus denounces the unbelief of the cities in which he had done most of his miracles. John's doubt was not unbelief, but these people were not wrestling with doubt. They were completely indifferent, and their indifference was an expression of their utter disbelief. Jesus has done most of the miracles recorded by Matthew in Korazin, Bethsaida, and especially Capernaum. He healed the servant of a Roman centurion (Matt. 8:5–13), cured Peter's mother-in-law of a fever

(Matt. 8:14–15), cast out demons and healed other sick people (Matt. 8:16), healed a paralytic (Matt. 9:1–8), raised a dead girl to life (Matt. 9:18–26), restored sight to two blind men (Matt. 9:27–31), and cast a demon out of a mute person, enabling him to talk (Matt. 9:32–33). Those are only a selection of the many great works Jesus did.

Still the people of Korazin, Bethsaida, and Capernaum would not repent of their sin and come to him, and he pronounces a judgment on them.

> Woe to you, Korazin! Woe to you, Bethsaida! If the miracles that were performed in you had been performed in Tyre and Sidon, they would have repented long ago in sackcloth and ashes. But I tell you, it will be more bearable for Tyre and Sidon on the day of judgment than for you. And you, Capernaum, will you be lifted up to the skies? No, you will go down to the depths. If the miracles that were performed in you had been performed in Sodom, it would have remained to this day. But I tell you that it will be more bearable for Sodom on the day of judgment than for you.
>
> Matthew 11:21–24

Five Truths about Judgment

No one likes to think about judgment, and we are relieved that Jesus moves on from this point to talk about the electing grace of God and to issue a gospel invitation. Nevertheless, it is important to think about judgment sometimes, and this passage is one of the most helpful passages in the New Testament for understanding it. These verses teach us five difficult lessons.

1. *There will be a judgment.* The reason we do not like to think about judgment is that we do not want to admit there will be one. We imagine that if there is a judgment, we will come out all right since we are nice people. Or we hope that if we are condemned, it won't be so bad. Jesus does not treat judgment so lightly. He says it should be feared.

2. *There are degrees of punishment.* One of the most frightening ideas in this passage is its teaching about degrees of punishment. Jesus says that as terrible as the judgment of Tyre and Sidon will be, it will not be as bad as the judgment of Korazin and Bethsaida. And as terrible as the judgment of Sodom will be, it will not be as horrible as the judgment of Capernaum. The people of Tyre, Sidon, and Sodom were wicked and will be rightly punished for their sins. But they had never heard of Jesus as the cities of Christ's day had and thus would not suffer as severe a punishment as those cities.[1]

3. *The worst sin of all is unbelief.* We do not think this way, since unbelief is our chief sin. We prefer to point out the sins of others by observing how outrageous or inhumane they are. In your mind, who are history's greatest sinners? Probably people such as Hitler, Idi Amin, Stalin, and, if we think back far enough, Genghis Khan or Nero. They are the sinners highest on our lists. Yet there is no record of the people of Korazin, Bethsaida, or Capernaum having done anything particularly offensive or inhumane. They were just

people going about their business as we do. Yet they refused to repent and turn to Jesus, and Jesus said that their unbelief was a far worse evil than the sins of other notoriously wicked cities.

What was the root of their sin? Jesus suggests that it was pride and does so by linking the unbelief of Capernaum to the pride of the king of Babylon in verse 23. Verse 23 is an echo of Isaiah 14:13–15 in which the Babylonian king says, "I will ascend to heaven; I will raise my throne above the stars of God. . . . I will make myself like the Most High" (v. 13). God informs this proud ruler, "But you are brought down to the grave, to the depths of the pit" (v. 15).

4. *God's judgments take account of his contingent knowledge.* This means that God's judgments are based not only on what people have done but also on what they would have done if the conditions under which they had lived had been different. In this case, Jesus says that Tyre, Sidon, and Sodom would have repented if the miracles that had been done in Galilee had been done there. That is why their judgment will be less harsh. Or to put it another way, as D. A. Carson does in a comment that should be particularly sobering for us, "At the final judgment God will take into account not only North America's and every North American's moral standing and response to Jesus Christ and use of opportunities, as compared with, say, every Cuban's use of the same—but also what both parties would have done if their roles and advantages had been reversed."[2]

When I think of the opportunities to believe in Christ that have been given to the people of America in our day, I tremble for America. And for you, if you have not yet trusted in Jesus Christ. No nation has ever had the opportunities to repent and believe on Jesus Christ as we have had. "How shall we escape if we ignore such a great salvation?" (Heb. 2:3).

5. *God does not owe salvation to anyone.* This is the final hard lesson of these verses. Although the people of Tyre, Sidon, and Sodom would have repented and been saved if Jesus had done the miracles in those cities that he did in Korazin, Bethsaida, and Capernaum, he did not do them, and the people perished justly for their sins. We think God owes us mercy, but if mercy were owed, it would not be mercy. The only thing God actually owes us is justice, and we will get it if we do not commit our lives to Christ. God *is* merciful to many, but God *owes* mercy to none!

Amazing Grace

And yet God *is* merciful! This is a wonderful, uplifting, thrilling, and encouraging revelation. It is especially wonderful because it is our only hope of being saved. I think Charles H. Spurgeon was entirely right when he suggested that at this point in his teaching the heaviness that must have been on Jesus as he spoke of God's judgment on the cities of Galilee lifted a bit and his brow must have cleared. For having spoken of judgment, Jesus turned to the subject of election—to God's amazing, electing grace—and his words were a prayer, the tone of which is thanksgiving. As Spurgeon says, "with thanksgiving" is the only right way to think about election.[3]

"I praise you, Father, Lord of heaven and earth, because you have hidden these things from the wise and learned, and revealed them to little children. Yes, Father, for this was your good pleasure" (vv. 25–26).

When we talk about revelation, which is what Jesus says God's electing grace gives, we need to acknowledge that there are two kinds of revelation. There is a *natural or general revelation.* This refers to the revelation of certain truths about God in nature. It is the kind of revelation Paul wrote about in Romans 1, saying that it is sufficient to condemn all persons because they do not follow it in order to seek out and worship God. Paul said, "The wrath of God is being revealed from heaven against all the godlessness and wickedness of men who suppress the truth by their wickedness, since what may be known about God is plain to them, because God has made it plain to them" (vv. 18–19). The response of unregenerate persons to this revelation is that "although they knew God [in this way], they neither glorified him as God nor gave thanks to him" (v. 21).

The second kind of revelation, the kind Jesus actually speaks of here, is a *personal or specific revelation* by God to an individual as a result of which that person turns from sin and trusts Jesus Christ. Jesus says several important things about it: (1) the gospel—he calls it "these things"—is known to God only, since he alone is its author; (2) no one knows what God knows except Jesus, because the gospel has been committed to him by God and because, being God's Son, he alone knows the Father; (3) it is the Father's pleasure that the Son should reveal him to those the Son chooses.

This is an astonishing series of statements. In the first of these brief paragraphs the revelation is said to be given by God and according to God's "good pleasure" (v. 26), while in the second paragraph the same revelation is said to be given at the discretion of the Son (v. 27). In other words, God the Father and Jesus are placed on equal footing, and what is affirmed of each is that the salvation of the lost is due entirely to their good pleasure. What is more, the revelation has to do with Jesus and his teaching, and it is made not to those who consider themselves wise and learned, which the citizens of Korazin, Bethsaida, and Capernaum must have thought they were. Instead of being given to such "wise" persons, it is given to those Jesus calls "little children" (v. 25). Jesus does not mean actual children, of course, though children are not excluded, but those who are humble enough to look to him for salvation.

The man who said this was either insane, a deceiver, or precisely who he claimed to be, which is how the great English apologist C. S. Lewis listed the options in *Mere Christianity.*[4] Millions have wisely believed that Jesus is God and have trusted him for their salvation.

A Gospel Invitation

The chapter ends with a gospel invitation, an invitation to do what those who have believed in Jesus Christ have done. They have enrolled in Christ's school in order that they might learn and believe all that he will teach them. Here Jesus says, "Come to me, all you who are weary and burdened, and I will give you rest. Take my yoke upon you and learn from me, for I am gentle and humble in heart, and you will find rest for your souls. For my yoke is easy and my burden is light" (vv. 28–30).

It is difficult to think of an invitation more important or more gracious than this—and it comes from the lips of the one who has just pronounced the most withering judgment on the citizens of Korazin, Bethsaida, and Capernaum. There are several reasons why this invitation is so gracious.

1. *The invitation is for everyone.* Jesus' words are for people of all ages, all nationalities, and all temperaments, and he calls them exactly as they are. We should emphasize this because we tend to think that Jesus' call is for people who are somehow "suited" for religion or perhaps have "earned" a gospel invitation. But it is precisely here that the universal offer must be stressed, as it was by Jesus. Following Christ is, in a certain sense, the hardest thing anyone can ever do. But at the same time, it is possible for everyone, because Christ himself gives us the will to persist in our calling. What do you need to hear and obey the call of Christ? A hymn answers rightly:

> Let not conscience make you linger,
> Nor of fitness fondly dream;
> All the fitness he requires
> Is to feel your need of him.

The citizens of Capernaum may have had their "felt needs," as we do, but Jesus was not one of them. Therefore, they missed their opportunity and will perish in God's judgment. Only the needy find salvation.

2. *The invitation is for those who are burdened by sin.* The phrase "weary and burdened" does not refer to physical weaknesses or to what we might call the burdens of a difficult life, though it may include them. It chiefly refers to a sense of sin's burden and the need of a Savior. The context makes this clear, for the earlier verses describe the rejection of John the Baptist and Jesus by the Jewish masses, followed by the Lord's denunciation of Korazin, Bethsaida, and Capernaum for their failure to repent at Jesus' preaching. They were not burdened by sin. They were getting along just fine. Still, there were people who were burdened, and these people believed that Jesus could lift sin's weight and turned to him to do it. These people listened to him, trusted him, and found salvation. This is why times of great movement by God's Spirit are also times of great repentance.

If you are awed by large numbers of professing Christians, regardless of the moral tone or spiritual usefulness of their lives, you will think this is a wonderful age, since, as the Gallup poll tells us, there seem to be more than fifty million born-again Christians in the United States. If you are impressed by large churches, you will judge ours to be an age of exceptional blessing, since we have built the largest auditoriums in church history. If you are impressed with money, you must be nearly ecstatic today, since more money is being given to Christian causes than ever before. Even the liberal churches report annual revenue gains, though their membership rolls continue to decline.

But if you are looking for something else—for a mature knowledge of God and real godliness in Christian people—and are bemoaning the accelerating moral decadence of our time, even within fellowships of professing believers, then you must grieve for the state of today's church and sorrow for the lost. Where discipleship is present, people are sensitive to sin and turn from it. They turn to Jesus, where relief from sin's dreadful burden can be found.

3. *The invitation is to learn about Jesus.* When Jesus called his disciples to "follow" him, he was comparing Christianity to a path in which his followers were to walk, he going ahead of them. When he challenged his disciples to "learn from me," he was comparing Christianity to a school in which he was to be both the subject matter and the teacher. This is the school in which every true believer has matriculated and in which a lifelong course of study is prescribed.

The Authorized Version of Matthew 11:29 translates the words "learn from me" as "learn of me," thus making Jesus the subject matter of the Christian's study rather than the teacher.[5] This variation exists because the Greek preposition *apo,* which occurs here, has a variety of meanings, including "of" and "from," and English has no exactly comparable word. Translators must choose one idea or the other when actually both may be involved. Here the root idea is knowing Christ himself, in the sense of John 17:3, where Jesus prayed, "This is eternal life: that they may know you, the only true God, and Jesus Christ, whom you have sent." But having come to know Christ himself, we also need to continue to learn about him in this school.

4. *The invitation offers rest for tired people.* In fact, it offers rest twice. There is a rest that is given: "Come to me, all you who are weary and burdened, and I will *give* you rest" (v. 28). That rest comes instantly when we first trust in Christ. Then there is a rest that is found: "Take my yoke upon you and learn from me, for I am gentle and humble in heart, and you will *find* rest for your souls" (v. 29). That rest comes as we increasingly learn to follow Jesus in our daily lives.

Jesus is the only rest you or any other poor, struggling, burdened soul will ever need. You may be laboring onward like Pilgrim, distressed at the burden on your back. No earthly master will lift that burden. Many will add to it. The majority will ignore it because they have burdens of their own. You need Jesus. He is the only one who can actually help you. Why not turn to him right now? Turn from all inferior teachers to the one who alone can teach true godliness and whose teaching will save your soul.

24

Lord of the Sabbath

Matthew 12:1–21

At that time Jesus went through the grainfields on the Sabbath. His disciples were hungry and began to pick some heads of grain and eat them. When the Pharisees saw this, they said to him, "Look! Your disciples are doing what is unlawful on the Sabbath."

He answered, "Haven't you read what David did when he and his companions were hungry? He entered the house of God, and he and his companions ate the consecrated bread—which was not lawful for them to do, but only for the priests. Or haven't you read in the Law that on the Sabbath the priests in the temple desecrate the day and yet are innocent? I tell you that one greater than the temple is here. If you had known what these words mean, 'I desire mercy, not sacrifice,' you would not have condemned the innocent. For the Son of Man is Lord of the Sabbath."

For the last two chapters I have been writing about opposition to Jesus that began to develop in Israel after his early ministry in Galilee. But so far it has not been too bad. John the Baptist's doubt was not really opposition, and the unbelief of the Galileans was more a case of indifference than rejection. Now the situation changes as Matthew brings the fierce opposition of the Jewish leaders to the fore.

Chief among these leaders were the Pharisees, and it is this elite body of religious professionals that Matthew brings before us in chapter 12. These men are referred to explicitly in verses 2, 14, 24, and 38, but they are either speaking, maneuvering, or being addressed or directly rebuked by Jesus in most of the verses of this chapter. Matthew has already recorded the first stages of their opposition to Jesus (in 9:3, 11, 14, 34; 10:25; 11:19), but now their rejection erupts into open hatred, and they scheme together to have this meddlesome rabbi put to death.

The Pharisees' Heavy Burden

The immediate cause of the Pharisees' fierce opposition was Jesus' disregard of their detailed rules for how to keep the Sabbath, rules that were difficult to follow and a burden for anyone to bear.[1] Matthew suggests this by the way the first verse of chapter 12 follows significantly from the last verse of the preceding chapter. Jesus had invited the common people to follow him, promising, "My yoke is easy and my burden is light" (Matt. 11:30). But in the very next verse we read that Jesus and his disciples were going through the grainfields "on the Sabbath," and everyone who read that would immediately think of the burdensome Sabbath regulations.

There was justification for the leaders' proper concern for the Sabbath, of course. For one thing, the command to keep the Sabbath is the fourth (and longest) of the Ten Commandments, and no command of God can ever be treated lightly. The decalogue says:

> Remember the Sabbath day by keeping it holy. Six days you shall labor and do all your work, but the seventh day is a Sabbath to the Lord your God. On it you shall not do any work, neither you, nor your son or daughter, nor your manservant or maidservant, nor your animals, nor the alien within your gates. For in six days the Lord made the heavens and the earth, the sea, and all that is in them, but he rested on the seventh day. Therefore the Lord blessed the Sabbath day and made it holy.
>
> Exodus 20:8–11

Even today the solemnity of this command should challenge us concerning what we do on Sunday.

Second, the leaders could not forget that one of the reasons given for the exile of the people to Babylon was that they had not kept the Sabbath, and the exile lasted until the missed Sabbaths had been made up. At the end of 2 Chronicles we read that Cyrus "carried into exile to Babylon the remnant, who escaped from the sword, and they became servants to him and his sons until the kingdom of Persia came to power. [So] the land enjoyed its sabbath rests; all the time of its desolation it rested, until the seventy years were completed in fulfillment of the word of the LORD spoken by Jeremiah" (2 Chron. 36:20–21).

What had Jeremiah said? He had warned, "If you do not obey me to keep the Sabbath day holy by not carrying any load as you come through the gates of Jerusalem on the Sabbath day, then I will kindle an unquenchable fire in the gates of Jerusalem that will consume her fortresses" (Jer. 17:27). God did that, and the Pharisees did not want to suffer that terrible destruction and deportation again.

Many Jews undoubtedly kept the Sabbath in the right spirit, just as some Christians keep a strict observance of the Lord's Day today—out of love for God and a desire to set aside at least one day wholly for spiritual matters. What was the problem then? The problem was that the Pharisees had added man's regulations to God's law, reducing a right observance of the Sabbath to the most terrible forms of legalism. Here are some examples.

1. *The law said that one was not to travel on the Sabbath (Exod. 16:29).* Fair enough! "But what constitutes traveling?" the Pharisees asked. As an answer, they developed the concept of a Sabbath day's journey, roughly one thousand yards. A man could walk that far on the Sabbath, but if he went farther, it was sin. However, if a rope was tied across the end of a street, the whole street technically became one dwelling place, and in that case a person could walk one thousand yards beyond the rope. Or if he deposited some food at a given place on Friday night, on the next day he could walk to it, eat his meal (thereby technically establishing a new home), then could go one thousand yards beyond that. I suppose that if he were clever enough, a determined man could walk halfway across Palestine.

2. *The law forbade the carrying of a load (Jer. 17:21–27).* But what was a load? Was a piece of clothing a load? The Pharisees answered that if it was worn as clothing it was not, but if it was carried it was. So the way to get a jacket from one room of the house to another was obviously to put it on, walk to the second room, and take it off.

3. *The law forbade work.* The same logic worked this way. A man is out walking. He spits. Is that work? Answer: It depends on what happens to the spit. If it goes into the dirt and makes a slight furrow, then it is plowing, which is work. If it hits a rock, no work is done. Under this system, being a devout Jew seemed to depend in part on where one spit on Saturdays.[2]

In all, the Pharisees had established thirty-nine categories of work that was prohibited on the Sabbath, and "reaping," which became the chief bone of contention in this conflict with Jesus, was one of them (*Shabbath* 7:2).

The First Incident

In this story Matthew explains that Jesus and his disciples were passing through the grain fields on the Sabbath day, and because the disciples were hungry, they began to pick some heads of grain, rub them in their hands to separate the grain from the chaff, and eat the grain. There is no suggestion that the disciples were stealing. On the contrary, the right to pick and eat grain at the edges of fields was established by Deuteronomy 23:25. The sole issue was the Sabbath and the Pharisees' narrow rules for keeping it. Some years later the famous Jewish rabbi Maimonides said, "To pluck ears is a kind of reaping."[3] But the disciples were guilty of more than that, according to the Pharisees. By plucking grain they were guilty of *reaping*. By rubbing it in their hands they were guilty of *threshing*. By blowing off the chaff they were guilty of *winnowing*. And by the total of those acts they were guilty of *preparing a meal*—all of which was forbidden.

How did Jesus answer? He might have answered by making some useful and right distinctions. The disciples were not working, after all. Plucking a few heads of grain was not harvesting. In any case, they were disciples not farmers. But this was not what he said. His answer was quite different. He raised three matters.[4]

1. *The case of David (1 Sam. 21:1–6)*. Everyone was familiar with this story. David has been anointed to be king over Israel, but he was hated by Saul, who wanted to kill him, and he had fled to the priestly town of Nob to save his life. When David arrived, he was hungry, having no provisions, and when he asked the priest for food, all Ahimelech had was the "consecrated bread" that had been in the tabernacle before the ark. There were twelve loaves of bread, representing the twelve tribes of Israel, and they were placed in the tabernacle to signify the fellowship of the people with God and their being consecrated to him (Lev. 24:5–9). Ahimelech gave this bread to David, and David ate it and gave some to his men.

By introducing this with the words "haven't you read," Jesus was not suggesting that the Pharisees had never read the story but that they had not grasped its significance. If they had understood it, they would have known that their approach to the Sabbath was fundamentally wrong since they were unable to explain such an incident. If David was right, then his need at that moment superseded the normal rules that would have restricted the use of the consecrated bread for the priests. The Pharisees should have known that the law was given to help people not hinder them.

In Mark 2:27, in a verse Matthew does not include in his account of this same incident, Jesus explains that "the Sabbath was made for man, not man for the Sabbath." It is the point he makes here. The laws governing the Sabbath (as well as other laws) were made for our benefit and not to hurt us or make life difficult.

2. *The case of priests who were working in the temple.* Jesus' second point is one only Matthew records, no doubt because Matthew is a particularly Jewish Gospel and the temple was of paramount importance to the Jews. It is about the work the priests did on the Sabbath.

The priests worked on the Sabbath and so "profaned" it—Jesus uses the word *desecrate*—by burning incense (Lev. 24:7), changing the bread of the Presence (Lev. 24:8), and by offering a double burnt offering (Num. 28:9–10). By referring to this practice, Jesus showed that some work took precedence even over the Sabbath laws. Since Jesus went on to say that one greater than the temple was present, meaning himself, he was teaching that the work he was doing was more important than the Sabbath regulations. There is also a suggestion that the kingdom he was bringing would supersede the Old Testament dispensation.

3. *The teaching of Hosea 6:6.* Jesus' third point was a reference to Hosea 6:6, a text already cited once in Matthew 9:13: "I desire mercy, not sacrifice." The point is similar to Paul's valuation of love in 1 Corinthians 13:3: "If I . . . have not love, I gain nothing." If we do not have love (or show mercy), none of the other things, such as speaking in tongues, prophesying, knowledge, or faith, are of value. Yet if that is true of something as important as faith, how much more a set of Sabbath regulations.[5]

The Second Incident

Matthew now adds a second, related incident, the healing of a man with a shriveled hand. We might suppose from Matthew's account that it happened on the same day as the earlier incident, but Luke makes clear that it was "on another Sabbath" (Luke 6:6). Matthew includes it: (1) as another argument in support of Jesus' Sabbath interpretation, and (2) to validate it.

1. *It is always right to do good, even and especially on the Sabbath.* Matthew adds this fourth argument to the three found in the preceding story, probably because it builds so naturally on the last one having to do with mercy. In this story Jesus shows mercy to the handicapped man, which the Pharisees were not about to do. Jesus rebukes them for their hypocrisy. They permitted a person to rescue a trapped sheep on the Sabbath, especially if it was one of their own. So why couldn't Jesus rescue the man with the shriveled hand? Is a sheep more valuable than a human being? Obviously, a man is much more valuable than a sheep. Therefore, it was right for him to heal the man and, by extension, to do good anywhere or at any time. "It is lawful to do good on the Sabbath," Jesus said (v. 12).

2. *The healing of the damaged man proves that Jesus' interpretation of the Sabbath is correct.* This is the point at which the discussion ends, the case being the same as Jesus' healing of the paralyzed man in 9:1–8. When he healed the paralyzed man, having previously said, "Your sins are forgiven" (v. 2), the healing validated his claim to be able to forgive sins. In this story, when he healed the man's hand, clearly with God's power, he proved that his interpretation of the Sabbath and his acts of mercy on the Sabbath were right because they were approved by God.

The Pharisees' Reaction

When I was a boy, my father would sometimes say to me, "A man convinced against his will is of the same opinion still." That was a meaningful word of wisdom, and it was mostly correct, I assume. It was certainly true of the Pharisees in this story. Mark says they were silenced (Mark 3:4). Yes, but not convinced. In fact, the situation grew worse. Rather than being merely unconvinced, they were determined to kill Jesus (Matt. 12:14).

How terrible this was! Here were men who were being punctilious in the observance of their interpretation of God's law. They were as religious as religious people get. But because Jesus was not conforming to their Sabbath regulations, they began to hatch a plot to kill him. We should learn from this how horrible it is to have a religion of rules and ceremonies when the heart is actually far from God. Isn't it true that there is no evil so great that it has not been practiced by someone at some time in the name of religion? And is it not also true that there is nothing as tragic as the tendency of the human heart to seize upon some outward, useless, hypocritical ceremony and follow it to the letter without in any way actually turning to God for salvation?

Why did they hate the Lord Jesus Christ so much? He was breaking their rules, of course. They hated that. But underlying that hatred was the fact that Jesus was *holy,* and they were not; he was *good,* and they were not; he was exercising a true *authority* from God, and they were not.

Mark records an interesting detail at this point. He says that the Pharisees took council with the Herodians to plot how they might kill Jesus (Mark 3:6). The Herodians were a political party; their unifying policy was support of the Herodian dynasty. But what this detail shows is that at this point the religious and secular authorities were joining forces to get rid of this troublesome rabbi. It has often been that way: John Hus and Martin Luther are only two of the most prominent examples.

Church and state will always combine to get rid of anyone who is truly righteous and therefore truly influential. It is because such people are too disruptive, too effective in exposing human injustices and sin.

An Important Summary

In spite of the boldness he showed in healing the man with the withered hand on the Sabbath and doing it in the very teeth of his enemies, Jesus was not courting the leaders' opposition at this time. So now he did what each of the Gospels reports he did on several occasions. First, Jesus withdrew quietly in order to work elsewhere. Matthew says, "Jesus withdrew from that place" (v. 15). Second, he warned those he healed "not to tell who he was," in order not to stir up mistaken expectations (v. 16). Jesus was not a fanatic, nor was he courting either fame or opposition. He had come to make atonement for the sin of his people. He would do it at the proper time, but at this point his hour had not yet come.

This was a watershed moment in Christ's ministry, marking rejection by the leaders and a turning to a different kind of teaching, which will be introduced in chapter 13. So Matthew pauses here to sum up who Jesus was and to indicate the nature of his ministry by quoting a well-known messianic passage from Isaiah (Isa. 42:1–4; Matt. 12:18–21).

> Here is my servant whom I have chosen,
>   the one I love, in whom I delight;
> I will put my Spirit on him,
>   and he will proclaim justice to the nations.

He will not quarrel or cry out;
no one will hear his voice in the streets.
A bruised reed he will not break,
and a smoldering wick he will not snuff out,
till he leads justice to victory.
In his name the nations will put their hope.

This is the longest quotation from the Old Testament in Matthew, but it is not a word-for-word quotation. It is, as William Hendriksen says, "Isaiah 42:1–4 as interpreted by Christ's fully inspired apostle Matthew."[6] Matthew gets it right. Isaiah 42:1–4 is the first of four prophecies about the suffering "servant of the Lord" (see Isa. 49:1–9; 50:4–9; 52:13–53:12), and Matthew is correct in applying the first of them to Jesus here.[7]

These verses contain four great predictions:

1. The Messiah will bring justice to the earth (v. 18).
2. The Messiah will not cry out like a demagogue but instead will go about his work quietly and humbly (v. 19).
3. The Messiah will not trample on the weak or those who are poor in spirit (v. 20).
4. The Messiah will bring salvation to the Gentiles (v. 21).

What an amazing set of predictions. Yet Jesus did precisely these things. His actions, however, did not fulfill the expectations of his day. The Jews of Christ's day wanted a Messiah who would drive out the Romans and establish a revived Jewish state. The disciples themselves had such thoughts even after the resurrection (see Acts 1:6). Jesus went about his work quietly, teaching and at last dying for his people. The benefits of his atonement were offered to the Gentiles. As far as justice is concerned, this is something that is being proclaimed now through the church and will be realized perfectly in power when Jesus comes again.

"What is pictured is a ministry so gentle and compassionate that the weak are not trampled on and crushed till justice, the full righteousness of God, triumphs," as it certainly will in the end.[8]

If you are a Gentile, you have benefited from that prophesied messianic ministry. If you have been buffeted by life ("a bruised reed") or if you are weak in faith ("a smoldering wick"), you are in a position to benefit also. Have you been buffeted? Is your faith weak? If so, be encouraged. Jesus did not come to snuff out anything that is weak but instead to fan the smoldering wick into a flame and to straighten and strengthen the bent rod. Aren't you glad he did not come to execute justice at this time? That will happen in time. Justice will be done. Judgment is inevitable in a universe ruled by a just and holy God. But today is the day of God's grace, and we live because Jesus is the Savior. He alone saves, strengthens, and keeps all who will repent and turn to him.

25

Jesus and the Devil

Matthew 12:22–37

Then they brought him a demon-possessed man who was blind and mute, and Jesus healed him, so that he could both talk and see. All the people were astonished and said, "Could this be the Son of David?"

But when the Pharisees heard this, they said, "It is only by Beelzebub, the prince of demons, that this fellow drives out demons."

Jesus knew their thoughts and said to them, "Every kingdom divided against itself will be ruined, and every city or household divided against itself will not stand. If Satan drives out Satan, he is divided against himself. How then can his kingdom stand? And if I drive out demons by Beelzebub, by whom do your people drive them out? So then, they will be your judges. But if I drive out demons by the Spirit of God, then the kingdom of God has come upon you. . . .

"You brood of vipers, how can you who are evil say anything good? For out of the overflow of the heart the mouth speaks. The good man brings good things out of the good stored up in him, and the evil man brings evil things out of the evil stored up in him. But I tell you that men will have to give account on the day of judgment for every careless word they have spoken. For by your words you will be acquitted, and by your words you will be condemned."

I do not know which despot, king, or president first invented "the big lie" idea, but it has certainly been known and practiced a long time. "The big lie" means that if you repeat a lie loudly enough and often enough, people will believe you. Nero used it when he fingered the Christians for the fire that destroyed Rome. Adolf Hitler used it when he blamed Germany's post–World War I economic troubles on the Jews.

The Pharisees were using "the big lie" in the middle section of Matthew 12, verses 22–37. Jesus had healed another demon-possessed man, one who had been blind and mute, and the Pharisees denounced his power by repeating (only sharper this time) that he was getting his power from the devil: "It is only by Beelzebub, the prince of demons, that this fellow drives out demons" (v. 24). They had suggested this for the first time in Matthew 9:34, and they brought it up again here because of two new circumstances: (1) Jesus had performed another dramatic exorcism, and (2) the common people had begun to speculate that Jesus might actually be "the Son of David," that is, the Messiah (v. 23). The Pharisees were probably beginning to fear that they were losing their hold on the people.

The man had been in a truly dreadful condition, as all sin's captives are. The demon had possessed him, and as a result, the man could neither talk nor see. Matthew has already taught us to think of physical ailments in spiritual terms. Therefore, we observe that the man could not talk in order to call out to Jesus to save him, nor could he see his way to come to Jesus. His friends brought this helpless sinner to the Savior, and Jesus healed him immediately.

Jesus' Teaching about Satan

This narrative, however, is not given to teach us about demon possession or what it might signify. It is about the Pharisees' "big lie" and about how Jesus answered it. Significantly, Jesus' response was not different from what he had been doing all along. We have seen several times in our study that Jesus had come chiefly to teach and preach. Here he does both in his answer to the Pharisees. First, he teaches them. Then, second, he preaches to them, warning them to repent of their sin, believe on him, and be saved. It is what Jesus might say to us if we have similarly evil thoughts or objections.

We can summarize Jesus' teaching first. It is in verses 25–29.

1. *"I cannot be exorcising demons by demonic power, because then Satan would be fighting against himself, and if he should do that his kingdom would not stand."* Satan is much too shrewd to liberate persons he has enslaved.

2. *"If I am not driving out demons by the power of Satan, then I must be doing it by the power of God."* In spiritual matters God's power is the only other power that exists, and in any case, it takes the supreme power of God to overcome the great but not omnipotent power of the devil.

3. *"If I am driving out demons by the power of God, then the kingdom of God has come to you."* The tense of the verb "has come" is important. It is not future, as if Jesus were merely pointing to something that would be true one day. "Has come" is a present tense, pointing to a present reality. The kingdom has come, and the reason it has come is that Jesus has come.

4. *"If the kingdom has come because I have come, then I must be the king, the Messiah."* This is Jesus' obvious implication. In other words, the people's tentative conclusion in verse 23 was the right one.

Verse 27 does something else too. It shows the inconsistency of the Pharisees' position. They had disciples who claimed to be able to drive out demons, and if this were true (the Pharisees would certainly claim it was), it was certainly not by anything other than God's power. How could they claim that Jesus did his work by Satan's power while maintaining that they did the same thing by God's power?

We might question whether the Pharisees' disciples were actually able to perform exorcisms, but Josephus is one fairly reliable historian who says they did. In his *Antiquities* (VIII, ii, 5) and again in *The Jewish War* (VII, vi, 3), he provides several such accounts. In the first of these works he claims to have seen an exorcism himself: "I have seen a certain Eleazar, a countryman of mine, in the presence of Vespasian, his sons, tribunes and a number of other soldiers, free men possessed by demons." He reports in some detail how this was done.[1]

In verse 29 Jesus summarizes his teaching, indicating this by the words "or again." It is a way of saying that what follows is what he has already taught, but he is saying it again by way of an image. In this illustration Jesus pictures Satan as a strong man whose house contains treasures, which are the men and women whom he has taken prisoner. Jesus is stronger than Satan. Therefore, he is able to bind the strong man and rob his house. The illustration adds force to the interpretation of Matthew 11:12 given earlier; that is, in Jesus the kingdom of heaven has been forcefully advancing.[2]

Jesus' Preaching to the Pharisees

In an earlier study I called attention to the fact that apart from his works of healing, Jesus' ministry consisted of two things: teaching and preaching. I pointed out that teaching and preaching are not the same thing. Teaching is instruction; it has to do with content, and it is primary. Preaching contains instruction and is based on it, but it is more than mere instruction. It is also a passionate declaration of what the hearers need to do with the truth they have been given, and it calls for that response. True preaching is the point at which sound teaching becomes personal.

We find both in Jesus' words to the Pharisees. They had accused him of casting out demons by satanic power. Jesus had answered their attack with arguments, showing the absurdity of their position (vv. 25–29). That was his teaching. But now he also preaches to them, insisting that what he has taught demands changes in how they think and function. In these verses (vv. 30–35), he shows how important it is for them to properly assess him and what he is doing, and how fatal it is to judge wrongly.

Let's take this step by step, as we did with Jesus' teaching.

1. *You cannot be neutral about Jesus (v. 30).* If the kingdom has come in Jesus and the demands of the kingdom are that people submit to Jesus' rule as king, then neutrality is impossible. You may think you do not care about Jesus one way or another, but if you are not for him, you are actually opposing him. Jesus said, "He who is not with me is against me, and he who does not gather with me scatters" (v. 30). The reason for this is that Jesus always demands a decision. He requires a deliberate submission to his rule. He calls us to deny ourselves, take up our crosses, and follow him (Matt. 10:38). If we do not submit to Jesus' rule, we are not "for" Jesus. We are resisting him.

2. *Your refusal to believe is dangerous (vv. 31–32).* One sin leads to another, and rejection sometimes leads even to an unforgivable rejection. Such was the case with the Pharisees, for Jesus accused them of having done what was unforgivable. "And so I tell you, every sin and blasphemy will be forgiven men, but the blasphemy against the Spirit will not be forgiven. Anyone who speaks a word against the Son of Man will be forgiven, but anyone who speaks against the Holy Spirit will not be forgiven, either in this age or in the age to come" (vv. 31–32).

These are frightening words. They are intended to be. But they have also been unnecessarily alarming for some people. Most ministers have had people come to them wondering if they have committed the unforgivable sin when they have done nothing of the sort. In fact, the fear that they might have sinned unforgivably is the best possible proof that they have not.

Still, we dare not take the warning of these words lightly. How do we keep a proper balance? Obviously by being careful to understand what these verses actually mean. This is not overly difficult since the context makes clear what the unforgivable sin is. It is what the Pharisees had done. They had called good, evil, and evil, good. Or to put it another way, they had called the good work of God in delivering the demon-possessed man demonic. This is called a sin against the Holy Spirit because the deliverance was by the power of the Holy Spirit and because they were identifying him with Satan. It is unforgivable because it is a case of distorting reality so thoroughly that repentance is impossible, and without repentance there can be no forgiveness.

This is a difficult saying, but it is a reliable one since it is "the sober verdict of the only person who has authority on earth to forgive sins."[3] Of all teachers, Jesus must have known what he was talking about.

Here is how D. A. Carson explains these verses in his commentary:

> The distinction between blasphemy against the Son of Man and blasphemy against the Spirit is not that the Son of Man is less important than the Spirit, or that the first sin is prebaptismal and the second postbaptismal, still less that the first is against the Son of Man and the second rejects the authority of Christian prophets. Instead, within the context of the larger argument the first sin is rejection of the truth of the gospel (but there may be repentance and forgiveness for that), whereas the second sin is rejection of the same truth in full awareness that that is exactly what one is doing—thoughtfully, willfully,

> and self-consciously rejecting the work of the Spirit even though there can be no other explanation of Jesus' exorcisms than that.[4]

In my judgment, this is a close parallel to what Paul writes in the first chapter of Romans, where he traces the downward path of sin. The root problem is rejection of the truth about God, Paul says (vv. 18–20). But this soon leads to a downhill path of perversion ending with what he calls a "depraved mind" (v. 28). A depraved mind is the confirmed mental state of those who not only practice the vices listed in the final paragraph of Romans 1 but also "*approve* of those who practice them" (v. 32). Those who approve of evil are saying that those evil practices are right and that the contrary good acts must be evil.

This is what the Pharisees were doing. Therefore, if they were actually convinced (or merely wanted to convince themselves) that the good works of Jesus were evil, as they seemed to have been doing, there was no possibility of their repenting and embracing Christ since from their debased perspective repentance would be an irrational and therefore an impossible act.[5] Those who have declined to that level are beyond hope, and lest we dismiss this too readily, we must keep in mind that this is exactly what Paul says of a declining secular society such as our own. If people in our culture really consider evil things to be good and good to be evil, what possible chance of genuine repentance and conversion do they have?

3. *The problem is in us (vv. 33–35).* According to Jesus' preaching, we must not consider this an external problem. It is in the very nature of those who refuse to believe on Jesus. This describes us, and it describes the Pharisees, since for all their religious pretensions, they were fundamentally evil—a "brood of vipers" (v. 34). We know this is what they were because of their words. "For out of the overflow of the heart the mouth speaks. The good man brings good things out of the good stored up in him, and the evil man brings evil things out of the evil stored up in him" (vv. 34–35). It is always the case that the words we speak reveal our heart's condition.

A Final Warning for Everyone

This has been very good preaching, and since it has been directed at the Pharisees and their particular sin of blaspheming against the Holy Spirit, we are tempted to lean back and merely urge Jesus on. "Preach it, brother!" we might say. But Jesus' words are not only sobering for the Pharisees and any others who may have sinned in a particularly grievous way. They are sobering for us too, since in the last verses of this section Jesus speaks to people exactly like us.

Do you notice the change that comes in verses 36 and 37? We have a clue that this is something different and additional because verses 36 and 37 appear in Matthew only. They do not occur in the parallel accounts in Mark and Luke. But there are two other clues as well. The words before this are directed at the Pharisees, that "brood of vipers." Jesus even speaks to them directly using the word *you:* "How can *you* who are evil say anything good?" (v. 34). But in these last two verses what he says is directed to "all men," which includes us. When he says, "For by *your* words you will be acquitted, and by *your* words you will be condemned," it is to us that he is speaking. The final clue is the formal way verses 36 and 37 are introduced: "But I tell you . . ." This is close to the most formal introductory formula, usually translated "truly, truly" or "I tell you the truth." It is a way of setting up a particularly important saying.

And so it is! These verses are more sobering even than Jesus' teaching about the unforgivable sin. In the previous section the words he is talking about are evil or particularly malicious words, but here they are merely "careless" or idle words. They are something of which every one of us, not just especially depraved or evil persons, is guilty. But, says Jesus, even these words are sufficient to condemn you at God's judgment.

Can you understand how serious this is and how desperate it makes your case? A careless word would be the *least* offensive act you have committed. But if even that single careless word is sufficient to condemn you at God's judgment, how much more the other very evil evils you have done? How about your envy of other people? Or your greed? Or your depravity? How about strife, deceit, and malice? Or slander? Have you never slandered anyone? How about insolent words, arrogant words, or boastful words? How about the times you disobeyed or even dishonored your parents? What about your senseless, faithless, heartless, ruthless, or otherwise blatantly non-Christian behavior?

These are sins Paul lists at the end of that sobering first chapter of Romans, things that "deserve death" (v. 32). And we are guilty of all of them, not to mention the fact that we have not loved God with all our hearts, souls, minds, and strength, nor our neighbors as ourselves, which are the first and second great commandments (see Matt. 22:37, 39; Mark 12:28–31). If we have done those things, in addition to being careless with our words, how can we escape God's judgment?

We cannot, of course. We need a Savior. We need Jesus who died for words we have carelessly spoken, as well as for the more obvious sins we have committed. We need him who bore the punishment for all our sins on the cross.

> My sin—O, the bliss of this glorious thought—
> My sin, not in part but the whole,
> Is nailed to the cross, and I bear it no more.
> Praise the Lord. Praise the Lord, O my soul.

"The Big Lie" or "the Big Truth"?

Yet we also need to stop speaking those careless words. We tend to take words lightly. "Sticks and stones may break my bones, but words will never hurt me," we say. But words do hurt, and the Bible takes words spoken by

Christians very seriously. James wrote about the harm evil words can do, saying, "With the tongue we praise our Lord and Father, and with it we curse men, who have been made in God's likeness. Out of the same mouth come praise and cursing. My brothers, this should not be" (James 3:9–10).

What is the remedy? The only remedy is a radical change of heart, for as Jesus says, it is "out of the overflow of the heart the mouth speaks" (Matt. 12:34). We need a cleansed heart, a new heart. The only way we can receive a changed heart is by a new birth, which is a product of the work of God in salvation.

Consider Peter, a disciple who must have been present with Jesus as he preached to the rulers of the Jews on this occasion. If ever a disciple was guilty of foolish, careless words, it was Peter. When he was on the mountain with James, John, and Jesus, and Jesus was transformed, appearing before the disciples with Moses and Elijah, Peter thought it might be a good idea to build three little shrines: "If you wish, I will put up three shelters—one for you, one for Moses and one for Elijah" (Matt. 17:4). When Jesus foretold his future suffering, Peter rebuked him, saying, "Never, Lord! . . . This shall never happen to you" (Matt. 16:22). On that occasion Jesus had to rebuke Peter as if he were Satan, for his words were from Satan even though Peter did not know it. In the upper room Peter refused at first to let the Lord wash his feet (John 13:8).

But what a change regeneration makes! And what a change in Peter after Christ's resurrection and his gracious recommissioning to service. In that day Peter's words were no longer careless, idiotic, or mistaken. Peter began to speak truthfully and with power, as the Holy Spirit spoke through him. Moreover, he did it before the very men who had accused the Lord of casting out demons by demonic power, confronting them with "the big truth" even as they had embraced "the big lie." Peter told them, "Know this, you and all the people of Israel: It is by the name of Jesus Christ of Nazareth, whom you crucified but whom God raised from the dead, that this man stands before you healed. . . . Salvation is found in no one else, for there is no other name under heaven given to men by which we must be saved" (Acts 4:10–12).

Those words were not from Satan. They were from God and are the exact testimony of all who have found the Lord Jesus Christ as their Savior. Today millions prefer "the big lie," but we speak God's truth, knowing that the Spirit of truth will use the truth to bring many to the Savior.

26

The Sign of Jonah

Matthew 12:38–50

Then some of the Pharisees and teachers of the law said to him, "Teacher, we want to see a miraculous sign from you."

He answered, "A wicked and adulterous generation asks for a miraculous sign! But none will be given it except the sign of the prophet Jonah. For as Jonah was three days and three nights in the belly of a huge fish, so the Son of Man will be three days and three nights in the heart of the earth. The men of Nineveh will stand up at the judgment with this generation and condemn it; for they repented at the preaching of Jonah, and now one greater than Jonah is here. The Queen of the South will rise at the judgment with this generation and condemn it; for she came from the ends of the earth to listen to Solomon's wisdom, and now one greater than Solomon is here." . . .

While Jesus was still talking to the crowd, his mother and brothers stood outside, wanting to speak to him. Someone told him, "Your mother and brothers are standing outside, wanting to speak to you."

He replied to him, "Who is my mother, and who are my brothers?" Pointing to his disciples, he said, "Here are my mother and my brothers. For whoever does the will of my Father in heaven is my brother and sister and mother."

The Pharisees must have been smarting from their verbal defeat by Jesus. Jesus had shown that their evil explanation of his miracles—that he was casting out demons by the power of Satan—was both absurd and contradictory. His arguments should have moved them to reconsider their position, but they did not, of course. They hated

Jesus, so rather than altering their views, they merely came at him from another direction, demanding a miraculous sign.

A sign? Whatever were they thinking? Some scholars try to explain their demand by suggesting that they were asking for a different kind of sign from those Jesus had already given, a sign produced on demand perhaps. But what sign could Jesus have given in addition to the miracles he had done? He told the disciples of John the Baptist, "Go back and report to John what you hear and see: The blind receive sight, the lame walk, those who have leprosy are cured, the deaf hear, the dead are raised, and the good news is preached to the poor" (Matt. 11:4–5). These were true messianic signs, and Jesus had performed them, which means that in light of his miracles the demand for a "sign" was both insulting and impudent. It was also hypocritical, for regardless of what Jesus might have done to meet their demand, these men would merely have dug their heels in deeper and refused to believe him.

It is the same today, when many more signs than those seen by the men of that far distant day have been given. Today there is overpowering evidence for the claims of Jesus to be the unique Son of God and the Savior. People still will not believe, and it is an insult to God to claim that there is insufficient evidence. What kind of evidence would it take? I sometimes say that even if God rearranged the very stars of heaven to read, "Jesus is my Son with whom I am well pleased; believe on him," people would look at the stars, scratch their heads, and say, "Isn't that unusual? I wonder how the stars managed to rearrange themselves that way."

Yet Jesus did offer them a sign, at least one that would be given to the entire world in time. It was the sign of his death and resurrection. He called it the sign of the prophet Jonah, saying, "For as Jonah was three days and three nights in the belly of a huge fish, so the Son of Man will be three days and three nights in the heart of the earth" (Matt. 12:40).

Three Days and Three Nights

No one can read that today without understanding at once that it is a prophecy of Jesus' resurrection. It is an excellent preaching text for Easter Sunday, but it also involves a problem. In the traditional handling of the events of Passion Week, Jesus was crucified on a Friday and was raised from the dead on Sunday morning. All four Gospel writers placed the crucifixion on the day immediately preceding a normal Saturday Sabbath (see Matt. 27:62; Mark 15:42; Luke 23:54; and John 19:31).[1] Yet if that is a correct understanding of these events, how can it be said that Jesus spent "three days and three nights" in the earth?

According to Jewish idiom, the phrase "three days" does not necessarily mean a period of seventy-two hours. It can mean merely one whole day plus parts of two others. But while this observation helps us deal with texts that say "three days," it does not help us deal with Matthew's version of the prophecy, for here the phrase is not "three days" but rather "three days and three nights."

It is possible that parts of one day and one night are involved, rather than three full days and three full nights; nevertheless, three periods of light and three periods of darkness must be accounted for.[2] This requirement, regardless of anything else, is fatal to a Friday crucifixion theory. As one writer says, "Add to the indictment of Friday the statement of the two disciples on the way to Emmaus, spoken on the afternoon of Sunday (Luke 24:21), 'Today is the third day since these things were done,' and the case looks black indeed against Friday. Sunday is not the third day *since* Friday."[3]

There is another difficulty too, a difficulty apparent to anyone who has tried to sort out the events of the final Passover Week and assign them days. On an average, about one-third of the Gospels is taken up with the events of the last week of Christ's life. This means that the events of this week are given to us in fairly complete detail. Indeed, from the arrival of Jesus in Bethany, six days before the Passover, until the resurrection, every moment seems to be accounted for. Yet when the events of these days are pieced together into one connected whole, one entire day, and possibly two, is lacking. One of the missing days can be explained as the preceding Sabbath, a day in which Jesus rested in Bethany and received those who came to see him and Lazarus. But what of the other day? Can it really be that in a week as full as this one was, one entire day is unaccounted for? How can we explain this omission?

The difficulty of accounting for this day led no less careful a scholar than Frederick Godet to move the events of Palm Sunday to Monday, thereby compressing six days of activity into five. This is interesting, but the same effect can be achieved by moving the crucifixion back to Thursday rather than by moving the events of Palm Sunday forward.

A third difficulty is of a more recent development. The dating of historical events has been a complicated matter, involving the days and times of solar and lunar eclipses and new moons. But in recent years, thanks to the use of computers, much that was formerly uncertain is now known. Thus, to give an example, as recently as 1973 a work entitled *New and Full Moons* by Herman H. Goldstine was published, from which it is possible to calculate the days of the week on which the Jewish Passover fell in any given year during Christ's lifetime or thereafter. If such a calculation established a Saturday Passover and therefore a Friday crucifixion for any year near the time at which Jesus must have been crucified, it would provide excellent support for the traditional theory. But, in fact, it does not. Instead, the day before Passover falls on a Friday only in the year A.D. 26, which is too early, and in the year A.D. 33, which most scholars agree is too late.[4]

What are we to do with these problems? Is there a solution? I believe there is and that it is obviously *the* solution, once we get over the idea that the crucifixion must have been on a Friday, as tradition says. The solution is simply that two Sabbaths were involved in this last week of Christ's earthly ministry. One was the regular weekly Sabbath, which always fell on Saturday. The second was an extra Passover Sabbath, which, in this particular week, must have come on a Friday.

It needs to be said, in case it is not entirely self-evident, that the Passover Sabbath always came on the fifteenth of the month of Nisan and would therefore naturally fall on different days of the week in different years, as Christmas does in our day. However, it was always observed as a Sabbath. In my reconstruction Jesus would have been crucified on Thursday and would have been raised from the dead sometime before dawn on Sunday morning.

April 6, A.D. 30

What does this suggestion do to the problems we have already noted as a result of the traditional dating? It eliminates each one.

1. *There are three actual days and three nights.* Jesus had spoken of a period of time beginning with daylight and comprising the whole of three days and nights, with the possible qualification that the opening period of day and the closing period of night need not necessarily be a full twelve hours. This is provided for as follows. Jesus died on Thursday afternoon about three o'clock; hence, the hours from 3:00 P.M. until dusk qualify as the first day. This period is followed by Thursday night, Friday, Friday night, Saturday, and Saturday night; that is, a total of three days and three nights in that precise order. In this scheme of things, Jesus could have risen from the dead at any point after dark on Saturday evening. What we know is that he was raised sometime before the women got to the tomb at dawn on Sunday morning.

Several minor points reinforce this idea. First, when the soldiers tried to explain why they were unable to guard the tomb successfully they said, "His disciples came during the night and stole him away while we were asleep" (Matt. 28:13). That would be a natural way of speaking if the resurrection and the subsequent opening of the tomb by the angels took place at night.

Even more striking is the fact that in the original Greek, Matthew's account of the events of the resurrection morning begins, "In the end of the *sabbaths* (plural), as it began to dawn toward the first day of the week" (Matt. 28:1). The plural has been a puzzle to many translators, who usually change it to the singular, "sabbath." But the word is plural, and the plural is explained if there were two back-to-back Sabbaths in that week—the special Passover Sabbath, which fell on a Friday, and the regular Saturday Sabbath, which came the next day.

2. *Each day of the week is accounted for.* In this new arrangement of events we have the following:

Saturday (the Jewish Sabbath): Jesus does not travel on this day but rather remains in Bethany with his disciples and Lazarus. Many come to see Jesus and the man he raised from the dead.

Sunday: Jesus enters Jerusalem riding on a donkey after having first made arrangements to secure the animal. He goes to the temple area and looks about, but it is late by this time and he returns to Bethany without further recorded actions or teaching.

Monday: Jesus returns to Jerusalem. On the way he curses the fig tree as a symbol of the barrenness of Israel and as a prophecy of what was coming to the nation. In Jerusalem he cleanses the temple for a second, final time (see John 2:12–22) and returns again to Bethany, where he spends each night of this week save the last.

Tuesday: On the way back to Jerusalem the disciples find the fig tree withered and receive Christ's explanation. In the city the disciples comment on the magnificence of the temple and are told that the day is coming when it will be torn down. On the way home Jesus pauses on the Mount of Olives to give what has come to be called the Olivet Discourse concerning things to come. Prophecy dominates the teaching of this day.

Wednesday: Jesus sends the disciples to make preparations for the Passover, which is, however, eaten that evening without the Passover lamb. Jesus is arrested that same night as he deliberately tarries in the Garden of Gethsemane on what would have been his normal trip back to Bethany.

Thursday: Jesus is tried and eventually crucified. The trial begins on what we would call Wednesday night (but which is actually the early hours of Thursday by Jewish reckoning) and is completed in the morning. Jesus is crucified. Darkness covers the land from noon to 3:00 P.M. Jesus is buried this same evening by Nicodemus and Joseph of Arimathea. The women observe where Jesus is buried and buy spices, but as it is now the start of the Passover Sabbath (that is, the Friday Sabbath that began at dusk on Thursday evening), they are unable to anoint the body until Sunday morning.

Friday and Saturday: The body of Jesus remains in the tomb. The women and disciples observe the two Sabbaths. Jesus rises from the dead sometime between the coming of darkness on Saturday evening and the coming of the dawn on Sunday morning.

3. *The day of Christ's crucifixion.* The day before Passover, the fourteenth of Nisan, did not fall on a Friday between the years A.D. 26 and A.D. 33. But how about Thursday? Strikingly, the fourteenth of Nisan fell on a Thursday once during those years, and this one time perfectly fits the situation. The fourteenth of Nisan fell on a Thursday in the year A.D. 30, the most probable year of the crucifixion even by other calculations. Thus, we may conclude with reasonable certainty that the crucifixion of Jesus is to be dated as April 6, A.D. 30, and the resurrection dated April 9.[5]

This Wicked Generation

This discussion provides good, strong evidence for the truthfulness of Christianity and is why I have taken so much time to review it. It shows the accuracy of the Bible, the divine self-awareness and prophetic knowledge of

Jesus, and most of all perhaps, the importance of the resurrection as a verification of Christ's claims. The sign of Jonah is still the greatest of all signs.

Yet, sadly, signs are not always followed, and the evidence even for so great a matter as the truthfulness of Christianity is often not believed. This is what Jesus talks about next. The Pharisees had asked Jesus for a sign, and Jesus had given one, though it was a sign that would not be seen by them until the close of his earthly ministry and his return to heaven. Would they believe him then? Jesus was under no illusions on this point. He saw their reaction as clearly as he saw the resurrection itself, and what he saw was their utter unbelief. They had the sign of his resurrection, but they would respond in exactly the opposite way as did the men of Nineveh, who believed when Jonah preached to them, and as did "the Queen of the South," who came from far off Ethiopia to see and learn from Solomon.

The sign made a comparison between Jesus and Jonah. Both were signs because of their supernatural deliverance. But the similarities stop there, since the people of Nineveh repented at the preaching of Jonah, while in the case of Jesus, the hearts of the people were hardened. The people Jesus knew would not believe him. Building on what he had said earlier about Tyre, Sidon, and Sodom in his denunciation of the unbelief of the Galilean cities (Matt. 11:20–24), Jesus declared that the citizens of Nineveh would rise at the judgment to condemn his own generation since they repented at Jonah's preaching while the people of Jesus' day would not repent, even though a far greater person than Jonah was among them. The same was true of "the Queen of the South," that is, the queen of Sheba (1 Kings 10:1–13). She came to see Solomon and learn from him, and Jesus was far greater even than that great king of Israel.

When I read this I tremble for our own generation. Don't you? It is true that Jesus was present in that day, and he is not physically present on earth now. But there is far more evidence for the truth of Jesus' claims today, including his bodily resurrection, than there was in the first Christian century. I have read that more than twenty specific prophecies were fulfilled in the last twenty-four hours of Jesus' earthly life alone. And when he was raised from the dead on the third day and appeared to the apostles, they were so convinced of his resurrection and so captivated by his person that they began to work their way through the entire Roman world to tell other people about him. They kept at it even in the face of severe hardships, and most gave their lives for his cause. Thus has the gospel come to us. Jesus' story has been proclaimed with powerful and wonderful effects. Lives have been changed. History has been altered. Good has been done. All because of Jesus. What shall we say of a generation that is able to turn its back on that witness and suppose in its folly that it is the master of its destiny and that all is well with its soul?

Here is a frightening description of our age: Jesus' picture of a man who had been delivered of an evil spirit but who had nothing of value to put in the evil spirit's place. So afterward the evil spirit returned, and the man was possessed not by one evil spirit but by seven. Our contemporaries have heard the gospel, but most have rejected it. Is that true of you? Do you have nothing inside but the husks of an empty materialism or sensuality? If so, your last condition will be worse than your first, and you will perish along with all other unbelievers at the last judgment.

The Family of God

What a grim chapter this has been, and it looks as if it will end even more grimly when we read about Jesus' mother and brothers coming to where he was teaching, asking to speak with him (vv. 46–50).[6] Matthew reports this without further explanation, but in Mark 3:21 we discover why they came. They said, "He is out of his mind." This was the same judgment the Pharisees had been making, though they said it in less flattering terms: "He is possessed by Beelzebub!" (Mark 3:22; Matt. 12:24). It is not a very nice picture of Jesus' family, but what else could they conclude? How could any sane man claim to be greater than Jonah? Or King Solomon?

None, of course! Unless he was the Son of God, the Messiah!

That has been the concern of these chapters all along, from the beginning of chapter 11 to the end of chapter 12, and it is the right question to ask. Is Jesus really God's Messiah? Is he the King? At this point Jesus' mother and brothers were not able to answer by saying yes. They thought he had merely gone off the deep end. However, it is important to note that they all eventually did believe on him. Mary and his brothers appear along with all the other early believers in Acts 1:12–14, where they are observed worshiping together. As for James, he emerges in time as the leader of the first church council, reported in Acts 15.

Yet the important issue now is not whether *they* believed or not. The question is whether *you* believe and whether *you* will follow Jesus, for who are those who belong to Jesus' family? It is not those who were born into his natural family according to the flesh. Jesus makes that perfectly clear in these last verses. It is those who have become his disciples, those who have denied themselves, taken up their crosses, and followed him. Pointing to his disciples, Jesus said, "Here are my mother and my brothers. For whoever does the will of my Father in heaven is my brother and sister and mother" (vv. 49–50).

What is the will of the Father? By now you should know the answer to that as well as I do. It is that people everywhere might repent of their sin and believe on Jesus as King and Savior. That is what God wants you to do. In fact, he commands it. Will you commit yourself to Jesus Christ? It is the way of salvation and the path to life.

Part Five

The Parables of the Kingdom

27

The Parable of the Sower

Matthew 13:1–23

That same day Jesus went out of the house and sat by the lake. Such large crowds gathered around him that he got into a boat and sat in it, while all the people stood on the shore. Then he told them many things in parables, saying: "A farmer went out to sow his seed. As he was scattering the seed, some fell along the path, and the birds came and ate it up. Some fell on rocky places, where it did not have much soil. It sprang up quickly, because the soil was shallow. But when the sun came up, the plants were scorched, and they withered because they had no root. Other seed fell among thorns, which grew up and choked the plants. Still other seed fell on good soil, where it produced a crop—a hundred, sixty or thirty times what was sown. He who has ears, let him hear."

When my youngest daughter Jennifer was young and we were still doing biblical musicals with the children of Tenth Presbyterian Church, she learned a song that contained the line "Jesus was a story-tellin' man." When I first heard that I thought it was a bit flip, as many contemporary Christian songs are. But I realized that it contains a real truth: Although Jesus was much more than a storyteller, he was at least that, and as a result, the people of his day flocked to him and listened to him gladly (Mark 12:37).

Christ's words were always picturesque. He spoke of sheep among wolves (Matt. 10:16), of camels creeping through the eye of a needle (Matt. 19:24), of people trying to remove specks from other people's eyes while planks were in their own (Matt. 7:5). He referred to a house divided against itself, destined to fall down (Mark 3:25), of throwing children's bread to dogs (Mark 7:27). He warned against the "yeast" of the Pharisees (Mark 8:15). Strictly speaking, however, these imaginative pictures are not stories. The stories Jesus told all fall into a particular category of story known as *parables.*

A parable is a story from real life or a real-life situation from which a moral or spiritual truth is drawn. Examples are abundant: the prodigal son (Luke 15:11–32), the good Samaritan (Luke 10:25–37), the Pharisee and the tax collector (Luke 18:9–14), the wedding banquet (Matt. 22:1–14; Luke 14:15–24), the sheep and the goats (Matt. 25:31–46), and others, including the parables of the kingdom that we have come to now (Matt. 13:1–52). By my count there are twenty-seven parables in the four Gospels, though some are similar and may merely be different versions of the same root story.

Parables differ from fables in that a fable is not a real situation. An example of a fable is any of Aesop's stories, in which animals talk. In those stories the animals are simply people in disguise. Parables also differ from allegories, since in an allegory each or nearly each detail has a meaning. The best-known and probably the most successful allegory ever written is John Bunyan's *Pilgrim's Progress.* But there are others. C. S. Lewis's Chronicles of Narnia are essentially allegories. In the parables of Jesus not every detail has a meaning. In fact, to try to force meaning into each of the details produces strange and sometimes even demonstrably false doctrines. Parables are merely real-life stories from which one or possibly a few basic truths can be drawn.

Parables of the Kingdom

But there is more to Jesus' use of parables than what I have suggested so far, and we have to understand this because it is important to the way Matthew introduces these stories. For one thing, since Jesus is rightly known for his stories, it is striking that we have not encountered parables in Matthew's Gospel until now. We are at chapter 13, almost halfway through the Gospel, but this is the first place Jesus' parables are introduced. As verses 10–15 make clear, Jesus adopted the use of parables at this specific stage in his ministry for the deliberate purpose of withholding further truth about himself and the kingdom of heaven from the crowds.

Why should he do that? The answer is that masses of people had rejected him (Matt. 11:16–24) and therefore could not understand the deeper things that he now needed to reveal about the kingdom. The disciples, on the other hand, had begun to believe on him and were looking to him for teaching. Therefore, he taught his lessons in parables and then explained the stories to them. In fact, as Matthew makes clear, from this point on the explanation of the parables is always given to the disciples alone and never to the crowds.

R. V. G. Tasker explains the difference in this way:

> When such people heard a parable about the kingdom it would . . . be for them an interesting but pointless story conveying no revelation of divine truth. The

> disciples, on the other hand, had already grasped something of the supernatural character of their Master and of the kingdom he came to inaugurate. To them therefore he could explain the truth embodied in these parables, as in fact he did in the interpretations here recorded of the parables of the sower and the tares. The result was that their powers of spiritual understanding developed and the mysteries of the kingdom became clearer to them. In their case there was another illustration of the proverbial truth that *whosoever hath, to him shall be given, and he shall have more abundance,* just as in the case of the crowds the complementary truth was also being demonstrated that *whosoever hath not, from him shall be taken away even that he hath.*[1]

Matthew 13 is the third of the six major collections of teaching by Jesus in the Gospel. We have already studied two, those in chapters 5–7 and 10. The others are in chapters 18, 23, and 24–25.

Chapter 13 contains seven parables, all of which have one theme: the kingdom of God. They are called the "parables of the kingdom." It is no accident that these are the first parables encountered, since from the beginning Matthew has been writing about the coming of the kingdom of God in Jesus Christ. It is sometimes said that Matthew's Gospel presents Jesus as the "king of Israel," just as Mark presents him as the "Son of Man" and Luke as the "servant." But whether we give Matthew that specific emphasis or not, there is no doubt that Jesus' proclamation of the kingdom is the major theme of this Gospel. The very first verse introduces Jesus as "the son of David," Israel's great king. Jesus' forerunner, John the Baptist, is said to have come preaching "the kingdom of heaven" (Matt. 3:2). Jesus made that the initial theme of his itinerant ministry (Matt. 4:17). Some would regard the Sermon on the Mount (Matt. 5–7) as the ethics of the kingdom and consider chapters 8–12 as demonstrations of the kingdom's power. Since this is Matthew's emphasis, we should not be surprised that the first parables are on this subject.

It is also no accident that the parables are presented in the order in which we have them, although methods of grouping the seven stories differ. The most obvious division is into two sets of four and three respectively. In the first four (the sower and the seed, the enemy who sows tares, the mustard seed, and the yeast) Jesus speaks before the multitudes. The last three (the parables of the hidden treasure, the fine pearl, and the dragnet) are spoken before the disciples only. Others have grouped the parables in the following way: (1) the parables involving planting and harvesting, (2) the parables of the mustard seed and the leaven, (3) the parables about the treasure and the pearl, which stress the kingdom's value, and (4) the parable of the dragnet.

Each of these classifications suggests a development, but I prefer a third system of classification. To my mind the first parable stands alone, since it deals with the origin of the kingdom. The next three belong together, since (as I hope to demonstrate) they explain Satan's desire to thwart the kingdom's growth. Parables five and six go together to show the attitude of those who vigorously seek the kingdom in spite of Satan's wiles, and the last parable, the dragnet, shows the kingdom's consummation. Taken together the stories show the nature, origin, hindrances to, and victory of Christ's work of spreading his gospel through his messengers between the days of his first coming and his coming again.

The Parable of the Sower

The first parable is an ideal one with which to begin, since (obviously enough) it deals with the beginning or origins of the kingdom. Here it is compared to a farmer sowing seed. "A farmer went out to sow his seed" (Matt. 13:3–9). Not all of Christ's parables are explained. In fact, most are not. But this one is (vv. 18–23), and the explanation Jesus gives is our starting point. The seed is the gospel of the kingdom, and the soil is the human heart (v. 19). The emphasis is on the various kinds of hearts and how they reject or receive Christ's message.

The Hard Heart

The first type of soil represents the hard heart, of which there are many today as well as in Christ's time. It is described as soil along the path (v. 4). This ground has been trampled down by the many feet that have passed that way over scores of years. Because the soil is hard, the seed that falls there merely lies on the path and does not sink in, and the birds (which Christ compares to the devil or the devil's workers) soon snatch it away. What is it that makes the human heart hard? There can be only one answer: sin. Sin hardens the heart, and the heart that is hardened sins even more broadly and deliberately.

This type of person is described in the first chapter of Romans. The person begins by suppressing the truth about God that may be known from nature (vv. 18–20), plunges into the spiritual ignorance and degradation that inevitably follows (vv. 21–31), and at last comes not only to practice the sins of evil persons but to *approve* of them as well (v. 32). Here we see both halves of the circle: Sin leads to a rejection of God and God's truth, and the rejection of truth leads to even greater sin. What is it that leads such a person to reject the truth of God in the first place? According to Paul, it is a determined opposition to the nature of God himself, which the apostle describes as human "godlessness and wickedness" (Rom. 1:18).

Virtually all God's attributes—whether sovereignty, holiness, omniscience, immutability, or even divine love—are offensive to the natural man, if he rightly understands them. So rather than repent of sin and turn for mercy to a God who is altogether sovereign, holy, knowing, and unchangeable, men and women suppress the knowledge they have and refuse to seek out the additional knowledge that could and should be the salvation of their souls.

Some years ago I heard a conversation between two women in which one asked the other, "Why is America in such a declining moral state?"

Her friend replied, "Because the people love sin." I cannot think of anything more profound than that. That is the message of Romans 1 in five words: *Because the people love sin.* Sin hardens people's hearts. Therefore, they will not receive the gospel of the kingdom of God when it is preached to them.

The opposition of the unregenerate heart to God's sovereignty is particularly evident in the kingdom parables, for kingdom means *rule,* and rule is the same as *sovereignty.* When Jesus came preaching the kingdom of God, he came preaching God's right to rule over the minds and hearts of all people. But that is precisely what the people involved did not want. Adam did not want it. He had great freedom, but he was offended by what he saw as God's unreasonable and arbitrary restriction of his eating from the tree of the knowledge of good and evil. If God exercised his sovereignty at that point, well . . . it was there that Adam would rebel. So he did—and he fell into death, carrying the rest of the race with him. This spirit of rebellion against God's sovereignty worked itself out in history until eventually the Lord Jesus Christ himself came to earth and the response of his people was, "We will not have this man to rule over us."

So it is also today. This is probably the greatest reason for the rejection of the gospel of God's grace in Jesus Christ at this or any other time in history. I heard of a man who said, "I believe that Jesus is the Son of God and that he died for sinners. But I guess I just don't want to give him my life. I want to make my own decisions." To think like that is fatal. What you need to do is humble yourself and yield your life to Jesus.

The Shallow Heart

The second type of soil stands for the shallow heart. Jesus described it as soil covering rocky ground. When the seed fell there it sank in, but only to a very shallow depth. It sprang up quickly, but it also faded quickly in the sun's heat because it had no root. Jesus described that person by saying, "The one who received the seed that fell on rocky places is the man who hears the word and at once receives it with joy. But since he has no root, he lasts only a short time. When trouble or persecution comes because of the word, he quickly falls away" (vv. 20–21).

Many people fit this description too. We see them in our evangelical churches. Their shallow hearts are attracted to the excitement of a place where much seems to be happening. They hear the gospel and seem to fit in. They even make a profession of faith. But then some difficulty arises—the loss of a job, misunderstandings with other Christians, sickness, even a bad romance—and just as suddenly as they once seemed to embrace the faith, they fall away because they were never really born again.

Several years ago I noticed an extreme case. The newspapers reported the arrest in Lakeland, Florida, of a man named Joseph Paul Franklin. He was wanted for questioning concerning a year-long series of shootings in Salt Lake City, Johnstown (Pennsylvania), Fort Wayne, Cincinnati, Minneapolis, and Oklahoma City. He had grown up in a bad home, dropped out of school at seventeen, and begun getting into trouble, with several arrests for carrying concealed weapons and disorderly conduct. But then, as one magazine went on to say in tracing his early life, "he became an Evangelical Christian."[2] After that he became a Nazi and then a Ku Klux Klansman. At one point he told friends he was going to join Ian Smith's Rhodesian army.

I had been reading that news item with only minimal interest, but when I came to the line about his being an "Evangelical Christian" my attention perked up. I wondered why that had been slipped in and whether it was just one more attempt on the part of the magazine's editors to discredit genuine Christianity. Upon reflection, I do not think it was. I think Franklin had indeed gone through Christianity as one stage in his warped development, and the magazine was simply reporting that fact fairly. The tragedy is not that a thing such as this is reported but that there are far too many like Franklin in our churches. Just being in church, mouthing the things you hear other people say, does not make you a Christian. Yours may be an extremely shallow heart. Your heart may be like rocky soil.

The Strangled Heart

The third type of soil stands for a strangled heart—a heart strangled by things. The Lord describes those things as thorns and says, "The one who received the seed that fell among the thorns is the man who hears the word, but the worries of this life and the deceitfulness of wealth choke it, making it unfruitful" (v. 22). We know this was true in Jesus' day because of our Lord's many warnings against riches: "I tell you the truth, it is hard for a rich man to enter the kingdom of heaven" (Matt. 19:23) and "It is easier for a camel to go through the eye of a needle than for a rich man to enter the kingdom of God" (Mark 10:25).

On one occasion a rich young man turned away sorrowfully because Jesus told him to sell everything he had and give it to the poor and he was unwilling to do it (Luke 18:23). If that was true in Jesus' day among people whom we would regard for the most part as quite poor, how much truer must it be in ours. We are choked with riches—we who have cars and houses and boats and bank accounts and all the modern gadgets of our materialistic culture.

There is this point too: Riches do not choke a person all at once. It is a gradual process. Like the weeds in Christ's parable, riches grow up gradually. Slowly, slowly, they strangle the budding of spiritual life within. Beware of that if you either have great possessions or are on your way to acquiring them. Above all, beware if you are saying, "I need to provide for myself now. I'll think about spiritual things when I am older."

Jesus warned against that in another story about a man whose fields produced such a good crop that he tore down his barns and built bigger ones, saying to himself, "You have plenty of good things laid up for many years. Take life easy; eat, drink and be merry." Jesus' words were, "You fool! This very night your life will be demanded from you. Then who will get what you have prepared for yourself?" (see Luke 12:16–21).

The Open Heart

The last type of soil is the one to which the entire parable has been building. It is the open heart, the heart that receives the gospel like good soil receives seed. This soil produces a good crop, says Jesus, "yielding a hundred, sixty or thirty times what was sown" (v. 23).

Here many minor points might be made.

1. Only a portion (in the parable, one-fourth) of the preaching of the gospel bears fruit—in Christ's or any other age. We should remember that even Jesus did not get all people to believe on him, though many did, and if this is so, we must not think we have failed when people reject our message. On the other hand, we should be encouraged in our witnessing by knowing that some *will* believe.

2. The only sure evidence of a genuine reception of the Word of God in a person's life is spiritual fruit. Although we are not saved by our good works, the total absence of them indicates that we have never been truly saved.

3. The presence of fruit is the important thing, not the amount of it, at least in most cases.

But these points are all less important than the main one, namely, that it is only the open heart that receives the preaching of the gospel and is saved. Not the hard heart. Not the shallow heart. Not the strangled heart. The only heart that ever receives the truth of the gospel and is saved is the heart that opens itself to Jesus and his teaching.

Which leads to this most important question: Do you have an open heart? Are you receptive to God's truth? Have you allowed the teaching of the Bible to settle down into your life so that you have turned from sin, placed your whole faith in Jesus, and begun to produce the Holy Spirit's fruit? You may say, "I'm afraid not. I wish my heart were like that, but I'm afraid it is hard or shallow or strangled by this world's goods. What can I do? Is my case hopeless?"

No, it is not. It is true that you can do nothing, any more than soil can change its nature. But although you can do nothing, there is one who can: the divine Gardener. He can break up the hard ground, uproot the rocks, and remove the thorns. That is your hope—not you, but the Gardener. Notice what God said through the prophet Ezekiel, who wrote to the hard-hearted of his day. "I will sprinkle clean water on you, and you will be clean; I will cleanse you from all your impurities and from all your idols. I will give you a new heart and put a new spirit in you; I will remove from you your heart of stone and give you a heart of flesh. And I will put my Spirit in you and move you to follow my decrees and be careful to keep my laws" (Ezek. 36:25–27).

A few minutes ago I referred to the rich young man who turned from Jesus sorrowfully because he was unwilling to sell his riches. He seemed to be open to the gospel. He had even asked Jesus how he might be saved. But riches were choking him, and he was unable to leave them in order to become Christ's disciple. Jesus remarked on how difficult it is for the rich to enter God's kingdom, and the disciples asked, "Who then can be saved?" They were beginning to recognize the serious nature of the problem.

Jesus replied, "What is impossible with men is possible with God" (Luke 18:26–27). In other words, said Jesus, "With God all things are possible" (Matt. 19:26). And so they are! Not just for someone else either. They are possible for *you*, if God does the work. What you need to do is turn to Christ and allow him to give you an open heart that will receive the gospel. Admit that you have a hard, calloused, grasping, covetous, or even frivolous heart, and ask him to save you anyway.[3]

28

The Parables of the Weeds, Mustard Seed, and Yeast

Matthew 13:24–43

Jesus told them another parable: "The kingdom of heaven is like a man who sowed good seed in his field. But while everyone was sleeping, his enemy came and sowed weeds among the wheat, and went away. When the wheat sprouted and formed heads, then the weeds also appeared.

"The owner's servants came to him and said, 'Sir, didn't you sow good seed in your field? Where then did the weeds come from?'

"'An enemy did this,' he replied.

"The servants asked him, 'Do you want us to go and pull them up?'

"'No,' he answered, 'because while you are pulling the weeds, you may root up the wheat with them. Let both grow together until the harvest. At that time I will tell the harvesters: First collect the weeds and tie them in bundles to be burned; then gather the wheat and bring it into my barn.'"

He told them another parable: "The kingdom of heaven is like a mustard seed, which a man took and planted in his field. Though it is the smallest of all your seeds, yet when it grows, it is the largest of garden plants and becomes a tree, so that the birds of the air come and perch in its branches."

He told them still another parable: "The kingdom of heaven is like yeast that a woman took and mixed into a large amount of flour until it worked all through the dough."

Nothing good has ever come into the world without opposition, and that is especially true in spiritual matters. Here we face not only the hostility of mere people like ourselves but satanic opposition as well. That is why the Bible warns us to be on our guard against the devil, who, we are told, "prowls around like a roaring lion looking for someone to devour" (1 Peter 5:8). The Scripture alerts us to the devil's "schemes," because he must not be able to "outwit us" (2 Cor. 2:11).

Since we have an enemy who is so fiercely opposed to the extension of God's rule on earth, we should not be surprised to find the Lord warning us against his devices in the parables of the kingdom in Matthew 13. Jesus does this clearly in the second parable, showing how the devil, like the enemy of a certain farmer, sows weeds in God's field, meaning that he scatters non-Christians among believers. The weeds of this parable are almost certainly a plant called bearded darnel *(lolium temulentum)*, which is closely related to wheat and is difficult to distinguish from it when the plants are young. Moreover, the roots of the two plants entangle themselves so that pulling up one would necessarily mean pulling up the other. When the plants are older, it is easy to tell them apart. According to the parable, the separation will come only at the final judgment.

Jesus also warns against Satan's evil devices in the third and fourth parables, in my opinion, though Jesus speaks without explanation and many commentators interpret these parables differently than I do. Jesus tells of a mustard seed that grew up to be a great tree and of yeast that a woman mixed into a large amount of dough. Some see these tales as pictures of the steady growth and influence of the church, but in my judgment they alert us to two more strategies Satan uses to harm the church in the period between Christ's first coming and his second coming.

The Parable of the Weeds

The first of these parables is the easiest to interpret (though it has some difficult parts), both because much of it is self-evident and because the Lord explains it in verses 36–43. The parable is in verses 24–30.

In discussing this passage, some have made much of a detail in Christ's explanation, found in verse 38. In the previous verse Jesus had explained that "the one who sowed the good seed is the Son of Man"—an explanation that no doubt applies to the first parable as well and shows that the parables are all somewhat linked. Then he goes on to say, "The field is the world" (v. 38). Some have stressed that point, arguing that if the field is the world, it cannot be the church. Therefore, Christ's prohibition against trying to separate the weeds from the grain before the final judgment should not be applied to the church. We need church discipline.

The concern over that interpretation is a valid one, because the church should strive to maintain purity. Other passages in the New Testament instruct us to work for that goal. But to argue for that idea leads us off track as far as the interpretation of the parable is concerned. For one thing, it is impossible to make a rigid distinction between the world and the church in this parable since, a little farther on, Jesus speaks of the angels weeding "out of *his kingdom* everything that causes sin and all who do evil" (v. 41). God's kingdom is not the world in general, so any interpretation based exclusively on the phrase "the field is the world" should be suspect.

Again, what is the point of the devil planting children "in the world," if all it means is that the devil's children and God's children live side by side? At best that is self-evident. Besides, if that is what Jesus means, the parable is not even stating the situation in the best way. If the field is the world rather than the church, it would be more correct to say that the devil's people are in the world already and that it is Jesus, rather than Satan, who plants his seed among that which is already growing. It would be Jesus who does the new thing, not Satan. However, as Jesus tells the story, the point is what *Satan* is doing, and that is something done after Jesus has already sown his seed. In other words, the devil places his own counterfeit Christians among true believers to hinder God's work.

So that is the real message, and whether the field is the world or the church is actually irrelevant. The point is simply that the devil is going to bring forward people (whether in the church or out of it) so much like true Christians, though they are not Christians, that even the servants of God will not be able to tell them apart. Consequently, although we want a pure church and will certainly exercise church discipline to the best of our ability in clear cases, we must not think we will achieve our full desire in this age. Even in our exercise of valid church discipline we must be extremely careful not to discourage or damage some for whom Christ died.

I find the following applications in this parable.

1. *If the devil is mixing his people in among true Christians, then we should be alert to that fact.* We should be on our guard not to be taken in by those who pretend to be Christians but are not, and we should not be surprised if the devil's people show up in strange places or eventually show their true colors by abandoning Christianity entirely. In 2 Corinthians Paul gives just such a warning, pointing out that "Satan himself masquerades as an angel of light" and that "it is not surprising, then, if his servants masquerade as servants of righteousness" (2 Cor. 11:14–15). "Servants of righteousness" can describe ministers. So we have a proverb that says rightly, "When you look for the devil, don't forget to look in the pulpit."

Again, we are not to be surprised if some eventually repudiate the faith and leave the Christian fellowship. John also wrote about such people, saying, "They went out from us, but they did not really belong to us. For if they had belonged to us, they would have remained with us; but their going showed that none of them belonged to us" (1 John 2:19).

2. *The mixed nature of the Christian assembly should not be an excuse for unbelievers to refuse to come to Christ.* Jesus did not pretend (nor should we) that the Christian church is perfect. It is anything but. Sometimes those who are not Christians say, "I'm not a Christian because the church is filled with hypocrites." But that is itself a hypocritical statement. It implies that the one

making it is better than those whom he rejects, which is probably not true. At best it is not the whole truth since there are deeper reasons why people will not become Christians. Still, the real problem is that if the objection were to be met (that is, if hypocrisy and other sins were to be completely eliminated among the people of God), there would be no place for the objector! The critic, who is himself a sinner and a hypocrite, would not fit in. There is a place for him only because Jesus came "not . . . to call the righteous, but sinners" to repentance (Matt. 9:13).

3. *No one should take comfort in sin.* The church is impure because, as Luther said, every Christian is *simul justus et peccator* ("at the same time righteous and a sinner"). We cannot always distinguish between the wheat and tares in this age. But a day is coming when that distinction will be made. The harvest will happen, the wheat will be gathered into God's barn, and the tares will be burned. As a result, we should examine ourselves as to whether we are true children of God or not. We should be careful to make our "calling and election sure," as Peter indicates (2 Peter 1:10).

The Mustard Seed and Yeast

The next two of Christ's parables (vv. 31–33) belong together. Each should help us to understand the other. Of all the parables Jesus told, however, none has produced such diametrically opposed interpretations as these two. On the one hand, most Bible students understand these parables to be about the kingdom's steady expansion and growth, so that in time it will come to fill the whole world. On the other hand, others see them as warnings against two of the devices the devil will use to corrupt the church over time. The problem remains because nothing Jesus said either in the parables themselves or elsewhere explains clearly what they mean.

Representative of the first explanation is William M. Taylor, who wrote an excellent book on the parables. He said of the story of the mustard seed: "A great result from a small beginning, a large growth from a little germ—that is the one thought of the parable, and of that the Lord declares that the kingdom of heaven upon the earth is an instance." He writes of the yeast, "The great truth here illustrated, then, is that the Lord Jesus Christ, by his coming and work, introduced into humanity an element which works a change on it, that shall continue to operate until the whole is transformed—therein resembling leaven, hidden by a woman in three measures of meal until the whole was leavened."[1]

Most postmillennialists and many amillennialists take this view since it fits their eschatology—the kingdom's triumph in the world before Christ's return. But others hold to this view simply because they regard it as the obvious meaning of the stories. D. A. Carson argues that it fits the context best because it explains how Jesus' work is actually the inauguration of the kingdom in spite of its meager start. "In both parables it is clear that at present the kingdom of heaven operates, not apocalyptically, but quietly and from small beginnings."[2] Small now, but triumphant in time! And, of course, that is the way the Christian church has grown throughout history.

The other viewpoint is represented by Arno C. Gaebelein, who sees the parables as teaching an abnormal and harmful bureaucratic expansion of the church and the devil's work of undermining it by the infusion of sin, represented by the yeast. He writes, "All these parables show the growth of *evil*, and are prophecies extending over the entire age in which we live."[3]

What are we to think about these two interpretations?

We should say first that whatever our interpretation of the parables might be, there is much more theological agreement between people who take these two sides than the interpretations themselves would indicate. To be sure, there is a profound disagreement as to whether the kingdom of God is going to be victorious in this age. Postmillennialists would say yes. Premillennialists would say no. But even here there is a measure of agreement. Both acknowledge that Christians are sent into the whole world with the gospel—the essence of the Great Commission. Both would agree that there has been an effective and striking growth of Christianity from its small beginnings at the time of Christ's death to its position as a major world religion today. Both would acknowledge the evils in the church, which the second explanation highlights.

So we may begin by realizing that—with the sole exception of whether the church is to be victorious in the world or only affect a part of it—*most* of the points any one interpreter would insist on would be accepted by the other side. We can even say that either explanation can be justified in one way or another as fitting into the development of the parables of the kingdom in this chapter.

But we do have to think of the stories one way or the other. And since I have already indicated that I lump them together with the second parable that tells of the devil's work in sowing tares among God's wheat, let me give my reasons for interpreting them as I do.

1. *The growth of a mustard seed into a tree is abnormal.* That is, a mustard seed does not grow into a tree; it is a shrub.[4] Those to whom Christ spoke would know that. So when he spoke of the unusual growth of this seed, his hearers would have been alerted at once to the fact that something in the situation was profoundly abnormal or wrong. If Jesus had wanted to stress the "victorious church" view, he should have referred to an acorn growing up to be a mighty oak or a cedar seed growing up to be one of the lofty trees of Lebanon.

2. *In the context of Matthew 13 the birds, who (in this parable) rest in the mustard tree's branches (v. 32), have already (in parable one) been identified as the devil or the devil's messengers (v. 19).* It is true that an element of one parable need not necessarily carry the same meaning in the next, but it would be strange if an element that symbolized evil at the beginning of the chapter carried a totally different meaning just thirteen verses later. Besides, who are the birds who roost in the church's branches if not those evil persons whom the devil

has sown among believers? If they are not Satan's people, who they are is unexplained. On the other hand, if the birds are the devil's followers, then there is an immediate and obvious carry-over into the parable of the yeast, for the yeast would represent the same thing as the birds do in verse 32. The parable of the yeast would just add the thought that the presence of evil is pervasive, not merely in the hierarchical structures of the church but in its many members and its life.

3. *In nearly all cases in the Old Testament (and in Jewish life today) yeast is a symbol of evil.*[5] In the sacrificial laws of Israel it was excluded from every offering to the Lord made by fire. At the time of the feast of unleavened bread, every faithful Jew was to search his home for any trace of yeast and then get rid of it. That is done today by orthodox Jews and symbolizes for them, as it did earlier, the putting away of sin. Again, just three chapters after this Jesus speaks of the yeast of the Pharisees and Sadducees, meaning their evil influence (Matt. 16:12; see Mark 8:15, where he refers to "the yeast of the Pharisees and that of Herod"). Likewise, Paul described deviation from the truth of the gospel as Satan's evil persuasion, adding that believers should beware since "a little yeast works through the whole batch of dough" (Gal. 5:9; see 1 Cor. 5:6).

Some have argued that yeast is not always a symbol of evil, and that is true. Sometimes it is simply yeast. But when it has a symbolic meaning, it is nearly always used to represent something evil rather than something good. It is difficult to see how an important and thoroughly understood symbol of evil could be used by Jesus to represent the exact opposite, namely, the blessed impact of his gospel on the world.

4. *It is significant that these two parables are bracketed by that of the devil's work in sowing tares among the wheat (vv. 24–30) and Christ's explanation of that parable (vv. 36–43).* The structure suggests that they should be taken not as teaching something entirely different from the parable of the tares but as expanding on it.

The Secular Church

Let's bring this discussion to a close. As Christians, we must be on guard against Satan's tactics. We are warned not only against his infusion of his own people into the Christian community but also against the visible church's bureaucratic growth (which confuses money, size, and structure with spiritual fruit) and against the infusion of evil into the lives even of believing people (which confuses a loving and forgiving spirit with treason to Christ's cause). In other words, we are to beware of the church becoming secular, that is, of becoming like the world around it.

The secular church is a church that is conformed to the world, as much of the contemporary church is. It is characterized by the world's wisdom, the world's theology, the world's agenda, and the world's methods. When the evangelical church becomes worldly, it may still be trying to do God's work, but it will be trying to do it in the world's way. It looks to the media and money rather than to God and his power to advance the gospel.

What has hit me like a thunderbolt in recent years is the discovery that what I had been saying about the liberal churches at the end of the 1960s and the beginning of the 1970s now needs to be said about evangelicals too. A few years ago Martin Marty, always a shrewd observer of the American church scene, said in an interview that in his judgment by the end of the century evangelicals would be "the most worldly people in America." He was on target when he said that, except that he was probably a bit too sanguine, since many evangelicals were functioning in a secular way long before the year 2000.

How has that happened? Like the liberals before us, evangelicals use the Bible's words but give them new meaning, pouring bad secular content into spiritual terminology. Sin becomes dysfunctional behavior. Salvation becomes self-esteem or wholeness. Jesus becomes more of an example for right living than a Savior from sin. Again, people are told how to have happy marriages and raise nice children but not how to get right with an offended God. As far as a worldly agenda is concerned—forget world hunger, racism, or ecology—what we seem to want most in life is to be left in peace with sufficient prosperity to enjoy our well-deserved leisure. Far be it from us to preach a gospel that would expose people's sins, make them uncomfortable, and drive them to the Savior.

When you put these contemporary evangelical characteristics together, it is difficult to escape the feeling that Jesus' parable of the yeast has been fulfilled in us, and all too visibly.

What can we do if we find that we have been permeated by the "yeast" of Satan's strategies? Under normal circumstances, yeast that has begun to work cannot be eradicated. That is why it is such a good picture of the evil that will be in the church and world until the return of Jesus Christ. But although in baking we would never be able to rid dough of yeast, in the spiritual realm we can have important successes—at least where we ourselves (and perhaps our immediate families and churches) are concerned. Paul writes to the Corinthians, "Get rid of the old yeast that you may be a new batch without yeast" (1 Cor. 5:7). And in Galatians, where he has been talking about the yeast of legalism, he says, "It is for freedom that Christ has set us free. Stand firm, then, and do not let yourselves be burdened again by a yoke of slavery" (Gal. 5:1; see v. 9).

Satan is active. The yeast of the Pharisees does work. But "thanks be to God! He gives us the victory through our Lord Jesus Christ" (1 Cor. 15:57). God will purify his people. He will bring his church to complete maturity and holiness in time. Jesus does not leave these important points out of his teaching, which is why, in the next parables, we are going to see the divinely imparted character of those who seize the kingdom and work with God to achieve that kingdom's victory.[6]

29

The Parables of the Hidden Treasure, Pearl, and Net

Matthew 13:44–58

"The kingdom of heaven is like treasure hidden in a field. When a man found it, he hid it again, and then in his joy went and sold all he had and bought that field.

"Again, the kingdom of heaven is like a merchant looking for fine pearls. When he found one of great value, he went away and sold everything he had and bought it.

"Once again, the kingdom of heaven is like a net that was let down into the lake and caught all kinds of fish. When it was full, the fishermen pulled it up on the shore. Then they sat down and collected the good fish in baskets, but threw the bad away. This is how it will be at the end of the age. The angels will come and separate the wicked from the righteous and throw them into the fiery furnace, where there will be weeping and gnashing of teeth."

A caricature of Calvinism takes issue with the doctrines of election and "irresistible" grace. It imagines a case in which a certain individual—we'll call him George—does not want to be saved. George loves sin and never looks beyond it. Although he has heard the gospel of salvation by grace through faith in Jesus Christ, he has no interest in it. But God has elected this person. So although George does not want to be saved, he is nevertheless dragged by the scruff of his neck into heaven "kicking and screaming," a reluctant convert.

On the other hand, a second individual—let's call her Mary—wants to be saved. Every time Mary hears the gospel she is enraptured by it. Whenever an invitation is given, she is the first one out of her seat. But God has not elected her. She wants to be saved, but she cannot be saved. God says, "Mary, this salvation of mine through Christ is not for you. It is for others. You must remain where you are. You cannot come to heaven."

This is a misunderstanding of Calvinism, for in election and "irresistible" grace God does not disregard or act contrary to the will of any man or woman. Rather, he regenerates the individual, and as a result, a will is born that now desires what the old will previously despised. Before, George hated Christ. Now he loves him and comes willingly when the gospel is preached. Again, if Mary desires to come, it is not in spite of God's predetermination but because of it.

One commentator says:

> When [people are] made over again . . . they come running irresistibly because they would not have it any other way. You can put all kinds of obstacles in their path, but they are men of violence. They are going to take the kingdom by force! When they find this pearl they are going to sell everything they have and get it. That hidden treasure is going to be theirs. They are going to have, because they hunger and thirst after righteousness.[1]

The Treasure and the Pearl

I begin this way because the prior work of God in a person's heart is the underlying presupposition of the parables of the treasure and the pearl. These parables describe the kind of people who have already been made alive in Christ. To use the imagery of the first two parables, they are the ones in whom the seed of the gospel has already been planted and is beginning to bear fruit. In the first, a man finds a treasure in a field. "When [he] found it, he hid it again, and then in his joy went and sold all he had and bought that field" (v. 44) In the second, Jesus describes a merchant looking for pearls. "When he found one of great value, he went away and sold everything he had and bought it" (v. 46).

The point of these parables lies in the nature and the resulting action of those who discover the treasure, which is the gospel. In these matters the man who discovered the treasure and the merchant who found the pearl are identical. They make every effort to possess what they discovered. There is a contrast that should not be overlooked, however. The man who found the hidden treasure was apparently not looking for it—his discovery was what we would call an accident—but in the case of the merchant, the finding of the pearl was the result of a long and faithful quest.

That contrast aptly describes the past experiences of people who find salvation. Some were not particularly anxious to find Christ—in fact, they were not even very interested in religion. They were going on their way when suddenly an unexpected thing confronted them: the gospel. They had never really heard it before. They were not seeking it. But there it was, and at once, with that insight granted by God's internal work of regeneration, they saw that this was a prize of far greater value than anything that had ever come into their lives previously. They saw themselves as sinners in need of a Savior. They saw Jesus as that Savior. They recognized that if they had him, they had all else besides. So they turned to him and believed, on the spot. Their case illustrates Isaiah's words: "I revealed myself to those who did not ask for me; I was found by those who did not seek me" (Isa. 65:1).

The other type of person is one who had sought God, though he had found the way difficult. It could be said of him as it is said in this hymn:

> I sought the Lord, and afterward I knew
> He moved my soul to seek him, seeking me;
> It was not I that found, O Savior true;
> No, I was found of thee.

But this person did not know during those years of seeking that God was seeking him as well. Those were dark years. At times he nearly despaired, but then suddenly the pearl of great price was before him, and he laid everything else aside to secure that most valued object. These are the people of whom Jesus spoke when he said, "Ask and it will be given to you; seek and you will find; knock and the door will be opened to you" (Matt. 7:7).

Pursuing the Prize

Here is where the main lessons of the two parables are to be found, for although the early experiences of these two men were different, once they had come upon the treasure, which is the gospel, they acted in similar ways. What did they do? First, they recognized the value of what they had found. Second, they determined to have it. Third, they sold everything to make their purchase. Fourth, they acquired the treasure.

1. *The two men recognized the value of what they had found.* It is not surprising that the merchant recognized the value of the special pearl, for he had been seeking pearls and had presumably learned their value (or lack of value) through his seeking. Nor is it surprising that the man who discovered the hidden treasure saw its value. He was not seeking it, but we can hardly imagine him casually kicking at the treasure with his foot and walking on. A treasure *is* valuable, after all.

We are inclined to say that a person who discovers treasure anywhere or in any form and then walks away from it is a fool. But many do that with the gospel. The gospel is preached; it is the answer to all our individual and community needs, for this life and for eternity. But despite that fact, millions simply walk away and continue in their spiritual poverty.

Do you want to know the character of one who has been made alive by God? He says with David, "I would rather be a doorkeeper in the house of my God than dwell in the tents of the wicked" (Ps. 84:10). He says of God's laws, "They are more precious than gold, than much pure gold" (Ps. 19:10). He declares, "Because I love your commands more than gold, more than pure gold, and because I consider all your precepts right, I hate every wrong path" (Ps. 119:127–28). He cries, "Forgetting what is behind and straining toward what is ahead, I press on toward the goal to win the prize for which God has called me heavenward in Christ Jesus" (Phil. 3:13–14). Such a person has already had a change of values. He has recognized the poverty of all that comes from man and has seen the true splendor of the gospel.

2. *They determined to have it.* The second thing that characterized both the man who found the treasure and the merchant who discovered the pearl was their determination to have what they found. The stories do not spell it out, but imagine this contrast. Here is a person who sees the value of his discovery but decides, upon reflection, that it will be too much trouble to acquire the treasure for himself. He would have to adjust his priorities. He would have to sell his goods and change his lifestyle, and that would take time and effort. He might be misunderstood by his family or friends. True, the treasure would make him a rich man, but the changes required would be too difficult. We may imagine such a situation, but that is not the case with the ones described in these parables. These men determined to acquire the treasure or the pearl for themselves.

3. *They sold everything to make their purchase.* What did it take for each of them to possess these treasures? It required giving up other things. Having recognized the value of their discovery and having determined to have it, they sold all they had to make the purchase. Nothing in the stories should be construed as teaching that salvation can be bought, except in the sense of Isaiah 55:1: "Come, all you who are thirsty, come to the waters; and you who have no money, come, buy and eat! Come, buy wine and milk without money and without cost." But if that is the case, what is the point of the man and the merchant selling their goods? It is a picture of renouncing everything that might be a hindrance to attaining the prize. Martin Luther had it right when he wrote, "Let goods and kindred go, this mortal life also." Luther did not think for a moment that salvation could be purchased by works or the renunciation of valued people or possessions, but he was determined that nothing, not even life itself, should keep him from God's kingdom.

4. *They acquired the treasure.* Having recognized the value of their discovery and having sold everything in their desire to have it, the man who discovered the treasure and the merchant who discovered the pearl then made their purchase. They acquired that on which their desires had been set.

This speaks of individual appropriation. It tells us that salvation does not consist merely in seeing the value of Christ's work and wanting it for oneself. Christ must actually become ours by faith, which is the means of appropriation. Faith has three elements. There is an intellectual element, in which we recognize the truths of the gospel. There is an emotional or heart element, in which we find ourselves being drawn to what we recognize. There is also a volitional element, in which we actually make a commitment to him whom the gospel presents. Salvation is a personal matter. People are not saved by Jesus en masse. They are saved one by one as by the grace of God they recognize their need and come to Jesus, trusting that he is who he claimed to be (the Son of God) and that he did what he claimed he would do (provide for our salvation through his death on our behalf). The man in the field did not allow someone else to buy the treasure, hoping that he might share in it. The merchant did not form a cooperative to acquire the pearl of great price. Each made the purchase for himself.

Do not think, if you are teetering on the brink of decision, that having renounced everything for Jesus you will one day find yourself disappointed at what will have proved to be a bad bargain. You will not find yourself coming back with your treasure or pearl, hoping to get your property back. It is never that way. In the exchange described by these parables, the men who made their purchases received a bargain. They made the deal of their lives, their fortune, and they were happy.

So it will be for you. You are not called to poverty in Christ but to the greatest spiritual wealth. You are not called to disappointment but to fulfillment. You are not called to sorrow but to joy. How could it be otherwise when the treasure is the only Son of God? How can the outcome be bad when it means salvation?

The Parable of the Net

The last parable in Matthew 13 introduces a new life situation, fishing and fishermen, but it makes almost the same points as the parable of the wheat and tares growing up together until the harvest, when there is a gathering of both followed by a separation. In the last of these parables, a gathering of fish is followed by a separation of the good from the bad. In both parables we have the work of the angels who do the gathering and separating. We even have a repetition of key phrases: "the end of the age" (vv. 40, 49), and "throw them into the fiery furnace, where there will be weeping and gnashing of teeth" (vv. 42, 50).

What, then, does the last parable teach that has not already been taught? Or to put it another way, why is this parable included? Is there anything new in this last parable? We might think that the new element is our role in drawing men and women into the gospel net, but that is not the way Jesus interprets his story. He compares the fishermen to angels, not to his earthly messengers, and the setting is not the age of gospel proclamation but the judgment.

As we make the comparisons, there is a point at which the repetition itself becomes the "new" thing, and the unique emphasis is not so much in what is repeated but in what is left out. There is no explanation of how the fish got into the water in the first place. Nothing is said about their growth or lack of it. There are no human workers, not even a devil. The only thing we have is the separation of the good fish from the bad, the wicked from the righteous, and the suffering of those who are cast into hell. The only really new element is the warning to the wicked. It is as though Jesus is saying with all possible emphasis: *"There is a coming judgment, and the fate of the ungodly will be terrible in that day."*

A Final Separation

Jesus' picture of the final judgment as a separation of good from bad fish (or a separation of wheat from tares) hits on the essential nature of judgment, for the word *judgment* means "to separate." In Hebrew, judgment refers chiefly to the work of a judge or lawgiver. But one meaning of the Hebrew word is "to discriminate" or make distinctions, and in Greek, *krisis* literally means "to divide." Jesus described the judgment that way. It is always a thorough and eternal separation.

Here are four important facts about God's judgment.

1. *It is thorough.* The time for mixture in any form will be over. Here we have mixture all the time. We do some good things, but our good is always mixed with evil. There are redeemed people in the church, but there are also those who are the devil's children. However, when the Lord sends his angels to execute judgment, those days will be over, and human beings will find themselves in one camp or the other. Either they will be with the blessed in heaven, having been cleansed from all sin by the redeeming work of Christ, or they will be in hell without Christ and without hope. No one will be partially in one camp and partially in the other.

2. *It is determined.* The second fact about God's judgment is that it has been previously determined in the sense that the grounds for separation between those who are saved and those who are lost will already have been established on earth. It will be determined by whether we have received the good seed of the gospel, whether we have believed in Christ, whether we have laid everything else aside to gain the hidden treasure or purchase the pearl. You know whether you have done that. So I ask, in which camp are you? If you are not with Christ now, you will be without Christ then. If you are with him now, you will be with him in the day of judgment.

3. *It is permanent.* Nothing could be more permanent than the collecting of the good fish and the discarding of the bad, or throwing the tares into the fire to be burned. In that day the opportunity for repentance will be over. The day for trusting in Jesus Christ will be past.

I wish I could say that the reality will be different, but I cannot, for Jesus himself does not. There is only one person who will tell you that. He is the devil, and he has been spreading that lie for centuries. He has told millions that the day of reckoning is always far off and that there will always be time for repentance or religion or whatever at a later date. In that way he has lulled millions to sleep, and they now drift on, oblivious to their danger.

Do not listen to the devil's lies. He cares nothing for you. He is a condemned and evil being who, knowing that he must perish, takes his sole delight in drawing others after him to a common doom. Instead, listen to the Lord Jesus Christ, who speaks truth. He speaks it in this parable so you may know that judgment is real, separation is coming, and the time for repentance is now. Hear him! Believe him! Turn from anything that would keep you from Jesus and throw yourself upon him and his work only.

4. *The end of the wicked will be dreadful.* The final point of Jesus' parable is the terrible fate of those who have not trusted and followed after Jesus Christ. I am glad Jesus taught that rather than leaving it for his ministers to imagine. How could we say that the end will be so bad that it can only be adequately compared to an eternal burning? How could we say that it will produce an eternal "weeping and gnashing of teeth"? No mere human being would dare predict that fate for another human being. Yet that is what Jesus does. He has more to say about hell than does any other person in the Bible.

What is it that makes hell so terrible, according to Jesus Christ? The first thing is suffering. Jesus teaches this in the parable of the dragnet, for having described how the wicked are thrown into the fiery furnace, he then describes them as "weeping and gnashing" their teeth.

The second thing that makes hell terrible is remembering the blessings of one's previous life and lost chances. In another story Jesus told how Abraham spoke to a man who was in hell, saying, "Son, *remember* that in your lifetime you received your good things, while Lazarus received bad things, but now he is comforted here and you are in agony" (Luke 16:24–25). That is one of the most chilling statements in the Bible. The rich man is told to remember, and what he has to remember is how he enjoyed a lifetime of good things without any reference to God. Now those good things are gone forever. He had his heaven on earth, but he will never enter it again, while Lazarus had his taste of hell here and is now enjoying God's heaven.

If you are without Christ, you should realize that however disappointing you think your life is now, there will come a day when it will seem good compared to your suffering. And the memory of your good things will haunt you and increase your suffering, unless you repent now and come to Jesus.

A Final Question

After Jesus had finished telling the parables of the kingdom, he asked the disciples, "Have you understood all these things?" (Matt. 13:51). They answered, "Yes." I find that answer amusing, since the parables of the kingdom have always been one of the most puzzling sections of the Word of God to most readers. Hardly anyone today would dare to say that he or she understands *all* these things. But the disciples thought they did. "Yes," they said, as if the matter were not at all difficult.

Of course, their yes did not actually mean that they *understood* all that Jesus was teaching, only that they *believed* all they did understand and were prepared to act on it. That is not bad. In fact, that is what is required of all who hear the gospel message.

It is in that sense that I ask the same question of you now: Do you understand these things? No doubt there is much you do not understand, just as there is much I do not understand. But do you believe what you *do* understand, and are you prepared to act on your understanding and come to Jesus? Admit that you are a sinner, in rebellion against God, deserving his judgment. Believe that in spite of those facts God sent his Son to be your Savior. Then commit yourself to Jesus Christ, promising to follow him as your Master, Lord, and Savior. The man who found the treasure and the merchant who discovered the pearl acted quickly. Jesus said, "Now that you know these things, you will be blessed if you *do* them" (John 13:17).[2]

Part Six

The Withdrawal of the King

30

The Death of John the Baptist

Matthew 14:1–12

At that time Herod the tetrarch heard the reports about Jesus, and he said to his attendants, "This is John the Baptist; he has risen from the dead! That is why miraculous powers are at work in him."

Now Herod had arrested John and bound him and put him in prison because of Herodias, his brother Philip's wife, for John had been saying to him: "It is not lawful for you to have her." Herod wanted to kill John, but he was afraid of the people, because they considered him a prophet.

On Herod's birthday the daughter of Herodias danced for them and pleased Herod so much that he promised with an oath to give her whatever she asked. Prompted by her mother, she said, "Give me here on a platter the head of John the Baptist." The king was distressed, but because of his oaths and his dinner guests, he ordered that her request be granted and had John beheaded in the prison. His head was brought in on a platter and given to the girl, who carried it to her mother. John's disciples came and took his body and buried it. Then they went and told Jesus.

When people read the Gospels for the first time, especially if they do so superficially, as most do, the Gospels seem to be mere collections of stories and teachings with little to connect them besides the obvious flow of events that mark the life of Jesus Christ. Even the order of events is sometimes puzzling. Yet there is far more to the arrangement of the Gospel material than this, and the more we study the Gospels the more profound the arrangement of the material seems to be.

That is what happens as we come to Matthew 14, the beginning of a section I have titled "The Withdrawal of the King" (chaps. 14–17). The chapter begins with the death of John the Baptist, which does not seem to have much to do with the ongoing story of Jesus. And what is worse, John's death is not in the correct sequence historically since the account indicates by means of a past tense verb in verse 3 ("had arrested") that the death of John occurred not at this point but earlier. All that happens here is that Herod Antipas, the one who had John killed, hears about Jesus and thinks that Jesus is John risen from the dead. The best handling of the facts would suggest that John was probably killed about a year before this, in A.D. 29.

Yet there is more to the account than appears at first. To understand what is going on, we need to remember two things.

First, we have just worked through a chapter in which Jesus predicted there would be opposition to his kingdom. The parable of the sower taught that only a part of gospel preaching will bear fruit. The parable of the wheat and tares pointed to the work of Satan as the kingdom's enemy. If my understanding of the stories of the mustard and yeast are correct, even more violent opposition was to be expected. This is exactly what we find now. At the end of chapter 13 we are told that the people of Jesus' hometown were offended by him and therefore rejected him, and here in chapter 14 we are reminded that Jesus' forerunner was likewise rejected even to the point of being killed. Are we to suppose that Jesus will experience any different treatment from the authorities?

Second, we have noticed a change in Jesus' teaching. He has turned away from the public preaching that had marked his work earlier to teach his own disciples in private. The parables of chapter 13 show this, for Jesus told only the first four to the crowds, who did not even understand them. Jesus explained them to his disciples later. Jesus told the last three parables to his disciples only.

What we have here is an important transition, and the reason Matthew includes the account of John's death becomes clear by the way the last verse of the account leads into verse 13. Verse 12 explains that after they had buried John, his disciples "went and told Jesus," after which we read, "When Jesus heard what had happened, he withdrew by boat privately to a solitary place." After the death of John, the handwriting was on the wall, and Jesus responded by withdrawing from the crowds and beginning to teach privately those he was going to leave behind.

The Murder of John the Baptist

Who was Herod? There are several Herods in the New Testament, the best known being Herod the Great, the founder of the Herodian dynasty. Herod the Great ruled at the time of Jesus' birth and was the one responsible for the murder of the infants of Bethlehem. The man who killed John was Herod Antipas. He is called a "king" (v. 9), but he was actually the tetrarch of Galilee, which means that he had a lower status than a king. *Tetrarch* is from the Greek word *tetra,* meaning "four." Originally it meant "a ruler over a fourth part of a kingdom," but it had come to mean only a lesser prince or governor. Herod's territory included Galilee and Perea. Since John's work had been in the area of Perea (see John 1:28) and Jesus' early work was in Galilee, both fell under Herod's official jurisdiction.

Herod ruled for more than thirty years, most of the time from Tiberias on the southwest shore of Galilee, not far from Capernaum or Nazareth. But at this point he seems to have been at the fortress of Machaerus, about seven miles northeast of the Dead Sea, since that is where John was imprisoned.

Herod's first wife was the daughter of Aretas, an Arabian king of the Nabateans, whose land bordered Perea. Herod divorced this woman to marry Herodias, the wife who appears in this story. Herodias had been married to Herod Antipas' half brother, and when Herod divorced his first wife to marry her, he created an explosive political situation. In fact, some years later it led to a war between Herod and Aretas in which Herod was defeated and was only saved from total disaster by the Romans. Any criticism of Herod's second marriage would have been like throwing sparks on dry tinder. It explains why Herod was so sensitive to John's words.

When John denounced Herod for his immoral behavior, it probably had very little to do with his divorce, which was allowed under both Jewish and Roman law. The problem was Herod's incestuous second marriage to Herodias, who was his half brother's wife. A marriage of this nature is explicitly condemned in Leviticus 18:16 and 20:21. Moreover, John did not merely speak out once against the marriage of Herodias and Herod. The text says that John was continually speaking out against it, using the imperfect tense of the verb "to say" *(elegen)* in verse 4. We can suppose that Herod brought John to the fortress of Machaerus to hear him, was stunned by John's forthright denunciation of his marriage, and then simply kept him there in prison, wanting to kill him but afraid to do so because of the people who thought John the Baptist was a prophet.

We can also understand that Herodias hated John for criticizing her marriage in this way. Herodias may have been urging the king to kill John, but Herod was resisting. One day, however, Herodias' opportunity came. Herod threw a party for his birthday, and Herodias sent her daughter by Herod Philip, her first husband, to dance before Herod and his guests. Josephus, the celebrated Jewish historian of that time, tells us that the daughter's name was Salome *(Antiquities,* XVIII, v, 4). She would have been very young, in her early teens. What is worse, it was highly improper for a girl of her class to dance in such a setting. Women performed at all-male parties, but they were slave girls who were subject to the desires of the men who attended such banquets. Matthew does not say that Salome's dance was sensual in nature, but the debased moral standards of Herod's court lead us to think it was.

John A. Broadus says, "It was therefore a bold step which Herodias took in sending her daughter to dance before Herod and his grandees."[1] Herod could have been offended. But Herodias understood men and reasoned that Herod and his drunken friends would be aroused by the young girl's dancing, which is what happened. The dance pleased Herod to such an extent that he rose to pompous extravagance before his guests and promised Salome anything she wanted. Prompted by her mother, the girl asked for the head of John the Baptist. Herod had made a foolish vow. He should never have made it, and having made it, he should never have kept it. But he wanted to save face and therefore granted Salome's request and had John beheaded in the prison.

So died the last of the Old Testament prophets. The old age ends in violence, and the stage is set for the unfolding of the new covenant of God's grace in Jesus Christ.

The Character of John the Baptist

We have already learned about John's strange appearance and his message from earlier references in Matthew. Here we learn several things about John's character.

1. *John was a righteous man.* Mark makes this point in his parallel account, explaining that "Herodias nursed a grudge against John and wanted to kill him. But she was not able to, because Herod feared John and protected him, knowing him to be a righteous and holy man" (Mark 6:20). Although Herod was far from righteous himself, he recognized righteousness in John and tried to protect him. Matthew shortens Mark's account and does not mention John's righteousness explicitly. But he has Herod testify to the same thing indirectly by reporting his fear that John had been raised from the dead and now possessed miraculous powers (v. 2). He imagined that God had thus vindicated the character of his prophet.

2. *John was an outspoken man.* It is one thing to be righteous; it is another thing to be outspoken about it, especially when standing before the great and powerful of this world. John was both.

Charles Colson tells what he witnessed when he would bring visitors to meet Richard Nixon when Nixon was president of the United States and Colson was special legal counsel to the president. Colson would gather the guests in a room outside the Oval Office, where they would talk to each other about what they were going to tell the president when they were face to face. "It was always the same," Colson wrote. "In the reception room they would rehearse their angry lines and reassure one another. 'I'll tell him what's going on. He's got to do something.'

"When the aide came to escort us in, they'd set their jaws and march toward the door. But once it swung open, the aide announcing, 'The president will see you,' it was as if they had suddenly sniffed some intoxicating fragrance. Most became almost self-conscious about even stepping on the plush blue carpet on which was sculpted the Great Seal of the United States. And Mr. Nixon's voice and presence—like any president's—filled the room.

"Invariably, the lions of the waiting room became the lambs of the Oval Office," said Colson.[2]

It is sad to report that none were more meek than the religious leaders. Of all people, they should have been the most outspoken. But they too wilted in the face of worldly power. Such is the awe of majesty that high office evokes. But John the Baptist did not cower before worldly power. He spoke out boldly and continued to do so, repeatedly saying to Herod, "It is not lawful for you to have her" (v. 4).

3. *John was a courageous man.* John was also courageous, for he could not have failed to know the danger he was placing himself in by continuing to denounce Herod for his marriage. Kings do not like to be confronted. Even more dangerous was the hatred of Herodias. John knew people well enough to know what was happening, but he continued to speak out and eventually died for his convictions.

John's fate reminds us of the kind of world in which we live. It is a world that has rejected Jesus and will reject his best disciples too. The world does not want to be told that it is sinful, that it has broken the holy law of God, that it needs a Savior, who is Jesus. But those who walk in the footsteps of John and the other saints who have preceded us will be as bold as these men were. How are any to be saved if we do not speak the truth about sin and preach the gospel boldly?

The Character of King Herod

The story does not tell us only about John, however. It also tells us about Herod, and what it reveals is that he was the exact opposite of John at every point.

1. *Herod was wicked.* John was righteous, but Herod was an evil man, even though he was not a particularly bad king as kings go. He betrayed his corrupt nature not only by his own evil acts but by his guilty conscience. Herod had seduced his brother Philip's wife, had wrongly imprisoned John, and now in a weak and drunken moment consented to John's murder without any kind of a trial. The execution was an outrage by Roman as well as by Jewish law. Moreover, it was Herod's knowledge of this wrong that caused him to suspect John had somehow come back to life after his unmerited execution. Herod was a Sadducee; Sadducees did not believe in the resurrection. But Herod's guilty conscience reduced his skeptical creed to dust, and he trembled at the thought of God's final judgment of him for this and for what had certainly been other evil actions.

What a powerful thing a guilty conscience is. John Ryle wrote:

> There is a conscience in all men by nature. Let this not be forgotten. Fallen, lost [and] desperately wicked as we are all born into the world, God has taken

> care to leave himself a witness in our bosoms. It is a poor blind guide, without the Holy Ghost: it can save no one; it leads no one to Christ; it may be "seared" and trampled under foot. But there is such a thing as conscience in every man, accusing him or excusing him; and Scripture and experience alike declare it (Rom. 2:15).
>
> Conscience can make even kings miserable, when they have wilfully rejected its advice; it can fill the princes of this world with fear and trembling, as it did Felix, when Paul preached. . . . God's witnesses may be put out of the way, but their testimony often lives and works on long after they are dead. God's prophets live not forever, but their words often survive them.[3]

2. *Herod was sly.* John was outspoken, but Herod was crafty, shrewd, deceptive, hypocritical, and devious, wanting to kill John but afraid to do it for fear of the people.

Mark tells us that Herod "liked to listen" to John (Mark 6:20). So we can suppose they talked often and imagine what some of those sessions may have been like. John would have spoken on "righteousness, self-control and the judgment to come," as Paul did in a similar setting before Felix (Acts 24:25). Herod would have trembled, as Felix did. He might even have agreed with John partway: "I see what you are getting at, John; you certainly have a point. I would probably think as you do if I were in your shoes. You are a good man. I admire you." But Matthew says that Herod actually wanted to kill John and would have done it earlier except that he was afraid of the people who considered John a prophet.

3. *Herod was weak.* John was courageous, but Herod was feeble, as many are who are more concerned for their reputations than for what is just or right. Herod knew that John was a righteous man. He knew that ordering his execution was an evil act. He knew that he had blundered in promising Salome anything she wanted because he had been infatuated with her dancing. But he was too weak to admit his mistake and too frightened of his wife's tantrums to uphold the moral law, which was his duty as the tetrarch. Herod could take a firm stand on wrong things, but he was weak on right things. Even his stand for the wrong betrayed his weakness.

4. *Herod was superstitious.* Many people who reject God's truth but nevertheless have an awareness of right and wrong become superstitious when they do wrong, because they sense that this is a moral universe and things cannot possibly go well for evildoers. Many follow horoscopes and believe almost any bizarre "spiritual" idea that comes their way. This is sad, but it always happens when people reject God and his written revelation in the Bible. When people stop believing in God, they do not believe in nothing. They believe anything.

Still the King

What a collection of characters we have encountered in this story. They provide a sad glimpse into the high life of antiquity, as well as what people are like today. There is Herod with his evil conscience. There is Herodias, a wicked, vengeful woman. There is Salome, already corrupted at a young age by her evil mother. There are the sensuous friends of Herod. And against them all is John the Baptist, whom everyone knew to be an upright, outspoken, and courageous man.

There is one character we have not talked about. He does not enter into the specific action of this story, though he is the most important person of all. He is Jesus himself, mentioned in the first verse of the story ("At that time Herod the tetrarch heard the reports about Jesus") and in the last verse ("Then they went and told Jesus").

Several commentators have pointed out that every time someone is "scandalized" or "offended" by a person in the Bible (see Matt. 13:57), that person is always Jesus. We have a good example of it here. Neither the citizens of Nazareth, nor Herodias, nor Salome, nor the drunken guests of Herod were offended by King Herod, because they were all like him to one degree or another. Nor were they offended by one another, for the same reason. Sinners like other sinners because they feel at home with them, and if their consciences bother them for some past evil acts, they can always point to some other sinner who is worse. It is comforting to have someone as evil as King Herod around.

True. But you do not get help from other sinners. Other people do not enable you to live an upright life, nor do they provide salvation from your sins. Only Jesus does that. Only Jesus can.

All of this means that in the final analysis the real contrast in this story is not between Herod and John the Baptist, as interesting as that is, but between King Herod and King Jesus. What happened to Herod? Herod killed John. But a few years after this, when Herod's brother Agrippa (the Herod of Acts 12) had been appointed king over the former tetrarchy of Philip, Herodias, who was always ambitious, pestered her husband until he went to Rome to see if he could not also be appointed a king. Unfortunately, Agrippa wrote to Emperor Caligula accusing Herod of treasonable dealings with the Parthians, and instead of being made a king, Herod was deposed and banished to Gaul, where he died.[4]

Think of the contrast. Herod did what those in power do. He used his power to preserve his power, but in the end he lost it and died a pauper's death. Jesus laid his power aside to die for his people, but today he rules in glory and will rule forever.

Herod was a petty king, but he looked kingly. Jesus was the King of kings, but he appeared in the days of his flesh as a humble Galilean peasant. Deceiving, if you look only at the outward appearance! Yet if you look beyond the appearance to who Jesus really was and listen attentively to what Jesus said, you will find yourself agreeing with John's testimony about him. John said, "I have seen and I testify that this is the Son of God" (John 1:34) and "Look, the Lamb of God, who takes away the sin of the world" (v. 29). John trusted in Christ and stood for righteousness. He died for it. But now John is with Jesus and will rule with him one day along with all who willingly and joyfully confess Jesus Christ as Lord and Savior.

First Corinthians 1:18 speaks of the "foolishness" of the cross, which is the way it seems to unbelievers. But the cross is actually the power of God for salvation for those who are being saved. It is for you if you will have it. It is for all who believe on Jesus.

31

The Feeding of the Five Thousand

Matthew 14:13–21

When Jesus heard what had happened, he withdrew by boat privately to a solitary place. Hearing of this, the crowds followed him on foot from the towns. When Jesus landed and saw a large crowd, he had compassion on them and healed their sick.

As evening approached, the disciples came to him and said, "This is a remote place, and it's already getting late. Send the crowds away, so they can go to the villages and buy themselves some food."

Jesus replied, "They do not need to go away. You give them something to eat."

"We have here only five loaves of bread and two fish," they answered.

"Bring them here to me," he said. And he directed the people to sit down on the grass. Taking the five loaves and the two fish and looking up to heaven, he gave thanks and broke the loaves. Then he gave them to the disciples, and the disciples gave them to the people. They all ate and were satisfied, and the disciples picked up twelve basketfuls of broken pieces that were left over. The number of those who ate was about five thousand men, besides women and children.

For some time now we have been looking at the change in Jesus' ministry that is found in the middle chapters of Matthew's Gospel (chaps. 11–16). Yet it is only in Matthew 14:13 that we come to it explicitly for the first time. We read in that verse, "When Jesus heard what had happened, *he withdrew by boat privately to a solitary place.*" It is because of this verse that I have titled Matthew 14–16 "The Withdrawal of the King."

The change has been coming ever since Jesus spoke his warning to the cities of Galilee in chapter 11, denouncing them for their failure to repent and turn to him; he warned that it would be more bearable for the notoriously wicked cities of Tyre, Sidon, and Sodom on the day of judgment than for them (vv. 20–24). Chapter 12 is almost entirely about the Pharisees and teachers of the law, with similarly strong words. Jesus called them a "brood of vipers" (v. 34), the chief representatives of that "wicked and adulterous generation" that asks for a sign but will not come to faith (v. 39). After this, Jesus began to teach in parables, saying that "the secrets of the kingdom of heaven" must be kept from those whose hearts are calloused (Matt. 13:11–15). At the end of that chapter he is rejected by the people of his own home city of Nazareth (vv. 54–57). At the start of chapter 14 we read of Herod's murder of John the Baptist and that John's disciples reported John's death to Jesus. It is at this point that we are told, "When Jesus heard what had happened, he withdrew by boat privately."

This section is characterized by three things: (1) Jesus' private teaching of the twelve disciples, (2) repeated failures on the disciples' part to understand or respond to Jesus' teaching, and (3) glimmerings of true faith and growth. The climax comes in chapter 16 in Peter's great christological confession ("You are the Christ, the Son of the living God," v. 16) and Jesus' subsequent teaching about the need for him to die and rise again (v. 21).

Jesus and the Crowds

We might suppose at this point that Jesus would have no more dealings with the masses. But surprisingly, instead of rejecting the crowds, Jesus continues to teach those who want to be taught—and heal and feed them too!

Jesus had withdrawn to a remote area on the northeast corner of the Sea of Galilee, not far from Bethsaida (Mark 6:45), crossing to it from the western side by boat. He wanted to be alone with his disciples. But the people saw where he was heading, and many walked around the lake so that they were waiting for him when he and his disciples landed. We are told that "he had compassion on them and healed their sick" (v. 14). In this way Matthew sets the stage for the miracle of the feeding of the five thousand that follows.

The feeding of this great crowd is the only miracle found in each of the four Gospels (see Mark 6:30–44; Luke 9:10–17; John 6:1–15), so it must have made a tremendous impact on those who were present. However, each Gospel contains different emphases. Mark is the closest to Matthew. Luke says that Jesus used the occasion to teach the people about the kingdom of God (Luke 9:11), which he had commissioned the disciples to do themselves in the passage immediately before this. John's version is the most independent and detailed. He says that the miracle was performed before the Jewish Passover (John 6:4), and he follows his account with Jesus' discourse on the bread of life (vv. 25–59). John's points are obvious! Jesus is the new Moses who feeds his people with spiritual food, and if they eat it, they will live forever. John's account ends with Peter's double testimony: "You have the words of eternal life" and "We believe and know that you are the Holy One of God" (vv. 68–69).

Two Banquets

But we are studying Matthew, not John or one of the other Gospels, and we want to learn what Matthew is teaching through this incident. The first lesson is stated clearly: Jesus cares about people, especially those who are poor or suffering. Verse 14 says, "When Jesus landed and saw a large crowd, he had compassion on them and healed their sick."

There is probably more to it than this, however, important as the mere fact of Jesus' compassion is. We should remember that Matthew makes some of his best points by the way he links incidents together, and if he is doing that here, we can hardly overlook the contrast between the party King Herod threw on his birthday for his friends and the party Jesus throws in the wilderness for the crowds. The first party is given by a king in his palace, the second by a Galilean preacher in the desert. The first was for the important people of this world, the second for the masses. The first was for Herod; it was his birthday. The second was centered on the crowds. The first was a drunken orgy, the second a pleasant country meal. The first was immoral; the high point was Salome's provocative dance. The second followed holy, edifying teaching by the Lord. The first ended with the murder of John the Baptist, the second by the feeding of those who had no food. The first was for this world only; the second anticipated the heavenly marriage supper to which people from every tribe and nation are invited and to which the poor of many nations will come.

What explains this contrast? The answer is this: Herod cared for no one but himself—his actions were determined by his lust for power and a desire to save face before his friends—while Jesus cared for other people. Jesus took time to heal, teach, and feed them, even though his first desire was to be alone with his disciples and teach them. Jesus' compassion for the masses is a reiterated theme in Matthew (see 9:36; 15:32; 18:27, 33; 20:34).

The first clear lesson of this story, therefore, is that Jesus cares for you, even though most of the other people in the world, especially the great and powerful people, do not. Most people who have power, prestige, or money do not care about others at all, even though they may pretend to, unless they have been saved and changed by Jesus himself. Your coworkers probably do not care a great deal about you. Even your friends are more interested in themselves and their problems than about you and your problems. So why do you spend so much time worrying about what others think and so little time bringing your cares to Jesus?

Joseph Scriven's poem of 1855 asks a good question and provides the correct answer:

Are we weak and heavy-laden,
Cumbered with a load of care?
Precious Savior, still our refuge—
Take it to the Lord in prayer!
Do thy friends despise, forsake thee?
Take it to the Lord in prayer!
In his arms he'll take and shield thee;
Thou wilt find a solace there.

When we bring our problems to Jesus, we bring them to one who not only cares about us and is compassionate but who understands us and is able to help us in our need. Peter wrote, "Cast all your anxiety on him because he cares for you" (1 Peter 5:7).

We Can Do Nothing

The second point of the story is clear in each of the Gospels, though it is introduced in different ways. It is this: In spiritual matters we can do nothing apart from Jesus Christ. Jesus said it himself in John 15:5: "If a man remains in me and I in him, he will bear much fruit; apart from me you can do nothing."

In one way or another each of the Gospels indicates that Jesus pressed this point on the disciples. In John, Jesus initiates the lesson by asking Philip, "Where shall we buy bread for these people to eat?" (John 6:5). The next words explain, "He asked this only to test him, for he already had in mind what he was going to do" (v. 6). The story continues by showing how Philip assessed the situation from a human perspective, replying, "Eight months' wages would not buy enough bread for each one to have a bite" (v. 7). It is after this that Andrew brings forward the boy with the "five small barley loaves and two small fish" (v. 9), which Jesus then uses for the miracle of the feeding. The emphasis is on the poor quality of the bread, only barley bread, and the smallness both of the loaves and fish.

Mark repeats the assessment that it would take "eight months of a man's wages" to buy food for so many people (Mark 6:37), and in Luke the disciples say, "We have only five loaves of bread and two fish—unless we go and buy food for all this crowd" (Luke 9:13). The first three Gospels also record the disciples' opinion that it would be best to send the people away so they could go into the surrounding towns and villages and buy food for themselves (Matt. 14:15; Mark 6:35–36; Luke 9:12).

What seems to have stuck out most clearly in the minds of Matthew, Mark, and Luke is that Jesus told the disciples to do something to improve the situation. He said, "*You* give them something to eat" (Matt. 14:16; Mark 6:37; Luke 9:13). The emphasis does not come across as forcefully in the English translation as it does in Greek. In Greek there is the added and usually unnecessary pronoun *you*. The emphasis seems to have been, "You, you do it; why do you come to me?" Since Jesus knew the nature of the problem and was already aware of what he was going to do, the only reason he said what he did was to impress on the disciples that they could do nothing by themselves.

What a lesson for us to learn! We tend to think that we can do at least something and that at worse all we really need is some specialized help from Jesus. We need to remember what Martin Luther said when he was reflecting on our "nothing." He said that our nothing really is nothing and not "a little something."

Yet we do have what God has first given to us, and although we can do nothing of spiritual value with it by ourselves, we will find that it is useful and sufficient if we place it in Jesus' hands. That is what happened here, of course. The disciples could do nothing, but they had five small loaves and two fish, and when they gave them to Jesus, they found that they were all that was necessary.

What did Moses have when God sent him to Pharaoh with the demand, "Let my people go"? All he had was a staff in his hand. But although Moses could do nothing with the staff, when he gave it to God, God used it to perform the miracles that led to the emancipation of the people.

What did David have when he went up against Goliath? A sling and a few small stones. But they were enough when God guided David's missile.

What can you do for Jesus? You know the answer to that as well as I do: nothing at all. But God has given you something that can be used effectively if you place it in Jesus' hands.

When I was preparing this lesson, I came across a wonderful quotation from Charles H. Spurgeon, relating the matter of the loaves and fish to his preaching. Spurgeon wrote, "Truly, he who writes this comment has often felt as if he had neither loaf nor fish; and yet for some forty years and more he has been a full-handed waiter at the King's great banquet."[1] It is like that for anyone who recognizes his or her own spiritual impotence and places all he or she has been given in Christ's hands.

The Sufficiency of Jesus Christ

All I have said about our impotence leads directly to the next lesson, for the story is meant to direct us to the sufficiency of Jesus Christ. That is what John 15:5 says, after all. The last part stresses our inability to do anything, but it does this so we will draw on Jesus' resources: "If a man remains in me and I in him, he will bear much fruit." Only after that does it say, "apart from me you can do nothing."

We *can* bear fruit, indeed, "much fruit" (v. 5) and even "fruit that will last" (v. 16). But this will be the case only if Jesus is working through us since he alone is able to meet anyone's spiritual need.

In this story Jesus meets the needs of the crowds abundantly. He took the five loaves of bread and two fish, directed the people to sit down, and then, looking to heaven and thanking God for the food, broke the food and distributed it to the people. The story concludes by saying, "They all ate and were satisfied, and the disciples picked up twelve basketfuls of broken pieces that were left over. The number of those who ate was about five thousand men, besides women and children" (vv. 20–21).

That is worth some serious reflection. In the first place, having enough food was a serious matter in the ancient world, because the rains would often fail, crops would wither, and people would starve. In our day, when we want something to eat, all we have to do is go to the store and buy it. In biblical times, however, if a person had enough food to eat, it was a gift from God and something for which to be particularly thankful. People knew that God alone provided food. Isaiah told the people, "If you are willing and obedient, you will eat the best from the land" (Isa. 1:19). Likewise, David wrote of God's blessings, saying, "The poor will eat and be satisfied; they who seek the LORD will praise him" (Ps. 22:26).

Jesus was building on this natural anxiety and the awareness that it is God who supplies our daily bread when he told those of his day, "I am the bread of life. He who comes to me will never go hungry, and he who believes in me will never be thirsty" (John 6:35). He meant that we will never find full spiritual satisfaction unless we find it in him.

John develops this thought fully by following the miracle of the feeding of the five thousand with Jesus' sermon on the bread of life, but the other Gospels have the same truths in mind. Therefore, it is right to ask at this point: Have you found Jesus to be sufficient for your spiritual need? Have you come to him? Have you been fed by him? Do you come to him now on a regular basis expecting to be fed?

If you have and do, I am sure you have found that not only are you satisfied, but there is even an abundance left over, which is only a way of saying that we can never exhaust God. I admit that the needs of other people drain us. Some are so needy that the church staff sometimes refer to them as bottomless pits. But there is no pit so deep or hole so black that Jesus cannot fill it or bring light to it. He will satisfy you, if you go to him.

Maybe you are like the prodigal in a far country. You thought life was to be enjoyed without the presence of your heavenly Father. So you squandered the inheritance he gave you, and you are at the point when your stomach and heart are empty and you are filling yourself with the slop that is fed to pigs. You are starving, miserable, abandoned, and alone. You need to do what the prodigal did. He came to his senses, saying, "How many of my father's hired men have food to spare, and here I am starving to death! I will set out and go back to my father and say to him: Father, I have sinned against heaven and against you. I am no longer worthy to be called your son; make me like one of your hired men" (Luke 15:17–19). When he confessed his sin and returned to his father, he found his father waiting for him. The father received him with open arms and lavished the riches of his household on him.

Then they had a party. The father said, "Quick! Bring the best robe and put it on him. Put a ring on his finger and sandals on his feet. Bring the fattened calf and kill it. Let's have a feast and celebrate. For this son of mine was dead and is alive again; he was lost and is found" (vv. 22–24). I promise that if you go back to Jesus, you will never find that he is begrudging to you or insufficient for your need.

God Works through People

The fourth lesson of the miracle of the feeding of the five thousand is that God works through people. That is, although Jesus alone is sufficient for all human need, he nevertheless chooses to work through us as channels by which he meets that need. In this case, he worked through the disciples, who were given the broken loaves and fish, distributed them to the people, and gathered up the pieces left over.

Years ago I took part in a management seminar conducted by a company called ServiceMaster Industries. I found much of it helpful, but one thing especially I've remembered. It was a definition of management: "Management is getting the right things done through other people." I have tried to keep that definition in mind and profit from it over the years, but I have also often thought of it in connection with the work of Jesus, especially in this story, though it applies to other examples of Jesus' work too.

In this story Jesus demonstrated his managerial skill by working through the disciples in the distribution of the food. He could have called down manna from heaven, thereby imitating Moses; the fact that the miracle took place at the time of the Jewish Passover (John 6:4), which was meant to recall the Exodus and the years of wilderness wandering, would have made manna appropriate. Again, Jesus might have caused a loaf of bread and a fish to appear in each man or woman's pocket. There were probably other things he could have done. But Jesus did not proceed in any of these ways. Instead he worked through other people: through all the disciples, according to Matthew's account; especially through Philip, Andrew, and the boy with the five small loaves and two fish, according to John's Gospel.

In this respect, the distribution of the food by the disciples to the five thousand people of the story becomes an illustration of what Jesus was doing when he sent them to preach among the cities of Galilee, as recorded in chapter 10, or what he will do at the end of the Gospel when he declares, "All authority in heaven and on earth has been given to me. Therefore go and make disciples of all nations, baptizing them in the name of the Father and of the Son and of the Holy Spirit, and teaching them to obey everything I have commanded you. And surely I am with you always, to the very end of the age" (Matt. 28:18–20). We are to be the distributors of that blessing.

Here is a story that will tie this together. On one occasion Jesus described a man who was visited at midnight by a friend but who had no food to serve him. So he went to a neighbor, who was already in bed, and called out to him, "Friend, lend me three loaves of bread, because a friend of mine on a journey has come to me, and I have nothing to set before him" (Luke 11:5–6).

The host must not have had any food, or he would not have bothered his neighbor in the middle of the night. But he had nothing; he knew it, and he knew his neighbor could help. So he went to his neighbor to get what he needed.

We are in exactly that position. You and I have nothing, but we have a friend in heaven who is able to supply what our friends need. We go to God with empty hands and cry out, claiming that double friendship: "Friend, a friend has come." The wonderful thing we discover is that God then supplies our friend's need as he has supplied our own.

32

Faith and Little Faith

Matthew 14:22–36

Immediately Jesus made the disciples get into the boat and go on ahead of him to the other side, while he dismissed the crowd. After he had dismissed them, he went up on a mountainside by himself to pray. When evening came, he was there alone, but the boat was already a considerable distance from land, buffeted by the waves because the wind was against it.

During the fourth watch of the night Jesus went out to them, walking on the lake. When the disciples saw him walking on the lake, they were terrified. "It's a ghost," they said, and cried out in fear.

But Jesus immediately said to them: "Take courage! It is I. Don't be afraid."

"Lord, if it's you," Peter replied, "tell me to come to you on the water."

"Come," he said.

Then Peter got down out of the boat, walked on the water and came toward Jesus. But when he saw the wind, he was afraid and, beginning to sink, cried out, "Lord, save me!"

Immediately Jesus reached out his hand and caught him. "You of little faith," he said, "why did you doubt?"

And when they climbed into the boat, the wind died down. Then those who were in the boat worshiped him, saying, "Truly you are the Son of God."

When they had crossed over, they landed at Gennesaret. And when the men of that place recognized Jesus, they sent word to all the surrounding country. People brought all their sick to him and begged him to let the sick just touch the edge of his cloak, and all who touched him were healed.

In the last study I said that Matthew 14–16 is characterized by three important themes: (1) Jesus' private teaching of the twelve disciples, (2) repeated failures on the disciples' part to understand or respond to Jesus' teaching, and (3) some small glimmerings of true faith and growth. We saw Jesus teaching the disciples in the account of the feeding of the five thousand. When he told the disciples to feed the people, he was obviously impressing on them that they could do nothing on their own. When he then fed the masses from five small loaves of bread and two fish, he was imparting a lesson about his own utter sufficiency. When Jesus used the disciples to distribute the food to the people, he was teaching them about their role as messengers. They had nothing to offer, but they would become bearers of the bread of life to those who were starving spiritually.

We see the next step in Jesus' teaching when he walks on the Sea of Galilee and allows Peter to walk on the water too. This is a story about the disciples' slow growth in faith. Peter began in faith, but his faith wavered, and he began to sink. The story teaches that we will only grow strong in faith when we keep our eyes on Jesus, the source of our faith, and do not turn aside to fret over threatening circumstances.

The story of Peter walking on the water is unique to Matthew. Mark and John tell about Jesus walking on the water, but their stories do not include the incident with Peter.

A Volatile Moment

The story does not begin with Jesus walking on the water, however. It begins with Jesus sending the disciples away in a boat while he dismisses the crowds and goes up a mountain by himself to pray. Taken together, the Gospels give three reasons why Jesus stayed behind and dismissed his disciples: (1) He wanted to be alone to pray (Matt. 14:23; Mark 6:46), (2) he wanted to escape the crowds and get some rest (Mark 6:31–32), and (3) he wanted to defuse the popular movement that would have made him a king by force (John 6:15).

These fit together nicely and are obviously all part of one picture. If the people were beginning to talk about making Jesus a king, which is what John specifically reports, it was likely that the disciples would have been swayed by the grassroots movement. Jesus sent them off to isolate them from these popular sentiments and at the same time dismissed the crowds to keep this demand from growing.

It was a critical moment in his ministry, and Jesus must also have felt a need for serious prayer. The people were offering a smaller version of what the devil had offered in the wilderness: "all the kingdoms of the world and their splendor" (Matt. 4:8). All Jesus had to do was bow to popular opinion, as earlier he had been asked to worship Satan. In the first case Jesus had spent forty days in prayer before the devil came to him. Here he needed to spend at least a few hours.

Howard Vos wrote of this critical moment in Christ's ministry, "His need for prayer was evident in view of the temptation to swerve from a course of action that would make him the Sin-Bearer of the world and the anticipation of defection of many of his followers."[1]

Peter's Remarkable Faith

Jesus sent the disciples away and dismissed the crowds before it got dark, perhaps by 7:00 or 8:00 at night, and Jesus prayed from that hour until he came to the disciples during the fourth watch of the night (v. 25). Early in their history, the Jews had divided the night into three watches. At this point, however, they were following the Roman system, which included four watches and assigned to the fourth the hours between 3:00 and 6:00 A.M. This suggests that Jesus had been praying for six or seven hours and that the disciples had been rowing for the same length of time. Crossing the lake would normally not have taken that long, but a storm had come up suddenly, and the boat was being buffeted by waves and wind.

Jesus must have seen all this from the mountain. He did not need some supernatural insight to know what was happening. But Jesus did exercise his divine power when he went to them walking on the waves. The disciples were terrified when they saw him. They thought they were seeing a ghost, but that was probably not their only reason for being afraid. Most likely they took the apparition for an omen warning them that they were doomed men and were going to drown.

When Jesus came walking on the water, he was filling a role that in the Old Testament was reserved for God alone. An example is Job 9:8, which says, "[God] alone stretches out the heavens and treads on the waves of the sea." It may be too much to suggest that a verse such as this was on Matthew's mind as he recorded this story, even less that he expected his readers to make this connection. But there may be something to be said for this connection. For one thing, in Mark's parallel account he says that Jesus seemed to be about "to pass by them," using a verb that occurs in Job 9:11. Again, when Jesus calms the disciples' fear, using the words "It is I" (v. 27), what he utters is actually the personal name of God, Jehovah, which means "I am." "I am" is the literal rendering of Matthew's quotation.[2] The thought that Jesus was demonstrating his deity by walking on the water may have been a part of the oral tradition that both Matthew and Mark knew and were using.

As soon as the disciples understood that the figure they saw walking on the water was Jesus, Peter asked to come to him, walking on the water himself. "Lord, if it is you," he cried, "tell me to come to you on the water" (v. 28).

Charles H. Spurgeon, the great Baptist preacher, believed that Peter was out of line to make this request. "What did Peter want with walking on the waters?" Spurgeon queried. Spurgeon suggested that his name, Peter, which means "rock," might have warned him that "like a stone he would go to the bottom. . . . Surely, he wist not what he said." Spurgeon reasoned that when Jesus told Peter to walk toward him, knowing he would sink, it was to teach him a practical lesson. He was not to do anything as foolish as this in the future.[3]

Such an interpretation is probably a bit too harsh, since Jesus' rebuke in verse 31 is not for Peter's impetuous faith but for his vacillating faith once he had started out. Most people see Peter's request as brave and faithful, and they are probably right to understand the story that way. Whatever the case, we *are* sometimes too presumptuous. We *do* ask to do what we are not called to do and often flounder in our attempts.

The Nature of True Faith

What is most important in this story is what it teaches about the nature of true faith, which is certainly why Matthew included it. These chapters record the disciples' first feeble attempts to understand and trust Jesus.

What is faith? Faith is not merely knowing that Jesus is the Son of God and believing that he can save us from sin but actually committing ourselves to him. I have often highlighted the three essential elements of faith by using the Latin words for them: *notitia, assensus,* and *fiducia. Notitia* refers to faith's content. It concerns understanding the doctrines of the gospel, particularly who Jesus claimed to be and what he accomplished on the cross. *Assensus* means agreement, assenting to the doctrines that are taught. It is like saying, "I understand what the Bible teaches about Jesus, and I believe it. I believe that Jesus is the Son of God and that his death was a true atoning death for human sin." *Notitia* and *assensus* are two necessary parts of faith, but they are not yet saving faith in the full biblical sense. True faith also involves *fiducia,* which is an actual trust in Jesus as the Son of God and Savior. It means that a person actually commits himself or herself to Jesus. To use the image of the story, it means stepping out toward him in faith.

Peter's action demonstrates this well. He believed that the figure he saw on the water was Jesus and that Jesus had power to call him and hold him up as he walked toward him. It is as if Peter had said, using the words of the apostle Paul to the Philippians, "I can do everything through him who gives me strength" (Phil. 4:13). And he could! As long as Jesus told him to come and as long as he kept his eyes on the Savior! It was only when he turned his eyes away from Jesus that he began to sink.

Peter's Faltering Faith

When Peter looked around and became aware of the fierce wind and saw the rolling waves, he became afraid and started to sink. His faith faltered at this point. But it is important to recognize that Peter's faith did not fail utterly. He had lost faith in Jesus' ability to keep him above the water, but he still trusted Jesus at some level since he immediately called out to him for help. "Lord, save me," he said (v. 30).

I said a moment ago that this incident is a good illustration of the trusting nature of true faith, but it is also a good illustration of true but faltering faith, which is what the faith of most of us is like. If Peter had no true faith at all, his act of getting out of the boat would have been mere foolishness or bravado, and when he began to sink, he would have started to flail his arms about, desperately trying to get back into the boat. He would not have cried out to Jesus. The fact that he cried out is proof that he really did trust Jesus. On the other hand, his faith was weakened by the waves, just as our faith is often undermined by difficult circumstances or by tragedies in life. When Jesus rebuked him, it was not for having no faith at all but for having little faith. "You of little faith," Jesus said, "why did you doubt?" (v. 31).

A moment ago I disagreed with Spurgeon, believing that Peter's attempt to walk to Jesus was a bold but proper act. Spurgeon thought Peter was wrong to do it. Yet Spurgeon said something else with which I agree entirely. He said that "Peter was nearer his Lord when he was sinking than when he was walking."[4] It was when Peter was in trouble that he was driven to Jesus and was closest to him.

It is exactly the same with us, and it is why Jesus permits storms to come into our lives too. As long as life is going along smoothly, we may be genuinely trusting Jesus for our salvation as true Christians, but our faith can be somewhat distant, abstract, or even peripheral. We trust Jesus, true enough, but if the truth be told, we also trust ourselves and our abilities. We may even trust ourselves more than we trust Jesus. Let trouble come, and suddenly we are confronted with our own lack of ability and weakness, and we are driven to Jesus simply because we have nowhere else to turn. It is in times such as these that faith in Jesus grows strong.

The Jews were not seafaring people, so there are not many stories in the Bible about peril on the sea. But I can think of one! It is the story of Jonah, who tried to run away from the Lord by taking a ship from Joppa to Tarshish on the far side of the Mediterranean. He was not acting in faith as Peter was. He was defiantly disobedient. But when God sent the storm that threatened to sink the ship in which he was sailing and the sailors finally threw him overboard to drown, which he had told them to do, Jonah found himself inside the belly of a great fish and turned to God again in prayer and found salvation. Jonah wrote:

> In my distress I called to the LORD,
> and he answered me.
> From the depths of the grave I called for help,
> and you listened to my cry.
> You hurled me into the deep,
> into the very heart of the seas,
> and the currents swirled about me;
> all your waves and breakers
> swept over me. . . .
>
> When my life was ebbing away,
> I remembered you, LORD,
> and my prayer rose to you,
> to your holy temple.
>
> Jonah 2:2–3, 7

God heard Jonah from inside the great fish and saved him, just as Jesus saved Peter when he was sinking in the waves. It often takes such things to turn us from disobedience to obedience and change our failing faith into robust faith in the Savior.

Asaph, one of the great psalm writers, was almost thrown off balance by the apparent easy life of the wicked. He knew God had been good to Israel. "But as for me," he explains in Psalm 73,

> "my feet had almost slipped;
> I had nearly lost my foothold.
> For I envied the arrogant
> when I saw the prosperity of the wicked.
>
> They have no struggles;
> their bodies are healthy and strong.
> They are free from the burdens common to man;
> they are not plagued by human ills."
>
> verses 2–5

He goes on like that for several stanzas until he explains how his faltering faith was at last restored. It was when he "entered the sanctuary of God." Then he "understood their final destiny" (v. 17). The rest of the psalm says that God held him by his right hand, just as Jesus must have reached out to save Peter. The psalmist ends by claiming that from that time on he made the sovereign God his refuge (v. 28).

If you have been sinking in life because of troubles or because you doubt the wisdom and power of God, stop looking at the waves and look to Jesus.

He is the Lord of all circumstances, and he will be there to see you through them.

The Disciples' Growing Faith

After Jesus rescued Peter, the two of them climbed into the boat and the wind died down. That was impressive in itself. A similar effect had caused the disciples to react with awe on an earlier occasion (Matt. 8:23–27). But this is not the climax of the story in Matthew 14. The climax here is not the stilling of the waves or even Jesus' earlier words to Peter: "You of little faith, why did you doubt?" The climax is the disciples' confession of faith in Jesus and their worship of Jesus in verse 33: "Then those who were in the boat worshiped him, saying, 'Truly you are the Son of God.'"

This is the first time Jesus is called the Son of God by the disciples, and the words build on what they had said earlier. In chapter 8 they had asked, "What kind of man is this? Even the winds and the waves obey him" (v. 27). Here they say, "Truly you are the Son of God." They still have a long way to go. If Peter's confession in chapter 16 is the all-important breakthrough in the disciples' spiritual understanding, what they say here could not have had its full spiritual significance. Still, it was a step on the way. They were growing in their faith and understanding.

And let's not forget their worship. This is also the first time the disciples are said to have worshiped Jesus. In chapter 2 the Magi from the East worshiped Jesus (v. 11). Later a leper is said to have worshiped Jesus, though the New International Version translates the word merely as "knelt before him" (Matt. 8:2). A synagogue ruler does the same thing in chapter 9 (v. 18). But this is the first time the disciples worshiped, and it is important to note that their worship in 14:33 is joined to their confession. That is what worship is, of course! It is acknowledging who God is and praising him both for who he is and for what he has done. In this case the disciples took the first step and worshiped Jesus as God's Son.

I notice too that they focused on Jesus entirely in their worship. Peter had experienced a great deliverance, but they didn't ask Peter to give his testimony. The wind had died down, but they didn't hold a discussion about miracles. They worshiped Jesus, and they worshiped only him because they were entirely taken up with him.

The Work Goes On

Meanwhile, the work that Jesus had begun months before continued as he now moved into the region of Gennesaret and healed those who were sick. Apparently Jesus had not been here before, because the people did not know him by face. But when they recognized that this traveling teacher was Jesus, they brought their sick friends and relatives to him to be healed.

These people knew of his reputation, and one of the things they had probably heard was that the woman with uncontrolled bleeding had been healed merely by touching the edge of his garment (Matt. 9:20–22). This is what they did too. The text does not say that these masses of people believed on him, any more than those in the upper regions of Galilee. (Gennesaret was a plain between Tiberias in the south and Capernaum to the north.) They were using Jesus only for their own ends, just as the people who had been fed with the loaves and fish wanted to use him by making him a king. Nevertheless, the Lord had compassion on these people and healed them anyway.

Jesus has also been caring for you, even if you have not committed your life to him. The friends you have, the health you possess, the possessions you own, the job you work at, even the life you are living are God's good gifts to you. Do not be like the people of Gennesaret who stopped there, and so perish in your sins. Turn your eyes to Jesus. Trust Jesus. Commit yourself to Jesus. Say, as Peter did, "Lord, save me!" Cry out with the disciples, "Truly you are the Son of God." That is how a person passes from spiritual death to life.

33

Kosher Hearts

Matthew 15:1–20

Then some Pharisees and teachers of the law came to Jesus from Jerusalem and asked, "Why do your disciples break the tradition of the elders? They don't wash their hands before they eat!"

Jesus replied, "And why do you break the command of God for the sake of your tradition? For God said, 'Honor your father and mother' and 'Anyone who curses his father or mother must be put to death.' But you say that if a man says to his father or mother, 'Whatever help you might otherwise have received from me is a gift devoted to God,' he is not to 'honor his father' with it. Thus you nullify the word of God for the sake of your tradition. You hypocrites! Isaiah was right when he prophesied about you:

"'These people honor me with their lips,
but their hearts are far from me.
They worship me in vain;
their teachings are but rules taught by men.'"

Jesus called the crowd to him and said, "Listen and understand. What goes into a man's mouth does not make him 'unclean,' but what comes out of his mouth, that is what makes him 'unclean.'"

Everything Jesus said seems radical to us because Jesus is God and God's thoughts are not our thoughts, nor are his ways our ways (Isa. 55:8). Yet it is probably the case that nothing Jesus ever said was as radical in terms of the religion of his day and all human thoughts about religion and true worship as what he told the Pharisees, crowds, and disciples in the first half of Matthew 15. We can get a sense of how radical this was by remembering that the same issue is treated extensively in Acts in the narrative of God's preparation of Peter for carrying the gospel to the Gentiles (Acts 10:1–48), and that it is the theme of the longest of the closing application sections of Paul's great letter to the Romans (14:1–15:13).

These verses do not seem so startling to us, probably for two reasons. First, we are far removed from the situation of Jesus' day and do not have much of a feel for what was going on, and second, we think a great deal like the Pharisees and do not really absorb Jesus' teaching.

True and False Religion

These verses contain more teaching than narrative, but the story is the background and needs to be looked at first. Jesus had been searching for rest, first on the eastern side of the Sea of Galilee and then on the western side in the area of Gennesaret. But he was interrupted by the multitudes of people who were following him wherever he went and who had now circled the lake again and were pressing him with renewed demands for healings. While this was going on, some Pharisees and teachers of the law came from Jerusalem to ask about his disciples' failure to wash their hands before eating. This had nothing to do with whether their hands were free of dirt. It was a matter of the Pharisees' traditions, their ceremonies. That they came "from Jerusalem" (v. 1) probably indicates they were an official delegation.

Washing one's hands before meals was not required by the Old Testament, but it had become an important part of the Pharisees' teaching and was of paramount concern to them since their religion was based primarily on such matters. We can sense how important their laws about "cleanness" were by noting that they have been preserved in one whole tractate of the Mishnah, which deals with such washings *(Yadaim).*

What we learn in this story is how radically wrong Jesus insisted their position was. Jesus did not reply by some mild attempt to excuse his disciples: "They didn't have a chance to wash; we've been out hiking; I'm sure they'll do better next time." Or by mere discussion: "Let's talk about such washings; why do you think they're so important?" Instead, he attacked the Pharisees forcefully and directly for fussing about paltry matters while breaking God's law in essential matters by their traditions (vv. 3–6). He said that their entire understanding of religion was wrong, that their hearts were "far from" God, and that their worship of God was "vain" (vv. 8–9).

Even stronger, when his disciples warned him that the Pharisees were offended by what he said, Jesus called them "blind guides" leading blind men (v. 14) and plants that God had not planted that would eventually be "pulled up by the roots" (v. 13). In light of the recent parables of chapter

13, this can only mean that the Pharisees were plantings of Satan and would be destroyed by fire at the last judgment.

When we remember that the Pharisees were the most highly regarded men of religion of their day, we see how shocking this is. By these words Jesus was not only condemning their system, he was condemning the best of human religion, saying that all human efforts to please God are external and vain, and that the only thing that really matters is a radical change of heart, since it is what comes out of the heart that makes a man "unclean" (v. 18).

A moment ago I said that this same issue is dealt with extensively in Acts 10, where God prepares Peter to carry the gospel to the Gentiles. Acts 10 tells about the sheet let down from heaven containing different kinds of clean and unclean animals and God telling Peter, "Do not call anything impure that God has made clean" (v. 15). In an obviously parallel way, the teaching of Jesus about true "cleanness" in Matthew 15:1–20 is followed in verses 21–28 by his response to an "unclean" Gentile woman's prayer for help and in the last verses of the chapter (vv. 29–39) by his healing and feeding of a largely Gentile crowd. Thus the point of Matthew 15 as a whole is that the kingdom of God is for Gentiles as well as Jews because Christianity rests on an entirely different foundation than did Judaism.

Jesus' Response to the Pharisees

There are three teaching conversations in these verses: (1) between Jesus and the Pharisees, (2) between Jesus and the crowds, and (3) between Jesus and his disciples. The first is Jesus' response to those who had complained about the disciples' non-traditional practices. The Pharisees had asked, "Why do your disciples break the tradition of the elders? They don't wash their hands before they eat" (v. 2). According to the Pharisees' way of thinking, such action meant the disciples were "unclean" and therefore "non-religious." If Jesus were a true teacher, he would have straightened out these disciples, they thought.[1]

Jesus' response was twofold, as I indicated earlier. He confronted them directly in regard to their own religious practices, and he condemned their false understanding of religion.

1. *"You break the command of God for the sake of your tradition" (v. 3).* This was a direct counterattack, but it was not as if Jesus were merely saying, "If I am guilty, then you are guilty too." Rather, he shifted the issue from the matter of tradition to the revealed law of God. The Pharisees accused him of breaking the tradition of the elders, but he accused them of breaking God's commands because of their traditions.

The issue Jesus raised was a particularly despicable practice of that time. The fifth of the Ten Commandments, the first from the second table of the law, said that a man must "honor [his] father and mother" (v. 4; see Exod. 20:12). One chapter later Exodus states, "Anyone who curses his father or mother must be put to death" (Exod. 21:17). These verses add a specific divine command to a universally recognized human obligation, to provide for one's parent when a father or a mother is in need. But the Pharisees had devised a way of avoiding this obligation. They even had a word for it: *corban.* (The word is actually used in the parallel account of this exchange in Mark 7:11.) It referred to a gift dedicated to God, and it worked this way. If a parent approached one of these people asking to be helped and the person did not want to help, all he had to do was say "corban," meaning that the money that might have been used to relieve the parent's need had been dedicated to God and was no longer available.

What made this practice even worse, the greedy and uncaring son did not even have to give the money to God. It was enough that he had promised to give it. He could give it later, on his deathbed perhaps, or not at all. In this way the parents of such men were dishonored and God's law was broken. What concerned Jesus most was that by this false piety these men nullified the Bible, making it of no effect, which is the problem with traditions (v. 6). It is what human traditions almost always do.

2. *"These people honor me with their lips, but their hearts are far from me" (Isa. 29:13).* Jesus' second response was even stronger than the first, for he reminded his accusers of Isaiah 29:13, thus accusing them of hypocritical and therefore utterly false worship. He said that Isaiah had been prophesying about them when he wrote,

> "These people honor me with their lips,
> but their hearts are far from me.
> They worship me in vain;
> their teachings are but rules taught by men."

That is a damning accusation for people who were regarded as the best people of their day, but it was a just condemnation, for a love of tradition more than a genuine love of God always leads to false religion. In fact, it leads to self-righteousness, which was the chief characteristic of these men. Self-righteousness does not bring a person into heaven. Rather, it leads to judgment and death since the only possible basis for our justification before God is Christ's righteousness, not our own.

Jesus' Teaching of the Crowds

This point was so important that Jesus called the crowds to him and strongly applied what he had said. This is the second of the three teaching conversations. He told them, "What goes into a man's mouth does not make him 'unclean,' but what comes out of his mouth, that is what makes him 'unclean'" (v. 11). This was a direct contradiction of the Pharisees, for he was saying that what matters before God is not clean hands or kosher food, which is what they were concerned about, but a purified heart.

The teachers of the law should have known this because it is taught in the Old Testament. For example, Psalm 24 asks, "Who may ascend the hill of the Lord? Who may stand in his holy place?" (v. 3). It answers, "He who has clean hands and a pure heart, who does not lift up his soul to an idol or swear by what is false" (v. 4).

It is obvious from these verses that "clean hands" does not refer to removing physical dirt by ceremonial washings, but to a blameless way of life flowing from a transformed heart. A "pure heart" refers to inward holiness. It is what Jesus was speaking of in the Sermon on the Mount when he said, "Blessed are the pure in heart, for they will see God" (Matt. 5:8). "Clean hands" refers to one who is holy in outward actions as well as inwardly, because he has been changed within. It is the exact opposite of Pilate, who although he washed his hands publicly, saying, "I am innocent of this man's blood" (Matt. 27:24), nevertheless was guilty in his condemnation of the Lord. He was guilty of violating the laws of Rome and going against what his conscience told him was right by agreeing to the crucifixion of one he had three times declared innocent (cf. John 18:38; 19:4, 6).

The Pharisees should also have been aware of Psalm 15, which asks, "Lord, who may dwell in your sanctuary? Who may live on your holy hill?" (v. 1). Psalm 15 answers:

> He whose walk is blameless
> and who does what is righteous,
> who speaks the truth from his heart
> and has no slander on his tongue,
> who does his neighbor no wrong
> and casts no slur on his fellow man,
> who despises a vile man
> but honors those who fear the LORD,
> who keeps his oath
> even when it hurts,
> who lends his money without usury
> and does not accept a bribe against the innocent.
>
> verses 2–5

This is the character of those who please God, but the only people who will ever have such a character are those who have had their nature changed by God. Or to put it in the language Jesus used when he spoke to Nicodemus, "You must be born again" (John 3:7).

Jesus' Teaching of the Disciples

The last of the three conversations in these verses is between Jesus and his disciples, and it seems to have been private. The disciples come to Jesus to say that the Pharisees were offended by his teaching. I find that amusing.

Of course they were offended by his teaching! Self-righteous persons are always offended when we speak of their sin or their inability to please God by their own corrupt and wicked efforts. Truth is resented. But I also find this amusing because the disciples thought they had to clue Jesus in. He knew the situation very well, of course. He replies now with even stronger teaching.

1. *The fact that the Pharisees were offended is proof not only that they were false interpreters of the law but they were outside the kingdom altogether.* That is what being "pulled up by the roots" refers to. It is an application of the second parable of the kingdom (Matt. 13:24–30) in which the weeds are separated from the wheat at the last day and are burned.

Actually, there are two images for these men. First, they are called plants the "father has not planted" (v. 13). That is an apt description of many who are involved in Christian work. They pretend to have been called by God, but they have not been called by God. They claim to speak for God, but they do not speak for God. On the contrary, they teach the traditions of mere men and sometimes even the doctrines of the devil, who is the prince of darkness. What else are we to think of preachers who deny the deity of Jesus Christ, dismiss the value of his atoning sacrifice for sin, ridicule the resurrection, and defend as normal, sins that the Bible says will carry those who persist in them to damnation? We say they are plants the Father has not planted. More than that, they are tares sown in God's field to hinder God's work. Their condemnation will be just.

Second, Jesus calls the Pharisees and teachers of the law "blind guides" (v. 14). They were aspiring to lead others, but the only outcome was that both those who were leading and those who were following would fall into a pit. I do not think Jesus meant only a pit in the ground. He was probably referring to that bottomless pit in which there is an eternal darkness and a weeping and gnashing of teeth (Matt. 25:30).

2. *"The things that come out of the mouth come from the heart, and these make a man 'unclean'" (v. 18).* Jesus states what makes a person unclean. It is not what goes into his mouth or whether he eats with unwashed hands. It is what comes out, for what comes out of the mouth comes from the heart, and the heart, as any careful reader of the Old Testament should have known, is incorrigibly wicked. Jeremiah wrote, "The heart is deceitful above all things and beyond cure. Who can understand it?" (Jer. 17:9). What Jesus says here is that all sins come from the heart. He even names them: "For out of the heart come evil thoughts, murder, adultery, sexual immorality, theft, false testimony, slander. These are what make a man 'unclean'; but eating with unwashed hands does not make him 'unclean'" (vv. 19–20).

Mark concludes from these words that "Jesus declared all foods 'clean,'" thereby abolishing not only the Pharisaic but also the Levitical regulations (see Mark 7:19). Paul, who learned the same lesson, argues in Romans 14 that because of this teaching Christians are not to divide over matters of diet or even the observance or non-observance of certain holy days. Why? Because "the kingdom of God is not a matter of eating and drinking, but of righteousness, peace and joy in the Holy Spirit. . . . Anyone who serves Christ in this way is pleasing to God and approved by men" (vv. 17–18). Righteousness, peace, and joy in the Holy Spirit is true religion. It is what Jesus came to teach and establish. Righteousness, peace, and joy are the spiritual opposites of kosher cooking and eating with washed or unwashed hands.

Clean Hands or a Clean Heart?

As we come to the end of Jesus' radical words about the nature of true religion, which is the only religion God accepts, I ask the necessary question: Do you stand before God with clean hands only, that is, with mere ceremonial religion, or do you come with a new, clean heart?

Washing our hands in a religious way is not the issue today, of course, but the principle applies in other areas. For some this type of ceremonial religion means good works, perhaps giving money to help the poor or donating time to charity. A person like this supposes that he will be accepted by God for these works. Another person thinks in terms of religious observance, so she is faithful to attend church services. Another person places weight on standing or sitting for prayers, how he holds his prayer book, or whether he crosses himself in entering a church. My mother is a strong Christian today, but she says that when she looks back to her catechetical instruction in preparation for her first communion, all she can remember is how she was told to hold her prayer book and when she was to sit down and stand up.

If you have been understanding religion in these or similar ways, you may have discovered that ceremonial things do nothing to change the nature of your heart. Regardless of how often you go to church, it is still the case that out of your heart come such sins as "evil thoughts, . . . false testimony [and] slander," or even such sins as "murder, adultery, sexual immorality [and] theft" (Matt. 15:19).

You have two problems. You need forgiveness for your sins, and you need a new heart that will enable you to stop sinning and begin to serve God. Where can forgiveness be found? Where can a new heart be acquired? The good news is that Jesus came to give you both. He died on the cross so you might have forgiveness, he bore the punishment for your sins in your place, and he rose again to impart the Holy Spirit, who is the source of new life. It is God alone who can give you a heart capable of loving and serving him.

It is possible to talk about the whole of Christianity as possessing a transformed heart. John Ryle, the evangelical Anglican bishop, wrote:

> What is the first thing we need in order to be Christians? A new heart.—What is the sacrifice God asks us to bring to him? A broken and a contrite heart.—What is the true circumcision? The circumcision of the heart.—What is genuine obedience? To obey from the heart.—What is saving faith? To believe

> with the heart.—Where ought Christ to dwell? To dwell in our hearts by faith.—What is the chief request that Wisdom makes to every one? "My son, give me thine heart."[2]

That is a very wise summary of what true religion is about.

Do you want a new heart? The only place you will ever get it is from God the Father and from Jesus, who made the gift possible. Come to God. Ask Jesus for it. The Pharisees would not come, which is why they perished in their sins.

34

Faith and Feeding of the Gentiles

Matthew 15:21–39

Leaving that place, Jesus withdrew to the region of Tyre and Sidon. A Canaanite woman from that vicinity came to him, crying out, "Lord, Son of David, have mercy on me! My daughter is suffering terribly from demon-possession."

Jesus did not answer a word. So his disciples came to him and urged him, "Send her away, for she keeps crying out after us."

He answered, "I was sent only to the lost sheep of Israel."

The woman came and knelt before him. "Lord, help me!" she said.

He replied, "It is not right to take the children's bread and toss it to their dogs."

"Yes, Lord," she said, "but even the dogs eat the crumbs that fall from their masters' table."

Then Jesus answered, "Woman, you have great faith! Your request is granted." And her daughter was healed from that very hour.

Nothing troubled the religious leaders of Israel more than becoming ceremonially unclean, and nothing made them more unclean than contact with "unclean" Gentiles. Yet in this next section of Matthew, Jesus leaves Israel to enter Gentile territory, where he helps a Gentile woman.

Was this woman "unclean"? The Pharisees would have said so. But when they had complained that Jesus' disciples ate with "unclean" hands, Jesus had taught that it is not "unclean" hands or "unclean" food going into a person's mouth that makes a person unclean, but what comes out of it. "For out of the heart come evil thoughts, murder, adultery, sexual immorality, theft, false testimony, slander. These are what make a man 'unclean'; but eating with unwashed hands does not make him 'unclean'" (Matt. 15:19–20). By this standard the Pharisees were unclean, not the Gentile woman. The Pharisees hated Jesus and were plotting to have him killed, while the woman demonstrated her "clean" status by her humility and her faith in Jesus as the "Lord," the "Son of David," and her Savior (v. 22).

Hope for the Gentiles

We have already noted several times in these studies that in spite of being the most Jewish of the four Gospels, Matthew is also the most open to Gentiles. Gentile Magi came to worship the infant Christ as early as chapter 2, and the Gospel closes with Jesus' command to "make disciples of *all* nations" (Matt. 28:19). Here, in chapter 15, just over halfway through the Gospel, we find Jesus leaving the Jewish area of Galilee to go to Tyre and Sidon. The area is not specified in detail, but Tyre was about twenty-five miles north of Galilee, and Sidon was about twenty-five miles beyond that, so the journey there and back could have taken a considerable amount of time, perhaps months.[1] This is the only time in his ministry that Jesus traveled out of Jewish territory into Gentile lands.

This was important for Matthew. Not only does he mention Tyre and Sidon, he introduces the woman involved in this story as a "Canaanite," which was the name of the ancient tribal enemies of Israel. The Canaanites were the people the Israelites were to destroy when they conquered the Promised Land under Joshua, and this is the only place in the New Testament where we find the word. This is not without meaning, and William Barclay is correct when he says, "The supreme significance of this passage is that it foreshadows the going out of the gospel to the whole world; it shows us the beginning of the end of all barriers."[2]

We are going to see that the same emphasis dominates the story of the feeding of the four thousand that follows, for the unique element in that feeding, and why it is included, is that it was done in a Gentile region and that the majority of the people there were Gentiles.

Faith of the Canaanite Woman

Yet there is a serious problem here. If we are correct that these stories mark the beginning of the "going out of the gospel to the whole world" and "the end of all barriers," why did Jesus refuse to speak to the Canaanite woman initially? This seems contrary to the main point of the story. It is also unusual behavior for Jesus, but Matthew does not explain Jesus' silence.

There are several reasons why Jesus may have refused to speak to her.

1. *Jesus was not sent to Gentiles, so he wanted no dealings with the Gentile woman.* We see something similar in Jesus' conversation with the Samaritan woman. He told her, "Salvation is from the Jews" (John 4:22). Alexander Maclaren

approaches the account of the Canaanite woman this way, arguing that Jesus' refusal "was a real refusal, founded on the divine decree, which he was bound to obey."[3] The problem with this answer is that Jesus spoke to the Samaritan woman, and in the story Matthew tells, it would mean Jesus changed his mind since he not only spoke to the woman but also healed her daughter.

2. *Jesus wanted to test the woman's faith.* This is David Dickson's answer. He writes of "four means used for the trial of her faith: . . . Christ keeping silent when she prays, . . . the small assistance she has of the disciples' prayers, . . . our Lord's telling her that his commission reached only to the lost sheep of the house of Israel, . . . [and] by seeming to exclude her (as a heathen, or unclean dog outside the covenant) from all the benefits of the Messiah."[4] This is a good explanation, because the story emphasizes how strong and perceptive her faith was. It ends with Jesus telling her, "Woman, you have great faith! Your request is granted" (v. 28). Jesus did not speak that way to many people.

3. *Jesus wanted to strengthen her faith.* This view appeals to William Hendriksen: "He aimed to strengthen it by means of the very answer he had given her in verses 24 and 26; for she would now begin to realize, far better than if he had immediately healed her daughter, what an extraordinary blessing she was receiving."[5] The woman addressed Jesus as "Son of David," and his answer drew out the full meaning of those words. If he was the Jewish Messiah, as she said, his ministry was to Israel. Did she really understand that?

4. *Jesus wanted to highlight what he was about to do, namely, answer the prayer of a Gentile.* This is the explanation that appeals most to me, since what Jesus is chiefly doing in this middle section of Matthew is training his disciples. The opening to the Gentile woman leads to the story of the feeding of the four thousand Gentiles in verses 29–39 and to the confession of Peter in chapter 16, all of which were part of the disciples' training. The incidents were important enough that Matthew remembered them and included them in his Gospel.

"Gentile Dogs"

It is not only Jesus' silence that seems to be a problem, however. It is also the words he used when he spoke to the woman. His first words were, "I was sent only to the lost sheep of Israel" (v. 24), and he followed that "politically incorrect" statement with the explanation, "It is not right to take the children's bread and toss it to their dogs" (v. 26).

How harsh! How cruel! How parochial! In that day Jews were accustomed to speak of "Gentile dogs," "infidel dogs," and later "Christian dogs." But Barclay reminds us of two things, no doubt rightly. First, "the tone and the look with which a thing is said make all the difference. Even a thing which seems hard can be said with a disarming smile. . . . We can be quite sure that the smile on Jesus' face and the compassion in his eyes robbed the words of all insult and bitterness."[6] Second, Jesus did not use the word for the wild dogs of the streets, but *kunaria,* which referred to house dogs or pets. It was a clever play on the "dog" idea, and it was not lost on the woman, who immediately picked it up as an encouragement to her appeal.

Still, Jesus did use the word *dogs,* and it is not terribly nice even to be called a household pet. The only reason I can see for Jesus' harsh language is that he wanted to emphasize her Gentile status. She was, as Paul would later write to the Ephesians, "excluded from citizenship in Israel . . . [a foreigner] to the covenants of the promise, without hope and without God in the world" (Eph. 2:12). Yet she did have faith! She believed in Jesus and was helped by him. The story teaches that if she found grace, there is hope for you, whoever you are and however hopeless you may feel your cause is. Instead of turning from Jesus, turn to him as this Gentile woman did.

A Gentile's "Great Faith"

The story says that Jesus helped the woman in response to her great faith; he healed her daughter (v. 28). So what we want to ask next is what made this Canaanite woman's faith so great? What were its characteristics? The greatness of her faith is certainly an important emphasis since, although Matthew uses the word *great* often, this is the only place he joins the word to *faith.* Only this woman, a Canaanite, and the centurion of Matthew 8:10 are publicly praised for their faith by Jesus.

Here are several things to notice about the woman's faith.

1. *Her faith was in Jesus.* She called him "Lord" and "Son of David" (v. 22). In fact, the word *Lord* introduces each of her three recorded statements (vv. 22, 25, 27). In an earlier study I emphasized that genuine biblical faith contains three elements: content *(notitia),* agreement with that content *(assensus),* and trust in or commitment to Christ *(fiducia).* All are here. The woman knew who Jesus was, believed that he could help her, and placed her confidence in him. If you would be helped by Jesus, you must put your faith in him too. No one else can really help you.

2. *She appealed to Jesus solely on the basis of his mercy.* She cried, "Lord, Son of David, have mercy on me." And later, when Jesus spoke about Gentiles being "dogs," she gave an even stronger proof of her awareness that she had no claim to him by agreeing with his statement (v. 27). This is how everyone must come to Jesus: asking for mercy, laying aside all self-righteousness, making no claim to entitlement, making no demands. Are you willing to come on that basis? It is the only way you will ever receive a positive answer from Jesus since, as Paul told the Ephesians, "It is by grace you have been saved, through faith—and this not from yourselves, it is the gift of God—not by works, so that no one can boast" (Eph. 2:8–9).

3. *She was persistent.* She would not allow herself to be easily turned away. The story says that she kept "crying out after" him (v. 23) and "came and knelt before him" (v. 25). Even after Jesus had spoken about Gentile dogs, she replied, "Yes, Lord, but even the dogs eat the crumbs that fall from their masters' table" (v. 27).

Persistence in prayer was important to Jesus because he referred to it often. On one occasion he told the story of a persistent widow who kept coming to an unjust judge to get justice. She had no money to bribe him, so he ignored her for a long time. But at last he gave in saying, "Even though I don't fear God or care about men, yet because this widow keeps bothering me, I will see that she gets justice, so that she won't eventually wear me out with her coming." Jesus concluded, "And will not God bring about justice for his chosen ones, who cry out to him day and night?" (Luke 18:1–8). The story does not teach that God is unjust or indifferent. It does not teach that by persistence we can get everything we may ask for, for we often ask wrongly and are graciously denied. What it does teach is that when we ask rightly, God does hear and will answer in his own proper time.

I do not think there is much of this strong persistent prayer in our day, at least not in affluent Western lands. We are too busy to pray and too self-confident. It was different in previous centuries. The Great Awakening under Jonathan Edwards began with his famous call to prayer, and it was carried forward by prayer. The work of God among the North American Indians under David Brainerd, Edwards's friend, began in the nights Brainerd spent in prayer asking God to effect that great work. In the eighteenth century a revival began in a small town in Ireland that eventually spread through the entire country. It started with seven ministers who committed themselves to pray regularly, fervently, and persistently for revival. When John Wesley and George Whitefield began their work, England was in spiritual stupor, a moral abyss, but a little group of believers began to pray, and God sent a revival that transformed England and even spilled over into the New World. One reason we do not have great blessing today is that there is not much of that dogged prayer and persistent faith seen in the Canaanite woman.

R. V. G. Tasker wrote about her faith:

> She does not stay to argue that her claims are as good as anyone else's. She does not discuss whether Jew is better than Gentile, or Gentile as good as Jew. She does not dispute the justice of the mysterious ways by which God works out his divine purpose, choosing one race and rejecting another. All she knows is that her daughter is grievously tormented, that she needs supernatural help, and that here in the person of the *Lord*, the *son of David* is one who is able to give her that help; and she is confident that even if she is not entitled to sit down as a guest at the Messiah's table, Gentile "dog" that she is, yet at least she may be allowed to receive a crumb of the uncovenanted mercies of God.[7]

This is the nature of all true faith. It was the faith exercised by the man who came upon the pearl of great price and the one who found the treasure in the field (Matt. 13:44–46). They did everything in their power to possess those treasures. It is the faith of those "forceful men" who lay hold of the kingdom and will not be turned aside (Matt. 11:12).

The Feeding of the Four Thousand

In Matthew 15 the story of Jesus' response to the Canaanite woman is followed by an account of his feeding of four thousand people near the Sea of Galilee, much as he had fed a somewhat larger group earlier (Matt. 15:29–39). What are we to make of this story?

We begin by noting its similarity to the story of the feeding of the five thousand found in chapter 14. These accounts have been favorite texts for liberal scholars who do not have a high regard for Scripture and find support for their low views here. They regard them as examples of what they call a non-historical "doubling" pattern in Matthew's Gospel. They point to the two times Jesus is said to have calmed a storm on the Sea of Galilee (see Matt. 8:23–27; 14:22–36). They also point out that Matthew mentions two demon-possessed men from among the Gaderenes (Matt. 8:28–34), rather than just one, as in Mark and Luke's accounts; that he speaks of two blind men in 20:29–34, rather than of blind Bartimaeus alone (see Mark 10:46–52; Luke 18:35–43), and so on.

It is not a very significant list of examples, and they can be explained in other ways than by a theory of doubling. But whatever may be the case in these other incidents, it is clear that no mere doubling of the stories takes place in Matthew's accounts. Matthew has a purpose in what he is doing, and what is more, both feeding stories are also told in Mark, and no one has accused him of mere doubling.

Leon Morris points out that Matthew

> clearly regards the two incidents as distinct: the numbers of people are different in the two incidents, as are the quantities of food and the amounts left over; the words for "basket" are different; the people in this incident had been with Jesus for three days (v. 32) whereas in the earlier incident they had just gone around the lake to head him off (14:13–14). . . . The times appear to be different, the earlier feeding being when the grass was green (Mark 6:39), that is, in spring, while here there is no mention of grass and the ground appears to be hard (v. 35); in other words, it is late summer."[8]

The important thing is this: Matthew includes the story of the feeding of the four thousand because all or most of these people were Gentiles, which makes it a sequel to the story of the Canaanite woman. It is true that Matthew does not say explicitly to which side of the Sea of Galilee Jesus returned after having been in the region of Tyre and Sidon, but Mark says that it was to the Decapolis (Mark 7:31), a name referring to an area to the west of Galilee known for its ten Greek cities, and Matthew fits in with this when he says that the people praised the "God of Israel" (v. 31). That was a natural thing for Gentiles but not Jews to have said. That these were Gentiles rather than Jews has been a view in the church since St. Augustine.

Gentile "dogs"! Yes. But in spite of their being Gentiles: (1) these people were healed just as the Jews had been (vv. 29–31), (2) they were fed just as the Jews had been (vv. 32–37), and (3) the disciples were used to serve them just as they had been used to serve the Jewish gathering (vv. 36–37). What better way to teach that Gentiles are as important to God as Jews and that Christianity is a worldwide religion.

Four Important Lessons

I have spent most of this study showing what the stories of the Gentile woman and the feeding of the four thousand are about and how they fit together. But these stories also need to be applied to ourselves directly. They teach four important lessons.

1. *Faith may be found in unlikely places.* "It is grace, not place, which makes people believers," wrote John Ryle.[9] That is true. One would have expected to find strong faith among the people of Israel, who had the Old Testament and all the other benefits that went with being Jews (see Rom. 9:1–5). The last place one would have expected faith was in an utterly Gentile territory. But it is the Canaanite woman who believed, and strongly, and it was the people of Galilee who did not.

Do not say, "That person will never come to faith" or "That one is too far gone to believe." You do not know that, and it is often the most unlikely persons who come. Who would have expected Saul, that first great persecutor of the Christians, to be converted? Yet he became the great missionary to the Gentiles. John Newton, the converted slave trader, said on one occasion, "I have never despaired of any man since God saved me."

2. *Be encouraged to come to Jesus.* You may think you are too sinful to come to Jesus or that Jesus could never care for you. But that is completely wrong. If Gentile "dogs" can come, you can come. If you have never turned from sin to trust Jesus as your Savior or have never thrown all your cares on him, do it now. Jesus himself said, "Come to me, all you who are weary and burdened, and I will give you rest" (Matt. 11:28). He taught, "Whoever comes to me I will never drive away" (John 6:37).

3. *Come to Jesus especially if you are in trouble or hurting.* Jesus cares for people whatever their problems might be. The multitudes were hungry. Many were sick. The Canaanite woman had an afflicted daughter. Jesus fed the hungry, healed the sick, and cured the girl's demon possession. Will he do less for you?

4. *Needy people will often find more compassion in Jesus than in Jesus' people.* The disciples were not much help either with the woman or with the crowds, either one-on-one or with the masses. But that was only to be expected. They were just poor sinful people themselves. They were not the answer to these problems. It is the same today. Today's disciples are not always more helpful than these first followers. But what of that? If you have been disappointed by Christ's people, don't despair. They are probably trying; it is just that they are still sinners. Come to Jesus. It is what they would tell you to do anyway.

35

Watch Out for the Pharisees

Matthew 16:1–12

The Pharisees and Sadducees came to Jesus and tested him by asking him to show them a sign from heaven.

He replied, "When evening comes, you say, 'It will be fair weather, for the sky is red,' and in the morning, 'Today it will be stormy, for the sky is red and overcast.' You know how to interpret the appearance of the sky, but you cannot interpret the signs of the times. A wicked and adulterous generation looks for a miraculous sign, but none will be given it except the sign of Jonah." Jesus then left them and went away.

When they went across the lake, the disciples forgot to take bread. "Be careful," Jesus said to them. "Be on your guard against the yeast of the Pharisees and Sadducees."

Every chapter of the Bible is important, but you know what they say about all persons being born equal: "Some are equaler than others." So also with the Bible. Some chapters are more important than others, though all are important. Matthew 16 is one of these "more important" chapters. It is the central or critical chapter in Matthew's account of the life, death, and resurrection of Jesus Christ. Or to put it another way, it is the high point in Jesus' teaching and the disciples' growth in spiritual understanding.

Chapter 16 is the climax of those chapters in which Jesus withdraws from the crowds to teach his disciples privately. The change began in chapter 13, when Jesus began to teach in parables, explaining that this was so the crowds might not be able to understand his teaching while those who had been given to him by the Father would understand it. The chapters that follow (chaps. 14–16) contain private teaching through which the disciples make slow spiritual advances. In chapter 16 Peter makes the single most important confession of faith in Jesus thus far in Matthew—"You are the Christ, the Son of the living God" (v. 16)—after which Jesus begins to teach the disciples that it is necessary for him to die and then be raised again (v. 21).

Chapter 16 also contains the first mention of the church (v. 18), as well as Jesus' important teaching that anyone who would be his disciple must "deny himself and take up his cross and follow me" (v. 24). All in all, it is a critical collection of vital teaching in a small amount of material.

Strange Bedfellows

This teaching begins with a prelude that relates another confrontation with the religious leaders of Christ's day. Matthew identifies them as the Pharisees and Sadducees, saying that they came to test Jesus "by asking him to show them a sign from heaven" (v. 1).

This was an odd combination of forces, for the Pharisees and Sadducees held different views and were rivals and antagonists in the leadership of Israel. The Pharisees' very name means "separated," and they separated themselves by strict observance of the law and traditions of Israel. They were the most spiritual people of the time. Although their zeal for the law drew them into legalism and a sad preoccupation with minutia, which Jesus condemned, they nevertheless believed in all the right things: a supernatural written revelation from God (our Old Testament), miracles, the coming of the Messiah, the resurrection, and a final judgment at the end of time. The Sadducees were modernists. They did not believe in miracles, and although they looked for a Messiah, the Messiah they looked for was no more than an effective political leader. They were really politicians themselves, and their policy was to collaborate with and support whatever government happened to be in power at the time.[1]

War, like misery, makes strange bedfellows, however, and here both the Pharisees and Sadducees appear side by side in their opposition to Jesus. More than likely they were representing the Sanhedrin, which included both groups, and this was probably an official delegation. The narrative flow suggests that they were waiting in Galilee for Jesus, anticipating his return from the north, and that they confronted him as soon as he arrived. Matthew says that they wanted to discredit him by demanding a miracle that he either could not or would not perform.

It took a great deal of unbelief to ask for a sign from Jesus after he had already given so many. Matthew alone has told us about his healing the sick, casting out demons, calming storms on the Sea of Galilee, feeding the hungry, even raising the dead. Most, if not all, of these miracles must have been reported to these leaders, which is why they had come to challenge Jesus. But it was not really a sign they were after. They hated Jesus for who he was, and their demand was really only an attempt to discredit him.

"Show us a sign! Show us a sign from heaven!"

At this same point in the next Gospel, Mark tells us that Jesus "sighed deeply" (Mark. 8:12), so we may conclude that Jesus' answer came from a heavy heart. He was distressed at the fierce unbelief and lack of spiritual understanding of those who should have been leading Israel to believe on him as their Messiah. "When evening comes, you say, 'It will be fair weather, for the sky is red,' and in the morning, 'Today it will be stormy, for the sky is red and overcast.' You know how to interpret the appearance of the sky, but you cannot interpret the signs of the times," Jesus said. "A wicked and adulterous generation looks for a miraculous sign, but none will be given it except the sign of Jonah." Then he "left them and went away" (vv. 2–4). Those last words are ominous with meaning.

We have already studied the sign of Jonah, since Jesus spoke of it in nearly the same words as early as chapter 12 (v. 39). What is new here is his reference to the leaders' skill in predicting changes in the weather. We have almost the same saying: "Red sky at night: sailors' delight. Red sky at morning: sailors take warning." Yet we might be closer to Christ's meaning if we compare his saying to our preoccupation with weather reports. Some people watch the evening news on television chiefly to see the weather predictions, which are really quite amazing. We have satellite pictures that display cloud cover and moisture density; computer generated graphics of clouds, rain, and snow patterns; live pictures of hurricanes, floods, and blizzards; and five-day forecasts—all on a global scale, if we want it. It is quite remarkable.

Wouldn't Jesus say to us, if he were here to speak to us directly, "You know how to forecast the weather, but you cannot interpret the times in which you live. I came, I died for sin, I have been raised from the dead, and all that means nothing to most of you. You worry about whether it is going to rain tomorrow, but you don't give a single serious thought to where you will spend eternity."

What will it take to get through to such a wicked and adulterous generation as our own? Nothing, of course—if we will not believe on the basis of the sign of the prophet Jonah, which is a reference to Jesus' death and resurrection.

Dumb and Dumber

We can understand the failure of the Pharisees and Sadducees to perceive the signs of the times, of course. They were unable to understand because they would not understand. It is exactly why people are unable to believe on Jesus Christ today: They do not want to believe. What really is incomprehensible is the dense minds of the disciples. To reapply the title of a movie, the Pharisees may have been spiritually "dumb," but the disciples were "dumber." They were dumber because they had every reason to understand.

Again, this is set in the context of the story. After leaving the unbelieving leaders of the nation, Jesus went back across the Sea of Galilee, taking his disciples with him. He had withdrawn from Galilee before when he had traveled north to the region of Tyre and Sidon (Matt. 15:21). Now he left again. As we will learn when we get to verse 13, he was headed for the region of Caesarea Philippi, which was about as far from Jerusalem as it was possible to get going north. This was the last of Jesus' withdrawals before his final return to Jerusalem, where he was crucified.

What was Jesus thinking as he and the disciples made their way across the lake again? It is perfectly clear from the story. He was still pondering the unbelief and hostility of the religious leaders. They should have believed on him, but they would not. Moreover, they were doing what they could to keep other people from believing. We know Jesus was thinking along these lines, because he suddenly spoke up with a warning for the disciples. "Be careful," Jesus told them. "Be on your guard against the yeast of the Pharisees and Sadducees" (v. 6). Jesus was warning them about the dangers of the legalism of the Pharisees and the modernism of the Sadducees.

What were the disciples thinking as they crossed the lake with Jesus? The answer to that question is obvious from the story too. They were thinking about food. The problem was that they had forgotten to bring along the necessary bread. Mark says that they had only one loaf (Mark 8:14). So when Jesus said, "Be on your guard against the yeast of the Pharisees and Sadducees" (v. 6), all they could think of was lunch. Their thinking must have gone something like this: "Yeast! Yeast is used to make bread! We don't have any bread! We forgot to bring bread!" They figured it out: "Jesus must be upset with us because we forgot to bring enough food."

In Mark's account we are told only that Jesus sighed at the unbelief of the Pharisees and Sadducees. But I think Jesus must have sighed even more deeply here as he realized the level on which the twelve disciples were still thinking. With all that had happened, how could they still be so dull as to miss what he was teaching?

As for bread itself, why should they be troubling their heads about that? Wasn't he able to take care of them with or without bread? "Don't you remember the five loaves for the five thousand, and how many basketfuls you gathered? Or the seven loaves for the four thousand, and how many basketfuls you gathered?" (vv. 9–10). If Jesus had been able to feed these two great groups of people so that they were not only fed but that baskets of food were left over, wouldn't he be able to see that this small group of twelve had what they needed for food? Why couldn't they trust him and leave it all in his hands?

Yet even that was not the worst failure on the disciples' part. They had been thinking about food and had failed to trust Jesus for it, but what was worse was their failure to understand what he was saying about the religious teachers. He wasn't talking about bread when he said, "Be on your guard against the yeast of the Pharisees and Sadducees." Couldn't they see that? He was talking about the Pharisees' doctrine. Matthew says that when he told them he was not talking about bread, they finally understood "that he was not telling them to guard against the yeast used in bread, but against the teaching of the Pharisees and Sadducees" (v. 12).

The Pharisees' and Sadducees' Teaching

We might think, since the disciples finally understood that Jesus was warning them about the Pharisees' teaching, that they understood what was wrong with the Pharisees' teaching. But if we are to judge from discussion in the various commentaries on Matthew, the specific matter he was speaking about is not so obvious. What was the specific nature of this wrong teaching?

D. A. Carson approaches this question from the context of the Gospel, which is probably the best way to start, and he sees the problem as "an attitude of unbelief toward divine revelation that could not perceive Jesus to be the Messiah (vv. 1–4) but that tried to control and tame the Messiah they claimed to await." He says that is why the next section of the chapter (vv. 13–20) is so important, because there "Peter makes the confession that Jesus is the Messiah, not on the basis of manipulative signs, but by revelation from the Father."[2]

Craig S. Keener, another contemporary writer, thinks the yeast of the Pharisees and Sadducees was cynicism, adding that "the disciples' passive unbelief (v. 8) suggests that the threat of Pharisaic leaven is closer to them than they would have guessed."[3]

R. T. France's view is similar: "It was the insidious effect of the attitude revealed in the request for a sign that Jesus warned his disciples against."[4]

In a parallel passage in the third Gospel, Luke calls the Pharisees' and Sadducees' error hypocrisy (Luke 12:56).

What are we to make of these diverse interpretations? We need to take Luke's explanation seriously. He is an inspired Gospel writer, after all. But we also need to think of the context of the passage in Matthew, as D. A. Carson does. The only thing I would add to Carson's analysis is that there is more to the context of these verses than chapter 16. There is also chapter 15 in which Jesus rebuked the Pharisees for their adherence to the traditions of men rather than the actual Word of God. They had been adding human legalisms to God's revelation, which is why they were unable to accept the Lord when he came. He came with a gospel of pure grace, but they thought they had to earn their salvation by such legalistic behavior as keeping the Sabbath and observing a kosher diet. Jesus said of them,

> These people honor me with their lips,
> but their hearts are far from me.
> They worship me in vain;
> their teachings are but rules taught by men.
>
> Matthew 15:8–9; quoting Isaiah 29:13

What about the Sadducees? If the error of the Pharisees was to add to the biblical revelation, the error of the Sadducees was to take away from it. They dismissed the miracles. Even worse, they dismissed the Bible's basically other-worldly outlook. They did not believe in a resurrection of believers. All they really had to live for was success and prosperity here and now.

In either case, whether by a legalism that added to the gospel or a modernism that subtracted from it, these men rejected and wanted to do away with Jesus. It is why they had come to test him by asking for a sign.

These two errors are always present in the church as well as in religion generally, which means they are a constant danger. One error is to try to live by law rather than by grace. It is the error of people who take their relationship with God seriously but do not understand the depths of their own depravity. They imagine somehow that they can add to Christ's work by their own good works or keep themselves in a state of grace by their good deeds. Paul encountered this error among the Galatians and warned them against "beginning with the Spirit" but then "trying to attain your goal by human effort" (Gal. 3:3). Paul argued that living by grace and trying to live by works are two incompatible systems and that salvation is by grace alone.

The other error is just as insidious. The Pharisees were intensely religious and erred by adding to the gospel human understandings of what religion should be. The Sadducees were not religious, but they erred by rejecting anything that was too other-worldly or too demanding, as was Jesus' teaching. This error is more common in our day than legalism. We do have legalists, both in the church and out, but most people in our day imbibe a modern approach to everything and live as if this world and what it has to offer are all that ever really matter.

Jesus warns against both views, and he is warning us as well as the disciples when he says, "Be on your guard against the yeast of the Pharisees and Sadducees." We can miss the gospel of God's grace in Christ as much by legalistic as by modernistic unbelief. The only gospel that will do us any good is the gospel of justification by grace alone because of Christ alone, which is received by faith alone.

Knowing the Times

Let me close by going back to what Jesus told the Pharisees. He faulted them because they were unable to "interpret the signs of the times" (Matt. 16:3). Are you able to interpret the times? Above all, are you able to interpret the times well enough to come to faith in Christ? Romans 13:11 uses this imagery when it says, "Do this, understanding the present time. The hour has come for you to wake up from your slumber, because our salvation is nearer now than when we first believed."

What does it mean for someone to understand the times? It is not a matter of understanding world events or politics or economics. Rather, it is a spiritual matter. Let me remind you of four points.

1. *Galatians 1:4 says that Jesus died "to rescue us from the present evil age."* This means time as a whole. Paul is telling us that ours is an evil time out of which we need to be redeemed.

You are never going to make any true progress in wisdom unless you begin by realizing that this world, with all its cultural systems, is hostile to God and opposed to any desires for godliness on the part of God's people. Jesus said it clearly. He told his disciples just before his arrest and crucifixion, "If the world hates you, keep in mind that it hated me first. If you belonged to the world, it would love you as its own. As it is, you do not belong to the world, but I have chosen you out of the world. That is why the world hates you" (John 15:18–19). Later in his high priestly prayer, he said, "My prayer is not that you take them out of the world but that you protect them from the evil one" (John 17:15). If you are to understand the times, you must begin by understanding that the present age is evil.

2. *In 2 Corinthians 6:2, Paul writes, "I tell you, now is the time of God's favor."* In other words, although this is indeed an evil age, it is nevertheless also an age in which God has acted in Christ to accomplish our salvation. Paul also wrote, "But when the time had fully come, God sent his Son, born of a woman, born under law, to redeem those under law, that we might receive the full rights of sons" (Gal. 4:4–5).

3. *A third text that describes our times is Luke 19:44.* Jesus was approaching Jerusalem on what we call Palm Sunday, and we are told that when he observed it he began to weep, saying, "The days will come upon you when your enemies will build an embankment against you and encircle you and hem you in on every side. They will dash you to the ground, you and the children within your walls. They will not leave one stone on another, because you did not recognize the time of God's coming to you" (vv. 43–44).

He was saying that the people had been given time to repent of their sins and turn to him and be saved, but they had refused to do it. As a result, the time of their opportunity was drawing to an end. This brings us to our fourth and last verse.

4. *1 Corinthians 7:29 says, "The time is short."* In other words, this is indeed a day of God's grace. It is a time to repent and turn to Christ. It is a time to serve him too. But it will not last forever. The day of God's grace will be followed by the day of God's judgment, and when that happens, the opportunity to believe on Jesus will be lost. If you are wise enough to interpret the times correctly, you will turn to Jesus now. St. Augustine did. God pointed him to Romans 13:11–14 while he was in the garden of a friend's estate in Italy. He was convicted by those words, interpreted the times correctly, turned from his sin, trusted Christ as his Savior, and became, by God's grace, the greatest theologian of his generation.

36

Peter's Great Confession

Matthew 16:13–20

When Jesus came to the region of Caesarea Philippi, he asked his disciples, "Who do people say the Son of Man is?"

They replied, "Some say John the Baptist; others say Elijah; and still others, Jeremiah or one of the prophets."

"But what about you?" he asked. "Who do you say I am?"

Simon Peter answered, "You are the Christ, the Son of the living God."

Jesus replied, "Blessed are you, Simon son of Jonah, for this was not revealed to you by man, but by my Father in heaven. And I tell you that you are Peter, and on this rock I will build my church, and the gates of Hades will not overcome it. I will give you the keys of the kingdom of heaven; whatever you bind on earth will be bound in heaven, and whatever you loose on earth will be loosed in heaven." Then he warned his disciples not to tell anyone that he was the Christ.

Jesus Christ is the heart of Christianity. Christianity *is* Christ. But to know Jesus we must understand two great things about him: who he is and what he did. In theological textbooks these two points are referred to as the person of Christ and the work of Christ. They emerge here in Matthew 16 explicitly for the first time.

This means that Matthew 16 is an important, critical chapter in this Gospel, what I called in the last study the climax or high point of the chapters in which Jesus has withdrawn from the masses and is specifically teaching his disciples.

In this chapter we learn that Jesus is "the Christ, the Son of the living God," that he came to suffer and die and on the third day rise again, and that those who would be his disciples must follow him by taking up their own crosses daily. Yet strikingly, many commentators have offered widely diverse interpretations of lesser points found in this chapter. Hundreds of books have been written to answer questions such as, Who is the rock on which Jesus says he will build his church? What are the gates of hell? What did Jesus promise Peter when he said he would give him the keys of the kingdom of heaven?

Peter's Great Confession

Not everything in Matthew 16 is puzzling, of course. The most important things are not, and foremost among these teachings is Peter's confession of Jesus as the Christ. Jesus approached the matter indirectly by asking his disciples two probing questions.

First, "Who do people say the Son of Man is?" (v. 13). The disciples would have been in a better position than Jesus to have known what people were saying about him, but Jesus did not need to elicit this information from his followers. These identifications were standard speculations for anyone who stood out above the common people. They were raised about John the Baptist, when he was asked whether he was the Christ and, if not, whether he was Elijah or "the Prophet" mentioned in Deuteronomy 18:15 and 18. John denied being any of these figures, claiming to be only a "voice . . . calling in the desert" (John 1:19–23).

Some time has passed, however, and now one of the popular speculations was that Jesus was John the Baptist himself. John had been killed by Herod (Matt. 14:1–12), but even Herod was wondering whether Jesus was somehow John the Baptist resurrected (v. 2). A second speculation was that Jesus was Elijah. Elijah was always on the list because of the last verses of the Old Testament: Malachi 4:5–6. "See, I will send you the prophet Elijah before that great and dreadful day of the LORD comes. He will turn the hearts of the fathers to their children, and the hearts of the children to their fathers; or else I will come and strike the land with a curse." Jeremiah was mentioned because the Jews had a tradition, preserved in 2 Maccabees 2:4–8, that he had hidden the ark of the covenant and altar of incense at the time of the destruction of Jerusalem by the Babylonians and that he would come again to restore them at the start of the messianic age.[1] Some were throwing out names of other prophets (Matt. 16:14).

The surprising thing is that no one was suggesting that Jesus was the Messiah, though that speculation had been made of John the Baptist. Apparently Jesus did not match up to anyone's messianic expectations.

Now Jesus asked his second question: "But what about you? Who do you say I am?" (v. 15). It was at this point that Peter spoke for the rest and gave his classic answer: "You are the Christ, the Son of the living God" (v. 16). Peter's answer did two things, both forcefully. First, it identified Jesus as the

Messiah, the one who was to reign forever on the throne of his great ancestor David. Second, and even more important, it identified Jesus as divine: "the Son of the living God." It is that combination of ideas that makes Peter's confession so important, for he was confessing that Jesus was no mere man but God himself come to save his people.

In the Greek text this is as forceful as any confession could be. It is only ten words, but in it the definite article occurs four times, like this: "You are *the* Christ, *the* Son of *the* God, *the* living One." This was so true and so important a confession that Jesus pointed out that it was not in the same category as other things Peter was in the habit of blurting out, most of which were wrong. He told Peter, "Blessed are you, Simon son of Jonah, for this was not revealed to you by man, but by my Father in heaven" (v. 17). It was the result of a specific divine revelation.

So also today. The first and most important thing any person needs to understand about Jesus is that he is the Son of God, "very God of very God," as one of the ancient creeds puts it. That is because the value of his work, dying for sin, depends on who he is. If he is not God, his death would have no more value than any other person's death. But because he is God his death has infinite value and is able to take away sins.

Do you see that? Can you believe it? If you can, it is because God has revealed it to you. It is because he is blessing you by bringing you from death to spiritual life, just as he was blessing Peter. Salvation is God's work from the beginning to the end.

On This Rock

So far so good. But now, what do we do about the problems that everyone knows are in these verses? To begin with, what did Jesus mean when he said to Peter, "And I tell you that you are Peter, and on this rock I will build my church"?[2] There are three main interpretations.

1. *Peter is the rock.* The Roman Catholic Church concludes from this verse that Jesus appointed Peter and his successors to be head of the church, the popes. But it is possible to believe that "rock" refers to Peter without the implications Catholics draw from it. Quite a few Protestant interpreters are willing to think of Peter as the rock but only in the sense that he was the first to make this confession and thus became, along with the other apostles, a foundation on which the church would eventually be built. Paul described the church as "built on the foundation of the apostles and prophets, with Christ Jesus himself as the chief cornerstone" (Eph. 2:20). D. A. Carson and William Hendriksen think this is the right interpretation, though they make clear that "the text says nothing about Peter's successors, infallibility, or exclusive authority."[3]

2. *Peter's confession is the rock.* This has been the majority view among Protestants. R. V. G. Tasker wrote, "The faith that was expressed by him was the rock upon which he would build his church."[4] Surprisingly, this was also the view of a large number of the early Catholic fathers. John A. Broadus is

informative here. He quotes Chrysostom as saying, "On this rock; that is, on the faith of his confession. . . . He did not say upon Peter, for it was not upon man, but upon his faith." Broadus also cites Gregory of Nyssa, Isidore of Pelusium, Hilary, Theodoret, Theophanes, Theophylact, and John of Damascus as having held this interpretation.[5]

3. *Christ is the rock.* This is a minority view among evangelicals, usually explained by saying that Jesus was making a pun on Peter's name. Peter's name is *petros,* a masculine noun meaning "rock" or "stone." (Peter's Hebrew name, *Cephas,* also means "rock.") But when Jesus referred to "this rock," he used the feminine form of the same word, *petra,* which this view says means "bed rock" or "foundation rock." The idea is that Peter was only a little stone, perhaps only a pebble, but that Jesus is the foundation on which the church is built.

This view has some weaknesses. One is that Jesus spoke in Aramaic, not Greek, and that even the Greek words do not necessarily have these different connotations. On the other hand, Jesus and his teaching have already been described as a foundation rock in Matthew at the end of the Sermon on the Mount, where Jesus called the man who builds his house on the rock wise (Matt. 7:25). Later Jesus will also speak of himself as "the stone the builders rejected" but which "has become the capstone," quoting Psalm 118:22 (Matt. 21:42). Nowhere does Matthew even hint that Peter is the rock.

There is a theological argument too. Throughout the Old Testament God is frequently described as the Rock of Israel, which is appropriate since he alone is the strength and fortress of his people. It is appropriate too that Jesus, who is also God, should be the rock and that we should think of the church being built on him. But Peter? Vacillating Peter? A mere man? It must have been considerations such as these that impressed St. Augustine, the greatest theologian of the early Catholic Church, for in his "Retractions," written late in life, Augustine acknowledged that in an early work against the Donatists he referred to Peter as the rock but that he had since come to believe that the rock could only be Christ.[6]

As for myself, I could believe that Jesus called Peter the rock in the careful and limited sense that many evangelical scholars suggest. But what persuades me that this third interpretation is right—that Jesus is the rock—is Peter's own testimony in his first letter.

How did Peter understand Jesus' words? First Peter 2:4–8 provides a definitive answer to that question, because there, as in his great sermon before the Jewish Sanhedrin (Acts 4:8–12), Peter does not suggest even for a moment that he is the rock on which the church is built. Rather, he insists that the foundation stone is actually Jesus Christ. Peter refers to Jesus as "the living Stone" on which those who believe are, "like living stones," being built into a spiritual house or temple. Therefore, if others, like Peter himself, are to be called stones in any sense, it is only because they have been built on Jesus, who is the actual foundation.

Peter proves his point by three Old Testament quotations.

Isaiah 28:16. This verse is probably placed first because it is the clearest of the three in identifying Jesus as the "precious cornerstone" of God's temple. In verse 4, Peter introduced the subject by referring to Jesus as one who had been "rejected by men but chosen by God and precious to him." Isaiah 28:16 shows us where he got two of those three ideas: (1) Jesus was "chosen by God," and (2) he was "precious" to God. In addition, it tells how human beings are to be related to Jesus. It is by faith, for they are to "trust in him." By believing on Jesus we are built into the church God is constructing.

Psalm 118:22. To those who believe, Jesus has become "precious." Yet that is not the only possible response to Jesus. It is also possible to reject him. This is the third of the ideas Peter introduced in verse 4 ("rejected by men"). He proves it by this second quotation.

Jesus had applied Psalm 118:22 to himself during his earthly ministry, so Peter had probably learned to interpret the verse this way from Jesus. Jesus had told a parable about farmers to whom the owner of a vineyard had leased a field. They were to care for it and give the owner his share of the profit when the time came. The owner sent servants to collect his profit, but the tenants beat, stoned, and killed them. Finally, the owner sent his son, thinking they would respect him. They killed him instead. Jesus then asked the chief priests and scribes to whom he was telling the story, "When the owner of the vineyard comes, what will he do to those tenants?"

They answered, "He will bring those wretches to a wretched end, and he will rent the vineyard to other tenants, who will give him his share of the crop at harvest time" (Matt. 21:41). This was the right answer, of course, but Jesus then applied it to himself by quoting these important verses from the psalm:

> "Have you never read in the Scriptures:
>
> 'The stone the builders rejected
> has become the capstone;
> the Lord has done this,
> and it is marvelous in our eyes'?"
>
> Matthew 21:42

There can be no question as to how Jesus understood these verses. God is the owner of the vineyard. The leaders of Israel are the evil tenant farmers. The servants are the prophets, and the son who was killed was Jesus himself, the Son of God. Therefore, he is also the stone rejected by the builders who was to become the capstone of revealed religion. Peter also cites Psalm 118:22 in Acts 4:11.

Isaiah 8:14. In the last of his Old Testament quotations, Peter returned to Isaiah again, using Isaiah 8:14 to add the thought of stumbling to the prior thought of rejecting Jesus. He meant that rejecting him is no small matter. It has a serious consequence, which is to fall down spiritually or be lost forever.

Clearly, Peter seems to have understood that the church was to be built on Jesus and nowhere claims or even suggests it could be otherwise. He would be the last of all people to suggest that he was the foundation.

The Gates of Hades

What about "the gates of Hades" not being able to overcome Christ's church? Several different interpretations exist. The most common view is that "the gates of Hades" refers to attacks on the church by Satan and his demonic forces and that this is a promise that Satan will not succeed. The problem is with the word *gates,* which is a strange way to refer to an attacking army. It suggests a defensive situation, and the natural way of understanding it is that hell will not be able to resist the forces of the church when the church is assaulting it. Unfortunately, although the Bible recognizes the reality of spiritual warfare, it does not speak of evangelism in those exact terms.

The other understanding of these words is that they refer merely to death, for passing through hell's gates was a common Jewish way of referring to death. If this is what Jesus means, the idea would be that not even death, whether in its natural form or in times of great mass persecutions, would be able to destroy the church Christ is building.

In any case, the idea is that in spite of attacks from various quarters, the church will be invincible, and the reason for its invincibility is that it is built on Christ. I suggest that this interpretation supports the view of "this rock" that I have taken, for we remember that when Satan requested permission to blow on Peter at the time of Jesus' crucifixion, Peter was able to recover only because Jesus took care of him and prayed for him. Jesus told Peter, "Simon, Simon, Satan has asked to sift you as wheat. But I have prayed for you, Simon, that your faith may not fail" (Luke 22:31–32). Because Peter was founded on the rock, which was Christ, he survived the temptation.

The Keys of the Kingdom

Peter was not the rock, but he did have an important role to play. Specifically, he was given "the keys of the kingdom of heaven" with the added promise, "whatever you bind on earth will be bound in heaven, and whatever you loose on earth will be loosed in heaven" (v. 19). Does that mean Peter was given the exclusive and daunting privilege of determining who would go to heaven and who would not?

Here again, three major interpretations exist.

1. *Peter and his successors have been given authority to receive or exclude individual people from salvation.* This is the position of the Roman Catholic Church. Strict Catholicism teaches that there is no salvation apart from the fellowship of the church. Therefore, exclusion from the church by excommunication means one is severed from the body of Christ; a person dying in that

state will go to hell. Priests have this authority over their flock, but ultimately it resides in the pope alone.

2. *Ministers have authority to announce forgiveness of sins to those who repent of sin and trust Christ.* This is the Protestant position, and it finds expression in the parts of Protestant services called the confession of sin and the declaration of pardon. The Heidelberg Catechism contains a classic statement regarding this position. "How is the kingdom of heaven opened and shut by the preaching of the gospel?" Answer: "By proclaiming and openly witnessing, according to the command of Christ, to believers, one and all, that, whenever they receive the promise of the gospel by a true faith, all their sins are really forgiven them of God for the sake of Christ's merits; and on the contrary, by proclaiming and witnessing to all unbelievers and such as do not sincerely repent that the wrath of God and eternal condemnation abide on them so long as they are not converted" (answer to question 84).

3. *Peter used the keys by opening the door of the gospel to Jews by his preaching at Pentecost, recorded in Acts 2, and by opening the door of the gospel to Gentiles by his preaching in the house of Cornelius, recorded in Acts 10.* Peter was the apostle to the Jews, so he preached to the Jews first. But although he was the apostle to the Jews, Peter was also the first to bring the gospel to a strictly Gentile audience.

This is a minority view among Protestants, but it is held by the distinguished evangelical scholar John Stott, among others. Writing on Acts 10, Stott says, "We have already watched [Peter] use these keys effectively, opening the kingdom to the Jews on the Day of Pentecost and then to the Sanhedrin soon afterwards. Now he is to use them again to open the kingdom to Gentiles; by evangelizing and baptizing Cornelius, the first Gentile convert."[7]

Jesus, the Christ

At the end of this section, Matthew records that Jesus warned his disciples not to tell anyone he was the Christ. He had good reason for doing so. The people had mistaken ideas about what the Messiah would be like and what he would do. Jesus did not want to be pressed into their false patterns of expectation, so he told his disciples not to announce who he was. Scholars have referred to this as "the messianic secret."

But that was then; this is now. Today there is no reason to preserve the secret. On the contrary, we have every reason and, in fact, Christ's own command, to proclaim it. Jesus is the Christ, the Son of the living God. He is the sinner's Savior. Therefore, to repent of sin and believe on him is to pass from death to life and to find salvation. To reject him is to perish forever. This is good news. Believe it, and tell others too.

37

The Way of the Cross

Matthew 16:21–28

From that time on Jesus began to explain to his disciples that he must go to Jerusalem and suffer many things at the hands of the elders, chief priests and teachers of the law, and that he must be killed and on the third day be raised to life.

Peter took him aside and began to rebuke him. "Never, Lord!" he said. "This shall never happen to you!"

Jesus turned and said to Peter, "Get behind me, Satan! You are a stumbling block to me; you do not have in mind the things of God, but the things of men."

Then Jesus said to his disciples, "If anyone would come after me, he must deny himself and take up his cross and follow me. For whoever wants to save his life will lose it, but whoever loses his life for me will find it. What good will it be for a man if he gains the whole world, yet forfeits his soul? Or what can a man give in exchange for his soul? For the Son of Man is going to come in his Father's glory with his angels, and then he will reward each person according to what he has done. I tell you the truth, some who are standing here will not taste death before they see the Son of Man coming in his kingdom."

I read in a book on etiquette that whenever you introduce two people you should give the name of each person and then tell something about him or her—where the person is from or what he does. "Sally, I would like you to meet Robert. He works with computers for Dupont." Or, "Robert, this is Sally. She's a doctor."

In a sense, in chapter 16 Matthew is introducing us to Jesus Christ in this way. He has been telling us about Jesus all along, of course, but here he gets to the heart of his introduction. Who is Jesus? Peter had the answer: "You are the Christ, the Son of the living God" (v. 16). Then, what does Jesus do? Jesus himself answered that part. "From that time on Jesus began to explain to his disciples that he must go to Jerusalem and suffer many things at the hands of the elders, chief priests and teachers of the law, and that he must be killed and on the third day be raised to life" (v. 21).

How do you introduce a person to Jesus Christ? You say, "This is Jesus Christ, the Son of God. He came to earth to suffer and die on the cross for your salvation and rise from the dead." You may have to say that more than once, of course, and explain it. Jesus had to do so more than once with his disciples. In fact, that is the significance of the words "from that time on" in verse 21. It is a turning point in the Gospel. Before this, Jesus had alluded to his death indirectly only once (Matt. 9:15) and to his resurrection only once (Matt. 12:39–40). Now he begins to teach the disciples openly and repeatedly. This teaching is so difficult for them to receive that Jesus comes back to it again and again (see Matt. 17:22–23; 20:18–19; 26:2, 12, 21, 31–32). Jesus explains that he will be betrayed, arrested, beaten, tried, and crucified in Jerusalem, but he promises that on the third day he will rise again.

Suffering, Death, and Resurrection

Did the disciples understand what Jesus was telling them? In one sense they didn't understand it at all, because when Jesus was arrested and killed, his death was a shock to them and they scattered immediately, each to his own home, like the Emmaus disciples (Luke 24:13–35). Not one of them understood the necessity of his death or anticipated his resurrection. In fact, most of them refused to believe in the resurrection even after they had heard about it. On the other hand, the disciples understood Jesus' words all too well. Otherwise, why would Peter have tried to dissuade Jesus from this "mistaken" way of thinking? "Never, Lord!" Peter said. "This shall never happen to you" (v. 22).

The problem was not their understanding of the words. The problem was that suffering did not fit into their ideas of what the Messiah should do. Like everyone else in their day, they thought the Messiah would be a strong political figure who would drive out the Romans and once again establish Israel as a free and independent nation.

None of this is surprising. The disciples were merely people of their time. What is surprising is Peter's arrogance in taking Jesus aside to rebuke him. It is an arrogance made even more shocking by his earlier confession of Jesus as the Messiah. If that meant anything, it meant that Jesus was Peter's Lord. But immediately after saying that Jesus was his Lord, Peter speaks as if he knows more about God's will for the Messiah than the Messiah does.

Something else is equally surprising—the sharpness of Jesus' rebuke of Peter. A moment before, Jesus had called him blessed: "Blessed are you, Simon son of Jonah, for this was not revealed to you by man, but by my Father in heaven" (v. 17). But now Jesus says, "Get behind me, Satan! You are a stumbling block to me; you do not have in mind the things of God, but the things of men" (v. 23). One moment Peter is God's mouthpiece. The next moment he is a mouthpiece for the devil.

Jesus recognized that this situation was exactly like the temptation Satan had made in the wilderness at the start of his ministry. It was a temptation to achieve worldly success without the cross. "All this [the kingdoms of the world and their splendor] I will give you, if you will bow down and worship me," Satan said (Matt. 4:9). Jesus' response was the same then as when he rebuked Peter: "Away from me, Satan!" (Matt. 4:10). He told Peter, "Get behind me, Satan!" (Matt. 16:23).

These verses contain at least two great lessons.

1. *Christianity without the cross is worthless.* Without the cross there is no salvation because there is no Savior. Christ's example helps no one, both because we cannot follow it and also because it is not an example we need but a Savior.

The English bishop John Ryle wrote:

> On matters of church government, and the form of worship, men may differ from us, and yet reach heaven in safety. On the matter of Christ's atoning death, as the way of peace, truth is only one. If we are wrong here, we are ruined forever. Error on many points is only a skin disease; error about Christ's death is a disease of the heart. Here let us take our stand. Let nothing move us from this ground. The sum of all our hopes must be, that "Christ has died for us" (1 Thess. 5:10). Give up that doctrine, and we have no solid hope at all.[1]

2. *It is easy for us to be exactly right one minute and terribly wrong the next.* One minute Peter is a prophet, a true spokesman for God. The next minute he is advancing the agenda of the devil, not realizing that in trying to deflect Jesus from the cross he is actually asking for his own damnation since apart from Jesus' death neither he, nor any of us, can be saved.

But Peter learned, and we shouldn't forget that either. The very man who said, "Never, Lord. This shall never happen to you," became one of the greatest expounders of the necessity of Christ's death. Once he got it right he never forgot it. It was Peter who told the Sanhedrin that Jesus Christ is "the stone you builders rejected, which has become the capstone" and "salvation is found in no one else, for there is no other name under heaven given to men by which we must be saved" (Acts 4:11–12). He wrote in his first letter, "He himself bore our sins in his body on the tree, so that we might die to sins and live for righteousness; by his wounds you have been healed" (1 Peter 2:24; see Acts 2:23; 3:18).

If we are going to be right in spiritual things, it will only be to the extent we study the Bible and grow in understanding. Whatever we may not fully understand, these two things at least will be clear: (1) Jesus died to save us from our sin, and (2) there is no salvation apart from him. We must go on from there, but without that starting point we are nowhere.

Taking Up the Cross

How many important lessons can a person learn at one time? Not many, probably. But on this occasion Jesus seized the moment and immediately went on to teach his disciples that not only did he have to go to the cross but in a sense they had to go to the cross too, dying to themselves and their own plans.

This was so important to Jesus that he repeated it again and again in his teaching, almost as often as he spoke about the necessity of his personal suffering.[2] He never suggested that his followers could die *for* sin, either their own or others' sins, as he would do, but he insisted that following him meant self-denial, suffering, rejection, and perhaps even physical death. The way of the cross is not only for Jesus but for us. Or to put it another way: Christ's death is of value only to those who are willing to die to themselves and follow him.

A great deficiency exists in today's evangelical church. Several years ago I wrote a book called *Christ's Call to Discipleship* in which I started by noting this fact:

> There is a defect, even a fatal defect, in the life of the church of Christ in the twentieth century: a lack of true discipleship. For the genuine Christian, discipleship means forsaking everything to follow Christ. But for many of today's supposed Christians—perhaps the majority—it is the case that while there is much talk about Christ and even much furious activity that is supposed to be done in his name, there is actually very little following of Christ himself. And that means that in some circles at least there is very little genuine Christianity. Many who fervently call him "Lord, Lord" are not Christians (Matt. 7:21).[3]

I wrote that in 1986, but the situation is no better today. In fact, it is probably worse. What is the problem? We do not like this kind of teaching. Prosperity? Yes. Victory? Yes. But suffering? Death? The cross? We do not like those things. Yet there is no genuine Christianity without them.

When Jesus tells his followers to deny themselves, take up their crosses, and follow him, he is saying that those items belong together as a composite picture of what being a disciple is all about. All three are necessary.

1. *Self-denial.* When we think about what it means to deny oneself, we are at once brought to the radical distinction between a God-oriented life and a life of unrepentant self-seeking or sin. Self-seeking is the opposite of self-denial, and the problem with self-seeking is that it has been the essence of sin from the beginning.

Self-seeking is what caused the fall of Satan. Satan said, "I want my way. I am going to displace God. I am going to rule the universe." God replied that Satan would actually be brought low (Isa. 14:12–15). By contrast, Jesus said, "I will go down in self-denial. I will abase myself in order that those I love might be lifted from sin to glory." As a result, God promised that Jesus

Christ would be exalted. He would be given that name which is above every name, so that every tongue would confess that "Jesus Christ is Lord" (Phil. 2:11).

2. *Taking up the cross.* Not only are we to say no to self, we are also to say yes to God, which is what taking up our cross involves. Some refer to cross-bearing as if it means enduring what is inevitable, but that is not the case at all. Several kinds of things we cannot avoid: a physical handicap, a deficient academic background, a drunken husband, a profligate wife. People sometimes refer to such inevitable limitations as "my cross," but they are not crosses. Real crosses involve the will. They involve saying yes to something difficult for Jesus' sake.

Cross-bearing involves prayer and Bible study. These necessary means of grace take time and must be voluntarily chosen and pursued, rather than other pastimes we might humanly prefer.

Cross-bearing involves the items Jesus lists in Matthew 25: feeding the hungry, giving drink to the thirsty, receiving the stranger, clothing the naked, caring for the sick, and visiting the one who is in prison (vv. 31–46). These actions are not easy. They involve denying one's self, time, money, and convenience. At times these actions seem pointless, because the gifts are abused or the one giving them is slighted by the one he helps. But we are to continue living in this way, because doing so means we are saying yes to Jesus. We are taking up our crosses in his service.

Taking up our cross involves witnessing. It means putting oneself out for the sake of those God sends into our lives.

Essentially, taking up our cross means accepting whatever God has given us and then offering it back to him (Rom. 12:1). Romans 12 describes us as God's priests making sacrifices that are "holy and pleasing" to him. Priests offer only what they have first received. They take the gifts of the worshiper and then offer them to God. We are in that position. The gifts we have are from God. We take these gifts—whatever they may be—and offer them back to God with thanksgiving.

3. *Following Jesus.* Discipleship is not simply a door to be entered but a path to be followed, and the disciple proves that his discipleship is genuine by following that path to the end. David wrote about it in Psalm 119. The section of the psalm that begins "Your word is a lamp to my feet and a light for my path" (v. 105) ends, "My heart is set on keeping your decrees *to the very end*" (v. 112). That is it! The true disciple is one who follows Christ to the very end.

Good or Bad Investment?

When the cost of being a Christian is put in these terms, which is the teaching of Jesus Christ himself, any sane person ought to ask whether this is a good investment or not. The cost is high. Is what we get out of it worth what we put in? Jesus seems to have been aware of that question, for he follows his demand for cross-bearing with three strong incentives for doing just that. These are obvious in the Greek text of Matthew 16, for each of them begins with the word *for* (in vv. 25–27; the New International Version eliminates "for" at the start of verse 26.) Why should any sane person deny himself to follow Jesus?

1. *Verse 25: Doing so means saving your soul and not doing so means losing your soul.* If all we are talking about here is worldly influence, wealth, or possessions, the devil's offer might be good: You can have the world; all you have to do is worship Satan. But those who worship Satan for the world he offers will perish with him. The devil can give you a paltry imitation of heaven now—"heaven on earth," we say—but you will experience hell hereafter. On the other hand, following Jesus now, though it requires self-denial and has its difficult moments, leads to heaven.

Further, in verse 25 Jesus does not even use the word *soul,* as if all he is speaking about is the life of the world to come. He speaks of life itself, meaning that even here fullness of life consists in following him and that the sure way to an empty life is to reject him.

2. *Verse 26: Your soul is more valuable than the entire world.* The world is not without value. Its charms are real. God created the world, after all. But the world is transitory. Jesus himself said that "heaven and earth will pass away" (Matt. 24:35). It is foolish to exchange your eternal soul for what will one day be gone.

3. *Verse 27: Those who follow Jesus will be rewarded by Jesus when he returns in glory with the holy angels.* Some people think the idea of rewards is an unworthy motivation. They think following Christ should be altruistic and idealistic, but Jesus knows our frailties and does not seem to be ashamed to hold out the promise of rewards. Deprivations and sorrows here, but rewards in heaven. Here a cross, but there a crown. Can anyone reasonably suppose that he or she will somehow come out on the short end by following Jesus Christ?

A Final Puzzling Sentence

I said when I began these studies of Matthew 16 that, although this is one of the richest and most important chapters in the Gospel, it is also one that seems to be a source of countless problems. Almost every sentence seems to have produced diverse interpretations among commentators. How is Peter the rock? What are the gates of Hades? What is the meaning of the keys? We do not escape problems even with the chapter's last verse, for no one seems entirely sure what Jesus meant when he said, "I tell you the truth, some who are standing here will not taste death before they see the Son of Man coming in his kingdom" (v. 28). Here are four suggestions.

1. *The disciples will see the kingdom come with power either at the resurrection of Christ or at Pentecost.* William Hendriksen writes, "The reference is in all probability to: *a.* his glorious resurrection, *b.* his return in the Spirit on the day of Pentecost, and in close connection with that event, *c.* his reign from his

position at the Father's right hand."[4] So also H. N. Ridderbos. "The beginnings of Christ's coming in his kingdom would indeed be seen by some of those who were listening to him. They would see these beginnings in his resurrection, in his ascension, and in the kingly manifestations of the exalted Lord that followed."[5]

2. *Jesus was referring to the fall of Jerusalem.* This is the view of John Broadus: "The most reasonable explanation, especially when we compare [this verse with] chapter 24, is to understand a reference to the destruction of Jerusalem, forty years afterwards."[6]

3. *Jesus was referring to the transfiguration.* Howard Vos says, "The prediction that some present would not die before they saw him coming in his kingdom is most naturally interpreted to refer to the three members of the inner circle. Shortly they were to witness the glorified Christ at the transfiguration, which was a foretaste of the coming of Christ in his kingdom."[7]

4. *Jesus expected the end of the world within a few years but was wrong to think so.* This has been a popular liberal view, but it is obviously unacceptable to those holding to the inerrancy of Christ and Scripture.

There is not much that seems to hinge on one's interpretation of this verse and any of the first three views is acceptable. Only the fourth is not. Nevertheless, as far as I am concerned, I think Jesus was referring to the transfiguration: (1) because the account of the transfiguration follows so closely, here as well as in Mark and Luke, and (2) because verse 27 is so closely linked to verse 26, where the emphasis is on Jesus coming in his "glory," as opposed to his humiliation. It is the glory that was revealed to the disciples on the mountain.

Lift High the Cross

We live in a day when a substantial part of the evangelical world wants a domesticated Jesus who "blesses, satisfies, fills, thrills, and strengthens his followers"[8] but does not insist on a cross. What we need is the genuine Jesus who demands that his followers die to self and actually follow him.

There was a time when Peter and the others did not understand this, though they did eventually. They proved it by the quality of their lives and by their faithfulness to Christ and the gospel unto death. We understand it now. We know what Jesus demands of us, or we would not be Christians. We know that we need to take up the cross and follow Jesus, but have we taken it up and are we bearing it daily? We know the value of the soul, but do we live as if we believed it? We have heard of Christ's return, but do we look forward to it joyfully? Those who are blessed by God will answer, "Yes, yes, yes," to those questions.

38

With Jesus on the Mountain

Matthew 17:1–13

After six days Jesus took with him Peter, James and John the brother of James, and led them up a high mountain by themselves. There he was transfigured before them. His face shone like the sun, and his clothes became as white as the light. Just then there appeared before them Moses and Elijah, talking with Jesus.

Peter said to Jesus, "Lord, it is good for us to be here. If you wish, I will put up three shelters—one for you, one for Moses and one for Elijah."

While he was still speaking, a bright cloud enveloped them, and a voice from the cloud said, "This is my Son, whom I love; with him I am well pleased. Listen to him!"

When the disciples heard this, they fell facedown to the ground, terrified. But Jesus came and touched them. "Get up," he said. "Don't be afraid." When they looked up, they saw no one except Jesus.

Many important things happen on mountains in the Bible, which means we are not wrong when we recall these events and speak of mountain-top experiences.

The most dramatic example is the appearance of God on Mount Sinai, first to Moses at the burning bush (Exod. 3:1–4:17), then later to the nation when the law was given accompanied by such terrifying physical phenomena as fire, darkness, storms, and thunder. It was so frightening that even Moses said, "I am trembling with fear" (Heb. 12:21). On Mount Carmel on the coast of the Mediterranean Sea God answered Elijah's prayer by sending fire to consume the sacrifice and even the altar, thereby defeating the claim of the false prophets of Baal (1 Kings 18:16–40). After that, God appeared to Elijah on Mount Sinai, as he had to Moses (1 Kings 19:9–18). Again, we can think of Satan's blatant temptation of the Lord Jesus Christ when he took him to "a very high mountain" and showed him all the kingdoms of the world and their glory, saying, "All this I will give you, if you will bow down and worship me" (Matt. 4:9). Jesus overcame Satan by reminding him that it was written in Deuteronomy 6:13, "Worship the Lord your God, and serve him only" (Matt. 4:10).

We come to another important mountain in this study. It is called the Mount of the Transfiguration, and it was the location of what was undoubtedly a mountain-top experience for the disciples who were with the Lord on this occasion.

Three disciples were present—Peter, James, and John—and Peter was so impressed by what he had seen that he wrote years later, "We did not follow cleverly invented stories when we told you about the power and coming of our Lord Jesus Christ, but we were eyewitnesses of his majesty. For he received honor and glory from God the Father when the voice came to him from the Majestic Glory, saying, 'This is my Son, whom I love; with him I am well pleased.' We ourselves heard this voice that came from heaven when we were with him on the sacred mountain" (2 Peter 1:16–18).

There are times in the lives of most of us when we wish we could have a mountain-top experience like that of these disciples.

On the Mountain

There is much about this story we do not know. We do not know what mountain this was, for instance. The "high mountain" of verse 1 has been traditionally identified as Mount Tabor, which lies south of Galilee. It has an elevation of nineteen hundred feet. But Mount Tabor seems to be located in the wrong place if Jesus was far to the north near Caesarea Philippi at this time. Besides, archaeologists tell us that in Jesus' day Mount Tabor had a fortress on the top, which would have made it an unlikely place for the private nature of the transfiguration.

Others have focused on Mount Hermon because of its high elevation (9,232 feet) and because it is just beyond Caesarea Philippi to the north. But it was outside Palestine proper in Gentile territory, and since Jesus and the disciples ran into "teachers of the law" as soon as they had come down (Mark 9:14), it seems an improbable location. The Jewish teachers would not likely have been in Gentile lands.

The best identification may be Mount Miron, which is the highest mountain in Palestine proper (elevation 3,926 feet) and lies midway between Caesarea Philippi and Capernaum. Yet all we can say is that it is a likely site. We do not really know where the transfiguration took place.

What we do know is that Jesus had gone up the mountain to pray, and while he was praying he was changed (Luke 9:28–29). "His face shone like the sun, and his clothes became as white as the light" (Matt. 17:2). The word for "transfigured" (v. 2) is used in 2 Corinthians 3:18 and Romans 12:2 to describe an inner transformation of the believer to Christ's likeness. Here it seems to have to do more with Jesus' outward, visible appearance. If we turn to Exodus 34:29–30, we find something similar. In that passage Moses' face is said to have shone so brightly that the people were unable to look at it, and Moses had to cover his face with a veil when he was with them. Yet there is a major difference. Moses' face shone because he was reflecting the glory of God, with whom he had been speaking. By contrast, Jesus' face shone because he was transfigured, which means it was his own glory that was being made visible for the disciples' benefit.

This difference also shows up in the appearance of Moses and Elijah. We are not told why Moses and Elijah were present rather than some other Old Testament figures. Since Moses was the great lawgiver and Elijah was the first of the great prophets, however, the two seem to represent the Law and the Prophets, the two chief divisions of the Old Testament, suggesting that what they stood for is now being fulfilled in Jesus.

Jesus had taught this himself, of course. He said, "Do not think that I have come to abolish the Law or the Prophets; I have not come to abolish them but to fulfill them" (Matt. 5:17). Again he said, "The Law and the Prophets were proclaimed until John. Since that time, the good news of the kingdom of God is being preached, and everyone is forcing his way into it" (Luke 16:16). This does not mean that the Law and the Prophets were to be abrogated by Jesus. The very next verse says, "It is easier for heaven and earth to disappear than for the least stroke of a pen to drop out of the Law" (v. 17). But it does mean that Jesus is the culmination of the entire Old Testament revelation and the fulfillment of everything these two great figures taught and represented.

Peter's Foolish Suggestion

The importance of Jesus as the fulfillment of what Moses and Elijah stood for comes out even more clearly in what happens next. Peter, the man of action, was not one to keep silent and merely marvel at what he was privileged to see. He thought he had to say something. So he blurted out, "Lord, it is good for us to be here. If you wish, I will put up three shelters—one for you, one for Moses and one for Elijah" (v. 4). This was exactly the wrong thing to say. The point of what was happening was that Jesus was the unique Son of God, the king of glory. Moses and Elijah were there to honor him. But Peter's suggestion had the effect of putting Jesus, Moses, and Elijah on the same footing. Or perhaps Peter even thought it was an honor for Jesus to speak to these other two great men.

This time it was God the Father himself who corrected Peter, rather than Jesus, who had corrected Peter earlier when he sought to deflect him from the cross (see Matt. 16:23). The text says, "A bright cloud enveloped them, and a voice from the cloud said, 'This is my Son, whom I love; with him I am well pleased. Listen to him!'" (v. 5).

It would be impossible for any Jewish reader to miss the importance of this cloud, for it would immediately suggest the Shekinah Glory cloud of the Old Testament and indicate that God himself was present to speak as he had spoken before on Mount Sinai. The Shekinah Glory was a striking phenomenon, and it is mentioned frequently in both the Old and New Testaments. In all it is referred to fifty-eight times in the Bible in at least ten different books.

The cloud is first mentioned at the Exodus when it appeared to lead the people. The text says, "By day the Lord went ahead of them in a pillar of cloud to guide them on their way and by night in a pillar of fire to give them light, so that they could travel by day or night. Neither the pillar of cloud by day nor the pillar of fire by night left its place in front of the people" (Exod. 13:21–22). The cloud protected the people from the pursuing Egyptians (Exod. 14:19–20). It was probably this cloud that descended on Sinai when Moses went up the mountain to receive the law from God (Exod. 19:16–20). When the wilderness tabernacle was completed, the cloud of glory filled it so that even Moses could not enter (Exod. 40:34–35). After this, the cloud is referred to many more times throughout the Pentateuch. It appeared at the dedication of Solomon's temple (1 Kings 8:10). It is even possible that the same phenomenon was involved in Jesus' ascension, when "a cloud hid him" from the disciples' sight (see Acts 1:9).[1]

Luke says that the disciples were afraid as the cloud began to envelop them (Luke 9:34), which is quite understandable, but they became even more terrified when they heard a voice that they knew was God's. What God said was similar to what he uttered at Jesus' baptism, recorded in Matthew 3:17: "This is my Son, whom I love; with him I am well pleased." It was an echo of Psalm 2:7 and Isaiah 42:1, which indicates that Jesus was both the Son of God, who is mentioned in the psalm, as well as the suffering servant, who is described in Isaiah, an important combination of ideas.[2] What is new here is the command: "Listen to him!"

Just as the first part of this instruction is an echo of Psalm 2:7 and Isaiah 42:1, so this part seems to echo Deuteronomy 18:15, where Moses told the people of Israel, "The Lord your God will raise up for you a prophet like me from among your own brothers. You must listen to him." This was an early messianic prophecy, indicating that the Messiah would function among other things as God's spokesman. Now this Messianic figure has been raised up. He is Jesus, and the duty of Peter as well as all others is to be quiet and listen to what Jesus has to say.

Could anything be more relevant today? We sometimes hear people say in a crisis situation, "Don't just stand there; do something." But one sharp theologian I know says, when he is thinking about the truths of God revealed in Scripture, "Don't just do something; stand there." He means that it is more important to stand firm on the truths of Scripture than to be active in Christian work. Similarly, we might say as we work at trying to understand what God said to Peter, "Don't just say something [which is what Peter was doing]; listen to Jesus."

I know that we need to speak. The Bible needs to be taught; it is what the ministers of the gospel are chiefly called to do. Every believer should be witnessing. But it is not activity we need so much as to hear the words of Jesus. It is not a vision we need so much as to learn from him. Charles H. Spurgeon said, "It is better to hear the Son of God than to see saints or to build tabernacles."[3]

Do you hear Jesus? Do you obey him? Or are you so caught up in the theories of mere men or even in otherwise worthwhile Christian activity that you miss that which alone is really needful (see Luke 10:38–42)?

Where Is Elijah?

On the way down the mountain the next morning, Jesus told the disciples to keep quiet about what they had seen until after the resurrection. The reason is obvious. He did not want them to relate stories that would fan a misguided messianic expectation. He needed to go to the cross before the nature of his work could be rightly and fully known.

But the disciples were still puzzling over what they had witnessed, and they countered with a question. They had seen Elijah with Jesus, and this caused them to wonder about Elijah's role as the Messiah's forerunner, which was prophesied in Malachi 4:5–6, the very last verses of the Old Testament. These verses say, "See, I will send you the prophet Elijah before that great and dreadful day of the LORD comes. He will turn the hearts of the fathers to their children, and the hearts of the children to their fathers; or else I will come and strike the land with a curse." Malachi 4:5–6 was used by the teachers of the law to say that Elijah had to come before the Messiah, as his forerunner. But how could that be if the Messiah, whom the disciples now believed Jesus to be, was already here and was about to consummate his work?

The disciples' question can be taken in two ways.

1. *As a chronological problem.* If you are the Messiah, what about Elijah? How can you be the Messiah if the teachers are right when they say that Elijah has to come first? How is this to be explained? Most people who read these accounts take the disciples' question this way because of the word *first,* which suggests the problem with the sequence.

2. *As a theological problem.* This understanding of the question comes from the anticipated nature of the forerunner's ministry. Malachi 4:6 taught that Elijah would bring about the restoration of all things (v. 11). But if Elijah was to do that, bringing the people to a right relationship with God as a precondition of the Messiah's coming, how was it that the Messiah would need to die? Who would reject him in such a happy age? D. A. Carson holds to this idea, saying, "Their confusion was not *merely* chronological—*who must*

come first—rather, it referred back to their fundamental inability to make sense of the combination of glory and suffering. At this stage, their witness of the transfiguration glory of Jesus had if anything confirmed them in their misapprehension."[4]

Whatever their question meant, both these puzzles were answered when Jesus replied, "To be sure, Elijah comes and will restore all things. But I tell you, Elijah has already come, and they did not recognize him, but have done to him everything they wished. In the same way the Son of Man is going to suffer at their hands" (vv. 11–12).

This means that the scribes were right to insist that Elijah must come before the Messiah, but they were wrong in failing to see that he had in fact come. They were wrong in their interpretation of the restoration too. They understood this as a promise of a perfect messianic age. But that was not a given fact, even in Malachi, since the last verse says that if the people do not repent at the forerunner's teaching, then God will return "and strike the land with a curse" (Mal. 4:6). Since Jesus is making clear that the work of Elijah had been done by John the Baptist and that the people had not repented at his teaching, the only thing they could reasonably expect from God now was this judgment.[5]

Moreover, since the leaders had mistreated and killed John the Baptist, why should Jesus expect any different treatment? By calling their attention to this pattern Jesus was reinforcing his teaching that it was necessary for him to be crucified. This was the second most important thing he had to teach them after he had taught who he was. Peter, James, and John had been given a glimpse of glory on the mountain, just as we have been given a glimpse of future glory in the last chapters of the Book of Revelation, but that is for later. This is now, and what is needed now is that the followers of Christ deny themselves, take up their crosses daily, and follow him. Before glory there must always be a cross.

Luke says that on the mountain Moses and Elijah were talking to Jesus "about his departure [that is, his death], which he was about to bring to fulfillment at Jerusalem" (Luke 9:31). So when the voice said, "Listen to him," one thing involved was their need to listen to what he had to say about his death and its meaning.

A Word More Certain

"Listen to him." That is what the voice from the cloud said to Peter and the others. That was all right for them, of course. But how are we to do that, since Jesus is not on earth with us, as he was with the disciples? It is no great mystery. The way we listen to Jesus today is by hearing what he has already said to us in the Bible.

"But that is so commonplace, so prosaic," you might say. "It is not much of a mountain-top experience. I want to see the bright light, be enveloped by the cloud, and hear the rolling thunder of God's voice. I want a personal revelation."

If that is what you are thinking, let me remind you of Peter's wise observations on this incident. Peter is the only one of the three disciples who has left a written record, and at the beginning of this study I quoted a part of it, his description of what he had seen on the mountain. He claimed that he was an "eyewitness . . . of his majesty" and that he heard the voice that came to Jesus "from the Majestic Glory." He heard God say, "This is my Son, whom I love; with him I am well pleased" (2 Peter 1:16–17). But do you know what Peter wrote next? Immediately after this he wrote, "And we have the word of the prophets made *more certain,* and you will do well to pay attention to it, as to a light shining in a dark place, until the day dawns and the morning star rises in your hearts" (2 Peter 1:19).

This means that Peter's experience on the mountain was an important one; he bears testimony to it. But he adds that there is something "more certain" even than this: the testimony of Scripture to which we must pay the most deliberate and rapt attention. He is saying that the Bible is more certain even than a voice from heaven, which, in this case, they did not doubt even for a moment was God's.

I do not know any truth of the Bible that is more relevant for believers in our day, since we live in an age when people appeal to their experience as the only sure measure of anything, not realizing that our experiences can be wrong or misleading.

We hear people justifying all types of unbiblical teaching or behavior by words such as, "God told me this is all right" or "I feel at peace with what I'm doing." But here is Peter—a prominent apostle of the Lord, a man who had a visual experience of Christ's transfiguration as well as having heard an audible word of God from heaven, experiences confirmed as true by the other apostles who were with him at the time—speaking of God's revelation in the Bible as being "more certain" even than his exceptional experience. He does it to remind us that we must evaluate our experiences by the Bible's teaching, rather than the other way around.

Do you do that? Or are you still longing for experiences that are being reserved for that future day when you are with the Lord in heaven? That day will come. You can be encouraged by it. But for now your duty is to read, mark, learn, and digest the words of God we have been given. If you do so and do so faithfully, carefully obeying what you read and understand, God will teach you all you need to live for him and serve him in this life until you die.

39

No Power and Little Understanding

Matthew 17:14–27

When they came to the crowd, a man approached Jesus and knelt before him. "Lord, have mercy on my son," he said. "He has seizures and is suffering greatly. He often falls into the fire or into the water. I brought him to your disciples, but they could not heal him."

"O unbelieving and perverse generation," Jesus replied, "how long shall I stay with you? How long shall I put up with you? Bring the boy here to me." Jesus rebuked the demon, and it came out of the boy, and he was healed from that moment.

Then the disciples came to Jesus in private and asked, "Why couldn't we drive it out?"

He replied, "Because you have so little faith. I tell you the truth, if you have faith as small as a mustard seed, you can say to this mountain, 'Move from here to there,' and it will move. Nothing will be impossible for you."

When they came together in Galilee, he said to them, "The Son of Man is going to be betrayed into the hands of men. They will kill him, and on the third day he will be raised to life."

In 1517, the same year in which Martin Luther posted his "Ninety-Five Theses" on the door of the Castle Church in Wittenberg, Raphael Sanzio began a painting of Christ's transfiguration. When he died in 1520 at the age of thirty-seven, the painting was not finished, but Raphael had completed enough for us to understand it. He showed Jesus on the mountain with Peter, James, and John. Everything is bathed with light. But in the same painting, at the bottom, Raphael shows the other nine disciples trying to cast a demon out of the epileptic boy and failing miserably. It is a way of saying that mountain-top experiences coexist with valleys and only by the power of the Son of God can we have victories in our lives.

The first half of Matthew 17 records Jesus' transfiguration; the second half records the failure of the disciples who remained below.

There are actually several failures. The first is their failure in the exorcism (vv. 14–21). A second is their failure to understand Jesus' words about his death and resurrection (vv. 22–23). A third failure involves only Peter, who is taught why Jesus is willing to pay the temple tax (vv. 24–27).

The flow of chapters 14–17 goes like this: Jesus teaches the disciples, they learn, but then they blunder badly. When the twelve see Jesus walking on the water in chapter 14, Peter asks to come to him and does so (vv. 28–29). It was a great step of faith, but then he looked at the churning water and began to sink (v. 30). The disciples begin to worship Jesus as God (v. 33), but in the next chapter they worry that Jesus' words may have offended the Pharisees (Matt. 15:12). Jesus teaches them that nothing that goes into a person's mouth makes him or her unclean, only what comes out (vv. 16–20), but they are ready to send away the believing but "unclean" Gentile woman who asks Jesus to heal her daughter (v. 23). In chapter 16 Peter's perception of Jesus' deity is followed by his failure to understand the need for Jesus' crucifixion (vv. 16, 22).

Understanding followed by misunderstanding. Progress followed by abject failure. This is the pattern. Yet it is our pattern too. We all move ahead spiritually but then fall back badly. When we realize how often we fail and how prone to sin we are, we marvel at the patience of God, who "knows how we are formed" and "remembers that we are dust" (Ps. 103:14). Jesus is a very patient teacher.

Failure Number 1: No Power

Although Mark's Gospel is shorter than Matthew's, Mark's stories are often longer than the parallel accounts in Matthew, which is the case here. Mark's story covers nineteen verses, including a lengthier description of the possessed boy's symptoms as well as the father's struggling faith. This is the man who told Jesus, "I do believe; help me overcome my unbelief" (Mark 9:24). Matthew eliminates these points to concentrate his account on the disciples' lack of faith.

At first glance it seems surprising that the disciples are unable to heal the epileptic boy, particularly since they had been given authority to cast out evil spirits earlier (Matt. 10:1, 8) and had actually done so (Mark 6:13). Here they fail. The obvious question is Why, which is what they ask Jesus: "Why couldn't we drive it out?" (v. 19).

Jesus tells them, "Because you have so little faith" (v. 20). In Mark he explains, "This kind can come out only by prayer" (Mark 9:29).[1] These are not two different explanations, and we can understand how they go together when we think about what Jesus is saying in Matthew. When Jesus tells the disciples that they have "so little faith," it is not a matter of quantity since he explains in the next verse that even faith "as small as a mustard seed" can move mountains. Moving mountains is a proverbial expression for overcoming difficulties (see Isa. 40:4; 49:11; 54:10). The disciples must have had at least that much faith in some sense or they would not have tried to do the exorcism. Instead of referring to an inadequate *amount* of faith, Jesus is referring to a faith that is *deficient.* That is, it is not the kind of faith that is effective. This is clear from Jesus' earlier words about an "unbelieving and perverse generation" (v. 17).[2] An *unbelieving* generation is a *faithless* generation, which is what the disciples and the others were being at this time.

When I write about faith, I usually say that biblical faith contains three elements: (1) the content of what must be believed, (2) assent to that content, and (3) trust in or commitment to Jesus Christ as the heart of the teaching. The third point (trust or commitment) is what makes faith personal and not just an intellectual or mechanical thing, and it is that personal element that was lacking here. It is why in Mark's account Jesus tells the disciples that the reason they had failed to exorcise the demon was that they had not supported their efforts by prayer.

The problem was that they were approaching the challenge with a formula, expecting inevitable results, the sort of error expressed in the Latin phrase *ex opere operato.* It means that the results follow from the mere doing of the work, like sacraments producing right results with or without faith, just because they are done. This is not biblical teaching. Neither the sacraments nor anything else achieves spiritual results mechanically since effective faith is a relationship in which we actually depend on God.

Here are two clear lessons from the story.

1. *To be effective in serving God we need a continuing relationship with God.* It is always easy for a genuine experience of God's grace and a genuine relationship with God to deteriorate into something merely mechanical. Because we had God's blessing in the past we think it will continue unchanged so long as we merely do the right things. We go to church. We read our Bibles. We even teach a class or preach sermons. But sadly we can do those and other worthwhile things without any real reliance on God, without true faith, and therefore fail badly. Nothing, however good in itself, can substitute for a personal, continuing, trusting relationship with God.

2. *There are no shortcuts to spiritual authority.* The disciples must have been seeking a shortcut when they came to the epileptic boy: do the right things, say the right words. But it did not work. They needed to go back to Jesus to learn why they were failing and what they needed to go on. When they did this they grew. Moreover, the time came somewhat later, after Jesus had sent out a much larger number of disciples, that they returned to him with joy, saying, "Lord, even the demons submit to us in your name" (Luke 10:17).

Just because you and I fail in a first effort does not mean our lives will always be characterized by failure.

Failure Number 2: Little Understanding

The second failure of the disciples in this section is handled briefly, probably because it has occurred before and will appear again several times more. It is their failure to understand Jesus' prediction of his death and resurrection. This is the second explicit prediction in Matthew, the first having occurred in the previous chapter, where it was the reason for Peter's foolish rebuke of his master (Matt. 16:22).

Here Jesus adds to what he had predicted earlier. In chapter 16 he had said that "he must go to Jerusalem and suffer many things at the hands of the elders, chief priests and teachers of the law, and that he must be killed and on the third day be raised to life" (v. 21). That stressed the *necessity* of his passion. Here Jesus emphasizes the *certainty* of his death, "must" being replaced by "will" ("they *will* kill him, and on the third day he *will* be raised to life," v. 23).

This is the first time Jesus mentions his betrayal. Later he adds that the chief priests and teachers of the law will "turn him over to the Gentiles to be mocked and flogged and crucified" (Matt. 20:18–19) and still later that Judas would be the one to betray him (Matt. 26:25; see Matt. 26:1–2).

Did the disciples understand any of this? Somewhat perhaps, since the verse ends by saying that the disciples "were filled with grief." They seemed to be getting the point that Jesus would be killed, that they would lose him. But they did not understand what his death meant or why it was necessary, and they certainly did not understand or believe in the resurrection. Mark says, "They did not understand what he meant and were afraid to ask him about it" (Mark 9:32). Luke adds that what he meant "was hidden from them, so that they did not grasp it" (Luke 9:45).

Failure Number 3: A Mistaken Defense

The last of these three failures was Peter's own, but it too came from a lack of understanding. When the apostolic band arrived back in Capernaum on what was now the final trip to Jerusalem, the collectors of the temple tax approached Peter to ask if Jesus had paid it. Peter seems to have risen to the Lord's defense—"Of course, he pays it"—but his words were too quick and too inappropriate, as Peter's outbursts often were.

The "two-drachma" tax was for the upkeep of the temple in Jerusalem, and it was based on Moses' instructions recorded in Exodus 30:11–16. The tax was fixed as a half shekel (two drachma equaled a half shekel), and it was required of every Jewish male over nineteen years of age. Nothing in Exodus says that the tax was to be paid annually, however, though that became the custom over time. As far as the law itself was concerned, it was imposed only one time—when a man became twenty years of age—and beyond that it was voluntary. Even more, rabbis were exempt, as were the priests who served in Jerusalem. The Sadducees generally disapproved of the tax, and the men of the Qumran community paid it only once in their lifetimes.

In Jesus' day there was no half shekel coin, so it was common for two men to go together and pay the tax with a single shekel coin, which is what Jesus told Peter he would find in the fish's mouth (v. 27).

What is this story about? Jesus explains it when he takes advantage of Peter's inappropriate response to teach him about his relationship to the temple. Peter may have seen Jesus pay the temple tax before, of course. It may be why he answered so quickly. But as soon as they were in the house together Jesus, who knew what had happened between Peter and the collectors of the tax, asked, "What do you think, Simon? From whom do the kings of the earth collect duty and taxes—from their own sons or from others?"

Peter answered correctly. "From others," he said.

"Then the sons are exempt," Jesus taught him. He meant that since kings do not collect taxes from their sons, no more would God the Father require a tax to support the temple from his Son, Jesus. At the most basic level the words are a statement about Jesus' unique deity. As the only begotten Son of God Jesus is exempt from temple taxes.

But there is more to the incident than this.

1. *The importance of inoffensive conduct.* Jesus explained that although he was exempt from the two-drachma tax, he would still pay it in order not to cause offense. It was not that he was unwilling to offend the temple authorities or anyone else when that was necessary, as it was when the truths of the Bible were at stake. The disciples had approached him earlier to explain that the Pharisees had been offended by his teaching about what is clean and what is not clean (Matt. 15:12). A right understanding of the Bible always matters. But in cases in which the issue is unimportant, as it was here, the right procedure is to act so as not to cause offense to other people.

In this verse the word translated "offense" is *skandalon. Skandalon* is never used in the New Testament for something that merely offends someone but always for something that causes the person to stumble spiritually or trip up. Jesus was saying that none of us should do anything that might cause another person to stumble over what is spiritually important. It is what Paul meant when he wrote to the Corinthians, "We put up with anything rather than hinder the gospel of Christ" (1 Cor. 9:12).

John Ryle asks his readers to think carefully about the words "lest we should offend them" and apply them to our duties as citizens, members of a church, and members of society. We do not have to approve of all the laws of the country in which we live to obey them. We do not have to approve of everything our local church or denomination does to support it. There may be things our neighbors do of which we strongly disapprove, but we should often overlook such things in order not to set up an unnecessary barrier to their hearing and responding to the gospel.

Ryle writes:

> There are matters in which Christ's people ought to sink their own opinions, and submit to requirements which they may not thoroughly approve, rather than give offence and "hinder the gospel of Christ." God's rights undoubtedly we ought never to give up; but we may sometimes safely give up our own. It may sound very fine and seem very heroic to be always standing out tenaciously for our rights! But it may well be doubted, with such a passage as this, whether such tenacity is always wise, and shows the mind of Christ. There are occasions when it shows more grace in a Christian to submit than to resist.[3]

2. *Christians ought to pay taxes.* Some commentators make a point of the facts that this tax was for the support of the temple in Jerusalem, and therefore was a matter of nationalistic pride, while taxes leveled by the Romans were resented by most of the conquered peoples, including Jews. But Jesus' words seem to reach beyond a merely Jewish tax. His illustration about kings and their taxes in verse 25 mentions both duty and taxes. "Duty" is the translation of the Greek word *tele,* which refers to the local taxes collected at the custom houses by *teloni,* the word for "tax collectors." "Taxes" is the translation of *kensos,* which was the word used for a head tax based on the tax rolls containing the names of those who were subject to it. It is from this word that we get the English word "census." This suggests that the principle of paying taxes so as not to give offense extends to all taxes rather than only to what we might think of as dues to support an approved religious function.

Moreover, if Matthew was written after A.D. 70, when the temple was destroyed by the Roman armies under Titus, which it may have been, it is important to remember that Vespasian ruled that the half shekel tax should then be paid to the treasury of the temple of Jupiter Capitolinus in Rome, which would have been a serious problem for Jews and Jewish Christians. How could they support a pagan religion? This account says they can.

The story is unique to Matthew, but it is understandable that he alone should record it since he had been a tax collector. He is saying that, however odious they seem, taxes even to the Roman government should be paid since what really matters is not the use pagans make of Christians' money but whether the state gives us freedom to keep on preaching the gospel.

Five chapters later Matthew makes the same point, telling how Jesus answered the question of the Pharisees who asked him, "Is it right to pay taxes to Caesar or not?" (Matt. 22:17). Jesus asked for a coin. When they produced it he asked whose picture was on the coin and whose inscription, and when they answered correctly that it was Caesar's, he told them, "Give to Caesar what is Caesar's, and to God what is God's" (v. 21). This limits the authority of Caesar since the state has no right to take from God what is God's. Christians must resist the state if it tries to do this. At the same time, however, it also establishes the legitimate authority of Caesar, which includes the right to levy taxes. Paul took exactly this position when he wrote to the believers in Rome, "Give everyone what you owe him: If you owe taxes, pay taxes; if revenue, then revenue; if respect, then respect; if honor, then honor" (Rom. 13:7).

I usually say that although the government does much we do not like, it also does much that is good and from which we profit. Our taxes support the armed forces that keep the peace and the courts that administer justice. Taxes maintain the national parks, pay food inspectors, fund the Federal Bureau of Investigation, support air traffic controllers, maintain the highway system, and undergird some education. State taxes support state universities, maintain highways, and pay for the courts. Local taxes provide for a city's schools, fire fighters, and police. Taxes make possible a stable society in which we can share the gospel.

A Summary of Chapter 17

I began this study by writing about coming down from the mountains to the valleys and about failures. The first we cannot avoid. There are always valleys. But as far as failures are concerned, although we will certainly also have those, we do not need to have as many as we do or experience them so often. Fortunately, Matthew 17 has provided pointers to the way we can overcome many of our failures.

1. *Listen to Jesus.* On the mountain in the excitement of the moment Peter thought he had to say something, so he blurted out his idea about constructing three shelters for Jesus, Moses, and Elijah. God told him to be quiet and listen to Jesus. That is exactly what you and I need to do. There is a time to speak, but we must listen to Jesus first, because it is only as we do that we will be able to say anything worthwhile.

2. *Take up the cross.* We like the glory, but we are not nearly so enthusiastic about cross-bearing. Yet what Jesus told his disciples repeatedly is that there is no crown without a cross. John the Baptist had to suffer, Jesus had to suffer, and so do we. It is only through much self-denial that we can be Christ's followers.

3. *Know your weakness.* We all have failures in our Christian lives, and one reason God allows so many of them is so we will learn that "apart from me [Jesus] you can do nothing," as Jesus said (John 15:5). We should remember Peter. Peter had a high opinion of himself. When Jesus explained that the disciples would abandon him at the time of his arrest, Peter was sure he would not do so. "Even if all fall away on account of you, I never will," he said (Matt. 26:33). But he did. He even denied the Lord three times. Like us, Peter needed to learn how weak he was and that if he was to stand, it had to be by Jesus' strength.

4. *Keep your faith personal.* The final lesson is that there can be no substitute for a personal faith in God, who is personal. Are the doctrines of the

Bible important? Of course they are. We do not know who God is, how sinful we are, or what God has done to save us in Christ apart from God's own revelation in Scripture. But knowledge alone saves no one. Christianity does not consist merely in collecting information. Is service important? Yes. The Bible says not only that we are ordained to salvation but also that we are ordained to good works (Eph. 2:10). We must do them. But the most important thing is that we get to know God, that we develop a personal relationship with him, and that we serve him because we love him.

Listen to Jesus. Take up your cross. Know your weaknesses. But above all, keep your faith personal. It is that relationship, more than anything else, that will keep you from these failures.

Notes

Chapter 1

1. D. A. Carson, "Matthew," in *The Expositor's Bible Commentary*, vol. 8, *Matthew, Mark, Luke* (Grand Rapids: Zondervan, 1984), 19.

2. Eusebius, *The Ecclesiastical History*, trans. Kirsopp Lake (Cambridge: Harvard University Press, 1965), vol. 1, 297.

3. For a list of these quotations, see William Hendriksen, *New Testament Commentary: Exposition of the Gospel According to Matthew* (Grand Rapids: Baker, 1985), 80–81.

4. J. Gresham Machen, *The Virgin Birth of Christ* (1930; reprint, London: James Clarke, 1958), 202–9.

5. Ibid., 209.

6. Donald Grey Barnhouse, *Man's Ruin: Exposition of Bible Doctrines, Taking the Epistle to the Romans as a Point of Departure*, vol. 1, *Romans 1:1–32* (Grand Rapids: Eerdmans, 1952), 45–47.

7. Part of this chapter is from an earlier study, "The Genealogies," in James Montgomery Boice, *The Christ of Christmas* (Chicago: Moody Press, 1983), 39–44.

Chapter 2

1. The Masoretic text does not have the word *they*, indicating that it is the mother who, perhaps first, would "call him Immanuel."

2. J. Gresham Machen, *The Virgin Birth of Christ* (1930; reprint, London: James Clarke, 1958), 46.

3. See Reuben A. Torrey, *The Bible and Its Christ* (New York: Revell, 1904), 58–85. See also Machen, *The Virgin Birth of Christ*, 188–209.

4. Parts of this chapter are taken from James Montgomery Boice, *The Christ of Christmas* (Chicago: Moody Press, 1983), 27, 33–38; and *The King Has Come* (Fearn, Scotland: Christian Focus Publications, 1992), 55, 60–61.

Chapter 3

1. These possibilities are discussed in most of the major commentaries. For example, D. A. Carson, "Matthew," in *The Expositor's Bible Commentary,* vol. 8, *Matthew, Mark, Luke* (Grand Rapids: Zondervan, 1984), 85–86; and William Barclay, *The Gospel of Matthew* (Philadelphia: Westminster Press, 1958), vol. 1, 17.

2. Barclay, *The Gospel of Matthew,* vol. 1, 23.

3. Donald Grey Barnhouse, *The Gift of Death* (Philadelphia: American Bible Conferences Association, 1935), 5.

4. Later, however, when he was hanging on the cross, Jesus called for a drink in order that Psalm 69:21 might be fulfilled. He was offered a sour wine vinegar raised to his lips on a sponge and took it, because in this case no myrrh was mixed with the wine (see John 19:29).

5. Barclay, *The Gospel of Matthew,* vol. 1, 240.

6. Parts of this chapter are taken from James Montgomery Boice, *The Christ of Christmas* (Chicago: Moody Press, 1983), 83–88; and *The King Has Come* (Fearn, Scotland: Christian Focus Publications, 1992), 155–65.

Chapter 4

1. Since Isaiah seems to be offering the birth of the child as a sign to King Ahaz ("before the boy knows enough to reject the wrong and choose the right, the land of the two kings you dread will be laid waste," Isa. 7:16), many commentators see this as the primary prophecy and the reference to the virgin birth of Jesus as secondary at best. However, J. A. Motyer ("Context and Content in the Interpretation of Isaiah 7:14," *Tyndale Bulletin* 21 [1970]: 118–25) argues that the prophecy is entirely futuristic, pointing Ahaz to a day when the Davidic dynasty would have lost the throne.

2. D. A. Carson, *God with Us: Themes from Matthew* (Ventura, Calif.: Regal Books, 1985), 17.

3. William Barclay, *The Gospel of Matthew* (Philadelphia: Westminster Press, 1958), vol. 1, 27. Barclay says that Matthew "is prepared to use as a prophecy about Jesus any text at all which can be made verbally to fit, even although originally it had nothing to do with the question in hand, and was never meant to have anything to do with it."

4. D. A. Carson, "Matthew," in *The Expositor's Bible Commentary,* vol. 8, *Matthew, Mark, Luke* (Grand Rapids: Zondervan, 1984), 95.

5. The New International Version uses the word *said* for the sake of good English form (v. 23), but the verb is not present in the Greek text.

Chapter 5

1. William Barclay, *The Gospel of Matthew* (Philadelphia: Westminster Press, 1958), vol. 1, 35.

2. H. A. Ironside, *Expository Notes on the Gospel of Matthew* (Neptune, N.J.: Loizeaux Brothers, 1948), 25.

3. For example, see Arno C. Gaebelein, *The Gospel of Matthew* (1910; reprint, New York: Loizeaux Brothers, 1961), 60–61.

4. D. A. Carson, "Matthew," in *The Expositor's Bible Commentary*, vol. 8, *Matthew, Mark, Luke* (Grand Rapids: Zondervan, 1984), 99.

5. William Hendriksen, *New Testament Commentary: Exposition of the Gospel According to Matthew* (Grand Rapids: Baker, 1985), 213.

6. For a discussion of these and other interpretations see Carson, "Matthew," 107–8; John A. Broadus, *Commentary on Matthew* (Grand Rapids: Kregel, 1990), 55–56; and others.

7. See James Montgomery Boice, *Foundations of the Christian Faith* (Downers Grove, Ill.: InterVarsity Press, 1986), 597–601.

8. Ironside, *Expository Notes on the Gospel of Matthew*, 29.

Chapter 6

1. R. V. G. Tasker, *The Gospel According to St. Matthew: An Introduction and Commentary* (Grand Rapids: Eerdmans, 1961), 52.

2. This is the view of E. Schuyler English ("Satan did not doubt Jesus' Deity. . . . It was in the sense of 'Since thou be the Son of God' that he appealed to him," *Studies in the Gospel According to Matthew* [New York: Revell, 1935], 37); H. N. Ridderbos ("Some think that the Devil here was trying to cause Jesus to doubt his sonship, but this interpretation is wrong. His aim rather was to seduce Jesus into misusing his messianic office," *Matthew* [Grand Rapids: Zondervan, 1987], 67); D. A. Carson ("Satan was not inviting Jesus to doubt his sonship but to reflect on its meaning," "Matthew," in *The Expositor's Bible Commentary*, vol. 8, *Matthew, Mark, Luke* [Grand Rapids: Zondervan, 1984], 112); and others.

3. R. C. Sproul, "Hath God Said?" in *Can We Trust the Bible?* ed. Earl D. Radmacher (Wheaton, Ill.: Tyndale House, 1979), 120–21.

4. In Luke's Gospel (Luke 4:1–13), where we have the only other biblical account of these temptations, the order of the second and third temptations are reversed. There does not seem to be any significant reason for this, though most commentators agree that Matthew's order shows the most deliberate sequence and is probably original.

5. See my study of Ephesians 6:17 in James Montgomery Boice, *Ephesians* (Grand Rapids: Baker, 1998), 250–57.

Chapter 7

1. Charles H. Spurgeon, *The Gospel of the Kingdom: A Popular Exposition of the Gospel According to Matthew* (Pasadena, Tex.: Pilgrim Publications, 1974), 19.

Chapter 8

1. Luke's version is called "the sermon on the plain" because Luke says it was delivered "on a level place" (Luke 6:17). But it is probably the same sermon, though less material is reported. Of the 107 verses in Matthew's account,

only 29 are in Luke, though 34 others are found elsewhere in the Gospel. For a helpful comparison of the two sermons, see William Barclay, *The Gospel of Matthew* (Philadelphia: Westminster Press, 1958), vol. 1, 80.

2. I. M. Haldeman, *The Kingdom of God* (New York: F. E. Fitch, 1931), 149.

3. For a fuller discussion of the dispensationalist approach to the Sermon on the Mount, see D. A. Carson, "Matthew," in *The Expositor's Bible Commentary*, vol. 8, *Matthew, Mark, Luke* (Grand Rapids: Zondervan, 1984), 127; and James Montgomery Boice, *The Sermon on the Mount: An Exposition* (Grand Rapids: Zondervan, 1972), 9–14.

4. The word *blessed* also occurs in verse 11 as a ninth blessing, but verses 11 and 12 stand apart from the preceding list as an elaboration and personal application of verse 10, which means that there are actually eight of these sayings. Luke's account of the sermon lists four beatitudes (Luke 6:20–22), followed by four woes (vv. 24–26).

5. Carson, "Matthew," 132.

Chapter 9

1. D. A. Carson, "Matthew," in *The Expositor's Bible Commentary*, vol. 8, *Matthew, Mark, Luke* (Grand Rapids: Zondervan, 1984), 141.

2. John A. Broadus, *Commentary on Matthew* (Grand Rapids: Kregel, 1990), 99. Broadus says, "The thought is, then, not to perform by his life but to complete by his teaching."

3. Carson, "Matthew," 143.

4. Ibid., 144.

5. R. T. France, *The Gospel According to Matthew: An Introduction and Commentary* (Grand Rapids: Eerdmans, 1985), 114.

6. "Have You Earned Heaven?" (Matt. 5:20) in James Montgomery Boice, *The Sermon on the Mount: An Exposition* (Grand Rapids: Zondervan, 1972), 98–104.

7. Carson, "Matthew," 147.

8. For a more extensive discussion of faith, justification, and works, see the chapter "Justification by Faith: The Place of Works" in James Montgomery Boice, *Foundations of the Christian Faith* (Downers Grove, Ill.: InterVarsity Press, 1986), 424–30.

Chapter 10

1. William Barclay, *The Gospel of Matthew* (Philadelphia: Westminster Press, 1958), vol. 1, 131.

2. William Hendriksen, *New Testament Commentary: Exposition of the Gospel According to Matthew* (Grand Rapids: Baker, 1985), 298–99.

3. C. S. Lewis, *Mere Christianity* (New York: Macmillan, 1958), 75.

4. Hendriksen, *New Testament Commentary*, 306.

5. For example, see James Patterson and Peter Kim, *The Day America Told the Truth: What People Really Believe about Everything That Really Matters* (New York: Prentice Hall Press, 1991), 6–8.

6. Verse 33 seems to refer most directly to Numbers 30:2 ("When a man makes a vow to the LORD or takes an oath to obligate himself by a pledge, he must not break his word but must do everything he said"), but it may also summarize other commands such as Exodus 20:7; Leviticus 19:12; Deuteronomy 5:11; 10:20.

7. Barclay, *The Gospel of Matthew,* 176.

8. R. V. G. Tasker, *The Gospel According to St. Matthew* (Grand Rapids: Eerdmans, 1961), 70.

9. H. A. Ironside, *Expository Notes on the Gospel of Matthew* (Neptune, N.J.: Loizeaux Brothers, 1948), 57.

10. In 1 Peter 1:15, for example.

11. D. A. Carson, "Matthew," in *The Expositor's Bible Commentary,* vol. 8, *Matthew, Mark, Luke* (Grand Rapids: Zondervan, 1984), 161.

Chapter 11

1. Cited by William Barclay, *The Gospel of Matthew* (Philadelphia: Westminster Press, 1958), vol. 1, 186.

2. D. A. Carson, "Matthew," in *The Expositor's Bible Commentary,* vol. 8, *Matthew, Mark, Luke* (Grand Rapids: Zondervan, 1984), 164.

3. The fact that there are two forms of this prayer (the version found in Matthew and a second in Luke 11:2–4) has led to much scholarly debate about the relationship between the two. But the settings are different, one public and the other private, and the simplest explanation is that Jesus gave this kind of instruction in many places and on many occasions. The variations also prove that Jesus intended the prayer as a model only. If he gave it on more than one occasion and in various ways, the variations show that it was not something to be repeated verbatim. Otherwise, the words would have been the same. If it was spoken on only one occasion, the variation in the reporting of it shows that the disciples at least did not understand it as a prayer to be memorized and repeated word for word, because they didn't do it. See Carson for a helpful discussion of the relation between Matthew's version and the parallel in Luke ("Matthew," 167–68).

4. Carson, "Matthew," 170–71.

5. Barclay, *The Gospel of Matthew,* 186.

6. H. N. Ridderbos, *Matthew,* trans. Ray Togtman (Grand Rapids: Zondervan, 1987), 132.

7. R. T. France, *The Gospel According to Matthew: An Introduction and Commentary* (Grand Rapids: Eerdmans, 1985), 137.

8. John A. Broadus gives a list of names on both sides of this debate *(Commentary on Matthew* [Grand Rapids: Kregel, 1990], 138–39). However, David Hill maintains that the word *evil* is never used for "the evil one" in either Hebrew or Aramaic; therefore, the use of the word in the Lord's Prayer should be referred chiefly to that spiritual or moral evil that may come to people in the present time *(The Gospel of Matthew* [Grand Rapids: Eerdmans, 1981], 139).

Chapter 12

1. William Barclay, *The Gospel of Matthew* (Philadelphia: Westminster Press, 1958), vol. 1, 245.
2. D. Martyn Lloyd-Jones, *Studies in the Sermon on the Mount* (Grand Rapids: Eerdmans, 1967), vol. 2, 95–96.
3. H. N. Ridderbos, *Matthew,* trans. Ray Togtman (Grand Rapids: Zondervan, 1987), 139.
4. Kenneth S. Wuest, *Wuest's Word Studies* (Grand Rapids: Eerdmans, 1966), vol. 4, 43.
5. Barclay, *The Gospel of Matthew,* 277–78.

Chapter 13

1. See James Montgomery Boice, *The Sermon on the Mount* (Grand Rapids: Zondervan, 1972), 287–88.
2. William Hendriksen, *New Testament Commentary: Exposition of the Gospel According to Matthew* (Grand Rapids: Baker, 1985), 367.
3. William Barclay, *The Gospel of Matthew* (Philadelphia: Westminster Press, 1958), vol. 1, 288.
4. The story is told by H. A. Ironside, *In the Heavenlies* (Neptune, N.J.: Loizeaux Brothers, 1937), 56–57.
5. The last paragraphs of this chapter are borrowed with alterations from James Montgomery Boice, *The Sermon on the Mount* (Grand Rapids: Zondervan, 1972), 318.

Chapter 14

1. William Barclay, *The Gospel of Matthew* (Philadelphia: Westminster Press, 1958), vol. 1, 302. The status of lepers is discussed on pages 300–301.
2. D. A. Carson, "Matthew," in *The Expositor's Bible Commentary,* vol. 8, *Matthew, Mark, Luke* (Grand Rapids: Zondervan, 1984), 201.
3. There are several differences between this account and the parallel account in Luke 7:1–10, the most noticeable being that in Matthew the centurion comes to Jesus himself while in Luke he sends elders of the Jews to ask that Jesus heal his servant. They plead the man's worthiness, explaining that he loved the Jews and had built them a synagogue. Luke's account is probably right in reporting that the centurion approached Jesus through intermediaries. Matthew eliminated that detail, assuming that what the ambassadors say, the one who sent them says. This would fit the emphasis on delegated authority, which is central to the account in Matthew. There is also an account of a healing from a distance in John 4:46–54, but John's story concerns the son of a royal official, not a centurion's servant, and should be considered a separate incident.
4. Howard F. Vos, *Matthew* (Grand Rapids: Zondervan, 1979), 69.
5. John Charles Ryle, *Expository Thoughts on the Gospels: St. Matthew* (Cambridge: James Clarke, 1974), 76.

Chapter 15

1. William Hendriksen, *New Testament Commentary: Exposition of the Gospel According to Matthew* (Grand Rapids: Baker, 1985), 403.
2. Dietrich Bonhoeffer, *The Cost of Discipleship* (1937; reprint, New York: Macmillan, 1966), 47.
3. Ibid., 47.
4. George Eldon Ladd, *Jesus and the Kingdom: The Eschatology of Biblical Realism* (New York: Harper & Row, 1964), 295–96.
5. John Charles Ryle, *Practical Religion: Being Plain Papers on the Daily Duties, Experience, Dangers and Privileges of Professing Christians* (Cambridge: James Clarke, 1959), 187–88.
6. Parts of the preceding are borrowed with changes from James Montgomery Boice, *Christ's Call to Discipleship* (Chicago: Moody Press, 1986), 118–22.
7. There is a helpful excursus on the meaning of the title "Son of Man" in D. A. Carson, "Matthew," in *The Expositor's Bible Commentary*, vol. 8, *Matthew, Mark, Luke* (Grand Rapids: Zondervan, 1984), 209–13. The title is also discussed extensively in other commentaries because of its prominence in the Gospels and in scholarly debate.

Chapter 16

1. John Charles Ryle, *Expository Thoughts on the Gospels: St. Matthew* (Cambridge: James Clarke, 1974), 79.
2. William Hendriksen, *New Testament Commentary: Exposition of the Gospel According to Matthew* (Grand Rapids: Baker, 1985), 413.
3. The Gospels have different names at this point, and the manuscripts of even a single Gospel vary. The best reading in Matthew is Gadarenes, Gadara being a town about six miles from the lake. The best reading in both Mark and Luke is Gerasenes, Gerasa being a town about thirty miles southeast of the lake. Gergesenes, which crept into the Greek manuscripts later, seems to be due to the influence of Origen, who was sure that neither Gadara nor Gerasa satisfied the requirements of the story. The explanation of these variants is probably, as Josephus reports, that Gadara was the regional capital and that it had smaller villages related to it on the border of the lake, one of which would have been Gerasa. Coins of Gadara sometimes display a ship. For further discussion, see D. A. Carson, *The Expositor's Bible Commentary*, vol. 8, *Matthew, Mark, Luke* (Grand Rapids: Zondervan, 1984), 219.
4. John A. Broadus attributes this observation to an ancient commentator named Theophylact (*Commentary on Matthew* [Grand Rapids: Kregel, 1990], 188).
5. Mark and Luke write about one man only, no doubt focusing on the most prominent and articulate of the two (Mark 5:2; Luke 8:27).

Chapter 17

1. D. A. Carson, *God with Us: Themes from Matthew* (Ventura, Calif.: Regal Books, 1985), 52.

2. In Mark and Luke's Gospels, Matthew is called Levi. Some have suggested that there is error or confusion here, but double names were not uncommon among the Jews. Thomas is also called Didymus (John 20:24), and Bartholomew is probably the same person as Nathanael (see John 1:45–49; 21:2). Again, it may be the case that Levi was Matthew's name before his conversion and that it was changed to Matthew afterward. Matthew is always the name that appears in verses giving an official listing of the Twelve (Matt. 10:2–4; Mark 3:16–19; Luke 6:13–16; Acts 1:13).

3. William Barclay, *The Gospel of Matthew* (Philadelphia: Westminster Press, 1958), vol. 1, 336–37.

4. This is the first historical indication of a movement involving the disciples of John apart from Christianity, following John's imprisonment and death. It continued into the time of the Acts (see Acts 18:25; 19:1–3).

Chapter 18

1. There is a certain amount of humor in these varying accounts. Mark says the woman had "suffered a great deal under the care of many doctors and had spent all she had" (Mark 5:26), words we might have expected from a layperson who could have been disappointed by doctors himself. But Luke, who was a doctor (Col. 4:14) and was probably a bit sensitive on this point, says that "no one could heal her" (Luke 8:43), meaning that her disease was incurable. If she could have been cured, he is sure the members of his profession would have done it.

2. Because Jesus told the mourners and crowd, "The girl is not dead but asleep," and because the word used for "sleep" *(katheudo)* is usually used literally, some have argued that this was not a real resurrection, merely a resuscitation from a coma. Those who say this are making the same mistake the people did. They took his words literally, though Jesus was speaking metaphorically. Even the disciples did it when Jesus used the expression in regard to Lazarus (John 11:11–14). Nevertheless, the girl was really dead and this was a true resurrection. Verse 18 should settle the matter: "My daughter has just died." The response of Jesus to John's disciples in Matthew 11:5–6 also presupposes some prior act of resurrection. This is the first resurrection Jesus performed and the only one recorded by Matthew. There are two others in other Gospels: the raising of the son of the widow of Nain in Luke 7:11–17 and the raising of Lazarus in John 11:1–44.

3. D. A. Carson, "Matthew," in *The Expositor's Bible Commentary,* vol. 8, *Matthew, Mark, Luke* (Grand Rapids: Zondervan, 1984), 233.

4. The word Matthew uses to describe the man's condition *(kophos)* meant: first, "deaf"; then, "dumb"; finally, a "deaf mute." All three senses appear in classical, Hellenistic, and biblical Greek (see Exod. 4:11; Isa. 43:8).

5. Verse 34 is missing from the Western textual tradition, but it has strong support elsewhere, and, in any case, it seems to be presupposed in verse 25

of the next chapter. Actually, the accusation is a high point of the opposition to Jesus that Matthew is introducing in these chapters.

Chapter 19

1. William Hendriksen, *New Testament Commentary: Exposition of the Gospel According to Matthew* (Grand Rapids: Baker, 1985), 449.

2. See Matthew 4:18–20; 14:25–31; 16:13–23; 17:1–8, 24–27; 18:21–22; 26:31–46, 58, 69–75; Mark 1:16–18, 29–31; 8:27–33; 9:1–10; 14:27–42, 54, 66–72; Luke 5:1–11; 9:18–20, 28–36; 22:31–34, 54–62; John 1:40–42, 44; 13:6–9, 36–38; 18:10–11, 15–18, 25–27; 20:1–9; 21:1–22; Acts 1:12–26; 2:14–41; 3:1–4:23; 5:1–11, 29–32; 8:14–25; 10:1–11:18; 12:1–19; 15:6–11.

3. See Matthew 4:21–22; 17:1–13; Mark 9:2–13; 10:35–40; Luke 5:1–10; 9:28–36; John 13:23; 19:25–27; 20:1–9; 21:20–24; Acts 4:1–3; Gal. 2:9; Rev. 1:1; 22:8.

4. Hendriksen, *New Testament Commentary,* 455.

Chapter 20

1. John Charles Ryle, *Expository Thoughts on the Gospels: St. Matthew* (Cambridge: James Clarke, 1974), 95.

2. John A. Broadus, *Commentary on Matthew* (1886; reprint, Grand Rapids: Kregel, 1990), 218.

3. There is no more important theme in the Gospel of Matthew than the kingdom of God. In fact, Matthew might well be called "the Gospel of the kingdom." There are fifty-four references to the kingdom in its pages.

4. Ryle, *Expository Thoughts on the Gospels,* 96–97.

5. Charles H. Spurgeon, *The Gospel of the Kingdom: A Popular Exposition of the Gospel According to Matthew* (Pasadena, Tex.: Pilgrim Publications, 1974), 70.

6. William Hendriksen, *New Testament Commentary: Exposition of the Gospel According to Matthew* (Grand Rapids: Baker, 1985), 461.

Chapter 21

1. D. A. Carson, "Matthew," in *The Expositor's Bible Commentary,* vol. 8, *Matthew, Mark, Luke* (Grand Rapids: Zondervan, 1984), 248.

2. Ibid., 250–53.

3. Ibid., 252.

4. Ibid., 253.

5. Beelzebub is probably derived from the Canaanite god mentioned in 2 Kings 1:2 in the form Baal-zebub ("Lord of flies"). The official title was probably Baal-zebul ("Baal the prince"), but in common Jewish usage this was the name of a senior devil, sometimes Satan himself (see Matt. 12:24–28).

6. William Barclay, *The Gospel of Matthew,* vol. 1 (Philadelphia: Westminster Press, 1958), 397.

7. Barclay, *The Gospel of Matthew,* 397.

8. See J. H. Merle D'Aubigne, *The Life and Times of Martin Luther,* trans. H. White (Chicago: Moody Press, 1958), 433.

Chapter 22

1. "The question did not arise from doubt or unbelief on the part of John. . . . It was asked for the benefit of his disciples" (John Charles Ryle, *Expository Thoughts on the Gospels: St. Matthew* [Cambridge: James Clarke, 1974], 109).

2. D. A. Carson, *God with Us: Themes from Matthew* (Ventura, Calif.: Regal Books, 1985), 62.

3. Ibid., 65.

4. D. A. Carson thinks "forceful men" are those who are opposing Christ's kingdom ("Matthew," in *The Expositor's Bible Commentary*, vol. 8, *Matthew, Mark, Luke* [Grand Rapids: Zondervan, 1984], 266–68). This does not flow from the context as well, in my judgment, but there would be an example of such "forceful men" in Herod, who had imprisoned John the Baptist. Carson thinks the reference to the kingdom being revealed to "children" in verse 25 excludes the idea of the kingdom being seized by what would be the opposite kind of persons.

5. Luke's equivalent verse has "by all her children" (Luke 7:35), that is, "by those who follow in wisdom's way" rather than "by what wisdom does." But these are not different things, even though they are expressed differently. Luke's words focus on the person of Jesus, whom we must follow, while Matthew focuses on what we must do. What is condemned in both cases is a refusal to believe in spite of evidence.

Chapter 23

1. Other passages that teach degrees of blessedness in heaven and degrees of torment in hell are Matthew 12:41; Luke 12:47–48; and Romans 2:5–16.

2. D. A. Carson, *God with Us: Themes from Matthew* (Ventura, Calif.: Regal Books, 1985), 66.

3. See Charles H. Spurgeon, *The Gospel of the Kingdom: A Popular Exposition of the Gospel According to Matthew* (Pasadena, Tex.: Pilgrim Publications, 1974), 82.

4. C. S. Lewis, *Mere Christianity* (New York: Macmillan, 1958), 41.

5. The New King James Version (1979) uses the New International Version's wording.

Chapter 24

1. Every one of the Gospels points to this as an initial and chief problem (see Mark 2:23–28; Luke 6:1–11; and John 5:1–18).

2. For more discussion of these points, see James Montgomery Boice, *The Gospel of John: An Expositional Commentary* (Grand Rapids: Baker, 1999), vol. 2, 363.

3. William Barclay, *The Gospel of Matthew* (Philadelphia: Westminster Press, 1958), vol. 2, 24.

4. William Hendriksen has an interesting note at this point. "In his answer Jesus, who elsewhere gave the true, spiritual interpretation of the first and second commandments (Exod. 20:1–6; cf. Matt. 22:37, 38, which summa-

rized the entire first table of the law), of the third commandment and the ninth (Exod. 20:7; Lev. 19:12; Num. 30:2; Deut. 23:21; cf. Matt. 5:33–37), the fifth and eighth (Exod. 20:12, 15; cf. Matt. 15:3–6), the sixth (Exod. 20:13; cf. Matt. 5:21–26, 38–42), the seventh (Exod. 20:14; cf. Matt. 5:27–32; 19:3–12), and the tenth (Exod. 20:17; cf. Luke 12:13–21; 16:14, 19–31; see also Matt. 22:39, in which the entire second table is summarized), now reveals the true meaning of the fourth commandment (Exod. 20:8–11)" (William Hendriksen, *New Testament Commentary: Exposition of the Gospel According to Matthew* [Grand Rapids: Baker, 1985], 512).

5. John Broadus points out that these three arguments, plus a fourth in the claim that Jesus is "Lord of the Sabbath" and a fifth in the following story (vv. 9–13) are supplemented by a sixth argument in Mark 2:27, a seventh in John 5:17, and an eighth in John 7:21–24 (John A. Broadus, *Commentary on Matthew* [Grand Rapids: Kregel, 1990], 258). That Jesus took such pains to defend his approach to the Sabbath shows how critical the issue was and how rightly the evangelists focus on it.

6. Hendriksen, *New Testament Commentary*, 519.

7. Howard F. Vos notes that verse 17 is an important claim to inspiration since it says that God himself spoke through Isaiah. Also, it "gives support to Isaiah's authorship of the latter half of the book that bears his name, a position commonly denied by liberal critics" (Howard F. Vos, *Matthew* [Grand Rapids: Zondervan, 1979], 95).

8. D. A. Carson, "Matthew," in *The Expositor's Bible Commentary*, vol. 8, *Matthew, Mark, Luke* (Grand Rapids: Zondervan, 1984), 287.

Chapter 25

1. There is another ancient exorcism account in Tobit 8:1–4.

2. William Hendriksen says that in verses 25–37, Jesus shows that the Pharisees' charge: (1) is absurd (vv. 25–26); (2) is inconsistent (v. 27); (3) obscures the truth (vv. 28–30); (4) is unpardonable (vv. 31–32); and (5) exposes the wickedness of those who make it (vv. 33–37). See William Hendriksen, *New Testament Commentary: Exposition of the Gospel According to Matthew* (Grand Rapids: Baker, 1985), 525.

3. D. A. Carson, *God with Us: Themes from Matthew* (Ventura, Calif.: Regal Books, 1985), 72.

4. D. A. Carson, "Matthew," in *The Expositor's Bible Commentary*, vol. 8, *Matthew, Mark, Luke* (Grand Rapids: Zondervan, 1984), 291–92.

5. There is something similar to Jesus' description of the "unforgivable sin" in Hebrews 6:4–6; 10:26–31; and 1 John 5:16. However, John is actually speaking of "a sin that leads to death," and the best way of thinking about his reference is that he is speaking of physical death, the kind of judgment that fell on Ananias and Sapphira and some others. Peter explained the sin of Ananias and Sapphira as their having lied to God (Acts 5:4). The verses in Hebrews are closer to the sin described in Matthew, but they are not quite the same.

Hebrews is speaking about people who have understood the gospel but have rejected it for something else. They will perish because there is no other sacrifice for sin but Christ's to be found.

Chapter 26

1. William Hendriksen argues that the crucifixion had to be on a Friday, because the word for the crucifixion day is *paraskeue,* and *paraskeue* is used "even in modern Greek to indicate Friday." But modern usage does not establish the usage in the time of Jesus, and most translations rightly render the term as "Preparation Day (that is, the day before the Sabbath)" (see Mark 15:42; also Luke 23:54; and John 19:14, 31, 42). Hendriksen's discussion is in his *New Testament Commentary: Exposition of the Gospel According to Matthew* (Grand Rapids: Baker, 1985), 534.

2. William Barclay responds to this difficulty by arguing that the saying is not Jesus' saying but Matthew's and that Matthew was mistaken. "Matthew understood wrongly the point of what Jesus had said" (William Barclay, *The Gospel of Matthew,* vol. 2, *Chapters 11–28* [Philadelphia: Westminster Press, 1958], 55). But that will not satisfy anyone who has a proper view of the Bible's divine authority and accuracy.

3. Roy M. Allen, *Three Days in the Grave* (New York: Loizeaux Brothers, 1942), 21–22.

4. See Roger Rusk, "The Day He Died," *Christianity Today,* 29 March 1974, 6.

5. The material on the dating of the crucifixion has been borrowed with a few changes from James Montgomery Boice, *The Gospel of John: An Expositional Commentary,* vol. 3, *John 9:1–12:50* (Grand Rapids: Zondervan, 1977), 318–22.

6. The natural way to understand "brothers" in verse 46 is that these were the natural children of Joseph by Mary. The Roman Catholic Church teaches the perpetual virginity of Mary, which would make this impossible. Thus, a variety of other interpretations have been offered. One supposes that these are children of Joseph by an earlier marriage. But if that were the case, one of these would have been Joseph's firstborn and thus the legal heir to David's throne, not Jesus. Another theory suggests that these were actually Jesus' cousins, sons of an otherwise unknown sister of Mary. But the wording links them to Jesus' mother, Mary, as her children. Any reading other than this is obviously only an attempt to support a spurious teaching that has no basis in the Bible. The names of these brothers are given in Matthew 13:55 and Mark 6:3 (James, Joseph, Simon, and Judas, and at least two sisters).

Chapter 27

1. R. V. G. Tasker, *The Gospel According to St. Matthew* (Grand Rapids: Eerdmans, 1961), 135.

2. *Time,* 10 November 1980, 22.

3. Sections of this chapter are adapted from James Montgomery Boice, *The Parables of Jesus* (Chicago: Moody Press, 1983), 13–20.

Chapter 28

1. William M. Taylor, *The Parables of Our Saviour Expounded and Illustrated* (New York: A. C. Armstrong and Son, 1900), 55, 60–61.

2. D. A. Carson, *The Expositor's Bible Commentary,* vol. 8, *Matthew, Mark, Luke* (Grand Rapids: Zondervan, 1984), 319.

3. Arno C. Gaebelein, *The Gospel of Matthew: An Exposition* (New York: Loizeaux Brothers, 1910), 292.

4. Some writers refer to claims that the mustard plant sometimes grows to a height of ten or more feet and that birds can sometimes be seen in its branches. But birds are seen even on the ground. Even a ten foot shrub is not a particularly good image for a sizeable religious institution.

5. D. A. Carson takes exception to this point, writing, "Efforts by most dispensationalists (e.g., Walvoord) to interpret the yeast as a symbol of evil are not very convincing in this setting because they require the introduction of anachronistic ideas like 'the professing church.' Moreover, though yeast is *normally* associated with evil in the OT, *this is not always so* (cf. Lev. 7:13; 23:15–18). Metaphors may have diverse uses" (Carson, *The Expositor's Bible Commentary,* 319).

6. Sections of this chapter are adapted from James Montgomery Boice, *The Parables of Jesus* (Chicago: Moody Press, 1983), 21–28.

Chapter 29

1. John H. Gerstner, "The Atonement and the Purpose of God," in *Our Savior God: Addresses Presented to the Philadelphia Conference on Reformed Theology, 1977–1979,* ed. James M. Boice (Grand Rapids: Baker, 1980), 115.

2. Sections of this chapter are adapted from James Montgomery Boice, *The Parables of Jesus* (Chicago: Moody Press, 1983), 29–44.

Chapter 30

1. John A. Broadus, *Commentary on Matthew* (Grand Rapids: Kregel, 1990), 318.

2. Charles Colson with Ellen Santilli Vaughn, *Kingdoms in Conflict* (Grand Rapids: William Morrow and Zondervan, 1987), 307.

3. John Charles Ryle, *Expository Thoughts on the Gospels: St. Matthew* (Cambridge: James Clark, 1974), 159.

4. Matthew 14:9 is the last place Herod is mentioned in this Gospel. He appears again, however, in Luke 13:31, where he is described as wanting to kill Jesus, and in Luke 23:6–12, where Jesus is sent to him by Pilate at the time of his trial.

Chapter 31

1. Charles Haddon Spurgeon, *Matthew: The Gospel of the Kingdom* (Pasadena, Tex.: Pilgrim Publications, 1974), 114.

Chapter 32

1. Howard F. Vos, *Matthew* (Grand Rapids: Zondervan, 1979), 110–11.
2. This is the way Jesus spoke at other moments of significant revelation (see Mark 14:62; Luke 24:39; John 8:58; 18:5–6).
3. Charles H. Spurgeon, *The Gospel of the Kingdom: A Popular Exposition of the Gospel According to Matthew* (Pasadena, Tex.: Pilgrim Publications, 1974), 118.
4. Ibid.

Chapter 33

1. The extent to which such ceremonial washings were carried out and the legal niceties that attended them are explained in Alfred Edersheim, *The Life and Times of Jesus the Messiah* (London: Longmans, Green and Co., 1883), vol. 3, 9–13.
2. John Charles Ryle, *Expository Thoughts on the Gospels: St. Matthew* (Cambridge: James Clarke, 1974), 174.

Chapter 34

1. The contrast between the green grass of the first feeding of the multitudes in Matthew 14 (see v. 19) and only the ground in the story of the second feeding in Matthew 15 (see v. 35) may reflect the passage of time from spring to late summer. I will mention this point again later.
2. William Barclay, *The Gospel of Matthew* (Philadelphia: Westminster Press, 1958), vol. 2, 133.
3. Alexander Maclaren, *The Gospel According to St. Matthew: Chapters 9 to 17* (London: Hodder and Stoughton, 1905), 318.
4. David Dickson, *A Brief Exposition of the Evangel of Jesus Christ According to Matthew* (1647; reprint, Edinburgh and Carlisle, Pa.: Banner of Truth Trust, 1981), 214–15.
5. William Hendriksen, *The Gospel of Matthew* (Grand Rapids: Baker, 1985), 624.
6. Barclay, *The Gospel of Matthew,* 135.
7. R. V. G. Tasker, *The Gospel According to St. Matthew* (Grand Rapids: Eerdmans, 1961), 151–52.
8. Leon Morris, *The Gospel According to Matthew* (Grand Rapids: Eerdmans; Leicester, England: Inter-Varsity Press, 1992), 406–7.
9. John Charles Ryle, *Expository Thoughts on the Gospels: St. Matthew* (Cambridge: James Clarke, 1974), 179–80.

Chapter 35

1. The Sadducees are not mentioned very often in the Gospels. In fact, they appear at only three places: (1) at the baptism of John (Matt. 3:7); (2) demanding a sign of Jesus, which is what they are doing here (Matt. 16:1); and (3) posing their trick question about the resurrection (Matt. 22:23; also Mark 12:18; Luke 20:27). Earlier in Matthew (Matt. 12:38), it was only the Pharisees and teachers of the law (scribes), who asked Jesus for a sign.

2. D. A. Carson, "Matthew," in *The Expositor's Bible Commentary*, vol. 8, *Matthew, Mark, Luke* (Grand Rapids: Zondervan, 1984), 362.

3. Craig S. Keener, *Matthew* (Downers Grove, Ill., and Leicester, England: Inter-Varsity Press, 1997), 268–69.

4. R. T. France, *The Gospel According to Matthew: An Introduction and Commentary* (Grand Rapids: Eerdmans, 1985), 251.

Chapter 36

1. Only Matthew mentions Jeremiah as a possible identification of Jesus.

2. The literature on these verses embraces hundreds if not thousands of books and articles. William Hendriksen has a representative list in his commentary *New Testament Commentary: Exposition of the Gospel According to Matthew* (Grand Rapids: Baker, 1985), 644.

3. D. A. Carson, "Matthew," in *The Expositor's Bible Commentary*, vol. 8, *Matthew, Mark, Luke* (Grand Rapids: Zondervan, 1984), 368; and Hendriksen, *New Testament Commentary*, 647.

4. R. V. G. Tasker, *The Gospel According to St. Matthew* (Grand Rapids: Eerdmans, 1961), 158.

5. John A. Broadus, *Commentary on Matthew* (Grand Rapids: Kregel, 1990), 356.

6. Ibid.

7. John R. W. Stott, *The Acts of the Apostles: To the Ends of the Earth* (Leicester, England: Inter-Varsity Press, 1990), 184.

Chapter 37

1. John Charles Ryle, *Expository Thoughts on the Gospels: St. Matthew* (Cambridge: James Clarke, 1974), 200–201.

2. See Matthew 10:37–39; Mark 8:34–37; Luke 9:23–27; 14:25–27; 17:33; John 12:25–26.

3. James Montgomery Boice, *Christ's Call to Discipleship* (Chicago: Moody Press, 1986), 13.

4. William Hendriksen, *New Testament Commentary: Exposition of the Gospel According to Matthew* (Grand Rapids: Baker, 1985), 659–60.

5. H. N. Ridderbos, *Matthew*, trans. Ray Togtman (Grand Rapids: Zondervan, 1987), 315.

6. John A. Broadus, *Commentary on Matthew* (Grand Rapids: Kregel, 1990), 368.

7. Howard F. Vos, *Matthew* (Grand Rapids: Zondervan, 1979), 123.

8. D. A. Carson, *God with Us: Themes from Matthew* (Ventura, Calif.: Regal Books, 1985), 101.

Chapter 38

1. The Shekinah is mentioned in these key passages: Exodus 13:21; 16:10; and 40:34–38; 1 Kings 8:10–11; Nehemiah 9:19; Psalm 78:14; and Revelation 14:14–16; as well as others.

2. The significance of this statement has been discussed in chapter 5, "A Voice in the Desert (Matthew 3:1–17)."

3. Charles H. Spurgeon, *Matthew: The Gospel of the Kingdom* (Pasadena, Tex.: Pilgrim Publications, 1974), 141.

4. D. A. Carson, *God with Us: Themes from Matthew* (Ventura, Calif.: Regal Books, 1985), 106.

5. Some have wondered how John could have denied that he was Elijah and Jesus could have said John was Elijah, as he does here. A balanced understanding comes from taking the references together. These three references are important: John 1:21 ("They asked him, '. . . Are you Elijah?' He said, 'I am not.'"); Matthew 11:14 ("And if you are willing to accept it, he is the Elijah who was to come"); and Luke 1:17 ("He will go on before the Lord, in the spirit and power of Elijah, to turn the hearts of the fathers to their children and the disobedient to the wisdom of the righteous—to make ready a people prepared for the Lord"). The last verse is a clear reference to Malachi 4:5–6 but makes clear that John was to fulfill Elijah's role in his spirit and power, but not as a literal reincarnation of the prophet. When Jesus said that John was Elijah "if you are willing to accept it," he meant that John would fulfill Elijah's role as restorer of all things if the people would repent. They did not, of course. So John's life, like that of Jesus, ended in rejection and death.

Chapter 39

1. This verse appears in a footnote in Matthew with the addition of "and fasting" (NIV) because it appears in some manuscripts. It is a case of the verse having been added by later copyists to make Matthew's text agree with Mark's. It is missing from many of the older Greek texts.

2. The words seem to be borrowed from Deuteronomy 32:5, 20.

3. John Charles Ryle, *Expository Thoughts on the Gospels: St. Matthew* (Cambridge: James Clarke, 1974), 217.

Subject Index

Scripture Index